C000111972

The Canterbury Preacher's Companion 2013

Some other books by Michael Counsell:

A Basic Bible Dictionary (Canterbury Press)

A Basic Christian Dictionary (Canterbury Press)

2000 Years of Prayer (Canterbury Press)

Every Pilgrim's Guide to the Journeys of the Apostles
(Canterbury Press)

Every Pilgrim's Guide to England's Holy Places
(Canterbury Press)

Every Pilgrim's Guide to Oberammergau and its Passion Play
(Canterbury Press) New edition 2008

The Little Book of Heavenly Humour by Syd Little with
Chris Gidney and Michael Counsell (Canterbury Press)

The
Canterbury Preacher's
Companion 2013

Sermons for Sundays, Holy Days,
Festivals and Special Occasions
Year C

Michael Counsell

CANTERBURY
PRESS
Norwich

© Canterbury Press 2012

First published in 2012 by the Canterbury Press Norwich
Editorial office
3rd Floor, Invicta House,
108–114 Golden Lane
London, EC1Y 0TG, UK

Canterbury Press is an imprint of Hymns Ancient &
Modern Ltd (a registered charity)
13a Hellesdon Park Road
Norwich, NR6 5DR, UK

www.canterburypress.co.uk
www.norwichbooksandmusic.co.uk

All rights reserved. No part of this publication may be
reproduced, stored in a retrieval system, or transmitted,
in any form or by any means, electronic, mechanical,
photocopying or otherwise, without the prior permission of
the publisher, Canterbury Press

Michael Counsell has asserted his right under the Copyright,
Designs and Patents Act, 1988, to be identified as the author
of this Work

British Library Cataloguing in Publication data

A catalogue record for this book is available
from the British Library

Scripture quotations are mainly drawn from the New Revised
Standard Version Bible © 1989 by the Division of Christian
Education of the National Council of Churches of
Christ in the USA

Readings are from *Common Worship: Services and Prayers
for the Church of England,* which is copyright © The
Archbishops' Council 2000: extracts and edited extracts are
used by permission.
Readings for days not covered by that book are from
Exciting Holiness, second edition 2003, edited by Brother
Tristram, copyright © European Province of the Society of
Saint Francis, 1997, 1999, 2003, published by Canterbury
Press, Norwich; see www.excitingholiness.org

ISBN 978 1 84825 059 8

Typeset by Regent Typesetting, London
Printed and bound by CPI Group (UK) Ltd, Croydon, CR0 4YY

LIST OF ADVERTISERS

Canterbury Press
Children's Society
Church of England Pensions
  Board
Church House Bookshop
Church Times
English Clergy Association
Holdings
Holy Faith
Peter Chalk
Prayer Book Society

RAF Chaplaincy
SCM Press
Sing Praise
Society of Catholic Priests
The Sign
Third Way
TMC
Towergate
Vanpoulles
WJK

**Do you value
Anglican Services
and music where the
Book of Common
Prayer is used**

One of the Society's aims is to ensure its continued use for
this and future generations. To this end it promotes the
prestigious Cranmer Awards for Young People.
Every member receives five magazines a year.

**To find out more and to obtain a membership form please contact
Ian Woohead on 01380 870384 or join online at: www.pbs.org.uk**

The Prayer Book Society Registered Charity No. 1099295. Co. Limited by Guarantee No. 4786973

HOLDINGS

Specialists in Clergy Taxation

Preferred advisors of

Ecclesiastical Insurance Group

Free initial consultation in your own home.

Year round, fixed fee service with a free advice line.

Rental income, child tax credits, no problem!

The Very Reverend Nicholas Coulton: "Until 2005 I had dealt with my own tax returns. Then the Eccesiastical Insurance adviser recommended Holdings and I've been grateful for their assistance ever since."

Reverend Heather Humphrey: "What a wonderful, amazing result!! Thank you so much for your prompt and efficient works. Wow!"

www.clergytax.eu

0844 4145 120

Contents

SUNDAYS

Unless otherwise stated, the readings and the verse numbers of the psalms are taken from *Common Worship: Services and Prayers for the Church of England* (Church House Publishing, 2000), with revisions, and are for Year C.

PETER CHALK & RPP TAXATION SERVICES LTD

Specialists in Taxation for the Clergy

Let Us Help YOU

Let us take away the strain of your yearly Tax Return completion

✓Personal service with over 37 years combined adviser experience

✓Affordable fixed price fee, payable by instalments if required

✓Over forty venues nationwide

✓Postal/Telephone service, if required

✓Free presentations for Colleges, courses and Clergy Groups

✓Financial advice through our sister company Towergate Russell Plaice

✓Authorised HM Revenue & Customs filing by Internet agents

✓Free Tax Credit advice/completion

If you would like to contact us to discuss your requirements please do so on the number below or take a look at our website

www.peterchalkco.co.uk

Do not hesitate, call us today!

**01476 591333/0844 980 8448 (local rate)
PO Box 6607, Grantham, Lincs, NG31 7NR**

Peter Chalk & RPP Taxation Services Ltd
Registered in England.   Company Number 4551413

towergate
financial

formerly Russell Plaice & Partners

Our advisers have been providing advice and service to the clergy for over 15 years.

Pensions & Annuities	ISA's & Investments
Life & Protection Needs	Inheritance Tax Planning
Income & Portfolio Planning	Mortgages

Contact us by phone **01476 560 662**
or via email at **TFGranthamEnquiries@towergate.co.uk**

TFG310

70a Castlegate
Grantham NG31 6SH
www.towergatefinancial.co.uk

Towergate Financial is a trading style of Towergate Financial (East) Ltd, which is authorised
and regulated by The Financial Services Authority

vii

viii

VANPOULLES Ltd
Complete Church Furnishers
Est. 1908

Telford Place, Crawley, West Sussex, RH10 1SZ

**Suppliers of
all church requisites**

Phone: 01 293 590100
Fax: 01 293 590115
sales@vanpoulles.co.uk
www.vanpoulles.co.uk

FEASTING on the WORD.

Preaching the Revised Common Lectionary

David L. Bartlett and Barbara Brown Taylor, editors

Named Book of the Year!
The Association of Theological Booksellers

"A unique and remarkable commentary that stands head and shoulders above the rest."
— *The Living Church*

"A monumental contribution. It will richly repay your investment."
— *The Christian Century*

Feasting on the Word is one of the most extensive and well-respected resources for preaching on the market today. Now complete, the twelve volumes cover all of the Sundays in the three-year lectionary cycle, along with moveable occasions. Each lectionary year consists of four volumes: one for the Advent and Christmas season, one for Lent and Easter, and one for each half of Ordinary Time. For each lectionary text, preachers will find brief essays—one each on the exegetical, theological, pastoral, and homiletical challenges of the text.

NOW COMPLETE!

COMPLETE SETS NOW AVAILABLE!

Feasting on the Word: Complete 12-Volume Set
9780664237134 • £309.99

Feasting on the Word: Year A, 4-Volume Set
9780664237141 • £103.99

Feasting on the Word: Year B, 4-Volume Set
9780664237158 • £103.99

Feasting on the Word: Year C, 4-Volume Set
9780664237165 • £103.99

Individual volumes each available for £27.99

FEASTING ON THE WORD:
Complete 12-Volume Set
on CD-ROM

9780664238124
£240.99

AVAILABLE FROM CHURCH HOUSE BOOKSHOP
TEL: +44(0)20 7799 4064   FAX: +44(0)20 7340 9997
EMAIL: BOOKSHOP@CHBOOKSHOP.CO.UK   WEBSITE: WWW.CHBOOKSHOP.CO.UK

xi

SERMONS FOR SAINTS' DAYS AND SPECIAL OCCASIONS

Readings are from *Common Worship,* or from *Exciting Holiness* by Brother Tristam SSF, second edition, Canterbury Press, 2003.

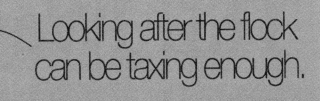

Looking after the flock can be taxing enough.

So let us take care of the finance for you.

As a busy member of the clergy you have enough to do without having to worry about your tax affairs.

TMC is here to help. We were established to provide a tax management service to the clergy and are now one of the largest such specialist advisers in the UK. Our team travels around the country to one of our regional venues so that we can discuss, face-to-face, your individual needs with:

General tax advice | Completion of tax returns
Tax credits | Payroll administration | Property accounts
Student advice | Annual Diocesan return

tmc

tax management for clergy

Call us on 01476 539000

Email: enquiries@clergytaxuk.com Visit: www.clergytaxuk.com

PO BOX 6621 Grantham Lincolnshire NG32 3SX

Third**Way**

Christian comment on culture

FREE SAMPLE COPY

Third Way is the long-established monthly magazine looking at culture, politics and the arts from a Christian viewpoint. Tony Blair, Thom Yorke, Tracey Emin and Desmond Tutu have all shared stimulating insights with us. Don't miss our wide-ranging news, features and reviews section plus *Third Way* is now bigger, glossier and more colourful.

Order now — quote 'TW1202'

Phone: 01603 785910; Email: subs@thirdway.org.uk
or send a postcard to Third Way Subscriptions,
13a Hellesdon Park Road, Norwich NR6 5DR

www.thirdwaymagazine.co.uk

REFLECTIONS FOR DAILY PRAYER

Reflections for Daily Prayer is designed to enhance your spiritual journey through the rich landscape of the Church's year.

Covering Monday to Saturday each week, it offers accessible reflections from popular writers, experienced ministers, biblical scholars and theologians, combining creative insight with high levels of scholarship.

Each day includes:
+ Full lectionary details for Morning Prayer
+ A reflection on one of the Bible readings
+ A Collect for the day

This unique series is for anyone who values both the companionship of daily Bible notes and the structure of the Lectionary.

Advent 2012 to eve of Advent 2013 edition | 978 0 7151 4249 3 | £16.99
Also available for the Kindle, and as an app for Apple devices from the iTunes store.

To order: tel: +44 (0)1603 785923, fax: +44 (0)1603 785915, write to: Norwich Books and Music, 13a Hellesdon Park Road, Norwich, Norfolk NR6 5DR, email: orders@norwichbooksandmusic.co.uk, or visit: www.dailyprayer.org.uk
UK orders: to cover p&p, £2.50 on orders below £25; £5 for orders between £25-£75: P&P is free for orders over £75. For details of overseas carriage, please contact our Norwich office or email: admin@norwichbooksandmusic.co.uk

 CHURCH HOUSE PUBLISHING   www.dailyprayer.org.uk

Looking for inspiration?

Jesus placed children at the heart of God's Kingdom.

Inspire your congregation to make childhood better by:

- **joining our campaigns**
- **supporting our work and mission.**

Work in partnership with us to involve and encourage children and young people, and use our worship resources to pray for the children we support.

Find out more:
Visit **www.childrenssociety.org.uk/church**
Email: **supportercare@childrenssociety.org.uk**
Tel: **0300 303 7000**

Charity Registration No. 221124

A better childhood. For every child.   www.childrenssociety.org.uk

SAVE MONEY ON SOME OF THE UK'S BEST LOVED HYMN BOOKS ...

Common Praise

(2000)

The definitive hymn book for the Christian year

Full music:
978 1 85311 264 5 | £27.00
WITH 25% GRANT £20.25

Melody & words:
978 1 85311 265 2 | £15.00
WITH 25% GRANT £11.25

Words (cased):
978 1 85311 266 9 | £11.50
WITH 25% GRANT £8.63

Large print words only:
978 1 85311 467 0 | £22.00
WITH 25% GRANT £16.50

Sing Praise

Hymns and Songs for Refreshing Worship (2010)

Full music:
978 1 84825 034 5 | £24.99
WITH 30% GRANT £17.50

Melody:
978 1 84825 038 3 | £14.99
WITH 30% GRANT £10.50

Words only:
978 1 84825 033 8 | £8.99
WITH 30% GRANT £6.30

Electronic words:
978 1 84825 0352 | £30.00
NOT IN GRANT SCHEME

Published by Canterbury Press & RSCM.
For further information visit:
www.singpraise.info

Hymns Ancient & Modern

New Standard Edition (1983)

Full music & words:
978 0 90754 737 2 | £24.00
WITH 25% GRANT £18.00

Melody & words:
978 0 90754 738 9 | £13.50
WITH 25% GRANT £10.13

Words only (standard size):
978 0 90754 739 6 | £11.00
WITH 25% GRANT £8.25

Large print words only:
978 0 90754 747 1 | £18.50
WITH 25% GRANT £13.88

Hymns of Glory, Songs of Praise

(2008)

Full music:
978 1 85311 900 2 | £27.50
SPECIAL OFFER | £8.50

Words only:
978 1 85311 901 9 | £12.00
SPECIAL OFFER | £5.00

NRSV Holy Bible

New Revised Standard Version, Anglicized Edition

978 1 85311 831 9 | £16.99
SPECIAL OFFER £8.00

TERMS AND CONDITIONS: Discounts off hymnals apply when a grant application form is supplied and a minimum of 20 units are purchased: form is available from Norwich Books and Music on +44 (0)1603 785925 or email: admin@norwichbooksandmusic.co.uk – or visit www.canterburypress.co.uk (and see under Grant Form): UK P&P – please add £2.50 on orders below £25; £5 for orders between £25-£75; P&P is free for orders over £75. For credit/debit card orders call +44 (0)1603 785925. Prices correct at time of publication but can change at any time; all whilst stocks last.

Hymns Ancient & Modern Ltd is a Regd. Charity No. 270060. Regd. in England No. 1220696.
Regd. Office: 13a Hellesdon Park Road, Norwich, Norfolk NR6 5DR. VAT Reg. No. GB 283 2968 24.

60 Years of Retirement Housing

With supported housing, nursing and dementia care and help to those on a low income, the Church of England Pensions Board provides security and peace of mind in retirement to those who have given their lives towards helping others in the name of Christ, including Clergy Widows and Licensed Lay Workers.

We rely on donations and legacies to continue this much needed work.

PLEASE HELP US IN ANY WAY YOU CAN

The Church of England Pensions Board (PC)
FREEPOST 898, LONDON SW1P 3YS
Tel: 020 7898 1800
Web: www.cepb.org.uk/appeals
Email: cepbappeals@churchofengland.org
Registered Charity Number: 236627

FREE SAMPLE COPY

no longer Occupied
St Paul's is cleared
gardener's quiet world
weeding out the noise

PLUS: who can tell what other cradle ... ?

News – UK and overseas; editorial comment and debate; stimulating features; humour; book and arts reviews; latest clerical vacancies.

The Church Times is an independent newspaper: not answerable to the bishops, or any interest group – just to its readers.

Order now — quote 'CT1204'

Call: 01603 785 911;
Email: subs@churchtimes.co.uk
or send a postcard to Church Times
Subscriptions, 13a Hellesdon Park
Road, Norwich NR6 5DR

www.churchtimes.co.uk

Preface

A preacher wrote to Canterbury Press, saying in a jocular way that he appreciates the *Canterbury Preacher's Companion*, but was becoming irritated by the number of words which are abbreviated: I've for I have, we'll for we shall, and that sort of thing. I am most grateful to this correspondent; his letter is very helpful. I aim to produce a book every year which is useful to people who have to prepare sermons, and any letter to me c/o the Canterbury Press is welcome. I agree with the writer; and last year and this year I have been through the text and removed many abbreviations, or, as they are known to grammarians, 'contractions'. But when I was discussing this with the senior editor, and we found ourselves worrying about 'the frequency of the contractions', we laughed as we realized that our language was becoming much too obstetric!

But this is a symptom of a deeper problem. Unlike most books, which are seen only by the reader's eyes, these sermons are heard with the ears of those in the congregation; and therefore have to be written in 'spoken English'. Phrases which look fine on the printed page are often heard by the listener in the pew as stilted and stiff. Even if you write your own sermon notes based on ideas found in my sermons, you need to write them in a form which will make your spoken words sound natural. Some effects of this are obvious: the correct possessive of Jesus on the page is Jesus', but in the spoken word you cannot hear an apostrophe, so I always use Jesus's, which everyone uses when speaking. I also use far more commas than would be necessary in a printed communication, to tell myself where to pause and divide the clauses.

Deciding which contractions are best avoided depends on the context, the preacher's own style of speaking, and the size of the building. If we are speaking the word of God to the people, we must make sure that what we say is audible and comprehensible. In a large building we need to speak slowly and e-nun-ci-ate care-ful-ly, as many people have hearing loss in the upper frequencies, where the consonants are, without realizing it. In a large church, colloquial English would be hard to follow, whereas in a small building formal language would sound stiff, stilted and boring. We must never be boring when handling God's words. Experienced preachers adjust their style instinctively to the acoustics, but it is worth thinking about it in advance when you write out the words of your sermons, even if you do so in note form. God bless you in your preaching ministry.

Michael Counsell

How to Remember the Last Supper

Jesus met his friends in the Upper Room and shared a meal with them; he said, 'Do this in remembrance of me.' The service of Holy Communion, The Eucharist, The Mass, The Holy Liturgy or The Lord's Supper is celebrated in direct obedience to this command. If Maundy Thursday and Corpus Christi are celebrated in your church, these festivals give us two opportunities to think about what it means: Jesus was giving us a visual aid to help us understand what he was doing on the cross. For Roman Catholics, and members of the Eastern Orthodox Churches, the Mass or Liturgy have always been at the centre of their worship. In the 1920s and 1930s the 'Parish Communion Movement' was very influential. Previously the Communion had been celebrated in most Protestant Churches once a quarter, or early in the morning attended by a faithful few, with no music. But, influenced by this movement, many Anglican and other churches made the Holy Communion the main service of the day, attended by the whole local community. This included the children, though they might go out after the opening hymn to a crèche or Sunday school, returning to join the rest of the congregation later. Many churches invite members of any denomination who are accustomed to sharing the bread and wine in their own church to receive the sacrament in the church where they are visitors. Where members of their own congregations were supposed not to receive the elements until they had been confirmed, there is now a debate about the age at which confirmation should be administered, and whether children of believing parents should be admitted to communion before they are confirmed. In many churches, the whole congregation worships together at least once a month in what is called 'All-age worship', which may or may not be a Eucharist; in this book the sermon for the Principal Service on Sundays is followed by a short note suggesting an activity which young people may share in, either during all-age worship or in a separate room for Sunday school.

More recently, the shortage of ordained ministers in most denominations has made it difficult for churches which insist that the celebrant must always be ordained to continue the ideal of having a Holy Communion in every church every Sunday; some clergy follow an exhausting round of celebrating in several churches one after another, without any time to chat to the congregation afterwards. These churches are being forced to choose between ordaining members of the congregation as Ministers in Secular Employment, or returning to a monthly communion, with non-eucharistic services led by laypeople on other Sundays. This has the advantage that many more people will discover that they have gifts in leading worship; and if they begin to preach, I hope this book will help them at first by giving them ideas for the subject of their sermons, and examples of how to tackle those ideas in a fresh way.

Jesus may have used some of the traditional words from the Jewish Passover ceremonies at the Last Supper, and it has been suggested that 'Lift up your hearts' may come from the words used at shared meals among the Pharisees; and these words may have passed over into the common meals which Christians held, probably in the atrium of the house of one of their richer members. Days ran from sunset to sunset in those times, so their meetings 'on the first day of the week' were probably after dark on Saturday evenings. They will have sung psalms, and begun to make up their own hymns. But most of their prayers will have been extempore. This may have led to a rather rowdy assembly, and St Paul appealed for all things to be done 'decently and in order'. Early examples of Christian prayer are found in the Acts of the Apostles and the Letters in the New Testament; in the Letters of St Clement of Rome; the *Didache*; the so-called *Letter of Barnabas*; and the Letter of Polycarp. Justin Martyr, writing in the mid-second century, describes the usual form of Christian worship in his day:

On Sundays there is an assembly of all who live in towns or in the country, and the memoirs of the apostles or the writings of the prophets are read for as long as time allows. Then the reading is brought to an end, and the president delivers an address in which he admonishes and encourages us to imitate in our own lives the beautiful lessons we have heard read. Then we all stand up together and pray; when we have finished the prayer, as I have said, bread and wine and water are brought up; the president offers prayers and thanksgiving as best he can, and the people say 'Amen' as an expression of their agreement. Then follows the distribution of the food over which the prayer of thanksgiving has been recited; all present receive some of it, and the deacons carry some to those who are absent.

While the city congregations contained many well-educated members who would find extempore prayer easy, country congregations might be led by a farmer who, even with the inspiration of the Holy Spirit, was scarcely articulate. We can imagine such an elder, on a visit to the nearest city, begging the bishop there to write out a Eucharistic Prayer for him to read to his own congregation. In this way, what we call 'liturgy' was born. St Hippolytus, in his book *The Apostolic Tradition*, written in about AD 200, includes a long Eucharistic Prayer which has greatly influenced modern liturgies.

Churches today which principally use extempore prayer need to guard against being ungrammatical, which is fine in private prayer but a hindrance in public worship; and against being repetitious, using the same clichés week after week in their prayers. For them, studying the prayer books of liturgical churches may help them to choose judicious phrases which will make their prayers easier for the worshippers to follow. Liturgy is a blessing because when worshippers know what is coming they can follow it in their own devotions, and when their minds wander, can bring the problems they were thinking about back into the worship of the congregation, picking up the common thread of their prayers without difficulty. But imagination is constantly needed to prevent liturgical worship becoming boring. The Sunday worship may have to come from an authorized service book, but this usually allows plenty of variation. But on a parish quiet day or pilgrimage, it may be possible to experiment with extempore prayer, which will make the worshippers think about what they are doing. Anglican clergy at their licensing vow to use in church 'services authorized by the bishop, and none other'; but away from the parish church there may be opportunities to experiment with 'none other'!

Dom Gregory Dix, an Anglican Benedictine monk, wrote a book in 1945 called *The Shape of the Liturgy*. In this he pointed out that Jesus did four things at the Last Supper, which we repeat in our Eucharists: he took bread and wine, he gave thanks, broke the bread, and gave it to his disciples. So the climax of our services is when we do what Jesus did at the Last Supper. But before that we copy what Jesus did when he went to the synagogues: he read the Scriptures, expounded them and prayed about them, with the singing of psalms. So Bible readings are the focus of the first half of our services. We prepare for this by recollection and confession, and respond to it by exposition, belief, and prayer. Similarly the second part of the service, repeating the actions of the Last Supper, has preparation (fellowship, self-offering) and response (after a party you wash up, say thank you, and say goodbye; and we do the same at the end of our worship). So the shape of our Holy Communion, whether it is liturgical or extempore, should be:

1 Getting ready: prayer for purity; confession and forgiveness.
2 What God did, as recounted in the Scriptures.
3 Our response, in sermon, creed and prayer.
4 Getting ready, by shaking hands with each other, *Taking* the bread and wine, and offering our lives to God symbolized by our gifts of money.
5 What Jesus did at the Last Supper: *Gave thanks; Broke;* and *Gave.*
6 Our response: ablutions, thanksgiving, blessing and dismissal.

Now I add some paragraphs which are only for the Church of England:

Common Worship offers a choice of eight Communion Prayers. You can use any of them at any service, and it is good to vary them to keep the worshippers' interest. But you may like to think about the distinctive characteristics of each, to help you choose one which is appropriate to a particular service. Memorable phrases may resonate with something in the readings:

A This prayer is based on Prayers 1 and 2 in *The Alternative Service Book*. There are optional responses. The opening statement of faith may be omitted when a proper preface is used, and extended prefaces (CW pp. 294 and 300–29) may be used with prayers A, B and E. Prayer A is suggested for Ordinary Time. Memorable phrases: 'slavery of sin'; 'born of a woman'; cross, resurrection and ascension; 'high priest'; 'sacrifice of praise'; renew, inspire and unite us.
B A revision of ASB Prayer 3, which was itself based on the prayer of St Hippolytus (see above). Extended prefaces may be used; suggested for Festivals. Memorable phrases: 'opened his arms on the cross'; 'put an end to death'; 'looking for his coming in glory'; 'gather into one in your kingdom'; 'in the company of N and all the saints'.

C A revision of ASB Prayer 4, which was based on the Book of Common Prayer. Suggested for Advent and Lent. Memorable phrases: 'source of light and life'; 'made us in your image'; 'suffer death on the cross for our redemption'; 'full, perfect and sufficient sacrifice'; 'although we are unworthy'.

D Uses short sentences and responses, and tells a story, so suitable for children. There is no space to insert a proper preface. Memorable phrases: 'your word goes out to call us home to the city where angels sing'; 'to the darkness Jesus came as light'; 'touched the untouchables'; 'this is our story, this is our song' (Blessed assurance); 'celebrate the freedom'; 'defying death he rose again'; 'plead for all the world'; 'Send your Spirit ... opened eyes and hearts on fire'; 'welcomed at your feast in heaven'.

E Short, narrative style. Extended prefaces may be used; theme of mission and outreach. Memorable phrases: 'broken bread and wine outpoured'; 'work together for ... kingdom ... justice and mercy'; 'bring us with N and all the saints'.

F Based on the Eastern Orthodox Liturgy; with short responses, but no space to insert a proper preface. Memorable phrases: 'though we chose the path of rebellion'; 'law ... prophets ... justice, mercy and peace'; 'signs of your kingdom on earth'; 'made perfect in human weakness'. 'Embracing our humanity'; 'proclaim ... celebrate ... rejoice ... long'; 'Bless the earth, heal the sick, let the oppressed go free'; 'to feast with N and all the saints'; 'new creation'.

G Based on the modern Roman Catholic Mass (ICEL). There is no space for a proper preface. Memorable phrases: 'echo the silent music of your praise'; 'made us in your image, the crown of all creation'; 'as a mother tenderly embraces her children'; 'born of Mary ... living bread'; 'opened wide his arms'; 'Church in every land ... unity ... faith ... peace'; 'bring us with N and all the saints'.

H Very short, with varied responses, and the Sanctus at the end; no space for prefaces. Suitable for children and shortened services. Memorable phrases: 'When we turned away you did not reject us, but came to meet us'; 'You embraced us as your children and welcomed us to sit and eat'; 'he opened wide his arms on the cross'; 'eternal song of heaven'.

YEAR C, the Year of Luke

(Year C begins on Advent Sunday in 2012, 2015, 2018, etc.)

ADVENT

The Church year begins with Advent, the four Sundays leading up to Christmas. Advent means 'coming', so we think about Christ coming into the world at Christmas, coming into our lives every day, and coming to us at our death. To meet Jesus is a solemn event, especially if we have things on our conscience. So we use the season of Advent to confess our sins, and use the solemn colour of purple for the altar frontals and vestments in church (except that the Third Sunday of Advent may use rose colour). The services are solemn: 'Glory to God in the highest' is usually omitted, and apart from carol services, we save the Christmas music until Christmas. In this way we enjoy the Yuletide festival more because of the contrast. Candles are lit on an Advent wreath, one on the first Sunday, two on the second, and so on, leading up to five on Christmas Eve. A search of the internet will find suitable prayers to be said while the candles are lit.

First Sunday of Advent   2 December 2012
Principal Service   **The Church's Year**

Jer. 33.14–16 A King is promised; Ps. 25.1–9 Waiting for God; 1 Thess. 3.9–13 Prayer to be blameless at the coming of Christ; Luke 21.25–36 The coming of Christ

'Now when these things begin to take place, stand up and raise your heads, because your redemption is drawing near.' Luke 21.28

Rhythm

'I got rhythm,' goes the Gershwin song – 'who could ask for anything more?' A sense of rhythm adds joy to life, whether you're drumming with your fingers on the table, or dreaming of winning *Strictly Come Dancing*. A musician without rhythm quickly gets out of time with the others. There's an inbuilt, unconscious rhythm to breathing, walking, or stirring your tea. A natural rhythm helps you to relax. Hurrying is committing violence against God's time – trying to make God fit into your time. Yet it's no use trying to plan your rhythm far in advance; you have to march in time with God's rhythm. Someone wrote, 'The way to make God smile is to tell him your plans!' When our ancestors were all involved in agriculture, the rhythm of the seasons gave a steady pattern to their lives. Nowadays we need to find something else to replace the farming year. The calendar year is too boring, and the tax year is too threatening. Well, happy New Year, everybody! I've got the perfect pattern for structured living, and it begins today: the Church's year, starting on Advent Sunday.

Jesus's life

The Christian year follows the pattern of Jesus's life. It begins with Advent, which means 'coming', when we are eagerly awaiting the coming of Jesus, predicted by the prophets. At Christmas we celebrate his birth at Bethlehem. He was revealed to the wise men, whom we think of at Epiphany. In Lent, we study his teaching, and follow his forty days' fast in the wilderness. We follow him up to Jerusalem, and greet him with palms. Next, we imagine ourselves sharing with Jesus in the events of Holy Week – the Last Supper, and his death on the cross; and we greet his resurrection with Alleluias at Easter. We sit with his disciples, as he teaches them about life in the kingdom of God, for forty days. We share their bewilderment as Jesus vanishes from their sight on Ascension Day; but ten days later we realize that his work on earth hadn't finished. It continued when he gave the Holy Spirit to them at Pentecost; it continues as the Spirit works through us to spread God's love through God's world. Finally we put these different experiences together: of God, our Father and Creator; as the Son of God, our friend and redeemer; as the Spirit of God, guiding and empowering us with love. Yet they are not three Gods but one God, and on Trinity Sunday we ponder on the mystery of God's greatness, which no words are adequate to describe. Then the year continues in a period of steady growth in the Spirit, during the green Sundays after Trinity. You see how the Church's year follows the pattern of Jesus's life?

Our life

Not only that, the rhythm of the Christian year is the pattern of our lives, too. As we settle ourselves into the Church's routine, we can reflect on our own progress. In Advent we think how Jesus comes to us, in our birth, in the crises of daily living, and at our death. We welcome him to be born in our hearts at Christmas; in the Epiphany season we plan how we can share him with those who don't know him. During Lent we discipline ourselves like good soldiers, to manage on the minimum of luxury. During Holy Week and Easter, we remind ourselves that we, too, must some day die. But at Ascensiontide, we remember that our death is the prelude to our own ascension into heaven. In the meantime, guided and strengthened by God's Holy Spirit, we shall grow stronger in love and deeper in devotion to the Blessed Trinity, bound to the three persons as they are bound to each other by bonds of eternal love.

The Church year

Contemplating the pattern of your own life, by laying it alongside the life of Jesus, as you follow the rhythm of the Christian Year, helps you to get everything in perspective. It takes away the sense of rush and hurry, and helps us to look at our lives from God's point of view. Have you got rhythm – the deep rhythm of the Church year, beginning today? Its steady progress helps us to swing through life like an army unit on a route-march.

All-age worship

Make or mark up a calendar with the church seasons, simplifying the inside covers of this book.

Suggested hymns

Advent tells us Christ is near (look this hymn up on Google); *I cannot tell why he, whom angels worship; O come, O come Emmanuel; The advent of our God.*

First Sunday of Advent   2 December 2012
Second Service   The Need for Decision

Ps. 9 The Lord judges the world; Joel 3.9–21 The valley of decision; Rev. 14.13—15.4 Blessed are the dead; *Gospel at Holy Communion*: John 3.1–17 Nicodemus

> *'Multitudes, multitudes, in the valley of decision! For the day of the Lord is near in the valley of decision.' Joel 3.14*

End-times

A fundamentalist asked a more liberal believer, 'Do you accept that we're now living in the end-times?' 'Oh yes,' replied the other, 'we've been in the end-times since Jesus rose again, and may well be for many more thousands of years.' Certainly Jesus wanted to instil a sense of urgency. But he admitted that even he himself didn't know when the world will end. Everybody, whenever they live, needs to make up their mind for or against God sometime. Some 400 years before Christ, the prophet Joel warned that 'the day of the Lord is near in the valley of decision'. Without being morbid, any one of us could die today. So we can't put off our preparations till tomorrow. The end-times, as far as I'm concerned, began the day I was born!

Death

Many doubters will respond, 'You can't use fear of death to scare me into believing in God. When you die, you die, and that's it.' Christians feel very sorry for anyone who takes that view. If death is the end, life has no meaning or purpose, and your pleasures are only temporary distractions. But if there is eternal life, you can look forward joyfully to a richer life after you die, meeting again those you have loved, and meeting face to face with the Saviour who loves you. Of course nobody can give a scientific proof that there is an afterlife. But Jesus taught about eternal life, and many people claim to have spoken with him after his resurrection. You can try a very simple experiment: pray to Jesus to make you a better person, and if you let him, he will do it! Only a living Saviour could do that. Of course, that assumes that you are praying in faith, and faith involves commitment. This experiment won't work unless you are prepared to act on the result, by loving God and loving

4

your neighbour. But suppose you are not yet ready to make that commitment. You can't prove that we go to heaven when we die, neither can you prove that we are just snuffed out like a candle. If you were a gambler, which would you bet on? If you bet that there *is* an afterlife, and live a life of love for that reason, you will know a joy which transforms even the sad and difficult times. When you die, there will be no regrets; and if there's no heaven, you won't know anything about it. But if you bet on total extinction, you will have no reason not to live a life of total selfishness. I doubt whether you will be truly happy. And when you die, you will have missed the chance of a glorious eternity. If you are aware of that, you will be full of regrets for making the wrong choice; even if you know nothing about it, there may still be some who loved you who will be sorry not to be able to share the joys of eternal life with you. Some of them are here in this church, and they made a firm decision for Jesus many years ago.

Decision

If you have never made that decision before, now's the time to choose. Even not choosing is itself a choice: it means rejecting all the good things, in this life and the next, which God has promised to give you to enjoy. What does that decision involve, you ask? Just one simple prayer, something like this:

> Jesus, if you really are alive, please listen. I don't really understand, but I want to believe. I want to give my life to you, to love you and know that you love me. I'm sorry for the wrong things I've done, but I believe you have forgiven me. I give you my life today; from now on I belong to you. Guide me in this life, and give me joy in the life to come. Amen.

Don't delay

You don't have to get the words exactly right. But if you are ready to say 'Amen' to that prayer, come and see me afterwards, or ask somebody else that you trust to pray with you. Or how about tonight when you are alone and can think about it calmly? Then tell somebody what you have done, who will help you not to be a backslider. Just don't put it off until it's too late. Remember what Joel said, 'Multitudes, multitudes, in the valley of decision!' You stand in that valley now. An anonymous poet once wrote:

Procrastination is my sin;
it brings me greatest sorrow;
I really must stop doing it –
I think I'll start tomorrow!

Don't delay. Tomorrow never comes. Choose Jesus now.

Suggested hymns

Fear not, rejoice and be glad; O happy day; Take my life and let it be; Who is on the Lord's side?

Second Sunday of Advent   9 December
Principal Service   The Author of the Acts
Bar. 5.1–9 God will lead his people with joy, *or* Mal. 3.1–4
A messenger to prepare the way; *Canticle*: Luke 1.68–79
Benedictus; Phil. 1.3–11 Overflowing love; Luke 3.1–6 John the
Baptist

> *'In the fifteenth year of the reign of Emperor Tiberius ... the word of God came to John son of Zechariah in the wilderness.' Luke 3.1–2*

Structure

We read little snippets from the Gospels, and that's very dangerous. We concentrate so hard on the details, that we can't see the wood for the trees. The Gospel writers were artists, telling a story. It was a true story, but it needed all their artistry – inspired, we believe, by the Holy Spirit – to make it interesting and moving to the readers. So Matthew, Mark, Luke and John, each in their own way, fitted the different stories about Jesus – which they had been told by the eye-witnesses – into a framework. This year, most of the readings come from St Luke's Gospel, and that's very interesting, because Luke didn't just write one book in the New Testament, he wrote two. Luke is the author of the Acts of the Apostles, and we should see the Gospel and the Acts as two parts of a single work. Neither can be understood without the other.

History

The beginning of the third chapter of the Gospel of Luke, which we have just read, anchors the story at a particular moment of history, 'In the fifteenth year of the reign of Emperor Tiberius'. This isn't a made-up myth; it's a faithful recounting of historical events. In fact Luke tries to show how these particular events make sense of the whole of world history; and he succeeds. The Gospel is the culmination of the process of preparation, described in the Old Testament – a process driven by the Holy Spirit. It describes the ministry of the Holy Spirit through Jesus; and it leads on into the ministry of the Holy Spirit through the Church, described in Acts, and which is continuing still through you and me.

Israel

The story of Israel, told in the Old Testament, is the story of the law and the prophets. Before Moses, everyone did what was right in their own eyes. Idols could be placated with sacrifices, and bribed to support their followers in battle, but nobody thought they were interested in the way we behave to each other. The prophets proclaimed that God requires obedience. They were called, through the Spirit, to prepare the way of the Lord. John the Baptist is often described as the last of the prophets. He prepared the way for the coming of Jesus, the next phase in God's plan of salvation, which is why Luke's Gospel begins with the birth of John and of Jesus. Then, in chapter three, John is shown to be fulfilling the prophecy of Isaiah.

Jesus

Throughout the Gospel Luke describes the life and teaching of Jesus, first in Galilee, then journeying to Jerusalem. It begins with the descent of the Holy Spirit on Jesus at his baptism, and continues with his teaching about the Holy Spirit, as he gathers a band of disciples around him. The Gospel climaxes with Jesus's death and burial in Jerusalem. Then follows the story of the resurrection, which leads to the ascension. The ascension story is repeated in Acts, because it's the beginning of the final phase.

Outreach

The ascension is when Jesus sends his disciples to be his witnesses, beginning in Jerusalem, and continuing to the ends of the earth. They are empowered by the gift of the Holy Spirit in Acts chapter two, and the next three chapters describe the growth of the church in Jerusalem. That growth continues into Judaea and Samaria, then onwards into the Greek and Roman world outside Palestine. St Paul continues the work through his missionary journeys in Turkey and Greece, and then decides to go to Rome, which, as far as the Jews were concerned, really was the end of the earth. Although he arrived there under arrest, he was able to preach openly and unhindered. Paul's death isn't mentioned, because the spread of the gospel is now up to others.

Vision

What a panorama! What a grasp St Luke has of the whole history of the world! The exciting thing is that there's a place for you in this story. You have a significant role to play in witnessing to the love of God the Father, the life and death of Jesus, and the power of the Holy Spirit. In the perspective given to us by St Luke, we can see that each one of us, like John the Baptist, has a part in preparing the way of the Lord.

All-age worship

Draw a timeline of world history, from God's point of view.

Suggested hymns

Long ago, prophets knew; Make way, make way; On Jordan's bank the Baptist's cry; When Jesus came to Jordan.

Second Sunday of Advent   9 December
Second Service   **The Historical Jesus**
Ps. 75 I will judge [76 To save the oppressed]; Isa. 40.1–11 Comfort my people; Luke 1.1–25 John's birth foretold

> '*I ... decided, after investigating everything carefully from the very first, to write an orderly account for you ... so that you may*

know the truth concerning the things about which you have been instructed.' Luke 1.3–4

Pictures of Jesus

Look at a painting of Jesus. Seventeenth-century Italian artists drew him as a seventeenth-century Italian man; Chinese paint him as a Chinese; Africans as an African. Yet he was none of these things. It's right to think of Jesus as like us, one of us, and our friend. But we distort his message if we assume there were no differences between his attitudes and those which are now fashionable. Yet what *was* Jesus like?

Liberals

In the nineteenth century, German liberal-moralists thought they could understand Jesus by peering back through ages. But they were like people looking down a deep well, it was said, and seeing a reflection of their own faces, very small. They wrote as though Jesus was a liberal-moralist. Similarly, Marxists read him as a communist revolutionary.

Schweitzer

Another angle was provided by Albert Schweitzer, musician, missionary and theologian. Jesus, he said, didn't come to teach morality, he came to change history. Schweitzer pointed out that most of the teaching of Jesus is what we call 'apocalyptic'. It's about God intervening in human history: Jesus proclaimed that we'd come to 'the end of the age'. This is undoubtedly true; but Schweitzer made it appear as though Jesus expected the end of the world in his lifetime. If that's the case, then Jesus was mistaken. Others have suggested that it was Schweitzer who was mistaken: by the coming of the kingdom, Jesus meant not the end of time, but a turning point in history. But in Schweitzer's book, translated as *The Quest for the Historical Jesus*, he set Christians off on a search which still continues. What was Jesus *really* like?

Bultmann

In reaction to Schweitzer, Rudolf Bultmann wrote that we can't know anything about Jesus through history. The stories about Jesus

9

in the Gospels, according to Bultmann, are all myth. We can only know 'the Jesus of Faith'! Now it's certainly true that it is the personal knowledge of Jesus through prayer that matters most. I can't accept, however, that we know nothing whatever about the Jesus of history. Agreed, the Gospels were written, not as disinterested records of historical fact – in fact there's probably no such thing, because all history is interpretation by selection. But the Gospel writers knew that they were reporting historical events, and weren't free to distort them. The Gospels are a better record, closer to the events, than we have for most of the personalities in history. Yet we don't question that Napoleon was historical, and that he said roughly what the documents tell us he said.

Jesus Project

The American group called 'the Jesus Project' looked at other Gospels, outside the Bible, to see if they give evidence for the sayings of Jesus. A few of these may represent memories from the time of Jesus, but most are late. These so-called 'apocryphal gospels' argued that God is remote, and it's difficult to approach him: a process to which the heretical group which wrote them alone had the key. This is the very opposite of the teaching of Jesus in the New Testament. The Jesus Project, however, would only accept as 'authentic' those sayings which are in at least three 'gospels', original or apocryphal. Very few sayings are left when this rule is applied. So the Jesus Project, too, claimed we know hardly anything about what Jesus said.

Jesus of Faith

No matter, they say – we worship 'the Jesus of Faith'. The trouble with the Jesus of Faith is that he's like an idol with feet of clay: you can turn him round to face any direction you yourself want to go. He's a God who only seems to be a man. Yet people who follow a God who only *seems* to be human, only *seem* to love their neighbours – they don't actually need to *do* anything about it! Jesus said, on the contrary, that people's beliefs were to be judged by their actions: 'By their fruits you shall know them.'

The Jesus of history

The Jesus of Faith is important, but our idea of him must always be checked against the Jesus of History, or we shall misunderstand what he really meant. St Luke wrote, 'I ... decided, after investigating everything carefully from the very first, to write an orderly account for you ... so that you may know the truth concerning the things about which you have been instructed.' A historical Jesus is the only one in whom you can have faith.

Suggested hymns

A man there lived in Galilee; Come, thou long-expected Jesus; Hark, a herald voice is calling; What a friend we have in Jesus.

Third Sunday of Advent   16 December
Principal Service   **Do You Want the Good News First?**
Zeph. 3.14–20 Sing, daughter Zion, God is in your midst;
Canticle: Isa. 12.2–6 Great in your midst, *or* Ps. 146.4–10
Justice; Phil. 4.4–7 Rejoice in the Lord; Luke 3.7–18 The witness of John the Baptist

> *'So, with many other exhortations, [John the Baptist] proclaimed the good news to the people.' Luke 3.18*

Good news first?

People say to you, 'There's good news and bad news. Do you want to hear the good news or the bad news first?' Then you are in a quandary. Sometimes it's best to hear the good news first, because that will give us strength to cope with the bad news later. At other times we'd rather hear the bad news first, and get it out of the way, so that we can then concentrate on the more hopeful report which follows.

The Baptist

St Luke's Gospel tells us: 'With many other exhortations, [John the Baptist] proclaimed the good news to the people.' The exhortations were bad news. 'What should we do?' the people asked him. He gave a clear answer: God expects us to be kind to our neighbour,

11

in very practical ways. 'Whoever has two coats must share with anyone who has none,' he said, 'and whoever has food must share it with the hungry.' Tax-collectors must collect no more tax than the regulations lay down. Soldiers, acting as the police force, mustn't extort money from anyone by threats or false accusations, and they must be satisfied with their wages. What's more, God is marking us out of ten for how well we obey his commandments: 'every tree therefore that does not bear good fruit is cut down and thrown into the fire'. John brought a message of imminent judgement, which was definitely bad news.

Remission

But, the Bible says, John 'proclaimed the good news to the people'. What was the good news? It's wrapped up in that strange phrase which both John and his cousin Jesus used: 'the baptism of repentance for the remission of sins'. If we are really sorry for the unkind things we have done, they said, God will forgive us, and wipe the slate clean. Then we can make a fresh start, as innocent as newborn babes, or in other words, 'born again'. We express our remorse by making a clean breast of things, confessing our faults to God with a genuine intention of changing our ways. God symbolizes his forgiveness by washing us in the water of baptism. Of course, *then* John baptized whole families, grown-ups and children together. *These days* most of us were christened as children, with the understanding that we should be brought up in a Christian family, where we are taught both the good news and the bad news by our parents, godparents, and the local Sunday school.

Bad news first

But how can anyone repent unless they know that what they are doing is wrong? In this case, the bad news of God's judgement very definitely needs to come first. Otherwise we wouldn't see the need for repentance, or realize what a splendid gift God is making to us when he offers to forgive us our sins. So Advent, as we prepare to celebrate the good news of the birth of our Saviour, is nevertheless a penitential season. The robes and furnishings are in the solemn colour of purple, and we sing hymns about God's awful judgement throne. Then we shall be ready for the good news when it comes on Christmas day.

Relax

This Sunday, however, is the third in Advent. We are about halfway through our season of preparation for Christmas. In some churches with lots of vestments, the purple is replaced today by a rose colour, just as on Mid-Lent Sunday or Refreshment Sunday. This shows that we can relax a bit amid the solemnity, and remember that the good news and the bad news go together. We repent so that we may be forgiven; therefore rejoice!

Cause for rejoicing

The prophet Zephaniah cried out,

'Sing aloud, O daughter Zion;
    shout, O Israel!
Rejoice and exult with all your heart,
    O daughter Jerusalem!
The LORD has taken away the judgements against you ...
The king of Israel, the LORD, is in your midst.'

St Paul wrote to the Philippians, 'Rejoice in the Lord always; again I will say, Rejoice ... The Lord is near. Do not worry about anything!' John the Baptist brought us clear instructions on how to behave, which saves us from groping about in the dark. Jesus brought us the power of the Holy Spirit, who enables us to work out the answers for ourselves. In this case the good news comes last.

All-age worship

Make tablets of cardboard, and write on them 'The Ten Commandments: simple instructions for young Christians'. Make a cardboard dove and write on it 'The Holy Spirit, given to those who are sorry, to guide them'.

Suggested hymns

To God be the glory; Rejoice! The Lord is King; Rejoice in the Lord always; The Kingdom of God is justice and joy.

Third Sunday of Advent   16 December
Second Service   Our God Comes

Ps. 50.1–6 Our God comes [62 Wait for God in silence]; Isa. 35
Here is your God; Luke 1.57–66 The birth of the Baptist [67–80
Benedictus]

> 'Our God comes and will not keep silence.' Psalm 50.2 (Common
> Worship)

Theophany

What would you do if, in five minutes' time, God appeared, sitting
on a cloud in the sky, in all his glory? Yes, look for somewhere
to hide. Me, too! Yet there are plenty of verses in the Bible which
appear to warn us that this could happen at any time – and many
of them are read in church during the Advent season. We call the
appearance of God in this way a 'theophany', from Greek words
meaning 'God' and 'to appear clearly'. Compare the word 'theophany' to the modern word 'cellophane®', which is a film enabling
you to see clearly what's inside. I'm not sure when the idea that
God might appear in this way was first thought of, but it was probably the Jews who first had the idea, and they, too, were terrified
at the thought – at first. If you believe that God has given you Ten
Commandments about how you should behave, and that he is as
aware as you are that you have fallen far short of what he expects
of you, the idea that he will come to be our judge is very alarming.

On our side

But gradually, starting from their experience at the Exodus, the
Israelites realized that they were God's Chosen People. They didn't
ask themselves what they had been chosen to do, very often, but
they concluded that God must be on their side. All the other nations
would be condemned, and Israel would be declared innocent, when
God came to judge between them. So the coming of God was something to be awaited with joy, when God's people would be recom-
pensed for all their suffering, and vindicated for their faithfulness.
You can see that this might lead to a certain complacency.

Return from exile

When the Israelites were weeping by the waters of Babylon, they dreamt of a day when God would appear to set them free from their exile. Then he would lead them across the desert back to their own land. This new optimistic picture of the coming of God to save his people inspired some of the loveliest poetry in the Bible. The fiftieth Psalm proclaims that

> Our God comes and will not keep silence ...
> He calls the heavens above,
> and the earth, that he may judge his people:
> 'Gather to me my faithful,
> who have sealed my covenant with sacrifice' ...
> For God himself is judge.

And in the thirty-fifth chapter of Isaiah occur the lovely lines – I'm quoting from the Authorized Version:

> The wilderness and the solitary place shall be glad for them;
> and the desert shall rejoice, and blossom as the rose ...
> Strengthen ye the weak hands, and confirm the feeble knees.
> Say to them that are of a fearful heart, Be strong, fear not ...
> Then the eyes of the blind shall be opened,
> and the ears of the deaf shall be unstopped.
> Then shall the lame man leap as an hart,
> and the tongue of the dumb sing:
> for in the wilderness shall waters break out,
> and streams in the desert.
> And an highway shall be there ...
> and it shall be called The way of holiness ...
> No lion shall be there ...
> but ... the ransomed of the Lord shall return ...
> and sorrow and sighing shall flee away.

Messiah

But when the Jews eventually returned to Sion, their troubles were not ended. So they dreamt that the coming of the Lord was still in the future, when he would send a general to lead them to victory over their enemies. They waited and waited, but the triumphant Messiah never came. Then, at last, our God *did* come, but not in the form they had expected. The Messiah arrived, in the person of a weak and defenceless baby, lying in a manger. At that first Christmas, all the promises were fulfilled. And all their presuppositions were shattered. Still, today, people wait for the coming of God in power. Maybe, one day, that is how God will descend to us. But much more important for us now is to realize that God *has* come to earth, and the theophany occurred in Bethlehem. Paradoxically, when we got a glimpse of God's true nature, it was not God's power, but his vulnerability which was revealed. And the true celebrities, the people who resemble God, whom we should imitate, are not the rich and powerful. God's heroes make themselves vulnerable, claiming nothing for themselves, but devoting their lives to serving others; so they reveal the character of God. They are the true theophany. That, surely, is the message of Christmas.

Suggested hymns

How lovely on the mountains; Joy to the world, the Lord is come; O come, O come Emmanuel; The Lord will come and not be slow.

Fourth Sunday of Advent   23 December
Principal Service   **Jesus in the Womb**
Micah 5.2–5a A leader from Bethlehem; *Canticle*: Magnificat Luke 1.46–55, *or* Ps. 80.1–8 Come with salvation; Heb. 10.5–10 When Christ came into the world; Luke 1.39–45 [46–55] Mary visits Elizabeth

> 'When Christ came into the world, he said, "Sacrifices and offerings you have not desired, but a body you have prepared for me."' Hebrews 10.5

Entrails

What do you think of human insides? Yes, 'messy', I should say. An exhibition is going round showing human cadavers carefully dissected, preserved and put on display. Many people can't make up their minds whether to visit the exhibition, because in one way they'd find it repellent; yet there's no denying that discovering how our bodies work could be fascinating and useful. It depends how it's done. We are all made up of the same organs; we inherit these structures from our parents, and without them we couldn't live. Yet former generations were quite squeamish, and refused to talk about or even think of the workings of the human body, even in private. Especially the reproductive system was a taboo subject; yet it's the way we all came into the world.

Abhorrent

We should remember this when we sing the Christmas carol, 'Oh come, all ye faithful'. It contains the line, 'Lo, he abhors not the Virgin's womb.' Today, those words sound almost twee – why should Jesus shrink to enter a human uterus? Yet if you had lived at the time of Jesus, or soon afterwards, you would have found it quite shocking to think of the pure, immaculate Son of God being surrounded for nine months by human flesh and fluids, and then going through the messy process of childbirth. Some of the Greek philosophers found it quite, well, abhorrent. Some rejected Christianity altogether for this reason; others said that the incarnation was merely a myth; Jesus wasn't really human, he didn't want to get mixed up in all that stuff. He was a supernatural being, they said, a vision, floating through the world about six inches above the ground. How could the Divine become a foetus, they asked?

Missing the point

Yet the philosophers were shrinking away from reality. Jesus was truly human, as well as truly divine, as we proclaim every week in the Nicene Creed. There's a reason for insisting on this: the only way for God to save human beings was to become one. Jesus 'assumed' human nature, body, mind and soul – and the early Christians had a saying: 'what is not assumed cannot be redeemed'. So it was essential that Jesus should have a genuine human body, and be born in the same messy way that we all are, because otherwise he couldn't have redeemed us totally. A purely spiritual Saviour is no Saviour at all: he would be merely a vision or a spook. The philosophers were missing the point altogether.

Te Deum

So the Christians wrote a great hymn: 'We praise thee, O God' – in Latin, *Te Deum*. In the Book of Common Prayer it was to be said or sung at matins. It contains the great line, 'When thou tookest upon thee to deliver man, thou didst not abhor the Virgin's womb.' That's where the line in 'O come, all ye faithful' is quoted from. This was in direct contradiction to the philosophers: there's nothing shameful about pregnancy and childbirth, it says. Jesus didn't stop being divine when he came to earth; but he also became totally human, like you and me. As the Letter to the Hebrews puts it, 'When Christ came into the world, he said, "… a body you have prepared for me".' A real human body, like yours and mine.

The body

Sometimes we wish we hadn't got a human body. We should like to have superhuman powers, like Batman – the body is a source of tiredness, hunger and pain. Yet, just when we are getting fed up with being human, we remember that Jesus willingly shared our limitations, from when he entered the womb of the Blessed Virgin, till he hung in agony on the cross. He knows what it's like to be human; so we can lay on him all our human frailty and weariness, and he will share the burden with us. Jesus can be our friend, because he is neither distant nor remote. He gives us moral strength, because he has been tempted in all things, the same as we are. In the days before Christmas, as we think of the Virgin Mary, pregnant and exhausted, dragging her heavy body on a bumpy donkey-ride to Bethlehem, we can be grateful to her for what she went through, and thank Jesus that he didn't 'abhor the Virgin's womb'. It's because of that that we are saved: he became what we are, so that we might become what he is: both human and divine.

All-age worship

Play at 'Mothers and Babies'. Find out all you can about your nearest Maternity Hospital.

Suggested hymns

Hark, the glad sound! the Saviour comes; Meekness and majesty; O come, all ye faithful; Where is this stupendous stranger?

Fourth Sunday of Advent   23 December
Second Service   **Joseph's Song**

Ps. 123 As a maid looks to her mistress [131 My soul is like a weaned child]; Isa. 10.33—11.10 A shoot from the stump of Jesse; Matt. 1.18–25 Joseph's dream

> *'Now the birth of Jesus the Messiah took place in this way. When his mother Mary had been engaged to Joseph, but before they lived together, she was found to be with child from the Holy Spirit. Her husband Joseph, being a righteous man and unwilling to expose her to public disgrace, planned to dismiss her quietly.'*
> *Matthew 1.18–19*

Betrothal

Betrothal vows among the Jews were so strong that an engaged couple were considered for legal purposes as though they were already married. If an engaged woman had sex with another man, both of them were to be stoned to death, provided that the offended fiancé cast the first stone. So St Joseph could have demanded Mary's execution. But St Matthew assures us that Joseph was 'a righteous man', and decided to save her from death by divorcing her. The angel persuaded him instead to wait until the baby was born, and then to marry her and adopt the child.

Minor aristocracy

There are two other remarkable things about Joseph in the pages of Scripture. The first was that he was a member of the royal family. The Gospels tell us that Jesus was descended from King David, not through Mary but because he had been adopted by Joseph. Yet Joseph had sunk to the level of a poor carpenter in Nazareth. What a come-down for a royal!

Accent

The second curious thing is that he probably spoke with a working-class accent. According to St Matthew's Gospel, St Peter is hiding in the courtyard of the High Priest's palace while Jesus is inside, on trial for his life. Peter doesn't want anyone to know he is Jesus's disciple, lest he too is executed. Then, says the Gospel, 'The bystanders came up and said to Peter, "Certainly you are also one of them, for your accent betrays you.'" In other words, Peter and all the disciples spoke with an accent. Jesus too must have learnt the Galilee accent from his parents Joseph and Mary. The Province of Galilee was in the far north of Israel, and their accent was despised by the posh folk in Jerusalem; but probably they were proud of it. Joseph's royal ancestors came from Bethlehem, but he must have lived in Nazareth long enough to pick up the north-country accent.

Joseph's song

So a retired vicar called Michael Counsell wrote a poem in which Joseph speaks north-country. Forgive me if I make a pig's ear of the accent while I read it to you. Joseph was a good man, and he won't mind us laughing at how he got things wrong. The last line contains a lesson for us all.

Minor aristocracy

Now Joseph was a decent bloke,
who lived among North Country folk
but had the whole thing wrong –
till God's white angel put him right,
appearing in a dream at night –
and so he sang this song:
'When I were but a little lad,
I learnt this lesson from me Dad:
"To find a decent lass,
it doesn't do a bit of good
to say your folks 'ave got blue blood
if you've no bloomin' brass."

My pride is not 'ypocrisy –
we're minor aristocracy,
me family and me;
related to the royalty
to whom you all owe loyalty –
it's in me family tree.
But by some deft skulduggery,
and not a little thuggery,
me uncle's younger son
took much more than he merited
of what we'd all inherited,
and left our lot with none.

Resulting from this larceny
I 'ad to turn to carpentry –
a craftsman, as you see;
and earn me bread with 'ands of toil
not owning any land or soil,
oop north in Galilee.
No dowry gift could I 'ave paid,
but thought that I 'ad found a maid
of good repute to wed.
We got engaged the other day,
but now she's in the family way –
before we've been to bed!

And now, since I'm of David's line
I've got to waste me precious time,
oop sticks, and travel down
to royal Bethle'em again,
to register with other men
'oo're born in David's town.
So 'oo'll remember Joseph's fame –
in spite of me illustrious name –
the princeling 'oo was poor?
Deprived of wealth's security,
I'll sink into obscurity,
forgotten evermore!

When I were but a little lad,
I learnt this lesson from me Dad:
"To find a decent lass,
it doesn't do a bit of good
to say your folks 'ave got blue blood
if you've no bloomin' brass."'
The angel came to him and said,
'When will you get it in your head?
You never can afford
to guess what God is going to do,
or what he has in store for you,
when working for the Lord!'

Suggested hymns

As Joseph was a-walking, he heard an angel sing; Good Joseph had a garden; Joseph dearest, Joseph mine; Joseph was an old man.

CHRISTMAS, EPIPHANY AND CANDLEMAS

Christmas is a season of joy, as we celebrate the coming of God into the world he created, the Word made flesh in the shape of a child in a manger. Christmas and Easter are the two focal points of the Christian year, and both should be celebrated as festivals of light, to keep the rhythm of the year swinging along and taking our souls with it. It is the children's festival, so we have family services, sharing the awe of the children when they see that Jesus became a child like them; and the whole family of God gather at God's table to share in the family meal of Christmas communion. The hangings and the vestments in church are in gold, if possible, on Christmas Day, and white on the Sundays from Christmas to Candlemas. January 6 is Epiphany, which means revealing who Jesus is. The readings tell of times when the divine nature of Christ was revealed. The wise men were not Jewish, and were the first non-Jews to recognize Jesus as 'King, and God, and Sacrifice' for every nation. He was revealed as Son of God by the voice from heaven at his Baptism. Andrew brought his brother to see the Lamb of God, revealed to take away the sin of the whole world. When baby Jesus was 40 days old he was presented to God in the Temple, and the aged priest, Simeon, hailed him as the one who would bring light to the Gentiles. That is why the fortieth day after Christmas is called Candlemas. Yet Simeon foresaw that a sword of grief would pierce Mary's heart, so at this point we turn away from celebrating Christmas, and start preparing ourselves for Good Friday and Easter in the solemn season of Lent.

Christmas Day   25 December

Any of the following sets of readings may be used on the evening of Christmas Eve and on Christmas Day: Set III should be used at some service during the celebration.

Set I   Hark, the Herald Angels Sing

Isa. 9.2–7 A child is born; Ps. 96 Tell of his salvation; Titus 2.11–14 Salvation has come; Luke 2.1–14 [15–20] The birth and the shepherds

> 'And suddenly there was with the angel a multitude of the heavenly host, praising God and saying, "Glory to God in the highest

heaven, and on earth peace among those whom he favours!"'
Luke 2.13–14

Heavenly choirs

Happy Christmas! The story of Jesus begins and ends in music. The heavens were filled with angels singing, when the shepherds heard of his birth in Bethlehem. At the end of his time on earth, he ascended into heaven, where heavenly anthems are ringing the praise of God in eternity. We can be sure that when Jesus welcomes us into heaven, even the unmusical will enjoy what's going on.

Carols

Christmas carols are one type of music which almost everybody enjoys. They probably started life as interludes in the popular mystery plays of the Middle Ages, when different trade guilds would act scenes from the life of Jesus on carts around the town. The first carols were actually dances – the word carol is derived from the Italian *carola*, which means a ring-dance – perhaps the people danced their way through the streets, from one scene of the play to the next. One of the dancers would sing the verse, and the rest would join in the chorus as they stamped and clapped around in a circle. The words told the story of Christmas for those who couldn't read it for themselves. Then the Puritans banned dancing, and the old carols survived in sing-songs at the pub. In the churches only metrical settings of the psalms were allowed. When other forms of singing were introduced in the Nonconformist chapels, it was not the old carols, but newly written Christmas hymns.

Charles Wesley

One of the most prolific hymn-writers was Charles Wesley, who wrote more than 6,500. With his brother John Wesley he was one of the founders of Methodism, originally as a movement within the Church of England, and, after they died, as a separate denomination. They both wrote hymns, so that men and women might sing their way into faith; that those who were cultured might learn the Christian way of life, and the uneducated might be led into truth by means of melody and rhyme. Charles Wesley was ordained in 1735, and in 1738 he came to a personal knowledge of Jesus at a Moravian chapel in Aldersgate Street in London. His brother

John, four years older, felt his heart 'strangely warmed' and came to saving faith in the same place three days later.

Hark!

A year after that, Charles Wesley wrote a hymn with ten four-line verses, which originally began:

> Hark, how all the welkin rings,
> Glory to the King of kings!

It was published in this form in 1739, but in 1753 it was changed to:

> Hark, the herald-angels sing
> 'Glory to the new-born king'

According to one expert, this is one of the four most popular hymns in the English language.

Mendelssohn

The tune we sing it to was originally composed by Mendelssohn for his Festival Cantata to celebrate the four-hundredth anniversary of the invention of printing. Felix Mendelssohn-Bartholdy was born in 1809 into a Jewish-Christian family in Germany, and was a great favourite of Queen Victoria in England. The English music-scholar, Dr William Cummings, as a child, had once sung in a choir conducted by Mendelssohn, and he realized that with a little adaptation this magnificent tune could be made to fit Charles Wesley's words. Immediately all the other tunes to which they had been sung were forgotten, and this became the universal favourite. Curiously, Mendelsson himself described the tune as 'soldier-like and buxom', but more appropriate to bright and popular words than for religious use.

Best of both

Perhaps we have got the best of both worlds. 'Hark, the herald-angels sing' is certainly popular, and it tells the story of the virgin birth and the shepherds in the fields. But it also explains why this is so important to us. This humble child is in fact the divine Son of God, come to earth to save you and me from death and from guilt, fully human and completely divine. He was born, that, when our bodies die, our souls may be born again into the deathless life of heaven. If we imitate the humility of the babe in the manger, he will take us one day to live with him in the glory of heaven. When we understand the message of this carol, we can mean what we say, when we wish each other, 'Happy Christmas!'

All-age worship

Make Christmas cards with pictures of shepherds and angels on them.

Suggested carols

Angels from the realms of glory; Ding! dong! merrily on high; Hark, the herald angels sing; O little town of Bethlehem.

Christmas Day   25 December
Set II   Being Human, Being Divine
Isa. 62.6–12 Prepare a way; Ps. 97 God comes to rescue his people; Titus 3.4–7 Salvation by grace; Luke 2.[1–7] 8–20 Shepherds go to Bethlehem

> *'The angel said to [the shepherds], "… to you is born this day in the city of David a Saviour, who is the Messiah, the Lord. This will be a sign for you: you will find a child wrapped in bands of cloth and lying in a manger."' Luke 2.10–12*

Divine

The angels told the shepherds that Jesus was the Messiah, the Lord. The word 'Lord', in the Bible, always has a double meaning.

First, it's the English translation for the name of God, in the Old Testament.
    Second, it reminds us that God is our ruler, our king, who commands us what to do and we obey him.

So the angels explain that Jesus is in charge of our lives, the divine Son of God. But, they told the shepherds, he's a helpless baby, born to a poor family, unable to afford a proper cradle and lying among the hay of a manger. Thoroughly human, in fact. So what sort of divine leader is that?

Being human

The problem is that we haven't yet properly understood what being human means; nor yet what it means to be divine. The essence of being human isn't being powerful, beautiful and strong. A horse can be powerful, beautiful and strong, but that doesn't make it a human being. *Homo sapiens* is 'the crown of creation', but that doesn't mean that we are perfect in every way. Being human means having the power to think, and make conscious choices; that's what Jesus took upon himself when he became a human being. But he voluntarily took on human limitations – he couldn't be in more than one place at a time, he needed food and drink, he needed rest. He started life as a child, needing to be taught; he spoke a particular language, adopting its metaphors and figures of speech. He adopted Jewish assumptions and attitudes; he didn't have an encyclopaedic knowledge. He experienced profound human emotions: he was tempted, angry, afraid, he laughed and he wept, just like us. The Christian Church is often criticized for its failings and inadequacy. That's because we are human, not superhuman. We are forgetful, and sometimes mistaken. We make assumptions, and take things for granted. The person in the pulpit and the people in the pews aren't angels – yet. So the Church isn't perfect – you wouldn't expect it to be, because it's made up of fallible human beings. But at least, when we get things wrong, we say we are sorry, and promise to try harder in future. Jesus was human too. Yet human beings are free to disobey God, and Jesus never sinned; so sinning isn't an essential part of being human. The definitive human being is not Adam, it's Jesus. Jesus became a human being at Christmas, like us, but in so doing, he changed the definition of what being human means.

Being divine

Jesus also changed our understanding of what it means to be divine. Jesus united in himself humanity and divinity, so they can't be as incompatible as we assume. When we think of God, we imagine all the powerful forces in the universe rolled into one, omnipotent and omniscient. Of course, that's true. But God became human at Christmas, so the divine nature must have another, vulnerable side to it. If God is like Jesus, that means that God wants us to think of him as a person, and relate to him as we relate to our friends. God, too, must be willing to make sacrifices for those he loves. Without forgetting the almighty transcendence of our Creator and Lord, we combine with that the understanding that God loves us with a deep, personal love. The God revealed in Jesus is passionately devoted to the poor, radically open to the outcast, extraordinarily hospitable to sinners, and caustically critical of those in authority.

A pretty story

So Christmas is a pretty story, and it's good to approach the babe in the manger with childlike love and joy. But Christmas is also profoundly revolutionary, because the Christ-child changes our whole idea of what it means to be human, and what it means to be divine. If we want to be truly human, we have to be human in Jesus's way, not in the world's way. He came to where we live, and became what we are, in order to make us what he is, and take us to live where he lives. Jesus became human, so that you and I might become divine.

All-age worship

Make a cardboard manger, and write on it all the words you can think of to describe what Jesus was like when he lived on earth. That's what we're supposed to be like, too.

Suggested carols

From heaven you came, helpless babe; O come, all ye faithful (5 verses); On Christmas night all Christians sing; See, amid the winter's snow.

Christmas Day 25 December
Set III What Sort of Son?
Isa. 52.7–10 The messenger of peace; Ps. 98 God's victory; Heb. 1.1–4 [5–12] God speaks through a Son; John 1.1–14 The Word became flesh

> 'Long ago God spoke to our ancestors in many and various ways by the prophets, but in these last days he has spoken to us by a Son.' Hebrews 1.1–2

Speaking through a Son

How many times have you heard somebody say, 'I admire Jesus as a man, but I can't accept that he was the Son of God'? It's a common excuse for not going to church. But it ignores the very strong claims that the child who was born on Christmas Day made about himself when he grew up. And in the New Testament there's a book called 'A Letter to Hebrews'; a Jew writing to other Jews about Jesus the Jew. It begins: 'Long ago God spoke to our ancestors in many and various ways by the prophets, but in these last days he has spoken to us by a Son.' The first followers of Jesus believed that on that first Christmas Day, a completely new phase began in God's relationship with the world, because God was now speaking to us in a much more direct way: through Jesus, his Son.

Did Jesus believe it?

Did Jesus believe this himself? The answer has got to be yes, because of his words and his actions. But first we must ask, are the reports in the Gospels about what Jesus said completely accurate? Here again we can answer 'yes'. Would the New Testament writers have got away with fudging the whole story of Jesus's claims to sonship, when there were still many people alive who had heard him for themselves, and who would soon kick up a rumpus if anyone started telling lies about Jesus? Many of these authors were put to death for what they had written – is it likely that they would have gone willingly to die, when they could have saved their lives by admitting that what they had written was all lies? So the first thing to notice is that when Jesus prayed to God, he called him 'Abba', which means something like 'Father dearest'. Then, when Jesus asked Peter, 'Who do you say that I am?', Peter replied, 'You are the Messiah, the Son of the Living God.' Instead of rebuking Peter for speaking blasphemy, Jesus praised him, saying that it was 'my Father in heaven' who had revealed this truth. Jesus told a parable about tenants who killed all the messengers sent to them by the landowner, who represents God, until he said, 'Now I will send to them my son.' Jesus said that from his birth, the kingdom of God had come into the world. He didn't begin his ministry until after his baptism, when he heard God saying, 'This is my beloved Son'. And so on, and so on, there are dozens of places where Jesus quite clearly claims to be the Son of God.

Confirmed by actions

These claims were born out by his actions. Jesus took it upon himself to contradict the laws of Moses: 'It was said to people in the old days ... but *I* say to you ...' For this he incurred the wrath of the priests and Pharisees. He could so easily have deflected their anger by admitting that he was just a man. But when the High Priest challenged Jesus at his trial, 'Are you the Messiah, the Son of the Blessed One?', Jesus replied, 'I am.' Then the Romans crucified him under an inscription, 'The King of the Jews', a phrase they wouldn't have used if Jesus hadn't used some such words of himself.

What sort of Son?

So there's no doubt that Jesus called himself the Son of God. But in what sense did he mean those words? What sort of Son was he? It's an important question to ask on Christmas Day, because many religions tell stories of lustful gods coming to earth and begetting half-human offspring by human mothers. The Christmas story is nothing like that. The Holy Spirit 'overshadowed' Mary, but God was not Jesus's *physical* father. Jews and Muslims are shocked because they think that this is what Christians claim. No, it was a spiritual relationship. Human sons resemble their human fathers, in their appearance, words and actions. So, if we say that Jesus was the spiritual Son of God, it means that his character reflects the character of the Almighty. On Christmas Day we don't just tell a pretty story. We are describing a turning point in history. God's plan to reveal himself reached the point where the divine Son of God could come to earth and be born as a human being. Jesus is our Saviour and our Lord; he loves us, and wants us to love him for ever.

All-age worship

Make a collection of 'father-and-son' photographs.

Suggested carols

Lord Jesus Christ, you have come to us; Mary had a baby, yes Lord; Once in royal David's city; The angel Gabriel from heaven came.

Christmas Day 25 December
Second Service **A Partridge in a Pear Tree**
Morning Ps. 110 This day of your birth, 117 Steadfast love;
Evening Ps. 8 Out of the mouths of babes; Isa. 65.17–25 A new
creation; Phil. 2.5–11 Jesus emptied himself, *or* Luke 2.1–20
(if it has not been used at the Principal Service of the day)

> *'Like the days of a tree shall the days of my people be.'* *Isaiah 65.22*

An ancient rhyme

You all know the Christmas carol which begins, 'On the first day of Christmas, my true love gave to me, a partridge in a pear tree.' It may have been a song used at Twelfth Night parties: if you didn't remember the right gift, you had to pay a 'forfeit' by doing something mildly silly. It refers to the twelve days of Christmas, which begin on Christmas Day, when we think of the birth of Jesus, and end on the day before the feast of the Epiphany, when we remember the coming of the wise men. So this song has its roots in the Christian faith, though it appears to be a purely secular party-game. Yet some people have suggested a Christian meaning to the twelve gifts – I shall come to that in a moment. The song first appeared in print in England in 1780, but the partridge was first introduced into England from France in the 1770s, and three versions of this carol in French are known. The French word for a partridge is *perdrix* [pronounced pear-*dree*], so possibly this was a French song later translated into English.

Christian?

Is there, then, a Christian meaning to the rhyme? Some people assure you that this song was taught to Roman Catholic children after the Reformation, when being a Catholic was a capital offence in England, to help them to learn the Catholic faith without giving away what religion they belonged to. So it's alleged that each gift has a symbolic meaning which wouldn't be understood by non-Catholics. There are a number of weaknesses in this theory. When Queen Elizabeth the First succeeded her Catholic sister 'Bloody' Mary, she tried at first to reconcile Catholic and Protestant. Later in her reign, some Catholics, who apparently wanted to put a Spaniard on the English throne, were indeed executed. But the law turned a blind eye to many ordinary Catholics. And nothing in the suggested symbolism would have been in any way objectionable to members of the Church of England. The story of the Catholic origins of this carol was never heard before the 1990s, and seems to many people to be an 'urban legend'. Nevertheless, I think it's worthwhile for people of all denominations to learn the so-called Christian meaning of the song, because it helps us to remember some aspects of Christian teaching, and claims a bit of the secular celebration of Christmas back for Christ, whose birthday it is. Aled Jones is alleged to have said, 'If you take Christ out of Christmas, all you are left with is M & S'!

Meaning

I have even been able to find a text in today's readings which refers to the twelve days and the pear tree – well, almost – which is, 'like the days of a tree shall the days of my people be'! (Groan!) Try to remember the Christian meaning of the carol:

The *true-love* is God who gives good gifts to those he loves.

A *partridge* is alleged to be willing to sacrifice her life to save her chicks, so this represents Jesus, and the *pear-tree* is the tree of the cross.

The *two turtle-doves* symbolize the Old and New Testaments.

Three French hens may be the gifts brought by the three wise men to Jesus, or alternatively they may be the three 'theological virtues' of faith, hope and love.

Four calling birds is actually a mishearing of 'colly-birds', meaning coal-black or blackbirds. The Christian symbolism is said to be the four Gospels, Matthew, Mark, Luke and John; or the prophets Isaiah, Jeremiah, Ezekiel and Daniel; or the four horsemen of the apocalypse.

Five gold rings are probably the coloured rings around a pheasant's throat. But they remind Christians of the five books of Moses, from Genesis to Deuteronomy.

Six geese a-laying (creatively) are the six days in which God created the world.

Seven swans a-swimming (gracefully) are the seven gifts of the Holy Spirit: prophecy, service, teaching, encouraging, giving, leadership and mercy.

Eight maids a-milking represent Jesus's love for the humble poor, revealed in the eight beatitudes.

Nine ladies dancing are the fruits of the Spirit: love, joy, peace, patience, kindness, goodness, faithfulness, gentleness and self-control.

Ten lords a-leaping are the Ten Commandments.

Eleven pipers piping represent the proclamation of the eleven apostles remaining after Judas committed suicide.

And *twelve drummers drumming* are the twelve teachings of the Apostles' Creed.

There you have it! Test each other this evening, to see how much you remember. And a very happy Christmas to you.

Suggested carols

Away in a manger; Child in the manger, infant of Mary; Silent night, holy night; While shepherds watched their flocks by night.

First Sunday of Christmas   30 December
Principal Service   **Faces of God**
1 Sam. 2.18–20, 26 Giving children to God; Ps. 148 Young and old together; Col. 3.12–17 The Word of Christ; Luke 2.41–52 The child Jesus in the Temple

> '[Jesus said to his parents], "Wist ye not that I must be about my Father's business?"' Luke 2.49 (Authorized Version)

Ancient Christmas blessing

On a Christmas card was printed what was said to be an 'Ancient Christmas blessing'. It's a very profound prayer, and will give you plenty to think about. Listen prayerfully:

> O God, you who are the God of a thousand faces, yet whom nothing can reveal so completely as the face of the child in Bethlehem: continue in our lives the mystery of his birth; may your Son become flesh in us, so that we may be for all those whom we meet an experience of your love.

Faces of God

This prayer gives us at least three things to think about: the many faces of God; God revealed in the face of Jesus; and God revealed through you and me. What does it mean to say that he is a God of a thousand faces? Surely these are the multiple ways in which God reveals his presence and his love:

First of all, there's the beauty of his creation. In the delicate colours of the sunrise and the grandeur of the sunset we recognize the face of God. In the surge of the tides and the power of the thunderstorm we see revealed another side to God's character. In the myriad stars seen through our telescopes, and the multitude of life-forms revealed by the microscope, we behold another aspect of the Creator's activity.

In the sonorous phrases of great poetry, and the harmonies of music, God speaks to us. In the works of great artists, and the challenge of great literature, we see the face of God.

Through the stern warnings of our teachers, and the warm embrace of those who care, he reminds us that he loves us, and expects us to behave lovingly towards others.

In television dramas, and the comments of strangers, we hear God speaking.

In the stillness of an ancient church, and the lives of those who care for the needy, we recognize his presence.

The one God reveals himself to people of different races and varied faiths in ways they can understand, which they will teach us if we listen.

Supremely, in the words of the Holy Scriptures we hear the language of God, explaining our need, and awakening our faith.

Yet this is only the beginning. Day by day we find new faces of God in the people around us, if only we are open to recognize him at work.

Truly he is the God of a thousand faces.

Babe in a manger

Yet while we recognize the presence of God about us, we have only seen a fraction of his self-revelation. For, as the prayer puts it, 'nothing can reveal [God] so completely as the face of the child in Bethlehem'. The face of every small child reveals to us something of God, by its complete absorption in the task in hand, its overwhelming joys and its sudden sorrows, its utter trust in the child's parents. But in the face of baby Jesus, we see that God has revealed his humility, coming down from the splendours of heaven to the poverty of one peasant family. Greater than the grandeur of God's glory is his sensational self-abasement. Then, as Jesus shares a life like ours, he identifies with us in our pain, and vulnerability to temptation. This is a face of God that we had never seen before. In the final act of self-sacrifice on the cross, God reveals his love in Christ. As Jesus himself said, he was about his Father's business.

God in us

But if the greatness of God is described in the gracious acts of Jesus, how can we possibly say that God becomes flesh in us? Surely there's no comparison? Yet our neighbours depend on us to reveal God's love to them. The world is so full of suffering, that God's love is not immediately obvious to those with little or no faith. God can't reveal himself to them directly, or they would be overwhelmed, so he relies on you to display his love to them. Sometimes you will do this by talking about God. More often, however, it's by your sympathy, your willingness to listen to their troubles and your deeds of practical kindness, that your friends and neighbours recognize that there's something different about people who go to church. It's a colossal responsibility. But God is relying on you.

All-age worship

Arabs say God has a hundred names, yet there is only one God. Find a large ball on which you can write as many words as you can think of that we use to describe God.

Suggested carols

In the bleak midwinter; Love came down at Christmas; O little town of Bethlehem; See him lying on a bed of straw.

34

First Sunday of Christmas 30 December
Second Service Equality

Ps. 132 David's descendants; Isa. 61 The Spirit is upon me;
Gal. 3.27—4.7 Children of God; *Gospel at Holy Communion*:
Luke 2.15–21 He was called Jesus

*'There is no longer Jew or Greek, there is no longer slave or free,
there is no longer male and female; for all of you are one in Christ
Jesus. And if you belong to Christ, then you are Abraham's offspring, heirs according to the promise.' Galatians 3.28–29*

Ancestry

'Who do you think you are?' That's the title of a television series
about discovering your ancestors. Researching one's family tree has
become much easier since the development of the internet. You can
go online, and gain immediate access to records of births, marriages
and deaths, and census returns, from the early nineteenth century,
and parish registers, some going back to the sixteenth century. Anyone who researches their family tree will find, with luck, there may
be someone famous among their ancestors; there's the occasional
villain or convict; local people who married immigrants, and for
many of our ancestors there's no record of them ever having been
married at all. Up until recently, many people clung to a myth of
racial purity: 'I'm descended from good English stock', or whatever.
Now the records, and genetic profiling, have shown that we are all
descended from a hodge-podge of different ancestors.

Abraham's children

There were similar myths in Bible times. Jews claimed with certainty that they were children of Abraham, forgetting that many
of their ancestors may have taken partners from outside the tribe.
According to Genesis, Abraham had two sons, one of whom was
the ancestor of the Jews and the other the ancestor of the Arabs.
The Bible also says that all the races of the earth are descended from
Noah, and before that from Adam and Eve. Before non-Jews could
be accepted as sharing in the promises that God made to Abraham's
descendants, St Paul had to argue that by being baptized into Jesus,
we have all become honorary Jews, and spiritual descendants of
Abraham. So all races are equal. This was a truly revolutionary
suggestion in the ancient world. Paul wrote to the Greek-speaking

Galatians, 'There is no longer Jew or Greek, there is no longer slave or free, there is no longer male and female; for all of you are one in Christ Jesus. And if you belong to Christ, then you are Abraham's offspring, heirs according to the promise.' To the Colossians, Paul wrote that when we became Christians we acquired a new self, in which 'there is no longer Greek and Jew, circumcised and uncircumcised, barbarian, Scythian, slave and free; but Christ is all and in all'. Scythians were the most despised among the barbarian races, and slaves had no legal rights at all! So there are no distinctions between races, between social classes, between genders, between the respectable and the outcast – since Christ came, all are equal.

Other faiths

Judaism was the only faith believing in only one God – together with Christianity, which was an offshoot of Judaism. Then Islam arose, another monotheistic faith calling themselves children of Abraham. For many centuries, Jews, Christians and Muslims, the three Abrahamic faiths, tolerated each other and co-operated as 'Children of the Book'. Later this broke down, but the blame certainly wasn't all on one side. Now we must work at re-establishing a dialogue between the faiths, because with all our differences we have so much in common. St Paul said that 'From one ancestor [God] made all nations to inhabit the whole earth ... so that they would search for God and perhaps grope for him and find him ... [A]s even some of your own poets have said, "For we too are his offspring."'

A prejudiced Church

Jesus, too, welcomed foreigners and affirmed the dignity of women. So why has the message of equality not been proclaimed loud and clear by his followers? Any Christian who stands before a sixth-form class talking about their faith is inevitably asked, 'Why then is your Church so sexist and homophobic, so unconcerned about injustice and the planet?' Although many Christians have been at the forefront of the struggle for equality, on the whole we come over to the rest of the world as deeply prejudiced. Of course, human beings aren't all equal in every respect. Everyone has special gifts and talents which others don't have, and can put them at the service of the rest. But this is very seldom anything to do with heredity, much more a matter of what opportunities, education and encouragement a child receives. Followers of Jesus, surely, ought to be seen as without exception supporters of racial, gender and every other sort of tolerance. Get out there, and join the marches and demonstrations, to show that we are not behind anyone else in welcoming all sorts and conditions as children of God, and worthy of equal respect, compassion and opportunity.

Suggested hymns

Christ is the world's true light; From the eastern mountains; In Christ there is no East or West; When I needed a neighbour.

Epiphany   Sunday 6 January
(When Epiphany falls on a Sunday, 13 Jan. has the readings for the Baptism of Christ; 20 Jan. is called Epiphany 3 and has the readings for Epiphany 2; 27 Jan. is called Epiphany 4 and has the readings for Epiphany 3.)
Principal Service   Incense
Isa. 60.1–6 Bringing gold and incense; Ps. 72.[1–9] 10–15 Kings will bow before him; Eph. 3.1–12 Preaching to Gentiles; Matt. 2.1–12 Visit of the Magi

'Opening their treasure-chests, they offered him gifts of gold, frankincense, and myrrh.' Matthew 2.11

Old Testament

The wise men offered to baby Jesus gifts of gold, frankincense and myrrh. Frankincense is a perfume, made by burning the resin which oozes from the bark of a tree which grows in Arabia. The word 'incense' is connected with 'incendiary', meaning burning; 'frank' means free or pure; frankincense gives out its perfume freely when it's burnt. The Egyptian Pharaohs used incense to drive away two very annoying things: bad smells and demons! It was used in Babylon when praying to their gods, and spread to India, China, Japan, Greece and Rome. It was used in the Temple in Jerusalem as a sacrifice to show honour to the Lord God; the first five books of the Old Testament mention incense more than fifty times, and the book of Exodus lists the mixture of different spices to be used in making it. Isaiah condemns incense when it's used in the worship of idols;

but in his great vision of God in the Temple, he describes 'the house filled with smoke'. Both Isaiah and Malachi predicted the coming of the wise men to Jesus – Isaiah wrote, 'All those from Sheba shall come. They shall bring gold and frankincense ...' Malachi foretold that foreigners would worship the Messiah: 'From the rising of the sun to its setting, my name is great among the nations, and in every place incense is offered to my name, and a pure offering ... says the LORD of hosts.'

New Testament

Incense is mentioned in the New Testament, not only as one of the gifts of the Magi, but also when Zechariah, the priest, is told that he will be the father of John the Baptist. It was his turn to make the incense-offering, when 'there appeared to him an angel of the Lord, standing at the right side of the altar of incense'. In St John's visions in the book of Revelation, the smoke rising up to heaven becomes a metaphor for the offering of prayer: 'the four living creatures and the twenty-four elders fell before the Lamb, each holding a harp and golden bowls full of incense, which are the prayers of the saints'. This image is borrowed from the book of Psalms: 'Let my prayer be counted as incense before you, and the lifting up of my hands as an evening sacrifice.'

Today

Incense helps you to relax: the book of Proverbs says that 'perfume and incense make the heart glad'. Eastern 'joss sticks' – a corruption of the Portuguese word *deos* meaning 'god' – may be mildly narcotic. Incense was originally used to drive away bad smells, so it was used at funerals to overpower the smell of decay, and was carried through the streets in front of Byzantine kings. A huge censer, the *Botafumeiro,* is swung the full width of the cathedral at Santiago de Compostella, to cover the travel smells of the hordes of pilgrims. Incense was hugely expensive, hence its use was limited to the rich. So it became a suitable gift to offer to a king, and therefore to an important god. Several of our hymns interpret the frankincense offered to baby Jesus as an acknowledgement that he was God incarnate: 'incense doth a God disclose'. Its use in church followed naturally, first in the churches of the East such as the Egyptian Coptic Church, and later in the Roman Catholic Church. Some Anglican and Lutheran churches use incense, too; the 'high-church' tradition is often humorously called 'bells and smells'. The charcoal is burnt in a metal 'thurible', carried by a 'thurifer', and the incense grains are spooned onto it from a container called, from its shape, a 'boat', carried by a 'boat-bearer'. Some churches which don't use incense during the rest of the year like to obtain some for Epiphany, though we must remember that some worshippers are actually allergic to it. The smoke represents our prayers rising to the presence of God, and it reminds us that Jesus is our King and our God. We use all five senses in our worship, offering them in thanksgiving to God. The part of the brain which recognizes smells is very close to the part which processes our memory, so the sweet smell of incense is very evocative. If you like to visit churches in this country and abroad, you may find that the first whiff of incense is redolent of many of the holiest places you have been to, and takes you back in memory to moments of deep awe and reverence.

All-age worship

Compare the effects of different essential oils and perfumes. Make a model thurible, or a joss-stick holder.

Suggested hymns

Brightest and best of the sons of the morning; Earth has many a noble city; O worship the Lord in the beauty of holiness; We three kings of orient are.

Epiphany   Sunday 6 January
Second Service   As with Gladness
Morning Ps. 132 David's descendants, 113 From the sun's rising; Evening Ps. 98 In the sight of the nations, 100 All the earth; Bar. 4.36—5.9 Look towards the east, *or* Isa. 60.1–9 Kings shall come; John 2.1–11 Jesus reveals his glory

> *'Nations shall come to your light,*
> *and kings to the brightness of your dawn …*
> *The wealth of the nations shall come to you.*
> *A multitude of camels shall cover you,*
> *the young camels of Midian and Ephah;*
> *all those from Sheba shall come.*

They shall bring gold and frankincense,
and shall proclaim the praise of the LORD.' Isaiah 60.3, 5–6

Prophecy

In the Old Testament, the prophet Isaiah said that when Israel's 'light' has come, kings will come on camels from Sheba and other countries to the east, bringing gold and frankincense. St Matthew in the New Testament wrote that wise men from the east – magi – followed the light of a star to where Jesus was born, and offered him gold, frankincense and myrrh. If you have a very strong faith, you will exclaim, 'A miracle! Isaiah had a vision, and the Lord told him to write those exact words about something which would happen 800 years in the future.' If you are a sceptic, however, you will say, 'Humbug! It was mere coincidence!' Well, if you can believe that you can believe anything. There are several hundred prophecies in the Old Testament which are fulfilled in the New Testament, and if you think that all those coincidences happened purely by chance, you are more gullible than the most superstitious Christian. Confounded by this argument, the sceptics will be forced to admit that it's unlikely to be a coincidence, but will defend themselves by arguing that there were no magi, Matthew made the whole thing up. In which case, we reply, why didn't Matthew call them kings from Sheba, and why did he include myrrh among their gifts? The New Testament doesn't mention kings, and Isaiah never talks about myrrh. Myrrh is mentioned in other places, but as a personal perfume, never as a gift. If Matthew was going to invent a fiction, why didn't he go the whole hog and make it an exact fulfilment? But there's a third possibility, if you are neither a complete sceptic nor a believer in miracles. Some Christians believe that the magi came, just as Matthew described it, but that the Holy Spirit inspired him to recognize that the similarity between this and what Isaiah wrote goes much deeper than the mere details. The Old Testament prophet foresaw that sometime in the future, people from other nations would come to the Jewish people to learn from them what God had revealed to them about himself. Then they would bring the gifts of their own culture and what they themselves had learnt of God, and contribute them to a greater religion in the future. And that was fulfilled at the birth of Jesus; people from many nations came to Jesus during his lifetime, and to his followers after he had ascended into heaven, to learn about the Christian God of Love. But the variety of the different cultural traditions which they brought with them has immeasurably enriched the Jewish religion of Jesus, and turned it into a tolerant, worldwide faith which can fulfil the hopes of everybody on earth.

As with gladness

This means that the traditional Christian story of the three kings, though it may not accurately correspond to the gospel narrative about the magi, does indeed go to the heart of it. The old carols are right when they interpret the gifts as recognizing Jesus as a King, a God, and a Sacrifice. 'As with gladness men of old' was written by William Chatterton Dix, the Bristol-born manager of an insurance company in Glasgow. Aged 29, he had been struck down by a near fatal illness, which confined him to bed for many months and left him very depressed. Then, on January the sixth in 1858, he read the Gospel of the day from his prayer book, and, as a devout Christian, he was struck afresh with the movingly simple and beautiful story of the babe in the manger, and the men who were wise enough to offer all they had at his feet. Each of us has a sort of 'inner Scrooge' which is tempted to scoff at those who have faith. At this time of year, when we are just about 'carolled out', and never want to taste another mince pie, carols like this one, or the awe on the face of a child kneeling by a crib, can bring back to us the sheer wonder of the Christmas story, of a God who was humble enough to come to earth, live and die like us, to bring shepherds and kings together, that we may live like him, and dwell together with him in heaven.

Suggested hymns

As with gladness men of old; Bethlehem, of noblest cities; The first Nowell; Who would think that what was needed?

Baptism of Christ
(see note on p. 37) 13 January
Principal Service   Turning Points

Isa. 43.1–7 When you pass through the waters; Ps. 29 The voice of the Lord is over the waters; Acts 8.14–17 Baptism and the Holy Spirit; Luke 3.15–17, 21–22 The Baptism of Jesus

> 'When all the people were baptized, and when Jesus also had been baptized and was praying, the heaven was opened, and the

Holy Spirit descended upon him in bodily form like a dove. And a voice came from heaven, "You are my Son, the Beloved; with you I am well pleased."' Luke 3.21–22

Turning points

For each of us, there come turning points in our life. Days after which nothing will ever be the same.

- It may be the day you started school – or when you moved to a new school.
- Maybe it was the day you first met your best friend, or your life-partner – the day you first realized that you were in love.
- The day you started in your first job, or when you were promoted to a post of responsibility.
- It may have been the day you discovered music, art or literature – or went to your first football match.

Great or small in their importance, these turning points had a long-term significance in your life which you may have only half-realized at the time. Some people give a secular explanation of why those days were important. Others say that God opened their eyes to some new truth, at each of those life-changing moments.

Jesus aged twelve

Jesus, too, had turning points in his life. The first came when he was 12 years old, when he went up to Jerusalem for the first time, and debated God's law with the experts. When his parents found him in the Temple, he explained himself in words which, literally translated, mean, 'Didn't you know I have to be about the things belonging to my father?' This is often translated as 'in my father's house', but 12 was the age when boys went to work in the family business, so it could mean, 'I must start working for God, my heavenly Father.' Either way, it was a turning point. He realized, probably for the first time, that his relationship with God was like that of father and son. Gradually he developed a deeper understanding of the special and unique relationship role he was to play in God's plans.

Jesus's baptism

However, until he was nearly 30 Jesus got on with the family business of carpentry. Then his cousin John started baptizing the crowds in the River Jordan, proclaiming that the kingdom of God was about to begin. Now Jesus realized that his hour had come. He was baptized, and as he came up from the water, he heard his Father's voice, exclaiming, 'You are my Son, the Beloved; with you I am well pleased.' These words were quoted from two different places in the Old Testament. 'You are my son' was from Psalm 2, and was spoken by God to the new king. So Jesus realized he was called to be the Messiah. But 'In you I am well pleased' comes from Isaiah 42, in what are called the Servant Songs. These poems climax in Isaiah 53, when it's made abundantly clear that anyone who serves God will have to suffer for it. So the track of Jesus's life was mapped out for him at this moment: he was to be not just the Messiah, but the crucified Saviour.

Conversion

For each of us, similar moments happen in our lives, and there's no going back. We have been heading for some goal, and we realize it's more important to take another direction altogether. The technical term for these turning points is 'conversion', but it takes many forms. Sometimes the life-changing experience comes like a bolt from the blue, and in a moment of deep emotion we give our lives to God. More often we work up to it gradually, until one day we wake up and realize that we are not the same person that we were six months ago. For every Christian, there comes a turning point when we realize that obeying God is more important than anything else – than being rich and famous, or even being happy. As was the case with Jesus, there may be a long gap between the day we commit ourselves, and the time when we realize what self-denial and suffering that may involve. But when the turning points come in your life, you will recognize them for what they are. And you will know, deep within yourself, that you can't ignore them – when God calls, you have to do what he asks you to. But, like Jesus again, with the call comes the gift of God's power, giving you the strength to do everything you have to. Just say yes and sign on the dotted line, and God will work out the details of your contract.

All-age worship

Make cards to give to your friends and family, reading 'God says, "You are my child; I'm pleased with you."'

Suggested hymns

O happy day; Spirit of the living God; When Jesus came to Jordan; Will you come and follow me?

Baptism of Christ

13 January

Second Service   **The River of Life**

Ps. 46 There is a river, 47 Clap your hands; Isa. 55.1–11 Come to the waters; Rom. 6.1–11 Baptized into Christ; *Gospel at Holy Communion*: Mark 1.4–11 The baptism of Jesus

> *'There is a river whose streams make glad the city of God, the holy place of the dwelling of the Most High.' Psalm 46.4 (Common Worship)*

Thirst

Have you ever been thirsty? I mean, really thirsty, knowing that if you don't get a drink of water soon you will die of dehydration. Sadly there are millions of people in the Third World who live like that most of the time. People who live on the edge of the desert; those who have a long trek to the nearest well, to bring back as much water as they can carry to slake the thirst of their family. Those for whom the nearest well is too polluted, who may have to leave their home to find another well where the water's cleaner and more abundant. With global warming, there may soon be millions more who know the meaning of thirst. Water is essential for life – you can go without food for weeks, but without water you will be dead within hours.

The Jordan

In Bible times, people settled near an abundant spring, or beside the River Jordan. A number of springs supplied the source of the river, in the north of the country, and it flowed down the great Rift

Valley, through Lake Galilee, irrigating the riverside fields on its way. It was truly living or life-giving water. Psalm 42 sings, 'As the deer longs for the water brooks, so longs my soul for you, O God', and Psalm 46 tells us, 'There is a river whose streams make glad the city of God, the holy place of the dwelling of the Most High.' The psalms often start with the idea of living, life-giving water, and praise the living, life-giving God. God is as essential to our survival as a good water-supply.

Jerusalem

But if 'the city of God' in that psalm refers to Jerusalem, the ironic thing is that Jerusalem is miles from the River Jordan. The water-supply has always been a problem in Jerusalem, and the city could only grow when new sources were developed. King David started with the Spring of Gishon; King Hezekiah took the water through a tunnel to the Pool of Siloam. Solomon and Pontius Pilate built aqueducts. So to sing of a river flowing from the Temple and irrigating the whole land, as St John did in the Revelation, was to dream of impossibilities.

Symbolic

Perhaps, then, these words aren't to be taken literally. Jesus was baptized in the River Jordan, because the river was the source of life for the land. So baptism symbolizes the beginning of a new life. Jesus said to the Samaritan woman at the well, 'I will give you living water ... those who drink of the water that I will give them will never be thirsty.' As the River Jordan is the source of physical life for the land, so baptism is the source of our spiritual life, and Jesus promises to give us this life abundantly, because he is the Son of the Living God, the true source of life. He received the Holy Spirit at his baptism – so those who believe in him are baptized into him, as St Paul says: 'All of us who have been baptized into Christ Jesus were baptized into his death ... but if we have died with Christ, we believe that we will also live with him.' So Jesus gives us his life, that we may be a source of life for others: 'The water that I will give will become in them a spring of water gushing up to eternal life.'

Sharing

These days, we are learning that we must share what we have with those who lack. If you have a tap which flows with clean water all day long, you should give to WaterAid or Practical Action, which work to build reliable water supplies for the thirsty throughout the world. If we have been baptized in water as Jesus was, and have received his life within us, then we must share it with those who don't know him, or haven't experienced the new life which he brings. Sitting on a source of running water and refusing to share it with the thirsty people around you is the sin of selfishness. Knowing that God has given you new and thirst-quenching life in Jesus, and failing to spread this good news to those who don't realize that God loves them, is the same or worse. Jesus was baptized in the River Jordan, and went out to call the whole nation to baptism; we have been baptized, and we must share this new life with friends, acquaintances, and strangers all over the world.

Suggested hymns

As the deer pants for the water; I heard the voice of Jesus say; Spirit of the living God (Iverson); When Jesus came to Jordan.

Third Sunday of Epiphany   20 January
(*When Epiphany falls on a Sunday, 20 January is called Epiphany 3 but has the readings for Epiphany 2.*)
See also 'Week of Prayer for Christian Unity', p. 292.
Principal Service   **From Everyday to Extraordinary**
Isa. 62.1–5 Nations shall see your salvation; Ps. 36.5–10 All peoples; 1 Cor. 12.1–11 Many gifts, one Spirit; John 2.1–11 The wedding at Cana

> 'When the steward tasted the water that had become wine, and did not know where it came from ... [he] called the bridegroom and said to him, "Everyone serves the good wine first, and then the inferior wine after the guests have become drunk. But you have kept the good wine until now."' John 2.9–10

Boredom

Boredom is a question of how you look at things. A theology student visited a tyre factory, and saw a young woman staring into a vat of water, through which inflated inner tubes were being passed three at a time. She had three buttons to press in front of her, and the student thought hers must be the most boring job imaginable. Years later, when he was an industrial chaplain, he visited the same factory and saw a middle-aged woman doing the very same thing. He realized to his horror that it was the same woman. 'What are you doing?' he asked her. 'Looking for the bubbles,' she replied. 'Do you know when that will happen?' asked the clergyman. 'No,' she answered – 'that's what makes life so exciting!'

Routine

Many of us claim that our life is boring. There are so many routine tasks to be done – cleaning the house, filling in forms, and so on – it makes you want to scream. Yet you can't escape them – much better to look at them in a new way. Is it possible to develop an attitude which enables you to find satisfaction even in the dull repetitive tasks of life?

Purification

I think the gospel story of Jesus turning the water into wine may give us a clue. The jars of water were standing there for the Jewish rites of purification. There are laws in the Old Testament which are basic common-sense hygiene – always wash your hands before you handle food, that sort of thing. But the religious experts had developed them into an elaborate ritual, which involved spending hours a day, every day, in washing hands and feet, head and body, clothes, plates, furniture and drinking vessels – in fact, anything that can be washed had to be cleansed in an elaborate way, not to make it clean, but because God would be angry if you didn't. So washing had become a bit of a bore. Unfortunately it had also become a religious duty. And religion was never meant to be boring.

Water into wine

There were six 30-gallon jars of water at the wedding feast. Jesus didn't pour them away. That would have been a waste of good water. Instead, he turned the water into wine. I don't know how he did it – but then, Jesus did a lot of things that I don't understand. I just rejoice that he did them, making a lot of sad people happy in the process. Wine – in moderation – is a symbol of enjoyment. Jesus tried to show us that religion isn't boring – it's a cause for celebration. It depends how you look at it.

From everyday to extraordinary

In fact, from this point of view, Jesus was turning the everyday into the extraordinary. All those dull daily routines can become a cause of deep satisfaction, if you look at them in the right way. If you clean the house so that your family will be happy to come home to such a lovely place, the routine will become enjoyable. Contrary to popular opinion, it isn't love that makes the world go round, it's the daily chores which do that. But if you do them for love's sake, the love turns the commonplace into the enjoyable.

For God's sake

It's the same if you do things for God. If you do your boring tasks to please God, and infuse them with your love of God, as an act of worship, all of a sudden they will take on a glory. The Pharisees washed things because they believed God would be angry if they didn't, but Christians wash them because we love God, and want his world to look beautiful. Then Jesus will turn the water you scrub with, in your mind, into the wine of joy and celebration. It all depends on how you look at it. If you have the right attitude, Jesus will convert the boring routine from the everyday into the extraordinary. Like the woman watching for the bubbles, you will be able to say, 'That's what makes life exciting.'

All-age worship

Play at doing some of the chores you hate. As you do them, repeat to yourself, 'I'm doing this because I love Jesus, as a sacrifice to please him.'

Suggested hymns

Brother, sister, let me serve you; Songs of thankfulness and praise; Teach me, my God and King; Will you come and follow me?

Third Sunday of Epiphany 20 January
Second Service **Tell of His Salvation**

Ps. 96 Tell of his salvation; 1 Sam. 3.1–20 The boy Samuel; Eph. 4.1–16 Unity in the Body of Christ; *Gospel at Holy Communion*: John 1.29–42 The first disciples

'Sing to the Lord and bless his name;
tell out his salvation from day to day.
Declare his glory among the nations
and his wonders among all peoples.'
Psalm 96.2–3 (Common Worship)

Muslims

Whenever Muslims speak of God they call him Allah. In many centuries of translation, the Bible Societies everywhere have chosen a word in the local language which is used for their god or the supreme god, to translate the Hebrew and Greek words for God in the Bible. This was simply a way of communicating with people who speak another language by using words they are familiar with. But some people in this country wrongly assume that Allah and the one we call God are different, rival gods.

Evangelism

You see, the Old Testament clearly holds up a hope that all nations will worship the one God whom Jews called Jehovah, Elohim or El – the name El is very close, linguistically, to the Arabic word 'Allah'. God's servant was to be 'a light to lighten the Gentiles'; 'all nations' were to come and worship him. The magi were Gentiles, and when they visited Jesus they held up a hope that every race would find in him the fulfilment of their fondest dreams. So the task of Christians became that of spreading the good news of God's love in Christ. The Psalmist sang: 'Sing to the Lord and bless his name; tell out his salvation from day to day. Declare his glory among the nations and his wonders among all peoples.'

Monotheism

Yet in those days the Jewish religion was the only example of monotheism in the world. Converting the heathen meant drawing them away from the worship of many gods, who were thought to

49

encourage violence and immorality in their followers. Christianity began by seeing itself as part of Judaism, though gradually they became estranged. But when Muhammad introduced the religion of Islam, it was firmly monotheistic, and even more concerned to draw infidels away from idolatry than we are. So it came about that there are three monotheistic faiths in the world – Judaism, Christianity and Islam, referred to in the Qur'an as 'the people of the book'. Should followers of one monotheistic religion, then, try to convert devotees of another monotheistic religion?

Character of God

Before you hurry to answer that question, think for a moment of the character of the one God described in the three monotheistic religions. All say remarkably similar things about God – not surprisingly, since all are developments of the faith of Abraham. But there are differences. Jews emphasize the need for a code of law; the Muslim Sharia law is not part of their scripture, the Qur'an. Muslims strongly emphasize the importance of submission to Allah – that's what the word 'Islam' means. Christians teach that Jesus fulfilled the inner meaning of the Law in his emphasis on grace and love. It's quite clear to Christians that we all worship the same God – after all, there *is* only one God – and we have a lot to learn from each other. So we shouldn't be using unfair pressure to compel those who disagree with us to change their faith. Rather we should be telling others of our experience of what Jesus has done for us – we should 'tell of his salvation day by day'.

Taking Jesus into their faith

A Christian working in Muslim lands used to say, 'we should be encouraging Muslims to take Jesus into their religion'. Without any suggestion that they might change their allegiance, which is what scares the Muslim leaders, we should help them to read for themselves the words of Jesus, whom they already recognize as a prophet. Some may then decide to commit themselves to following him, though in countries where conversion is illegal, they may have to do so quietly in the privacy of their hearts. 'Sing to the Lord and bless his name; tell out his salvation from day to day. Declare his glory among the nations and his wonders among all peoples.' That's all we have to do; not twist anybody's arm. Then they themselves can decide how to respond.

Suggested hymns

From the eastern mountains; God is working his purpose out; Tell out, my soul; We have a gospel to proclaim.

Fourth Sunday of Epiphany   27 January

(When Epiphany falls on a Sunday, 27 January is called Epiphany 4 and has the readings etc. for Epiphany 3.)

Principal Service   Law and Interpretation

Neh. 8.1–3, 5–6, 8–10 Joy in the Commandments; Ps. 19 The heavens declare God's glory; 1 Cor. 12.12–31a The unity of Christ's body the Church; Luke 4.14–21 Jesus reads the Scriptures at Nazareth

'They read from the book, from the law of God, with interpretation. They gave the sense, so that the people understood the reading.' Nehemiah 8.8

Nehemiah

The Old Testament book of Nehemiah paints a graphic picture. The kingdom of Judah had been defeated by the Babylonian army, Jerusalem was destroyed, and the majority of the population were taken into exile in Babylon. There they had lost hope, and forgotten what was contained in their Holy Scriptures. Then a man called Nehemiah persuaded King Cyrus to allow him to bring a few descendants of the original exiles across the desert, back home to Jerusalem. There they set about rebuilding the city and the Temple, with a trowel in one hand and a sword in the other, to defend themselves against their enemies. When it was completed, the people wept because the new Temple was smaller than the original. But a priest called Ezra stood up in a makeshift pulpit, and read to them the law books from the Old Testament. Then they rejoiced, because now they knew what it means to be a Jew, and could follow all the old traditions of their race. The Law isn't an oppressive burden, in the eyes of the Jews, but a generous revelation to his Chosen People of how God wishes them to live, if they want to avoid all the troubles that follow from lawlessness.

Interpretation

The book of Nehemiah says that 'They read from the book, from the law of God, with interpretation. They gave the sense, so that the people understood the reading.' Now that could mean simply that the Jewish language had changed since the laws were written, and somebody had to translate them into the new dialect of Aramaic, the language that Jesus spoke at home. But probably it means more than that. Society had changed, too, and rules which were helpful in a simple nomadic or agricultural society couldn't be applied to the new world of clashing civilizations in which they now lived. So somebody had to explain how the old laws must be reinterpreted in a new context. Applying Scripture to changed circumstances was essential then, and it's still needed now.

Scribes

That was the task of the scribes. When Jesus was 12, he went to the Temple and debated with the scribes about how the Old Testament was to be interpreted in their day. Later he had harsh words about the Pharisees, who clung fiercely to the old traditions, and neglected 'the weightier things of the law'. But some of them were enlightened: Rabbi Akiba said, '"You must love your neighbour as yourself" – this is the greatest general principle in the law.' Rabbi Hillel was challenged to teach the whole law while standing on one leg. He replied, 'Whatever you hate for yourself, don't do to your neighbour.' In the first five centuries after Christ, when the Temple had again been destroyed so that much of the old law couldn't be interpreted literally, they gathered together the reports of their debates in a book called the Talmud. Still today Jewish people love nothing better than arguing about how the old laws should be applied in modern life.

Law for Christians

So what does the law of the Old Testament mean for a Christian? As Jewish people have long known, nobody can apply it literally today. But if, like Nehemiah, we devote ourselves to the task of reinterpreting the Scriptures to modern life, selecting parts that are relevant and rejecting those which are outdated, we may rejoice to find that the Bible has much to teach us. The Jews taught a lawless world that there is one God, who cares about how we treat each other. Jesus went to the heart of the Scriptures when he said that we should love God and love our neighbours, 'on this all the law and the prophets depend'. But there's no escaping the task of debating how these principles are to be applied in the ever-changing circumstances of modern life. Jesus read from Isaiah a passage about setting free those who suffer from oppression, and commented, 'today this scripture has been fulfilled in your hearing'. There are plenty of oppressed people today whom Jesus is calling us to love as much as we love ourselves. Like Nehemiah and Ezra, we must 'read from the book, from the law of God, with interpretation' – giving the sense, so that we may understand the reading.

All-age worship

Discover the Bible reading notes for young people published by Scripture Union and others.

Suggested hymns

Brother, sister, let me serve you; Father of mercies, in thy word; Lord, thy word abideth; Will you come and follow me?

Fourth Sunday of Epiphany   27 January
Second Service   **The Big Bang**
Ps. 33 The greatness and goodness of God; Num. 9.15–23
The cloud of God's presence; 1 Cor. 7.17–24 The life that the
Lord has assigned; *Gospel at Holy Communion*: Mark 1.21–28
Authority over an unclean spirit

> *'By the word of the Lord were the heavens made
> and all their host by the breath of his mouth.'*
> Psalm 33.6 (Common Worship)

Stars

When our ancestors looked into the night sky they asked themselves, 'How did the stars get there? No man, nor race of men, could have made them; they must have been put there by someone superhuman, a god.' Some thought God took a long time over it: in the book of Job God talks of measuring the earth's foundations while the morning stars sang together. To promote the idea of the Sabbath, others described creation as happening in six 'days', with God resting on the seventh 'day', though St Peter reminds us that 'with the Lord one day is like a thousand years, and a thousand years are like one day'. Then the telescope was invented, showing millions of stars, spinning round in galaxies, millions of light years away. Surprise, surprise – they aren't oil lamps hanging from a flat surface! When a car passes you sounding its horn, the sound drops in pitch as it passes you – whee-oo! It's called the Doppler Effect; and the wavelength of light is affected in the same way if the source is moving very fast. Measuring what's called the 'red-shift' in the light emitted by the stars, we can calculate that they are all moving apart at high speeds – the further away they are, the faster they are travelling. From this you can calculate that they all started from a single point, called a 'singularity', more than 13 billion years ago. That figure can be confirmed by measuring the decay of radioactive isotopes. So all the energy in the universe must have been concentrated in one place, and burst out in what became known as the Big Bang. The echo of this can be heard in the radio 'noise' which fills all of space.

Who caused it?

By measuring the temperature of the stars, you can work out how long it took our sun to condense from the gas clouds; when the planets were formed; and when our planet was ready to support life. But I don't want to give you a science lecture, or discuss *how* it happened. I'm more interested in the *why* questions, which science can't answer. Why did the Big Bang happen? Everything has a cause, though sometimes we don't know what the cause was. But the cause of an event must always be earlier in time than its effect – nothing can be caused by something that hasn't happened yet. So what caused the Big Bang? Now that's a difficult question, because time and space are linked – where there's no space, there's no time. So if matter and space began in the Big Bang, time, too, began then. Therefore you can't say that the Big Bang was caused by something which happened 'beforehand'. The only possible answer is that the Big Bang was caused by something *outside time;* in other words, by something or someone in eternity. The only eternal being we know anything about is called God – *God* created the Big Bang. Therefore, God created the stars, as our ancestors told us. Only he took an unimaginably long time about it.

Logic

This isn't science – you can't test 'why-questions' by experiment and measurement. It's actually a very old argument in logic. Think of a chain of events, each caused by the one before. Imagine it as a real chain, each iron link hanging from the link above it, which caused it to happen. Now, chains don't just hang there, like the Indian rope trick; they must be suspended from a nail. What's the nail from which the chain of cause-and-effect hangs – the First Cause? Philosophers long ago realized that it must be the eternal God. This is a perfectly logical way of proving that God exists. So the Big Bang theory turns out to be on the side of religion!

What's God like?

Mind you, logic can't tell you what God is like, or how God wants us to behave. That can only come if God reveals himself to us, in the Scriptures, and in the life of Jesus. From all of that, we learn that God is like a loving father. But Christians have no need to be afraid when scientists tell us *how* the universe began; what the Bible tells us is *why*. The Big Bang theory confirms that 'By the word of the Lord were the heavens made, and all their host by the breath of his mouth.'

Suggested hymns

Eternal ruler of the ceaseless round; O Lord my God, when I in awesome wonder; The heavens declare thy glory, Lord; The spacious firmament on high.

Second Sunday before Lent
(or Candlemas; see p. 297)   3 February
Principal Service   **What Makes Us Human?**
Gen. 2.4b–9, 15–25 Creation; Ps. 65 Creation, harvest; Rev. 4 The living creatures cry 'Holy!'; Luke 8.22–25 Stilling the storm

> *'And the LORD God formed man of the dust of the ground, and breathed into his nostrils the breath of life; and man became a living soul.' Genesis 2.7 (Authorized Version)*

Soul

What makes human beings different from the animals? Many people would say it's because we alone possess an immortal soul. As a proof-text they may quote Genesis 2.7, which, in the Authorized Version of the Bible, tells us that God breathed into the newly created man the breath of life, 'and man became a living soul'. Unfortunately that's a mistranslation. Modern translations say that 'the man became a living being'. It's exactly the same word which is used in the previous chapter for the fish and the land animals; and all the animals and birds are described as 'everything that has the breath of life'. However there are a few verses in the New Testament which suggest that the soul is the part of a human being which can survive the death of the body. So what makes humans distinctive may be that God gives to some of us, at least, the gift of eternal life.

Human behaviour

It used to be said that what made human beings different was our ability to think. But the more we study animals, the more strongly evident it becomes that many have a brain power approaching ours. Indeed a newborn baby, or someone with a brain injury, may be less able to reason than many of the higher animals, but that doesn't make them any less human. Chimpanzees and gorillas have been seen to use sticks as tools; and the organization of an ants'-nest or a beehive is more sophisticated than many human societies. If you watch the wildlife programmes on television, you will have seen examples of mother animals torn by having to choose between preserving their own life and that of their offspring. So even emotion and the power of choice are not exclusively human. Violent human beings are often described as behaving like animals; so you can't make a clear separation between human beings and other animals simply on the grounds of behaviour.

Evolution

A small boy asked his Sunday school teacher, 'Is it true that God said, "From dust you have come, and to dust you shall return"?' 'Quite right,' answered the teacher. 'Well you should look under my bed,' said the boy, 'there's an awful lot of coming and returning going on down there!' The Bible also says God made *'adam'* out of 'adamah': human beings out of the dust. This is surely meant to stop us vaunting ourselves as being invariably better than the animals. It fits well with the theory of evolution, because it suggests that the human race has its origins in the basic natural processes of the earth. Intelligence is a natural progression from the first vertebrate animals up to the human brain. Human reason has evolved gradually down the millennia.

Sentient

We describe ourselves as 'sentient' animals. That means having the ability to feel and respond to stimuli. But we have seen that some animals approach us in their capacity for feelings. It's better to distinguish *Homo sapiens* by our highly evolved self-awareness, which probably comes from the faculty of speech. Many animals seem conscious of themselves as individuals, but we have this to a higher degree. That means we have a greater ability to choose, and above all, a greater potential for love. Every pet-owner knows that animals can be affectionate; so it's not a difference in kind – more one of degree.

Unlikely

Now there are many variables on a new planet which have to be 'just right' for life to emerge and survive: right distance from the sun, the temperature range, force of gravity just right, an atmosphere, presence of water, a moon, and so on. There may be other planets with life on them. But when you add together the improbability of a planet having the necessary conditions for life to emerge, and the unlikelihood of life evolving into self-aware, loving human beings by a succession of random mutations, you are almost forced to believe that God was involved. Perhaps he was just out of sight, controlling the apparently random evolutionary process so that he could have beings capable of knowing that God loves them, and of returning that love, so that we could live with him for ever. Which is not that far from the Genesis description of God breathing his spirit into the newly formed humans to give them a living soul, after all.

All-age worship

Cut pictures from magazines of computers, pets, children and parents. Sort out those which you can love, and those which can love you in return. Then sort out those which can love Jesus.

Suggested hymns

Above the moon earth rises; All creatures of our God and King; Every star shall sing a carol; Lord of beauty, thine the splendour.

Second Sunday before Lent   3 February
Second Service   **Lilies of the Field**
Ps. 147 Laws of nature, laws of God; Gen. 1.1—2.3 The creation; Matt. 6.25–34 Lilies of the field

> *'Strive first for the kingdom of God and his righteousness, and all these things will be given to you as well.' Matthew 6.33*

Obama

Barack Obama, before he was elected President of the USA, wondered how he could reconcile his Christian faith with his politics. Which passages of Scripture should be used to guide public policy? 'Should we go with Leviticus,' he asked, 'that suggests slavery is OK and eating shellfish is an abomination? Or we could go with Deuteronomy, that suggests stoning your child if he strays from the faith? Or should we just stick to the Sermon on the Mount – a passage so radical that it's doubtful our own Defence Department would survive its application.' There's no doubt he has a wry sense of humour! History will judge how well he applied Christian morality to the life of a great nation.

Sermon on the Mount

St Matthew has very helpfully gathered the moral teaching of Jesus together in chapters 5, 6 and 7 of his Gospel. It's doubtful whether Jesus made the mistake of preaching all that much material in one sermon – it's too much to take in, in one dose. Moreover none of the hills in the Galilee area is high enough to be described as 'the mountain'. Probably Matthew wanted to remind his readers of Moses bringing his followers the Ten Commandments at Mount Sinai – the simple teaching of Jesus fulfilled the complicated laws of the Old Testament, and replaced them with the guiding principle of love.

Priorities

In the passage chosen for today's reading, Jesus calls for a right set of priorities in our behaviour.

Do not worry about your life, [he said] – what you will eat or what you will drink, or about your body, what you will wear. Is not life more than food, and the body more than clothing? Look at the birds of the air; they neither sow nor reap nor gather into barns, and yet your heavenly Father feeds them. Are you not of more value than they? And can any of you by worrying add a single hour to your span of life? And why do you worry about clothing? Consider the lilies of the field, how they grow; they neither toil nor spin, yet I tell you, even Solomon in all his glory was not clothed like one of these. But if God so clothes the grass of the field, which is alive today and tomorrow is thrown into the oven, will he not much more clothe you – you of little faith? Therefore do not worry, saying, 'What will we eat?' or 'What will we drink?' or 'What will we wear?'

Faith

If we are worrying about material things, we have too little faith in God's love and care for us. We are putting our desire for food and drink, clothing and long life, above our quest for the rule of God in a just society. 'Strive first for the kingdom of God and his righteousness,' said Jesus, 'and all these things will be given to you as well.' The kingdom of God is wherever God is obeyed as King. We should be seeking to build up that obedient relationship with our heavenly Father in our own hearts, so that others will want to copy us. If everybody obeyed God, our lives would be filled with 'his righteousness', and his kingdom would come 'on earth as it is in heaven'.

A better place

Striving for God's kingdom isn't just longing for heaven; it involves trying, through our love, to make the earth a better place. So we must be prudent with material things, but concentrate on spiritual things. First we must empty our minds of distraction and worry, then make ourselves open to God's presence. We start with mental prayer or meditation, thinking as carefully and logically about God as we can. Then we find ourselves caught up in spiritual prayer or contemplation, when no words are used, but we just enjoy knowing that God is with us. This becomes so precious to us, that we no longer have time to worry about our material needs.

Joke

Jesus ended with a joke: 'Don't worry about tomorrow,' he said, 'for tomorrow will bring new worries of its own. Today's trouble is enough for today.' In other words, there's quite enough problems today, without starting to worry about tomorrow's in advance! God loves me, and he will see me safely through the day. So, whoo-hoo! What is there to worry about?

Suggested hymns

All things bright and beautiful; Seek ye first the kingdom of God; Sometimes a light surprises; We plough the fields, and scatter.

Sunday next before Lent   10 February
Principal Service   **Josephus on Jesus**
Ex. 34.29–35 Moses' face is shining; Ps. 99 God spoke in the cloud; 2 Cor. 3.12—4.2 The Spirit unveils God's truth; Luke 9.28–36 The transfiguration [37–43a The epileptic boy]

> 'Then from the cloud came a voice that said, "This is my Son, my Chosen; listen to him!"' Luke 9.35

Josephus

Here's a historical thriller for you – as far as we can tell, it's true. In the late 60s AD, the Jewish people rebelled against the occupying Roman army. One of the Jewish generals was a man called

Joseph. He and some companions were trapped in a cave, and the Roman soldiers invited them to surrender. The Jews refused, agreeing to kill each other instead until only Joseph was left alive. He decided he could do more good alive than dead, and surrendered to the Romans, who took him to Rome. There he became a Roman citizen, and changed his Jewish name to Josephus [Joe-SEE-fuss]. While the Romans were besieging Jerusalem in AD 70, Josephus tried to mediate between the Jews, who thought it better to die rather than surrender, and the Romans, who were ready to kill as many as it took to restore order. Josephus couldn't persuade either side to change their minds, and tens of thousands of Jews were slaughtered. He started writing books, hoping to get the Romans and Jews to understand and tolerate each other. His most famous books are *The Jewish Wars,* a detailed history of the battles of which he was an eyewitness, and *The Antiquities of the Jews,* telling the history of the Jews through the Old Testament up to his own day. He remained a practising and believing Jew; he was not a Christian, but in *The Antiquities* he wrote a long passage about John the Baptist, which is generally agreed to be historical, and twice he mentioned Jesus.

Josephus on Jesus

In chapter 20 of *The Antiquities*, Josephus describes the High Priest Annas assembling a panel of judges. He writes: '[Annas] brought before them James, the brother of Jesus, who was called Christ.' This passage is generally accepted as authentic, and it's clear historical evidence that Jesus existed, and was believed by many Jews to be the expected Messiah – though Josephus won't say whether he agreed with them. It was written sometime between AD 70 and 80, not long after the Gospels and the Acts of the Apostles. Most of the documents we rely on for ancient history are nothing like as close to the events as that.

Manuscripts

In chapter 18, Josephus has a longer passage about Jesus. Unfortunately, most old documents exist in different versions, with copying mistakes by various scribes. Historians have various techniques for comparing these manuscripts so as to eliminate the errors, so you can be sure that the modern versions are 99 per cent accurate to what the author originally wrote. Another Jew, Geza Vermes, happily still alive today, but very sceptical about Christianity, none-theless thinks that what Josephus wrote was this:

> About this time there lived Jesus, a wise man ... For he was one who performed paradoxical deeds and was the teacher of such people as accept the truth gladly. He won over many Jews and many Greeks. He was called the Christ. When Pilate, upon hear-ing him accused by men of the highest standing among us, had condemned him to be crucified, those who had in the first place come to love him did not give up their affection for him ... And the tribe of the Christians, so called after him, has still to this day not disappeared.'

Transfiguration

So the early writings of one Jew, confirmed by the scholarship of another Jew, neither of whom believe in Jesus, confirm that Jesus lived and was believed by many to be the Messiah. Human reason can't take you any further than that. Then you must depend on God revealing to us who Jesus really was. In today's Gospel reading, the disciples on the mountain-top heard God say, 'This is my Son, my Chosen; listen to him!' Jesus was a human, historical figure, as described by Josephus. What Josephus couldn't know, because he had never met any of those who believed in Jesus, was that the human Jesus was also the Son of God. But *we* have read the writ-ings of the apostles, and we know and believe what God told us: that Jesus was divine, and when we listen to the words of Jesus, we can hear God speaking. No Jewish historian can claim that for his or her writings, however fascinating they are as history.

All-age worship

Cut a circle from a piece of card, stick transparent film over the hole, and draw on it a picture of Jesus. Lay it on a table, and you see Jesus the man; hold it up to the light, you see the Son of God.

Suggested hymns

Christ is the world's true light; Christ, whose glory fills the skies; Lord, the light of your light is shining; 'Tis good, Lord, to be here.

Sunday next before Lent   10 February
Second Service   **Love is God's Meaning**
Ps. 89.1–18 The wonders of God; Ex. 3.1–6 The burning bush;
John 12.27–36a Glorify your name

> *'[The voice from the burning bush] said … "I am the God of your father, the God of Abraham, the God of Isaac, and the God of Jacob." And Moses hid his face, for he was afraid to look at God.'*
> *Exodus 3.6*

The meaning of life

The meaning of cricket is quite baffling to an American. What is a crease, a leg bye, what's silly mid-off? Show Americans the rule book and they will be none the wiser – 'a googly is an off break bowled with an apparent leg-break action by a right-arm bowler to a right-handed batsman, or conversely for a left-arm bowler' … What on earth's that all about? The meaning of a game is not found in the game itself, but in the people who play it. They say 'Cricket makes us proud to be British' … or Australian, as the case may be. Here's another question – what's the meaning of a credit card? You won't find it printed on the card – its meaning lies in the effect it has on computers thousands of miles away when you put your card into the cash machine. Thirdly, do you believe your life has meaning? Like cricket and credit cards, the meaning doesn't lie in the thing itself, but in its relationship with things outside it. The meaning of this beautiful universe can't be found anywhere in the universe – it must be outside the universe, in the heart of God himself.

The meaning of God

Asking for meaning is what makes us human. We are the only life-forms in the whole universe, so far as we know, able to ask the question 'Why?' Yet we can't believe that life is completely meaningless, or else why bother? To understand that God gives life meaning is the triumph of the Bible. Primitive human beings believed that there was a god in every tree and stone, and one for each tribe and family, frequently warring against each other. So everything that happens to us was due to happenstance, in a hostile universe. But the Jews invented monotheism, belief in one God and one God only. What God means us to do is right; what goes against God's will is evil. God means us to love one another, and love the

63

one God with all our heart, mind, soul and strength. As Julian of Norwich put it, 'Love is his meaning'; and God has put us here so that we can learn to understand that and to do it.

Moses

According to the Bible, Moses was looking for the meaning of life. He had killed an Egyptian who was attacking an Israelite, and fled for his life, far away from home to the region around Mount Horeb. There in the desert he saw a burning bush – burning, but not consumed by the fire – it was timeless. Moses turned aside to look, wanting to know the meaning of this thing. God spoke to Moses from the burning bush, saying, 'I am the God of your father, the God of Abraham, the God of Isaac, and the God of Jacob.' Not one god for one time, and another god for a later period; not one god for here and another god for over there; but one God and one God only for the whole universe. In the one, timeless, universal God, the universe and everything in it finds its meaning.

Love

So what did God mean by creating the universe, and us in it? The simplest answer to this question is to say that God made us all in love. We are not unconnected individuals; we are people in relationships. It's love which makes those relationships possible – love which rescues us from eternal loneliness. We are not alone; we are here because God loves us, and created us in love. God has given us the incredible privilege of free will, so that we can choose to love God, and choose to love each other, without being forced to, against our will. Love means giving the object of your love freedom; allowing us to develop in our own way, allowing each of us to develop our unique potential. If that's how God loves us, then surely that's how he means us to love each other, with generous tolerance for those who are different from us. God put us here so that we could learn to love one another with all our hearts, and then learn to love God in the same way. When we can do that, then we shan't be consumed by the changes and chances of this fleeting life, but will rise above them to join our Creator in that timeless world where all is love. And that's the meaning of life – love here on earth for a while, then outside this universe, together with each other and with the one God who gives it all meaning.

Suggested hymns

Be still, for the Spirit of the Lord; I, the Lord of sea and sky; Jesus, where'er thy people meet; The God of Abraham praise.

LENT

If we are to feel the rhythm of the seasons, we must have down times so as to appreciate more the upturns. Lent is a season of penitence ready for Easter. Easter was the time for baptism in the early Church, and those who were to be baptized had forty days of fasting and instruction to prepare them to become members of the Church. This was so popular that whole congregations clamoured to be allowed to join in. On Shrove Tuesday we are 'shriven', that is, the priest declares that God has forgiven us our sins. On Ash Wednesday we 'repent in dust and ashes'. Lent is an Old English word for 'spring', and the forty days from Ash Wednesday to Good Friday – not counting the Sundays, when the Lenten discipline is relaxed – commemorate the forty days when Jesus fasted in the wilderness, learning to resist the temptations of the world, the flesh and the devil. 'Giving up things for Lent' is a training in self-discipline, but to avoid the temptation to self-righteousness, we also do something positive: prayer, Bible reading, study groups and extra services. The altar frontal and vestments are in solemn purple, or unbleached linen to represent sackcloth.

Ash Wednesday   13 February
Keep Calm and Carry On

Joel 2.1–2, 12–17 Rend your hearts, *or* Isa. 58.1–12 Care for the needy; Ps. 51.1–18 Cleanse me from my sin; 2 Cor. 5.20b—6.10 Suffering of an apostle; Matt. 6.1–6, 16–21 Secret fasting, *or* John 8.1–11 Adultery and forgiveness

> *'Rend your hearts and not your clothing. Return to the LORD, your God, for he is gracious and merciful, slow to anger, and abounding in steadfast love, and relents from punishing.' Joel 2.13*

Keep calm

During the Second World War, an official Government Poster was distributed, in an eye-catching shade of red, complete with the royal crown at the top, and put up in factories and public buildings. It consisted of advice as to what to do in the case of an emergency – for instance if a bomb fell on the building you were working on. The solemn recommendation, in large white letters, was 'KEEP CALM AND CARRY ON'! We may smile now at this example of the British 'stiff upper lip', which was taken to extremes in this case. It reminds us of the film *Carry on up the Khyber,* where the British community continue with their formal dinner, even though the walls of the consulate are collapsing around them under enemy gunfire! But actually the only alternative is to panic, and as Corporal Jones of *Dad's Army* discovered, that does no good at all.

Open to our feelings

It's fashionable in some circles to recommend everybody to 'be open to their feelings'. It's true that repressing your emotions, and refusing to recognize that you have any (or 'denial' as it's called), is very dangerous. If not dealt with, deep emotions can unexpectedly well up and cause violent behaviour. Much better to face up to them and analyse them, and then set them to one side as you 'keep calm and carry on' with your life. If you feel a need to talk about your feelings, go to a skilled counsellor or somebody with a great deal of patience. Don't claim the right to pour your inner soul over every casual contact, or you will make yourself very unpopular, and very inefficient.

Joel

Is this what the prophet Joel meant, when he wrote, 'Rend your hearts and not your clothing'? There has been a plague of locusts – grasshoppers which suddenly swarm, breeding rapidly and flying from field to field, eating everything on which they land. The prophet calls for a day of solemn prayer to God, asking the Lord to take away the marauding insects. Or maybe this is a metaphor for an invading army, nobody is quite sure. In any case, Joel calls on the whole nation to 'Return to the Lord, your God.' God can't help a nation if many of them ignore his existence. They must repent their irreligion, confident that God is only waiting on that to forgive them utterly.

Restraint

But Joel calls on them not to 'go over the top'. 'Don't tear your clothes to shreds, in an artificial display of emotion,' he says, in effect. 'Let the emotion of penitence be sincere in your hearts, away from the public gaze.' 'Rend your hearts, and not your garments.' No showing off how deep your feelings are. In other words, 'Keep calm and carry on.' It's a good warning to us all against overt display of our emotions during Lent.

Hidden suffering

Many people suffer deeply in their lives, but don't let others know about it. Provided they have somewhere where they can let go, and release the floodgates of feeling, this restraint is admirable. Robert Louis Stevenson wrote, 'If we could see into one another's souls we'd be amazed at how cheerful we are.' How many of your friends, who haven't a care in the world, as far as you can see, are bravely hiding an inner grief? Don't question them about it; they will speak about it when they are ready, if they want to, and if you make it clear that you can listen patiently to others without talking about yourself instead.

Lent

The passage from Joel is read on Ash Wednesday, the beginning of Lent. In these forty days, leading up to Easter, we examine ourselves, and tell God we are sorry for the unkind things we have done, and the opportunities to be kind which we have missed. It's good, when you are alone, to make a list of the things you have on your conscience. Then tell God you are sorry, and believe with every fibre of your being that he has forgiven you. If you are in any doubt about that, or if you need help, confess to God in the presence of a minister, who will advise you and assure you of God's absolution. Tell others that you have the dignity of being a forgiven sinner, but don't tell *anyone* what you confessed. 'Rend your hearts and not your garments.' 'Keep calm and carry on.'

Suggested hymns

Christian, dost thou see them; Dear Lord and Father of mankind; O for a heart to praise my God; O Jesus, I have promised.

Posters available from the Imperial War Museum,
http://www.iwmshop.org.uk/category/671/Keep_Calm_and_Carry_
On_Gifts

First Sunday of Lent   17 February
Principal Service   **Forgiveness**
Deut. 26.1–11 First fruits; Ps. 91.1–2, 9–16 God's providence;
Rom. 10.8b–13 Faith, salvation and unity; Luke 4.1–13 The
temptation of Jesus

> *'Jesus, full of the Holy Spirit, returned from the Jordan and was
> led by the Spirit in the wilderness, where for forty days he was
> tempted by the devil.' Luke 4.1–2*

Temptation

Temptation is when you know something is wrong, but you half-
want to do it anyway. If we are honest, we must admit that each of
us has had moments like that. The morally wrong course of action
seems so attractive, and we think that it will bring us pleasure. Perhaps we are right – buying the kids a hamburger instead of cooking
them a healthy meal; or one more drink for the road; or seducing
the attractive stranger, any of these might be very pleasant – in the
short run. But eventually it will almost certainly bring disaster, and
a very much worse quality of life for us and for other people whom
we have harmed by our actions. Not to mention our feelings of guilt
for what we have done to them. Yet the long run seems so far away
that we hardly notice it when we are tempted to seek short-term
gain. That's why temptation is so insidious.

Jesus

The Gospel tells us that Jesus heard a voice from heaven calling him
God's Son. Then, at once, he was tempted for forty days. When you
think about it, that's truly shocking. How could the Son of God
be torn between good and evil? How could he actually *want* to do
something he knew to be wrong? Surely that's impossible? God's
Son is supposed to be perfect, and above all that kind of thing.
But no, that's what's so wonderful about divine love: the heavenly
Christ voluntarily came to earth, becoming human, and subjecting
himself to all the confusing and contradictory desires and tempta-

tions that human beings have to put up with – not just for forty days, but for the whole of his life. The only thing that was different about Jesus was that he battled against his temptations, and unlike us, he won every time. Luke gives us three examples of what Jesus wanted: turning stones into bread, ruling the world, and impressing people with his miracles. In other words, Jesus really wanted to be *prosperous*; to be *powerful*; and to be *popular*. And who doesn't? But at what cost? If it involves compromising your principles and using immoral methods, those desires are the very Devil, leading eventually to the loss of everything that makes us human.

Us

Yet which of us doesn't want nice food, beautiful clothes, a fine house and long holidays? If those things are won by hard work, and we are generous, well and good. But if we give in to the temptation to cheat and lie, and are mean, our money makes us monsters. We should like the power to set the world to rights; but if our power comes from treading on other people's shoulders and denying them their rights, power turns us into tyrants. And popularity? If you want to be universally liked, you have to agree with everybody, and never speak up for what's true and honest. Popular people soon lose their individuality, and with it departs their sense of right and wrong. No, we have to resist these temptations, just as Jesus did.

Grace

If we pray, Jesus will give us the strength to stand up against temptation. Lent is a time to practise. Training ourselves to say no to the little things – the chocolates, the hours in front of the TV – and devoting time to prayer, Bible study and healthy exercise, makes us stronger when the big temptations come. For everybody is tempted sometime, and you must be ready for the biggies before they hit you.

Forgiveness

There's nothing wrong with being tempted – wanting to do wrong things is what it means to be human. What we do need to feel guilty about is the number of times we give in. Yet all is not lost. After the Iraq war, the American commanders were instructed to set up 'Awakening Councils', inviting Iraqis to co-operate in bringing

69

peace to their province. A certain Colonel MacFarland was asked why, among the sheikhs he invited to form the committee in his area, there were some who had taken part in attacks on Americans. 'I'm a product of Catholic schools,' he replied, 'and I was taught that every saint has a past, and every sinner can have a future.' Think about it: all of us are tempted, and all of us have given in, sometimes. God wants us to feel penitent, but not perpetually guilty; he wants to forgive us. 'Every saint has a past, and every sinner can have a future.' God bless you.

All-age worship

Write in your best handwriting, 'Every saint has a past, and every sinner can have a future.'

Suggested hymns

Be thou my vision; Forty days and forty nights; O happy band of pilgrims; Seek ye first the Kingdom of God.

First Sunday of Lent   17 February
Second Service   **A Man Who Thinks He's Good**
Ps. 119.73–88 A wineskin in the smoke; Jonah 3 Nineveh converted; Luke 18.9–14 Pharisee and publican

> 'The Pharisee, standing by himself, was praying thus, "God, I thank you that I am not like other people: thieves, rogues, adulterers, or even like this tax-collector. I fast twice a week; I give a tenth of all my income."' Luke 18.11–12

Not religious

Sometimes people say to me, almost boastfully, 'My family never go to church – we are not religious.' To which I reply, 'Good, you are just the people Jesus needs in his church. He prefers the sinners, because people who think they are religious cause him so much trouble!' That makes them sit up! They don't like being called sinners, of course. But it's a surprise, because many people think Jesus is only interested in 'good people'. Some people speak of Jesus as though he spent most of his time going about telling people to be good. Did he?

Pharisees

If you mean that he was preachy, that he told people to be goody-goody, then nothing could be further from the truth. He was in constant conflict with 'religious' people, and told a parable of a very good man, a Pharisee, who thanked God that he was so much better than the tax-collector; yet Jesus said it was the tax-collector who went home 'justified'. Jesus spent much of his time warning people against the danger of judging others; it's like a man offering to take a speck out of his brother's eye when there is a great log sticking out of his own eye, he said! To tell other people how to live their lives, when you don't know how to live your own, is as absurd as one blind man leading another by the hand to show him the way. The parable ends with them both falling into the ditch. The crowd probably laughed at the knockabout humour of this; but then they realized that Jesus was not joking about blind people, but about those who think they can see better than others. Then, as in many of the parables, they probably came to the uncomfortable realization that the joke was against them, and they had been laughing at themselves, if they were in the habit of telling others to be good.

Carousel

Jesus would probably have agreed with the song in the musical *Carousel* in which the chorus sings that there is nothing so bad for a woman as a man who thinks he is good. Or for that matter, a woman who thinks she is good; and neither of them is much use to God, because God can't reach them through their pride.

Law

But perhaps the common picture of Jesus is that his emphasis was on telling people not to do bad things. Inevitably, when small children are growing up they have to be told from time to time not to be naughty. If the child has good parents, this will be how they warn their children that putting their finger on a hot surface will burn them, or hitting their brother over the head does *not* lead to a happy family life. Of course, some parents tell their children off for doing things which are not actually sinful, but just inconvenient to the parents – like crying when children have pains in their tummies. So, growing up with this image of what naughtiness is, and what parenting involves, it's small wonder that many people think of

God, whom Jesus described as Father, being constantly angry over petty actions in which we may be unable to see any harm. But it would be hard to find a verse in which Jesus tells people off for smoking, drinking, dancing, gambling, or any of the other things which so-called religious people commonly describe as sinful.

Love

Jesus did give his disciples commands, but they were almost always positive ones. He told us to love other people, to love our neighbour as ourselves. The important things, in his mind, were feeding the hungry, visiting the prisoners, and giving a cup of cold water to those who are thirsty.

Truly religious

So let's aim to be truly religious, in the sense that Jesus meant it. Not constantly criticizing others and blind to our own faults like the Pharisee; but humble, honest about ourselves, and aware of our need for God's forgiveness and help, like the tax-collector. He went home 'justified', meaning that he was the friend of God. So can we be, if we are tolerant, understanding and forgiving of others, as God is with us. Then we can go on our way rejoicing.

Suggested hymns

And can it be?; Forgive our sins as we forgive; God forgave my sin in Jesus' name; Just as I am, without one plea.

Second Sunday of Lent   24 February
Principal Service   **Rationalist Morality**
Gen. 15.1–12, 17–18 God's promise to Abraham; Ps. 27 Faith and providence; Phil. 3.17—4.1 Citizens of heaven; Luke 13.31–35 Jesus's lament over the city

> '[Jesus said], "Jerusalem, Jerusalem, the city that kills the prophets and stones those who are sent to it! How often have I desired to gather your children together as a hen gathers her brood under her wings, and you were not willing!"' Luke 13.34

Indoctrination

A man calling himself a 'rationalist' wrote to a British newspaper, demanding that the Church of England should apologize for indoctrinating generations of children with false superstition and irrational dogma. The words he used for his attack were certainly over the top, but actually he had a point. It's only recently that schools have seen the importance of teaching children to think for themselves, and make up their own minds. Before that the purpose of education was regarded by everybody as to impart knowledge, and train individuals to conform to the principles on which society was based. The poor were encouraged to better themselves by what was called 'Self-help'. Each child, by diligent study, was taught to get themselves a job a couple of rungs higher on the status ladder than their parents. Nobody would find work at all if they were rebellious and undisciplined. There was no room in a society like that for individual choice. The Christian faith was seen as a means of encouraging the type of behaviour which would turn children into useful citizens. If teaching children to be considerate to their neighbours is indoctrination, then that's what every school, and not only those sponsored by the C of E, was doing.

Individual rights

In the second half of the twentieth century, a change came over people's attitudes to education. Stress was laid on encouraging each child to develop their unique talents; to explore and discover the world of knowledge for themselves; and to protect the rights of the individual. Good teachers had always done this instinctively; now it became official policy. Church schools were in the forefront of this revolution. As a result, many children grew into strong individuals, able to make mature decisions, and with a wide range of interests.

Too far?

But many teachers, parents and members of the public felt that this had gone a step too far. The lack of discipline, and the absence of a clear ideal of moral behaviour, led some, though not all, pupils into antisocial behaviour, idleness and dissipation. The removal of clear Christian teaching on the way we should behave opened the path to a do-it-yourself system of ethics, with everyone using their own reason to work out their individual view on life. In other words, we moved to a rationalist morality. The trouble with that, and the emphasis on rights above duty, is that, if you eliminate any moral authority outside your own desires, then the only reason for behaving well is if it is to your own advantage to do so. If theft means other people stealing my possessions, that's wrong; but doubtful business deals and little white lies are simply 'looking after number one'. The lives of other people are only important as far as they contribute to my own happiness; if they no longer do that, let them be put down!

Jesus

Jesus looked at the society of his own day, and burst into tears. He had been trying to win them to follow his example of unselfish behaviour by means of love; and they had rejected him. 'Jerusalem, Jerusalem,' he cried out, 'the city that kills the prophets and stones those who are sent to it! How often have I desired to gather your children together as a hen gathers her brood under her wings, and you were not willing!' Christian morality is the opposite of selfish rationalist morality. It's based on the assumption that other people are as important as you are, because all are loved equally by God. Christian morality calls us to help and do good to others, because we love our neighbours as much as we love ourselves. Love will never force anyone to do anything against their will, so it protects individual freedom. But it tries to win them, by loving them, to see that certain types of behaviour are unacceptable because of the harm they do. Christian teaching shows people that God loves them, so that they will love God in return, and love the poor, the sick, the homeless and the immigrant for God's sake. So let's teach that sort of morality as urgently as we can, in our schools, in our homes, in the media and by personal example – its emphasis on responding to God's love is quite reasonable, but it's the very opposite of indoctrination. We don't want Jesus weeping over our loveless society as he wept over Jerusalem.

All-age worship

Make a poster outside the church, reading: 'Does your behaviour make Jesus cry about you?'

City of God, how broad and far; In the streets of every city; Love is his word, love is his way; O for a heart to praise my God.

Second Sunday of Lent   24 February
Second Service   **Thou Hast Not Donne**

Ps. 135 Praise for God's goodness; Jer. 22.1–9, 13–17 Call to repent; Luke 14.27–33 Counting the cost

> *'If you will not heed these words, I swear by myself, says the Lord, that this house shall become a desolation.' Jeremiah 22.5*

Naughty boy

Young John was a naughty boy. The son of a London ironmonger, he studied at Oxford and Cambridge, and took up law. He managed to get a job as a secretary. But he'd grown into an ardent lover, and wrote passionate and erotic verse. He playfully rebuked the sun for waking him when in bed with his beloved:

> Busy old fool, unruly Sun,
> Why dost thou thus,
> Through windows, and through curtains, call on us?
> Must to thy motions lovers' seasons run?

The girl was his employer's niece, Ann More, whom he had secretly married without permission. The poet was dismissed in disgrace and thrown into prison. His name was spelled D O N N E, but pronounced John Dun. He lived in the early seventeenth century.

Reform

Born a Roman Catholic, his doubts led him to leave that church. After struggling with his conscience – how could a sexy lover dare to face God? – he was persuaded by King James to seek ordination in the Church of England, and in 1621 he was made Dean of Saint Paul's Cathedral. The passion he had previously spent on the flesh he now converted into love for God. This is shown in some of his greatest poems, his brilliant sermons, and his book called *Devotions upon an Emergent Occasion*, written when he was lying sick in bed expecting to die, from which comes the famous quotation 'Ask not for whom the bell tolls ...'

Penitence

During Lent we are thinking about confessing our sins. John Donne wrote a poem about this, with a pun on his own surname: when God is done with forgiving the sins he has just admitted, he still hasn't captured John Donne's soul, for there are more sins to confess: 'When thou hast done, thou hast not done, for I have more.'

A Hymn to God the Father

In the first verse, the poet confesses to God his share in the guilt of Adam's sin, and the sins which he can't stop committing:

Wilt thou forgive that sin where I begun,
Which is my sin, though it were done before?
Wilt thou forgive that sin, through which I run,
And do run still: though still I do deplore?
When thou hast done, thou hast not done,
For I have more.

Verse 2 confesses that he has led others into sin, and the temptations which he resisted for a while, but then gave in to:

Wilt thou forgive that sin by which I have won
Others to sin? and made my sin their door?
Wilt thou forgive that sin which I did shun
A year, or two: but wallowed in, a score?
When thou hast done, thou hast not done,
For I have more.

In the final verse he confesses that he is afraid of dying unforgiven. He makes God promise that Jesus, the Son of God, will shine on him like the sun – another pun – to forgive him and welcome him:

I have a sin of fear, that when I have spun
My last thread, I shall perish on the shore;
Swear by thyself, that at my death thy Son
Shall shine as he shines now, and heretofore;
And, having done that, thou hast done,
I fear no more.

A great sinner, a great poet, and at last, a great saint.

Lessons

What lessons can we learn from John Donne, as we confess our sins this Lent? First, we need to be thorough. Once a sin has been confessed, we needn't mention it again. But looking back over our lives, most of us can find things we did which hurt other people, though we may not have realized it at the time. So confess them now, even if you forgot to then. Next, go over the year since last Lent, and, using pencil and paper, list the things you are ashamed of. Ignore the siren voices which try to persuade you the things you did weren't really sinful, or not very serious. List everything, accept your responsibility for them, confess them, then forget them. Second, confess your failure in resisting temptation; the times you led others into sin, and your habitual sins. Finally, confess that yielding to doubt is also a sin. God has promised to forgive you everything you confess; you may be forgiven a moment's uncertainty, but when you have confessed them, believe firmly that God has forgiven you. Believe that death holds no terrors for you now.

Example

When you confess your sins to God this Lent, will you do so as ardently, as thoroughly, and as confidently as John Donne did? When that is done, God's work is done, for you have no more to confess.

Suggested hymns

'Forgive our sins as we forgive'; God forgave my sin in Jesus' name; I will sing the wondrous story; Just as I am, without one plea.

Third Sunday of Lent   3 March
Principal Service   **Trials**
Isa. 55.1–9 A call to conversion; Ps. 63.1–9 Faith and providence; 1 Cor. 10.1–13 Temptation; Luke 13.1–9 The parable of the fig tree

> *'No testing has overtaken you that is not common to everyone. God is faithful, and he will not let you be tested beyond your strength, but with the testing he will also provide the way out so that you may be able to endure it.' 1 Corinthians 10.13*

Blacksmith

There's an old story of a blacksmith who became a convinced Christian. He was regular in worship, Bible reading and prayer, and lived a good Christian life. Yet from that day onward, everything seemed to go wrong in his life. He suffered pain where he'd never felt it before. He never had much money, and his family had to live frugally. One day, a non-Christian friend stopped at the forge to talk to him. The unbeliever sympathized with him in his trials and tribulations. 'It seems strange to me', he said, 'that so many bad things should happen to you, just when you have become a devout Christian. Your religion promises you God's blessings, yet everything is getting worse. You say you believe in a God of love; how could a loving God treat you like that?'

Tempering

The blacksmith didn't answer at once, and it was evident that he had often asked himself the same question. After a while, he gave this answer: 'You see there the raw iron out of which I make horseshoes? Do you know what I do with it? I take a piece of iron in the tongs and heat it in the fire until it's red-hot. Then I hammer it unmercifully until it's roughly the shape I want. Next I plunge it into a bucket of cold water; that's called tempering it. Then I heat it again and hammer it some more. I go on doing this over and over until at last the iron's in the shape I want. But sometimes', he went on, 'I find a piece of iron that can't stand up to this treatment. The heat and the hammering and the cold water are too much for it. I can tell that, for some reason, it will never make a good horseshoe. So I throw it onto that heap of scrap iron over there.'

Prayer

The blacksmith finished by comparing the story that he'd told to his own life. 'I know that God's been holding me in the flames of affliction and I have felt his hammer upon me. But I don't mind, so long as God can make what he wants out of me. So in all my trials and tribulations, my prayer to God is simply this: "Try me in any way you wish, dear Lord – only don't throw me on the scrap heap!"'

St Paul

St Paul wrote his first letter to the Christians in Corinth, who had suffered many difficulties in their lives. So had Paul: shipwrecks and sickness, attacks by his enemies and disloyalty from his friends. So he wrote to comfort the Corinthians and strengthen them, out of his own experience. Paul's words are very like the blacksmith's; he wrote, 'No testing has overtaken you that is not common to everyone. God is faithful, and he will not let you be tested beyond your strength, but with the testing he will also provide the way out, so that you may be able to endure it.'

Evolution

We see by looking at the natural world around us that every creature suffers the most appalling agonies, and nature is 'red in tooth and claw'. New species only come from the death of those that were not suited to survive. How can you reconcile Jesus's teaching about a loving father with all this suffering? The answer, said St Paul, is that every parent has to care for their children – but you can't protect them from every ill, without removing their freedom. They have to learn from their mistakes. Yet God knows your breaking point better than you do, and he will stop your suffering before you reach it. However much you suffer, God will always give you enough inner strength to bear it patiently, and learn to trust God more firmly. When you are having a bad day, and seem to be at the end of your tether, remember that God knows how much you can bear, and is using your pain to build up your faith. God will make you strong enough to bear it if you pray to him. Then say the blacksmith's prayer: 'Try me in any way you wish, dear Lord – only don't throw me on the scrap heap!'

All-age worship

Put some whipping cream into a cold bowl. Whip it by hand until it sets, then serve it on fruit. Say grace: 'Lord, thank you for this firm, smooth cream. Use the buffeting of my life to make me firm in my faith. Amen.'

Suggested hymns

Be thou my guardian and my guide; Christ triumphant, ever reigning; God moves in a mysterious way; The Church's one foundation.

Third Sunday of Lent   3 March
Second Service   **Say One for Me**

Ps. 12 No longer any godly, 13 How long?; Gen. 28.10–19a
Jacob's ladder; John 1.35–51 The call of Nathanael

> '[Jacob] dreamed that there was a ladder set up on the earth, the
> top of it reaching to heaven; and the angels of God were ascend-
> ing and descending on it.' Genesis 28.12

Say one for me

One of your friends, who isn't a churchgoer, hears that you attend
the services here. What do they say to you? Almost always, you will
hear them remark, half-jokingly, 'Say one for me, will you?' There's
a wistfulness there – your friends secretly wish they knew how to
pray for themselves, but have forgotten how or never learnt to – so
they hope that your prayers for them will be the next best thing.
This phrase is so commonly used that it was made the title of a Lent
course in some areas recently – 'Say one for me!'

Two-thirds

A recent survey showed that over two-thirds of the people in this
country said that they pray, at least occasionally. As well as the
firm believers like you and me – well ... fairly firm – who pray
because we have seen that it works, there must be an awful lot of
people who secretly want to believe. So they tick the box on the
questionnaire to say that they pray sometimes – or else they say to
somebody like us whom they know to be a believer, 'Say one for
me, please!'

Jacob's ladder

The Old Testament story of Jacob's ladder is about prayer. He fell
asleep, and dreamt of a great staircase from earth to heaven. Many
angels were going up and down. The word 'angel' means a mes-

senger, so these creatures were carrying messages for God. The ones going up were carrying the prayers of people on earth and bringing them before God. Those descending were bringing back the answers – quicker even than email! Jacob called the place where he had been sleeping 'Bethel', or 'The House of God'. Jesus mentioned this story when he met Nathanael. Jesus knew that Nathanael had been sitting under his fig tree, the traditional place for a Jew to pray. So Jesus said to him, 'you will see heaven opened and the angels of God ascending and descending upon the Son of Man'. In other words, Jesus himself is the House of God, the bottom rung of the ladder of prayer. Jesus will carry our prayers up to his heavenly Father, and bring back the answers. God always answers prayer: the answer can be yes; or wait; or 'No, I can't give you that, but I have got something even better to give you if you will only be patient.'

Prayer works

Prayer really works. It may not bring about the changes we asked for, but it always causes spiritual growth in the person who prays. Jesus promised the Holy Spirit to those who ask. The Spirit of God gives us the faith and perseverance to endure long periods of suffering, if needs be. We also receive spiritual power to change our own selfish characters, and that of the people round us through loving them, and in this way the world becomes a better place.

Learning to pray

But prayer is not easy, if you are out of practice. That's why our friends ask us to pray for them. You don't need to know the right words, as though it was a magic spell. God hears even the most stumbling, hesitant and ungrammatical prayers of his children if they chatter away to him. But you can always learn to pray better. We can learn to include prayers for others and ourselves, thanksgiving, penitence and worship. We can learn to sit in silence, listening for God's answers – usually in the form of a sudden certainty in our hearts about what he wants us to do. You can learn by reading books about prayer, or going to study groups and discussion groups in Lent; by being more regular in your worship, or by listening attentively to the sermons – *I said attentively ... wake up at the back there!*

81

We are angels

So as you grow in prayer, when you are even a little bit better at it than when you first started, you can become God's messenger. When your friend asks you to 'Say one for me', you should mention them to God by name in your silent prayers, in church or at home. You may not be very clear what their needs are, but God knows. Maybe God will use you to bring back the answer to them, or maybe the answer won't be apparent for several years. Yet the people who pray – you and me – are the angels on Jacob's ladder, carrying the messages for other people up to God and back down again to earth. You have always wanted to be an angel, haven't you? Well, now's your chance.

Suggested hymns

As Jacob with travel was weary one day; Blessed assurance, Jesus is mine; Prayer is the soul's sincere desire; What a friend we have in Jesus!

Fourth Sunday of Lent   10 March

(For Mothering Sunday, see the Second Service.)
Principal Service   **The Prodigal Father**

Joshua 5.9–12 Passover in Canaan; Ps. 32 Repentance; 2 Cor. 5.16–21 Forgiveness and reconciliation; Luke 15.1–3, 11b–32 The prodigal son

> *'While [his son] was still far off, his father saw him and was filled with compassion; he ran and put his arms around him and kissed him.' Luke 15.20*

Prodigal son

Jesus told a story of a younger son, who demanded his share of the family wealth in cash, then went off and blew the lot. We call it the parable of the prodigal son, but actually all the emphasis is on the strange behaviour of his father. The law-abiding Pharisees thought the life of the nation depends on everybody sticking to the rules. If people do what they like, society falls apart and everybody suffers. Everyone must invest their share of the village's wealth in planting new crops. The younger son was entitled to one-third of the family fortune, *when his father died*. If he squandered it far away, the villagers might starve. The Pharisees thought the father had a duty to refuse his son's request.

Discipline

Dr Ken Bailey, who spent over forty years in the Middle East, once asked some Arabs, 'Has anyone in your village ever asked for his share in the family capital, to take it away with him?' 'Never!' they replied. 'Could anyone ever make such a request?' 'Impossible!' 'If anyone did, what would happen?' 'His father would beat him, of course!' 'Why?' 'This request means *he wants his father dead!*' It was the father's task to maintain discipline, for the good of all. In this way, human fathers stood in the same relationship to their children as God does to his Chosen People, they thought – God is a tyrant, who punishes disobedience, for the good of society. Many people today still view God as a tough disciplinarian.

The prodigal father

So when Jesus told the story of a father who was so unbelievably generous, he was implying that God doesn't follow the rules of common sense. Everybody was deeply shocked at this blasphemy. The younger son squandered his cash on wine, women and song, and we call him prodigal, which means someone who is wasteful with their money, a lavish spendthrift. But wasn't the father also being wasteful, by letting his son get away with it? Ought we not to call the story the Parable of the Prodigal Father? Is Jesus saying that God is like that, a wastrel, squandering his love and resources on people who don't deserve it? Astonishingly enough, yes, he is, thank God!

The son returns

Predictably, the younger son soon runs out of cash, and has to take the demeaning position, for a Jew, of herdsman to a flock of pigs. He comes to his senses, and heads back home. He has a vague idea that he won't be welcomed, because he has upset his father, but if he applies for a job as a wage-earner, they will surely accept him.

83

His father welcomes him

The father had been broken-hearted when his son went off. Astonishingly, though, he still loves him, and every day he peers down the road to see if the wastrel is returning. One day he sees a figure in the distance, and the father breaks into a run. How undignified! Before the rascal can apologize, Dad throws a party for him, he is so happy to have him back. 'And that', thought the Pharisees, 'is what Jesus wants us to think God's like? Not a disciplinarian, but a God who comes searching for even the most dissipated of his children and throws his arms around them? That's blasphemy!'

The older brother

When Dad welcomes the scoundrel, Big Brother is furious. But more than kid brother's wastefulness, Dad was hurt by his elder son's intolerance. Just like the Pharisees' intolerance towards the tax-collectors and sinners. And that's the point of the story, for you and me as much as for the Pharisees. God loves all his children, and for the well-being of all, he wants us to live in love and tolerance with each other. It hurts God when you do something unkind, but he still loves you. You are quite undeserving of God's love, of course, but that doesn't stop the Prodigal God from pouring his love all over you. But what really wounds him is when you compare other people unfavourably with yourself. Criticizing others is the sin of intolerance. That breaks God's heart. The only way he can show you how much it hurts him, is to die on a cross in front of you. Then, perhaps, you will come home and let the Prodigal God throw his arms around you.

All-age worship

Pin to a large blanket the words 'God loves all his children'; then snuggle in it.

Suggested hymns

Amazing grace; Hear us, O Lord, have mercy upon us; I cannot tell why he whom angels worship; There's a wideness in God's mercy/ Souls of men.

Mothering Sunday   10 March
Mrs Alexander
(This is the second set of readings for Mothering Sunday from *Common Worship*.)
1 Sam. 1.20–28 His mother offers Samuel to the Lord; Ps. 127.1–4 Children a gift from the Lord; Col. 3.12–17 Love and care; John 19.25b–27 Mary is your mother

> *'Above all, clothe yourselves with love, which binds everything together in perfect harmony. And let the peace of Christ rule in your hearts, to which indeed you were called in the one body. And be thankful.' Colossians 3.14–15*

Love and care

Mothering Sunday is a day for saying thank you to mothers, for how much they love us and care for us. The two words which come to mind when we think of mothers are love and care. In one of his letters, St Paul wrote we should love everybody with the love and care we have experienced from our mothers: 'Above all, clothe yourselves with love, which binds everything together in perfect harmony ... And be thankful.'

Hymns

Hymns about love are suitable for Mothering Sunday – God's love for us, and God's call to love our neighbour as much as ourselves. There are also some hymns about Jesus's home life with Mary his mother, such as 'Lord of the home, your only Son received a mother's tender care.' 'For the beauty of the earth' has a lovely verse thanking God 'For the joy of human love, brother, sister, parent, child'. And then there's 'All things bright and beautiful', about God creating everything on earth for us to enjoy. They say that beauty's in the eye of the beholder, and I think most people would say that the smile on a mother's face is one of the most beautiful things in creation.

Mrs Alexander

'All things bright and beautiful' was written by a wife and mother, Mrs Alexander. She was given two Christian names: Cecil Frances;

and her name before she was married was Humphreys. She was born in 1818, the daughter of an ex-army officer who managed the estates of the Earl of Wicklow. Most of her hymns were written before she married, for the children of the Sunday school classes she taught. Many were meant to illustrate phrases from the Apostles' Creed: 'Once in Royal David's city' explains about the birth of Jesus, and 'There is a green hill far away' is about his death on the cross. 'All things bright and beautiful' is about God the Creator, and was written in County Tyrone; the 'river running by' was the River Mourne. Other hymns were to illustrate the collects in the Book of Common Prayer, including 'Jesus calls us o'er the tumult', and she translated the hymn known as St Patrick's Breastplate, beginning 'I bind unto myself today'. They were collected in a book called *Hymns for Little Children* which was published in 1848 and went into a hundred editions, the profits all going to a school for children who couldn't hear or speak, in Londonderry.

Rich and poor

Cecil Frances Humphreys was a beautiful woman, and two men both wanted to marry her. She couldn't make up her mind which to choose, but sadly the first one died, so she married a poor clergyman, the Reverend William Alexander. Later Mrs Alexander's husband became Bishop of Derry, and later still Archbishop of Armagh. 'All things bright and beautiful' is popular at all sorts of occasions because so many people learnt it at school. It's often criticized because it used to include a verse reading:

The rich man in his castle,
the poor man at his gate,
God made them, high or lowly,
and ordered their estate.

This verse was dropped from the hymnbooks quite soon after it was written, because some people misunderstood it. It could be interpreted as discouraging people from trying to change their position in life. But the Victorian age was one of great social mobility, as is shown by Mrs Alexander's own life story. The comma in the third line of her hymn is all-important: 'God made them, (comma) high or lowly.' It's a statement that whatever our position in life, we are all equal in the sight of our Creator. Whether we are stars, or only have a bit-part, each has an important role in the drama of life.

86

Mother-love

Mrs Alexander had four children – like most mothers, I expect she tried to love them all equally, the outwardly successful and the stay-at-homes alike. It's from our mothers that we learn that none of us is a nobody; we are all important to our mothers. If Mother loves me, that means God thinks I'm worthy of love, too; and we learn our ideas of God's love from what we have experienced in the home.

All-age worship

Learn one of these hymns by heart, and sing it when you give some-one flowers.

Hymns by Mrs Alexander

All things bright and beautiful; Jesus calls us – o'er the tumult; Once in royal David's city; There is a green hill far away.

Fifth Sunday of Lent   17 March
(Eve of St Patrick's Day, transferred)
Principal Service   **Silence**
Isa. 43.16–21 Salvation; Ps. 126 Salvation and joy; Phil. 3.4b–14 Perseverance; John 12.1–8 Mary and Martha

> *'Martha served, and Lazarus was one of those at the table with [Jesus.] Mary took a pound of costly perfume made of pure nard, anointed Jesus' feet, and wiped them with her hair. The house was filled with the fragrance of the perfume.' John 12.2–3*

Mary and Martha

There was a house in Bethany where Jesus loved to relax, away from the cares of the world. It was the home of his friend Lazarus – whom Jesus loved – and his sisters Mary and Martha. Martha was busy preparing the meal; but Mary liked to sit in silence at the feet of the Master and listen. Martha grumbled at this, but Jesus said that Mary had found the one thing that was necessary in life. Mary poured some very expensive perfume over Jesus's feet, and the house was filled with the odour of the ointment. It was as though

87

prayer in silence in the presence of Jesus had given their lives a completely new atmosphere.

Busy

But Martha was busy with the domestic chores. Sometimes our lives are too busy. Through never having time to stop and think, we become inefficient at our jobs. We realize that something is missing from our lives, but don't know what it is. The trouble is that, often without realizing it, we all have an inner thirst for silence. Yet we live in a world of noise. Some people have the telly on all the time they are at home. We talk on our mobile phones, whether or not we have anything to say. We are glued to our computers, sending and receiving emails, or 'social-networking'. Even if we have been told that God is with us always, we are no more aware of his presence than we are of the non-stop Muzak® in the superstore.

Silence

We need to make time for silence. At least once a week, we should set aside anything from five minutes to an hour to be completely quiet. We each need to find a place where we can rely on being uninterrupted. It may be in church; in your bedroom; in the garden; or in an isolated spot in the countryside. Some people find it helps them to focus on God in the silence to have some visual aid, like a picture or a candle. The great Quaker, William Penn, said, 'True silence is the rest of the mind; it is to the spirit what sleep is to the body: nourishment and refreshment.'

Jesus

Elijah found that God was not in the storm or the earthquake, but in 'a still small voice' – a better translation of those words would be to say he found God in 'the sound of silence'. Centuries ago, Christians who went off into the desert to be quiet used to say, 'To live without speaking is better than to speak without living.' The Dalai Lama, when asked by his followers how they should answer the questions of those who came to them, replied, 'Remember that silence is sometimes the best answer.' Mother Teresa of Calcutta said, 'We need to find God, and he cannot be found in noise and restlessness. God is the friend of silence.' Jesus, too, at crucial moments, retreated into the desert to be silent. He was silent before his accusers, 'like a lamb who before its shearers is dumb'. Then Jesus was silent on the cross for three hours, except for those seven phrases which form his last words.

Awareness

All our searching for God is fruitless, because God is already here in our hearts; all we have to do is quieten down and listen to the silence. Sometimes we may hear God speaking; more often we become aware of God in our hearts, giving us a strong feeling about what he wants us to do. The purpose of prayer isn't to talk at God until you persuade him to change his mind – the Danish Christian philosopher Søren Kierkegaard wrote, 'Prayer does not change God, it changes the person who prays.' We should aim to be more like Mary, who made time to listen to Jesus in silence, and was changed, until 'the house was filled with the fragrance of the perfume'.

Contemplation

Silent contemplation is the ultimate aim of all prayer, and monks spend years in silence learning to contemplate the presence of God. Yet the peace and power which contemplation offers is available to the simplest Christian beginner who makes time to be silent. God speaks to you in the words of the psalms, saying 'Be still and know that I am God.'

All-age worship

Close your eyes and imagine Jesus standing in front of you. How long can you sit enjoying his love like that? Talk for a bit, then try to sit in silence for a longer time.

Suggested hymns

Be still and know that I am God; Be still, for the presence of the Lord; Dear Lord and Father of mankind; Spirit of the living God.

Fifth Sunday of Lent   17 March
Second Service   **The Hammersmith Flyover**

Ps. 35 You deliver the weak; 2 Chron. 35.1–6, 10–16 Josiah's
Passover; Luke 22.1–13 Preparing for Passover

> *'Say to the owner of the house, "The teacher asks you, 'Where is the guest room, where I may eat the Passover with my disciples?'"' Luke 22.11*

The Hammersmith Flyover

If you want to enter or leave London on the west side by road, you will almost certainly have to go over a bridge called 'the Hammersmith Flyover'. This section of elevated highway rises up on pillars, taking the traffic over all the congested side streets which previously hindered the free movement of vehicles. 'Flyover' is a marvellous name to give to this feature – you can picture in your mind's eye each lorry and car sprouting wings, and soaring over all the hindrances which would otherwise have delayed its progress!

Passover

The word 'flyover' is quite like another word, which you find in the Bible: the word 'Passover'. The picture behind the two words is quite similar, too. The Jews were slaves in Egypt, and Pharaoh refused to release them. Moses had run out of carrots to persuade the king to 'Let my people go.' Now he had to change from carrots to sticks, making threats of what God would do if Pharaoh didn't obey him. The king had ignored all the plagues with which God punished his obstinacy, so at last Moses had to make the worst threat of all – the death of the firstborn. If the Egyptians didn't free their Hebrew slaves, God would send his angel to kill the oldest son in each family, and the firstborn male of all their animals too. But the angel of death, as it flew overhead, was instructed not to kill any Jewish boys, so there had to be a sign to identify the Jewish houses – it sounds almost as though the angel was short-sighted! So every household was to meet together for a family meal of lamb, and the blood of the lamb was to be painted on the doorposts of the house as a T-shaped cross. Whenever God's angel saw the cross of blood, it was instructed to 'pass over' that house without killing either human or animal there. Jewish families were instructed to celebrate the Passover meal every year, thanking God for saving them from death. Then God helped Moses and the Israelites to pass over the Red Sea towards the Promised Land. So the meal also reminds them that God has saved them from slavery.

Family sermon

A preacher was trying to explain this story to a congregation of children and adults in a London suburban church once. He compared the Passover to the Hammersmith flyover, just as I have done. Then he pretended to mix the words up, and every time he wanted to describe the festival he said 'the Feast of the Hammersmith flyover ... oops! Sorry, I mean the Feast of the Passover.' This tickled the sense of humour of one little lad, who had been driven over the flyover many times in the past eight years, and he started to giggle – in fact he never stopped giggling till the service was over, and the congregation couldn't help laughing with him. It was one service which that congregation will never forget! I'm not going to resort to any such cheap tricks to raise a laugh today – but if I hear anyone giggling I'll know you are thinking about the Feast of the Hammersmith flyover!

The Last Supper

The Last Supper which Jesus held with his disciples, on the evening before he was crucified, was a Passover supper, or *seder* as it's called in Hebrew. He taught them that his death would save them from death and slavery in a completely new way. God wants everyone to live with him in eternity, but we have to accept his invitation by faith in Jesus. Jesus died and rose again, so that, united with him by faith, we too, when we die, might rise again to eternal life. We are slaves to bad and selfish habits, and to feelings of guilt for what we have done. Jesus's death was like the Passover lamb, sacrificed to assure us that God has forgiven us, and given us power to resist temptation by the Holy Spirit. Jesus is the Lamb of God, who takes away the sin of the world. Marked by the blood of the lamb, we too pass over from death to life, from slavery to freedom. So drink the wine at Holy Communion, symbolizing the blood of Jesus, and have faith in him, and he will lead you into the Promised Land of heaven, as we eat together the holy meal of the Ham ... er, s-sorry, of the Passover. Then we can pass over all the obstacles and fly into heaven! Won't that be wonderful?

Suggested hymns

At the Lamb's high feast we sing; Now my tongue, the mystery telling; Sing, my tongue, the glorious battle; When Israel dwelt in Egypt's land (Go down, Moses).

HOLY WEEK

'Passiontide' is the name for the solemn week from Palm Sunday to Easter, because we remember the suffering – *passio* in Latin – of Jesus on the cross, from love for us. We also call it Holy Week, because we see into the mysterious love of God. On Palm Sunday we think of those who waved branches from palm trees, as Jesus rode into Jerusalem as the King on a donkey, and we bless palm crosses for people to take home with them. On Maundy Thursday we remember the Last Supper, a Passover meal which Jesus celebrated in the Upper Room with his disciples: the name comes from the 'new com-*mand*-ment' which Jesus gave us, to love one another as he has loved us. The Eucharist on this day may include the foot-washing and stripping of the altars, reminding us how Jesus was stripped of his clothes by the mocking soldiers. Good Friday is a strange name to give to the day when we remember the appalling death of Jesus on the cross, but on that day he absorbed our sin and brought us forgiveness and reconciliation with God, promising that death will be followed by eternal life.

Palm Sunday 24 March
Principal Service **Someone Needs to Pay**
Liturgy of the Palms: Luke 19.28–40 Triumphal entry; Ps. 118.1–2, 19–29 Blessed is he who comes; *Liturgy of the Passion*: Isa. 50.4–9a I gave my back to the smiters; Ps. 31.9–16 Assurance in suffering; Phil. 2.5–11 Obedience unto death; Luke 22.14—23.56 The Last Supper to the burial, *or* Luke 23.1–49 The trial to the cross

'I gave my back to those who struck me,
  and my cheeks to those who pulled out the beard;
I did not hide my face from insult and spitting.' Isaiah 50.6

Someone needs to pay

Picture a school teacher coming into the classroom and it's an absolute tip. The children rushed off without tidying up. The teacher is furious. She or he will either have to clear up the mess themselves, or persuade the caretaker to, or make the children do it. 'Someone needs to pay for this,' the teacher raged. This isn't about money – paying the caretaker or mending damaged property are trivial matters. A serious offence has been committed, and justice won't be satisfied till someone is given an equally serious punishment. If you can't identify the culprit, a scapegoat must be chosen to pay the penalty instead.

Who needs it?

But wait a moment. Who 'needs' this to happen? Does the guilty party need it? Or does the teacher need it? Or do the rest of the class need a scapegoat? When you think of it, each of these *imagines* they need it, but in fact they don't. Thinking this issue through may help us understand why Jesus died on the cross.

Judge and jury

Our imaginary teacher has appointed themselves judge and jury – 'upholding justice'. But actually the teacher wants revenge. True justice is when oppressed people, unable to protect themselves, are delivered from their oppressors. Yet nobody is oppressed in this situation. The teacher, who is considerably inconvenienced, can make the whole class clear up the mess, without needing to get into a rage. People often read in a newspaper about a crime committed miles away from their home, and shout, 'Someone needs to pay for this!' But it's nothing to do with them – they are calling for revenge, and that's not nice. The Pharisees and their supporters were furious that liberal ideas of love were attacking their powerful position in society. They needed a scapegoat, and Jesus had to pay. As Isaiah said, God's suffering servant always becomes the scapegoat when people howl for revenge.

Classmates

The entire class of schoolchildren in the story knew they were guilty, but they didn't want to be punished. They, too, found a satisfactory solution in the scapegoat. So did the crowd when they cried for Jesus to be crucified. The argument that 'someone needs to pay' is often a way of evading our own guilt. What the bystanders really need is a warning or a severe shock which stops them, in turn, from committing the offence the accused is charged with.

The offender

But what about someone who really is guilty of what they are accused of? Often they have a feeling that they need to be punished, to get rid of the nagging sense of guilt. But life doesn't work that way; the only way to overcome guilty feelings is to face up to what you have done, apologize to those you have offended, and ask for their forgiveness. You won't do that until you realize what harm you have caused. That's where the scapegoat idea really works. When we see Jesus bleeding on the cross, we understand the seriousness of our sins. But the scapegoat must have *voluntarily* sacrificed themselves in our place.

Atonement

There are many ways of explaining what Jesus did on the cross. Choose the atonement theory which works for you, and ignore the rest. Christians often speak of God demanding that 'someone needs to pay' for human sin. I describe this as the 'transaction theory'. It's as though God calculates how much pain pays for so much sin, and then loads the lot onto Jesus. I find that a deeply offensive picture of God. But if Jesus, the Son of God, *voluntarily* offered himself to be the scapegoat, this means that God himself is the one who pays for your sins and mine. Realize that, and it gives you a jolt! Who could help loving the Saviour, whose love rescues us from guilt at such a cost? Now we shall try our hardest not to cause him further pain. Love breeds love, and our loving gratitude to the crucified helps us to love ourselves, and to love other sinners for Jesus's sake. When Jesus rode a donkey into Jerusalem to be our Saviour, he alone knew what it was going to cost him.

All-age worship

Make a roll of newspaper. Cut the end to resemble a palm leaf. Wave it in a Palm Sunday procession.

Suggested hymns

Ah, holy Jesus, how hast thou offended?; All glory, laud and honour; Ride on, ride on in majesty; There is a green hill far away.

Palm Sunday 24 March
Second Service **The Lightning Conductor**
Ps. 69.1–20 Zeal for your house consumes me; Isa. 5.1–7 The Song of the Vineyard; Luke 20.9–19 The parable of the wicked tenants

> *'The owner of the vineyard said, "What shall I do? I will send my beloved son; perhaps they will respect him." But when the tenants saw him, they discussed it among themselves and said, "This is the heir; let us kill him so that the inheritance may be ours." So they threw him out of the vineyard and killed him.' Luke 20.13–15*

Kenosis

'He saved others,' jeered the crowd when Jesus was crucified, 'but he can't save himself!' Jesus had become a famous healer, bringing freedom from pain to those who were suffering, which they found nowhere else. Yet the crowd was right – he couldn't save himself. The Son of God had chosen to become human, with all that this entails. As St Paul wrote in his letter to the Philippians,

> though he was in the form of God,
> [he] did not regard equality with God
> as something to be exploited,
> but emptied himself,
> taking the form of a slave,
> being born in human likeness.
> And being found in human form,
> he humbled himself
> and became obedient to the point of death –
> even death on a cross.

Being human means having to put up with pain and suffering – so if God's Son chooses to become a mortal man, that means he's bound to endure suffering and death.

Foresight

'Does that mean that Jesus knew in advance that he would be cruci-fied?' you ask. Well, the incarnation's a mystery beyond human power to understand. For thirty years Jesus 'emptied himself' of his divine omniscience. But even as a human being he was very close to his heavenly Father, who could have told him what God can see in the future. For God is above time, and all times are 'the present' to God. Yet even to a mere human, it was perfectly obvious that the Jews couldn't go on as they were. They were subjects of the Roman Empire, yet they were constantly murdering Roman soldiers, and plotting an insurrection. In fact the Jews, then, behaved towards the Romans in much the same way as Jews of today complain that the Arabs treat them! It was perfectly obvious to most people that the Romans wouldn't put up with such treatment for much longer. Soon they'd clamp down, and many Jews would die. So Jesus decided to draw down the wrath of Rome on himself, and save his people from the inevitable Roman revenge.

Stories

So Jesus told stories, gripping and unforgettable stories, to help his listeners to understand what was going on around them. We heard one of these stories in the Gospel reading today. Once upon a time, said Jesus, there was a man who travelled far away from home. He owned a vineyard, and left it in the hands of some tenants, in return for a share of the harvest. When he sent messengers to collect the rent, however, the tenants beat them up and sent them away empty-handed. So the owner decided to send his oldest son; but the tenants threw him out and killed him. End of story. But every Jew knew that in their Scriptures, the nation of Israel is called God's vineyard. Jesus was saying that God's own people would make God's Son an outcast and kill him. Jesus knew that his own death was inevitable.

The lightning conductor

To use a modern analogy, Jesus was like a lightning conductor. In a thunderstorm, a colossal electrical charge builds up in the clouds. Any tree or building will attract that charge, and the electricity will be released as a thunderbolt, possibly destroying the structure and killing anyone sheltering there. Pointed structures in particular attract the charged ions; but if a spike is connected by a copper cable or strip to the ground, the electricity will be harmlessly discharged to earth. Jesus knew that he was the lightning conductor. By attracting the wrath of the Pharisees and the Romans, it could be discharged through him, and the rest of the people would remain unharmed.

The Saviour

It's a memorable image. Of course, it would have meant nothing to the people of Jesus's time, because they didn't know the science. But maybe it will help you to understand better what it means to call Jesus our Saviour. By allowing himself to become an outcast, and condemned to a shameful death, Jesus absorbs the hatred which bad people feel towards good people, and so protects us from their vengeance. Some Christians are called to the same ministry – to soak up the jealous hatred which everyone feels for people whose goodness they envy. Accept that lot humbly if God calls you to it. And when you say your prayers, give praise to Jesus for being our lightning conductor.

Suggested hymns

From heaven you came, helpless babe; In the cross of Christ I glory; Morning glory, starlit sky; O love, how deep, how broad, how high.

First three days in Holy Week   25–27 March
Behold the Man!

(*Following are the Wednesday readings but this sermon may be used on any day this week.*)
Isa. 50.4–9a I gave my back to the smiters; Ps. 70 Those who say Aha! Aha!; Heb. 12.1–3 Suffering and perseverance on the cross; John 13.21–32 Judas betrays Jesus

> '*After saying this Jesus was troubled in spirit, and declared, "Very truly, I tell you, one of you will betray me." The disciples looked at one another, uncertain of whom he was speaking.' John 13.21–22*

97

Feelings

Until recently, English-speaking folk were notoriously bad at speaking about feelings. Yet bottling up your emotions can be dangerous, in case they burst out of you in unexpected and dangerous ways. Best to find a good friend, listen to each other, laugh or cry together, and you will both feel better.

Jesus's feelings

But because we don't like talking about our own feelings, we can be insensitive to other people's. We become so self-centred, wrapped up in our own troubles, that we don't notice the suffering of others. We blunder about, wounding and offending people, without realizing what hurt we are causing them. God has feelings, too, and God suffers when we disobey him, in a way we shall never understand. But God sent his only Son, who feels the same as God does, so that we should see how much we hurt the most loving of all hearts. Yet even then, we often don't notice. Jesus wasn't a buttoned-up Britisher, he wore his heart on his sleeve. The words are there in the Gospels, but often we don't even see them.

Last Supper

For instance, at the Last Supper, he knew he was going to die the next day. 'Now my soul is *troubled*,' he said. 'And what should I say – "Father, save me from this hour"? No, it is for this reason that I have come to this hour.' His disciples were arguing and squabbling about which of them was more important, and they didn't see how sad their Master was. He knew that one of them was going to betray him to death, but they pooh-poohed the idea. 'After this,' we read, 'Jesus was *troubled* in spirit.' Anyone with an ounce of humanity in them would be, too, in those circumstances. In the Garden of Gethsemane, he told his three best friends, 'I am deeply *grieved*, even to death; remain here, and keep awake.' They promptly fell asleep! The sweat poured off him, so frightened was he of dying, but nobody noticed.

Pilate

For a moment, Pontius Pilate felt pity for what Jesus was going through. He brought Jesus before the crowd, thinking that the sight of him would stir their sympathy. 'Behold the man!' he cried. *Ecce homo!* We ought to say the same when we read the Passion story. Forget the divine Son of God for a moment – behold the *man*! His physical pain was real and acute. Yet because he was human, his mental agony was even greater. Try and imagine what was going through the mind of Jesus as he hung on the cross. His friends had deserted him – at one point he even felt as though God had abandoned him. He was human, for God's sake! Perhaps he worried that his life had been a failure. Battling with his human emotions, it must have taken tremendous courage to keep going. At last, by the skin of his teeth, he won through. With the cry of victory, 'It is finished!' he yielded up his spirit to his Father.

Only human

Any human being, when their life hangs by a thread, would feel as Jesus did. 'After all,' we say, 'we are only human.' We shan't understand the events of Holy Week unless we take literally the humanity of Jesus. He was, on earth, completely human, from the moment he was conceived – with all humanity's weakness, doubt and fear. But he wasn't 'only human'. Inside that frail human nature was a spark of divinity which enabled Jesus to keep going. Because we believe in Jesus, the divine spark enters our hearts too, and his Holy Spirit enables us to endure the bad times as patiently as he did. 'He became what we are, that we might become what he is.' With the Spirit in us, we aren't '*only* human', either. We *are* fully human – God knows that, and looks at us saying, 'Behold the man' ... or woman, or child. But we are not limited by our human nature; the Spirit's power will make us strong enough to cope with anything. Look at Jesus, and say, 'Behold the man!' Then look at yourself in the mirror, saying, 'See a human being, indeed, with human emotions – but one inspired with the Spirit of Jesus, and ready for anything our Father calls me to undergo.'

Suggested hymns

I cannot tell why he whom angels worshipped; Meekness and majesty; My song is love unknown; When I survey.

Maundy Thursday   28 March
Sacraments

Ex. 12.1–4 [5–10] 11–14 The Passover; Ps. 116.1, 10–17
The cup of salvation; 1 Cor. 11.23–26 The Last Supper; John
13.1–17, 31b–35 Foot-washing

> 'During supper, Jesus, knowing that the Father had given all
> things into his hands, and that he had come from God and was
> going to God, got up from the table, took off his outer robe, and
> tied a towel around himself. Then he poured water into a basin
> and began to wash the disciples' feet and to wipe them with the
> towel that was tied around him.' John 13.2–5

Communicating

There are many ways of communicating. A story is better than a
lecture, and a picture is worth a thousand words. So when Jesus
wanted to get a new idea into the minds of those who were reluctant
to accept it, he told them a parable. And when he wanted to explain
to the disciples the difficult idea of why he had to die, he acted it
out before them. Perhaps you didn't realize that was why he invited
them to the Last Supper? Think about it. It was a Passover meal,
though it may have been brought forward a day because Passover
clashed with the Sabbath that year. It was customary at that meal
to eat unleavened bread, as a reminder that when the Israelites fled
from Egypt, they didn't even have time to let the fermenting dough
rise which they made their bread from. They drank wine to remind
them of the Passover lamb, sacrificed, and its blood painted on the
doorposts. This was to save them from dying when the angel of
death passed over their house to kill the Egyptians. So the meal was
full of symbolism, implying salvation from slavery and from death.

Eucharist

Then Jesus added another layer of symbolism: he broke the bread,
he poured out the wine, pointed at them and said, 'This – my body.
And this – my blood.' Perhaps it wasn't until later that they realized
what he meant. When they did, they would never forget what he
had done. His body, he was saying – the warm, human body which
had healed them and embraced them – this body was going to be
broken until it was a corpse, the victim of extreme violence. His
lifeblood, they realized, was to be poured out of multiple wounds

to form a pool on the ground. And in this way Jesus resembled the Passover lamb; he was sacrificing his life, to save them from captivity to sin and the fear of death. Those ideas take a bit of thinking about, before we can absorb their full meaning. So Jesus told them to repeat the actions over and over again – not only at Passover time, but every time they met to remember how he died. We continue to act out the death of Christ still, week by week. In this Eucharist Jesus speaks to us in a way that goes beyond words. Repeating these actions tells us again and again: Jesus died *for you* – a sacrifice to set you free from bad habits and spiritual death.

Sacraments

Actions speak louder than words. If Jesus tried to explain his death to us in words, we might never grasp its meaning. But by seeing it acted out before us time and time again, gradually the wonder of it sinks in. So we have invented a new word to define this sort of communication. We call the Holy Communion a sacrament. The Book of Common Prayer says a sacrament is 'an outward and visible sign of an inward and spiritual grace, given unto us, ordained by Christ himself, as a means whereby we receive [his grace], and a pledge to assure us thereof'. In other words, you can't see God's love; but Jesus gives us something we can see – bread broken and wine outpoured – to make us certain that he loves us. A sacrament is often compared to a kiss: you can't see your mother's love, so she gives you a kiss – love made visible – so that you should never doubt that she loves you.

Seven

Once you have grasped the idea of a sacrament, all sorts of things take on a symbolic meaning: a flag which you salute, a Bible on which you swear to tell the truth, even the holy act by which a child is conceived – they are all 'earthly signs with heavenly meanings'. Sometimes the Church says there are seven sacraments. There's nothing magical in the number, but it's easy to remember. Traditionally they are:

Holy Communion
Baptism
Confirmation
Marriage

Healing
Confession and forgiveness
Ordination to the ministry.

All of them share in the new form of communication which Jesus invented at the Last Supper, of actions speaking louder than words, and making the invisible love of God visible before our very eyes.

Suggested hymns

And now, O Father, mindful of the love; Broken for me, broken for you; Sweet sacrament divine; The heavenly Word, proceeding forth.

Good Friday   29 March
Famous Last Words

(This could be used as the sermon at a Good Friday service with the usual readings; or as the outline for an hour's worship; or expanded into a Three Hours' Devotion. Each section may be followed by silence and a prayer.)

HYMN *When I survey the wondrous cross*

There's a widespread belief that the last words somebody says before they die sum up the total experience of their life. It isn't always true, but when it is, they are often quoted as 'famous last words'. As Shakespeare said, 'The tongues of dying men enforce attention like deep harmony.' According to the four Gospels, Jesus spoke several times when he was being crucified. Considering the pain involved, it's amazing that he was able to talk at all. If you add all the four Gospels together, we have seven famous last words of Jesus on the record; there may well have been more. They are called the seven words from the cross; and each one tells us something about how we should live, and hope to die.

Luke 23.27–34 The crucifixion
Father, forgive

The first of the seven words from the cross was spoken, according to Luke, while the soldiers were nailing Jesus to the cross. 'Then

Jesus said, "Father, forgive them; for they do not know what they are doing."' It was not only the soldiers – each one of us often does things which hurt Jesus. But he forgives us; bringing forgiveness was the purpose of his life and death.

HYMN *Were you there when they crucified my Lord?*
Luke 23.39–43 With me in paradise
In paradise

To the penitent thief, Jesus said 'Truly I tell you, today you will be with me in paradise.' Here was forgiveness at its most demanding; Jesus forgives someone who may well have been a murderer, but who, at the last minute, showed a flash of faith. Nobody's beyond redemption. Jesus encouraged him with the promise of eternal life.

John 19.23–27 Behold your son
Here is your mother

According to John, when Jesus saw his mother, and the disciple whom he loved standing beside her, he said to his mother, 'Woman, here is your son.' Then he said to the disciple, 'Here is your mother.' And from that hour the disciple took her into his own home. At times of intense pain, most of us are only capable of thinking of ourselves; Jesus was unselfishly caring for his mother and his best friend.

HYMN *O sacred head, surrounded*
Matthew 27.45–49 Why have you forsaken me?
Forsaken

St Mark writes, 'At three o'clock Jesus cried out with a loud voice, "Eloi, Eloi, lema sabachthani?" which means, "My God, my God, why have you forsaken me?"' Matthew has the same thing in slightly different words. Jesus entered fully into our human experience, even to the extent of feeling as though God had deserted him. Yet the words were a quotation from Psalm 22, which ends on a joyful note. It's as though he had to work bravely through his despair in order to return to hope.

John 19.28–29 I am thirsty
Thirst

'After this,' writes St John, 'when Jesus knew that all was now finished, he said (in order to fulfil the scripture), "I am thirsty."' Psalm 69 includes the words, 'When I was thirsty, they gave me vinegar to drink.' Jesus, who was fully human, was dehydrated after three hours in the heat of the noonday sun. But he was also fully divine, and he was thirsting to obey his Father's will, and to win our souls for heaven.

HYMN It is a thing most wonderful
John 19.30 It is finished
It is finished

'When Jesus had received the wine, he said, "It is finished."' This is a cry of triumph; Jesus seized victory from the jaws of defeat. 'Love's redeeming work is done.'

Luke 23.44–49 Into your hands
Commending his spirit

'Then Jesus,' concludes St Luke, 'crying with a loud voice, said, "Father, into your hands I commend my spirit." Having said this, he breathed his last.' This is a quotation from Psalm 31, and may well have been the prayer of faith which Jesus, in common with many other people, used to say just before he went to sleep each night.

Matthew 27.57–61 Burial
The Lord's Prayer

Christ crucified draw you to himself, to find in him a sure ground for faith, a firm support for hope, and the assurance of sins forgiven; and the blessing of God Almighty, the Father, the Son, and the Holy Spirit, be with you all, now and evermore. **Amen.**

(*Common Worship*)

HYMN There is a green hill

All-age worship

Make a cardboard cut-out in the rough shape of Jesus's body. With a hammer and tin tacks, nail it to a large wooden cross. Discuss what the soldiers were feeling, and what Jesus felt.

EASTER

The Easter festival and the forty days which follow are the other high point, together with Christmas, in the rhythm of the Church's year. Jesus died on Good Friday, but his disciples became convinced that he was now alive again, and would bring eternal life to all who believe in him. The altar frontals and vestments are white, or gold on Easter Day, and the Easter hymns resound with alleluias. If 'Glory to God in the highest' has been omitted in Lent, it is sung again for the first time on the evening before Easter. At the vigil, a new fire is lit, symbolizing the new life which began at the resurrection of Jesus; and the Easter candle, lit from it, symbolizes Christ the light of the world, and burns at all the services from Easter till Ascension Day, and at baptisms in the rest of the year. At Easter we may renew our baptism promises. We may make an Easter garden with a model of the empty tomb.

Easter Vigil   30–31 March
Point Scoring

(*A minimum of three Old Testament readings should be chosen. The reading from Ex. 14 should always be used.*)
Gen. 1.1—2.4a Creation, Ps. 136.1–9, 23–26; Gen. 7.1–5, 11–18, 8.6–18, 9.8–13 Noah, Ps. 46 Our refuge and strength; Gen. 22.1–18 Sacrifice of Isaac, Ps. 16 The path of life; Ex. 14.10–31, 15.20–21 The Exodus, *Canticle*: Ex. 15.1b–13, 17–18 The song of Moses; Isa. 55.1–11 Come to the waters, *Canticle*: Isa. 12.2–6 Great in your midst; Bar. 3.9–15, 32—4.4 God gives the light of Wisdom, *or* Prov. 8.1–8, 19–21; 9.4b–6 Wisdom, Ps. 19 The heavens declare God's glory; Ezek. 36.24–28 I will sprinkle clean water on you, Ps. 42 and 43 Faith and hope; Ezek. 37.1–14 The valley of dry bones, Ps. 143 A

prayer for deliverance; Zeph. 3.14–20 I will bring you home, Ps. 98 Salvation and justice; Rom. 6.3–11 Baptism, death and resurrection, Ps. 114 The Exodus; Luke 24.1–12 The empty tomb

> 'The [angels] said to [the women at the tomb], "Why do you look for the living among the dead? He is not here, but has risen ..." ... Returning from the tomb, they told all this to the eleven and to all the rest ... But these words seemed to them an idle tale, and they did not believe them.' Luke 24.5–11

Against it

If you see a protest march near your home, it's very tempting to join it, and only then to ask what they are protesting against. There a story of one marcher who told a reporter, 'I don't know what this march is about, but I'm definitely against it!' In fact it's much easier to say what you are opposed to than to stand up for something positive. A political party, which was elected because it was opposed to the policy of the government before them, suddenly finds that it has to think out clearly what it's standing for, now it's in power. Many movements seem to exist with the sole purpose of scoring points against their opponents. This is a great weakness, because unless they are strongly *for* something positive they will do little good in the world.

Atheists

This criticism applies to some atheists, who have written books recently, which became best-sellers because they angrily condemned all forms of religion. They claim that religious people are responsible for all the evil in the world. This pays little attention to the facts of history, or the experience of religious people today. Of course, if someone is violent and selfish, and becomes an adherent of a religious movement, they will make their faith an excuse for behaving in an objectionable manner. But it's not really the religion which is to blame, it's the sin in the heart of those who claim to be religious but ignore the message of love which is at the heart of all religions. The atheists don't see this; they gain popularity by being strongly against religion, but they never explain what they would put in its place.

Resurrection

The Christian belief in the resurrection of Jesus, which we celebrate tonight, is the very opposite of this. It makes a very positive assertion, that Jesus is alive today, and that his gift of eternal life is available to everyone who trusts in him. Christianity doesn't try to score points by being opposed to other faiths. It simply makes an offer of God's eternal love, which brings joy and happiness to anyone who will accept it. In our Easter hymns, enemies are said to be defeated, but these enemies are the fear of death and our hopelessness in the face of our own mortality. Without Jesus, life is short and meaningless, and there's no reason for trying to make anything of it. For those who believe, however, their faith offers them strength and hope in their struggle against these ancient enemies.

Beliefs

When the women returned from the tomb, the male disciples at first didn't believe them. Yet the eminent psychologist William James said that everyone has beliefs – what he called 'working hypotheses', which help us to make sense of our lives. These beliefs are vital to our existence; but they lie beyond logical or scientific proof. For instance, the United Nations in 1948 'reaffirmed their faith in fundamental human rights'. No scientific experiment can prove that everyone has the right to freedom and the pursuit of happiness, yet we all believe it to be so. This is a positive belief, and it creates human solidarity. So does the belief that Jesus is alive, whereas those who claim there is no God simply lash out at those who do, leading to the fragmentation of society. I know which side I would rather be on. Alleluia, Christ is risen! He is risen indeed! Alleluia!

Suggested hymns

I serve a risen Saviour; Jesus lives! thy terrors now; Light's glittering morn bedecks the sky; The strife is o'er, the battle done.

Easter Day   31 March
Principal Service   **The Divine Gardener**

Acts 10.34–43 Peter and other witnesses to the resurrection, *or* Isa. 65.17–25 New heavens and a new earth; Ps. 118.1–2, 14–24 I shall not die but live; 1 Cor. 15.19–26 The last enemy destroyed is death, *or* Acts 10.34–43; John 20.1–18 Magdalene at the tomb, *or* Luke 24.1–12 The women see Jesus

> *'Supposing him to be the gardener, she said to him, "Sir, if you have carried him away, tell me where you have laid him, and I will take him away."' John 20.15*

Gardening

Mary Magdalene met the risen Christ, and thought he was a gardener. Which of course he is – he tends our souls as a gardener tends the plants, baptizing us with water, feeding us with love, pruning us when our souls grow lank and straggly, while protecting us from more harm than we can cope with before we have grown firm and strong. A gardener depends on the facts of science about the growth of plants, but a good gardener needs much more than that. An artistic sense is necessary to see where each plant will look its best, and relate well with the others; and a deep passion for growing things must fill the heart of the gardener. So it was with Christ – he helps our souls to grow because he cares deeply about us – because he loves us. A good gardener is an artist; and so is Jesus.

Feelings

The Easter story is all about the triumph of love over logic, of passion over prudence. It's about people allowing their personal judgement to override the received judgements of authority, pragmatism, money, power, and even common sense. Caiaphas was reasonable in his decision to hand Jesus over to Pilate, to prevent revolution in Jerusalem, and so was Pilate – what he did was necessary to protect the Roman Empire. Peter's denial of Jesus arose from fear of the power of others. Thomas's reason told him that Jesus was dead, until he allowed his feelings to convince him that the dead man stood before him. Those who opposed Jesus made reasonable decisions – decisions we would probably have made ourselves in the same circumstances. So the Easter story challenges us to examine how we decide – in a limited, logical way, or allowing the full force of our artistic, intuitive feelings to drive us to the more creative conclusions? Jesus, the gardener, rose like a plant in springtime from the dead earth, to help our souls to grow – out of the dull world of commerce and greed, until we bloom with the beauty of love.

Beyond reason

Don't get me wrong – there's nothing illogical about belief in the resurrection. But experimental science can tell us nothing of what would happen if God came down to earth, because it's never happened before. Yet the world of faith goes beyond reason, because it supplements our logical minds with feelings of art, beauty and love. In this way, religion appeals not just to the brain, but to the whole person. Religion is meant to balance out the barren world of the materialist, by adding the extra dimension of the emotions. Jesus overcame the kingdom of this world by pointing to the alternative kingdom of heaven, which, as he rightly pointed out, is within us. So he appealed to the inner world of feelings to take us beyond the getting and spending, the haste and waste of daily life.

Almost persuaded

Jeanette Winterson, the novelist, wrote a few years ago that she wouldn't call herself a believer, but reading the Easter story each year persuades her that the world of the spirit is the only answer to the sense of imprisonment that so many have in modern life. It liberates us by appealing to the world of feelings which is the power behind art and literature. The Easter story, she wrote, allows her to escape from the false opposition of rational against irrational, of what can and can't happen, and to live in a three-dimensional world of the feelings. It might even, she admits, take her through that three-dimensional world into another world, where questions of what can and can't exist, what is and isn't possible, no longer have any meaning.

Growing plants

There must be many people like that, dissatisfied with a merely material explanation of life, but not yet convinced that Christianity is the answer. Like King Agrippa when St Paul preached to him, they are 'almost persuaded' to believe in an afterlife. So Jesus, the

Divine Gardener, tends our souls like growing plants, until we burst into bud like spring flowers, and achieve our full potential as spiritual and eternal beings.

All-age worship

Bring some pot-plants to church, and learn what we must do to help them thrive. Write on the pots, 'Jesus is our gardener'.

Suggested hymns

Alleluia, alleluia! Hearts to heaven and voices raise; Come, ye faithful, raise the strain; Good Joseph had a garden; Now the green blade riseth.

Easter Day   31 March
Second Service   Hands and Side
Morning Ps. 114 The Exodus, 117 Praise the Lord; Evening Ps. 105 The Exodus, *or* 66.1–11 God holds our souls in life; Isa. 43.1–21 You are my witnesses; 1 Cor. 15.1–11 Witnesses of the resurrection, *or* John 20.19–23 Sunday evening appearance

> 'When it was evening on that day, the first day of the week, and the doors of the house where the disciples had met were locked for fear of the Jews, Jesus came and stood among them and said, "Peace be with you." After he said this, he showed them his hands and his side. Then the disciples rejoiced when they saw the Lord.' John 20.19–20

The disciples

The disciples knew that Jesus was dead. The nails had been driven through his hands, near the wrists, so that he should hang from the cross. Death from crucifixion could take a very long time, so, in order that the body shouldn't hang there on the Sabbath, the Roman soldier drove his spear into Jesus's side, near the heart, till blood and water flowed out. Then, to their astonishment, Jesus appeared before the disciples in the Upper Room that night. At first they may have thought they had only seen a ghost. After all, the doors of the house where they had met were locked for fear that the Jewish leaders might send soldiers to arrest them too. But they realized it was a real live person, when Jesus showed them his hands and his side. His *hands*, and his *side*! This proved to them that Jesus was no ghost. The body which they saw was the same body that had been crucified, wounded in those very significant places, his hands and his side. So they came to believe that it wasn't a dream, there really can be life after death. Gradually they came to believe that Jesus, though undoubtedly human, may also in some sense have been divine.

Symbolism

So the wounds in Jesus's hands and side became the proof of the resurrection, for us as well as for the disciples. The following Sunday Jesus said, 'blessed are those who have not seen, but yet have believed'. Jesus was talking about you when he said that. But 'hands and side' are also full of symbolic meaning. They remind us of how and where Jesus was wounded, through the nerves which pass through the wrist into the hands, and through the heart, which causes heavy bleeding and death. They are perhaps the two most sensitive points in the body, and Jesus knew this when he went up to Jerusalem to be crucified. His was a voluntary sacrifice, made in full knowledge of what he would have to endure. But they were also the symbols of the two reasons that Jesus came down to earth – the hands, so that he could serve us, and his heart, so that he could love us.

Heart

To the Jews, the heart was the very core of our being, the centre of our personality. They were commanded to love God with all their heart, all their mind, all their soul, and all their strength. The heart, then, became thought of as the seat of our emotions, and Jesus was wounded to the heart, struck to the core of his being. You could say, then, that Jesus showed them the wound in his side to remind his disciples that human disobedience always breaks God's heart.

Hands

He showed them the marks of the nails in his hands, to point out to us that the crucifixion was the climax of humankind's ongoing warfare against our Creator. Yet hands are what we use to serve others; and, as the children's chorus tells us, 'Jesus's hands were kind hands, doing good to all.' Jesus laid his healing hands on lepers, a deaf man, Jairus's daughter, and Peter's mother-in-law. Often, when they brought sick people to him, Jesus 'took them by the hand' to give them confidence, before he healed them. But when the woman touched the hem of his robe and was cured, Jesus felt strength going out of him. Perhaps when Jesus showed his disciples the marks of pain on his hands, it was a subtle reminder about how much it costs God to heal and wait upon us, his handiwork.

Homage

Nowadays, when the Queen confers a knighthood on one of her subjects, it's traditional for the one who has been honoured to kiss her hand in homage. The final symbolic meaning we can take from these references to his hands, is to remember that Jesus, the Servant King, has honoured us by serving us, so we must return the honour by promising our loving obedience for evermore. Perhaps you would like to close your eyes, and picture the risen Christ standing there in front of you, showing you his heart of love which you have pierced, and holding out his wounded hand. Then imagine yourself taking his hand gratefully, and kissing it in a promise of eternal obedience.

Suggested hymns

Alleluia! O sons and daughters, let us sing; Angel-voices ever singing; From heaven you came; That Eastertide with joy was bright (Part 3 of Light's glittering morn).

Second Sunday of Easter   7 April
(Eve of the Annunciation, transferred)
Principal Service   Acts of the Risen Christ
Ex. 14.10–31; 15.20–21 The Exodus (*if used, the reading from Acts must be used as the second reading*), or Acts 5.27–32 Peter witnesses to the resurrection; Ps. 118.14–29 I shall not die but live, *or* Ps. 150 Praise in Heaven; Rev. 1.4–8 The firstborn from the dead; John 20.19–31 Thomas's doubt and faith

'Peter and the apostles answered, "We must obey God rather than any human authority."' Acts 5.29

Words

Words change their meanings. Sometimes a word which used to be exciting has now become boring. The word 'Gospel', originally meant 'Good News'. Now it's some pages in a dusty black book, written in old-fashioned English. If we called the four Gospels, 'What Jesus did', they might get read more often. Read one of the Gospels straight through, and you will be begging for more. 'What an exciting book,' you will say; 'but why stop there? Did the story of what Jesus did end when he was taken away from us into heaven?' And the answer is, no! The sequel comes next in the Bible, entitled, the Acts of the Apostles. That, too, could sound boring! Let's call it 'What the Apostles did'.

Acts

We read from the book of Acts, every Sunday in Eastertide, in our lectionary. That's a long haul, and sounds like a dull read, yet in fact it's a thrilling adventure story. But what do you think when you hear the word 'apostle'? A jury of twelve grumpy old men, whose frozen mug-shots are in ancient stained-glass windows? No, these were pioneer travellers, heroes willing to risk their lives for what they believed in. The word 'apostle' means 'missionary'. Let's call them 'messengers', people sent by their home church to carry the good news of Jesus to people who don't know that God loves them. So you *could* call the fifth book in the New Testament, 'What the Messengers did'. Or even, maybe, 'Adventures of Christ's Messengers'.

Through us

But I haven't finished yet. With Christian humility, the apostles would want to shift the focus away from themselves onto Jesus. What's important isn't what they achieved, but what Jesus did through them, using the apostles as his instruments. So the book of Acts is a fitting sequel to the story of 'What Jesus did'. It's about what Jesus did after he'd gone up to heaven, working through his messengers. And that's exciting!

Peter

The apostles whose adventures the book recounts weren't all members of the close circle of twelve that Jesus appointed. More than half of Acts is about St Paul, who wasn't even a Christian when Jesus died. Today's reading continues the adventures of Simon Peter. Yes, the same man who ran away when Jesus was arrested, and was so terrified he wouldn't even admit to knowing Jesus, when a chit of a girl challenged him. The first thing Jesus did with Peter was to turn the tongue-tied bungler into a brilliant speaker and debater. After the disciples had received the Holy Spirit, Peter and John healed a crippled beggar in the Jerusalem Temple, and preached about Jesus to the curious crowd that gathered around them. The priests sent and arrested them, accusing them of unauthorized rabble-rousing. Peter replied, 'We must obey God rather than any human authority. The God of our ancestors raised up Jesus ... God exalted him at his right hand as Leader and Saviour, so that he might give repentance ... and forgiveness of sins. And we are witnesses to these things.'

Lessons

So we see from the book of Acts that the heroic apostles were brave when threatened, persistent in bearing witness to the resurrection of Jesus, and obedient to God our Creator in all things. Yet the achievement was not theirs, but from God working through them. So the story of 'What Jesus did through his messengers' turns out to be a promise of what God can do through you and me. If you are loyal to Jesus our Saviour, and do your best to love God and your neighbour, then Jesus will strengthen you. He will help you to ignore the threats of those who feel themselves menaced by the message of repentance and forgiveness which we proclaim. He will give you courage to speak out for what you believe, and the power of the Spirit to love everyone equally. Then the story of your life will turn out to be an account of 'What Jesus did through Joe Bloggs' – or Jane Bloggs, or whatever your name is. It's bound to be a story of high adventure, with a happy ending, in the next world if not in this one.

All-age worship

Tell, or write, your life story so far, trying to show how God used you to help other people.

114

Suggested hymns

I danced in the morning; Jesus, stand among us; We have a gospel to proclaim; Will you come and follow me?

Second Sunday of Easter 7 April
Second Service **Recognizing Jesus**
Ps. 16 The path of life; Isa. 52.13—53.12, *or* 53.1–6, 9–12 The Suffering Servant; Luke 24.13–35 The road to Emmaus

'While they were talking and discussing, Jesus himself came near and went with them, but their eyes were kept from recognizing him ... When he was at the table with them, he took bread, blessed and broke it, and gave it to them. Then their eyes were opened, and they recognized him; and he vanished from their sight.' Luke 24.15–16, 30–31

Emmaus

Jesus walked all the way to Emmaus with two of his disciples, but at first they didn't recognize him. Not until he broke bread with them did they realize who this stranger really was. We smile at their blindness, but put yourself into their situation – would you have recognized Jesus in those circumstances? One of the two was called Cleopas – a name not otherwise found in the New Testament. Yet one of the women standing near the cross when Jesus died was 'his mother's sister, Mary the wife of Clopas'. Cleopas could easily become Clopas, so maybe it was Clopas and his wife Mary, Jesus's aunt, who walked along the road to Emmaus, that Sunday evening. They must have known Jesus well, and they had no excuse for not recognizing him.

Disguise

Yet it's true of all of us – we all do the same. Jesus is with us, making himself known to us, and we fail to recognize him. It may seem as though he delights in wearing a disguise, or in being invisible, but it's not his fault, it's ours. We have preconceived notions of how Jesus will communicate with us, but when he actually has something he wants to say to us, he does so in such unexpected ways that we don't realize that he is with us all the time. The first problem on the road to Emmaus was that the disciples knew that Jesus had died – Mary the wife of Clopas, if it was indeed she, had actually seen Jesus die on the cross. So they were just not ready to accept that the living person walking the dusty road beside them that Sunday evening might actually be the same Jesus who had died on Friday. We, too, fail to hear him speaking to us because, no matter how many times we say the creeds, and however joyful we are at Easter time, somewhere deep down we don't really believe that he rose again. It seems so unscientific and so unlikely. So, despite the evidence of friends who say they have experienced Jesus at work in their lives today, we are blind to his presence. When Jesus speaks to our subconscious minds, we put down the words we hear in the night to a bad dream or indigestion. Wisely we decide to have nothing to do with spiritualism, because some so-called mediums can be manipulative; so if somebody we love, who has died, tries to reassure us that they are all right, we call our dream mere wish fulfilment. Jesus speaks to us through the nagging of our conscience, or in moments when we are transported by joy, and again we fail to recognize him. Friends say wise things to us, which we needed to hear at that moment, and afterwards admit they don't know where those wise words came from. We fail to recognize that Jesus can speak to us even through the mouths of other human beings.

What sort of resurrection?

The second problem that the disciples had on the road to Emmaus was that they were not quite sure what they meant by resurrection. They had heard other Jews proclaiming that when Messiah comes, all good Jews will return to physical life on earth in the new kingdom of God. But when the one they had hoped was he was painfully executed, there were no hoards of dead bodies crawling out of their graves. So the disciples decided that Jesus couldn't have been the one they were waiting for. For us, too, Jesus on the cross is so different from the King we had been dreaming of, that we find his promises of a happy afterlife to be too good to be true.

Preconceptions

You see, we have all built up preconceptions of what Jesus ought to look like and what he wants to say to us. Jesus delights to overturn preconceptions. What he is saying is, 'It's me. Your friend, who died. Death leads to new life. So stop worrying – everything is going to be all right!' Jesus says that to you, today. Do you recognize his accents, even in the words of the preacher? Or are you too wrapped up in what you think the Son of God should look like, and what words we should use to describe eternal life. Like Jesus's Aunty Mary, and Clopas her husband, at Emmaus, do you fail to recognize the reassuring voice of Jesus, when it comes to you from an unexpected mouth?

Suggested hymns

Abide with me; At the lamb's high feast we sing; Jesus, stand among us; Will you come and follow me?

Third Sunday of Easter   14 April
Principal Service   **A Letter to Paul**

Zeph. 3.14–20 The Lord is in your midst (*if used, the reading from Acts must be used as the second reading*), or Acts 9.1–6 [7–20] Paul's conversion; Ps. 30 God brought me up from Death; Rev. 5.11–14 Worshipping the Lamb; John 21.1–19 The lakeshore

> 'Saul ... went to the high priest and asked him for letters to the synagogues at Damascus ...' Acts 9.1–2

Following the request made to the High Priest Caiaphas, from our respected friend Saul of Tarsus, for letters of authority to take with him to Damascus, the secretary of the Council – the scribe Athaniah ben-Uzzi – was instructed to write to Saul as follows:

To Saul, whom we appoint as our representative, knowing that you see eye to eye with us on everything, brought up as you were, loyal to the traditions of the Pharisees – greetings! When there was a risk of the people rising up against the Roman occupying army, under that blasphemous revolutionary, Jesus of Nazareth, you helped us. He taught them that even 'sinners' could pray direct to the Blessed One, and receive forgiveness for their sins, without needing to sacrifice in our holy Temple. If the crowds had followed the Nazarene, the Romans would have massacred them all, and where would that have left us? With no authority, no jobs! When that fool of a Governor looked like letting him go, you stirred up the crowd to demand Jesus bar-Abbas instead.

As you are fluent in the Greek language, this makes you very useful, because so many of our present troubles come from the Hellenists, the Greek-speaking Jews. Explain to the synagogues in Damascus that our problems here in Jerusalem all began when some Greek-speaking Jews joined the followers of the Nazarene. There were fierce arguments between the two language groups. Over money, as usual. The Jesus people appointed seven new leaders, who all speak Greek and have Greek names. When they started spreading the Jesus-heresy among the filthy foreigners also, that is when we realized how useful you could be to us. You argued them down, showing them that you can't be a party to the covenant without obeying the Law – the whole Law.

Explain in Damascus that one of them, with the Greek name of Stephen, tried to argue that we had been wrong to have this Jesus crucified. And that you don't need the Temple for priests to offer sacrifices in. No, he said the death of Jesus was a ... sacrifice! Need we say more?

Everyone knows that we are the Chosen People. The condition of our choosing is that we should keep the commandments – all of them. So if these Jesus-babblers start telling people to disobey the commandments about sacrifice, the kingdom of the Blessed One will never come. At the stoning of Stephen, your report reminds us, you held the clothes of the men who carried out the execution. Since then, you have been questioning people till they admit to being Jesus-followers, and then putting them in chains. We congratulate you, but it doesn't go far enough. We think you should have them put to death. If they destroy the community of Israel, prison is too good for them.

And now we hear it's broken out in Damascus. This loathsome heresy. We hear that some of the followers of Jesus are teaching in the synagogues there, that anyone who believes in Jesus doesn't need to obey the Law. Now the Covenant will be completely destroyed!

So, when you get to Damascus, take this letter to the rulers of the synagogues there. Tell them to start a rigorous enquiry. Question every member. Find out if any are thinking of joining 'the Way', as they call it. Then you must bring a case of blasphemy against each one.

If this heresy spreads, there will be no Temple, no priests, no council. The Damascus road, Saul, will probably give you a new vision of the way in which we should be heading. Above all, resist any temptation to compromise. We can't afford to lose you, or

the whole world will be claiming equal rights with God's Chosen
People.

*[Footnote: Hullo, Saul, Azariah the scribe here. After dictating that,
they started arguing among themselves. The Pharisees wanted to go
into life on earth after the resurrection, and the Sadducees, who don't
believe in resurrection, were worried about offending the Romans.
So the meeting broke up in disorder, and there was nobody to sign
the minutes. All I can do is wish you success in eradicating what
you obviously see to be an evil; you will receive a warm welcome if*

you visit the Council again, after successfully completing the task. Oh, and keep all the letters you receive, together with copies of the letters you write – they might make you famous one day – signed, Azariah ben-Uzzi, scribe]

All-age worship

Copy the picture on page 119. Identify the Council chamber, Pharisees, Sadducees, scribe, the Holy of holies, sacrifices, Roman fortress.

Suggested hymns

And can it be?; Beneath the cross of Jesus; O happy day; We sing the glorious conquest.

Third Sunday of Easter   14 April
Second Service   The Dream of Gerontius

Ps. 86 You have delivered me from death; Isa. 38.9–20 The living thank you; John 11.[17–26] 27–44 The raising of Lazarus

> '[Jesus] cried with a loud voice, "Lazarus, come out!" The dead man came out, his hands and feet bound with strips of cloth, and his face wrapped in a cloth. Jesus said to them, "Unbind him, and let him go."' John 11.43–44

John Henry Newman

In the early nineteenth century, many people seemed to regard the Church of England as merely a department of state. John Henry Newman joined a group of scholarly clergymen in Oxford in arguing that the Church is a divine society. This high view of the Church led to them being called High Churchmen, though what we now call 'high church' worship was introduced by the ritualists a generation later. Infuriated when the government disestablished the Anglican Church in Ireland, they wrote a series of papers called *Tracts for the Times,* several of which came from the pen of Newman. They were also called Tractarians, or Puseyites after one of their leaders. Most remained in the Church of England, but Newman and a few others became Roman Catholics. He was a scholar, and his book *The Idea of a University* influenced intellectuals from many disciplines. But he was also a poet, and his hymn, 'Lead, kindly light', is especially moving. He was eventually made a cardinal, after surviving many disagreements with Cardinal Manning. In 2010 the Pope set in motion the process leading to Newman being declared a saint. Many people see this as a gesture of reconciliation between the Roman Catholic Church and the Church of England. For Newman was a member of both churches, yet was never really happy in either. He had an ideal concept of what God's Church should be, and no actual denomination could live up to it.

The Dream of Gerontius

Newman's greatest work of art was the long poem he called *The Dream of Gerontius,* later set to transcendent music by Sir Edward Elgar. It illustrates and develops what Jesus taught about resurrection, and especially the hope he gave us when he raised his friend Lazarus. 'Gerontius' means an old man, and he dreams of what it might be like to die, and what follows death. His friends are gathered round his deathbed, and join the priest in praying for the dying man's soul. The old man prays for strength to endure his last agony, and proclaims his faith in the words of the creed: 'Firmly I believe and truly ...' He commends his spirit into God's hands, and his friends pray 'Go forth upon thy journey, Christian soul ... may thy place today be found in peace, and may thy dwelling be the Holy Mount of Sion.' The soul of Gerontius awakes, realizing that he is being carried along by his guardian angel, who sings 'Alleluia!'

Demons and angels

They then hear a chorus of demons, complaining that the heavenly crowns which should have been theirs have been given to mere human beings. The soul asks whether he will see God when he reaches the judgement seat. 'Yes,' replies the angel, 'but only for a moment ... the flame of the Everlasting Love doth burn ere it transform.' They hear a chorus of angels singing the well-known words, 'Praise to the holiest in the height.' The soul sees God, then gladly surrenders to the healing waters of purgatory. The souls in purgatory sing, 'Lord, thou hast been our refuge', while the angel says farewell: 'Swiftly shall pass thy night of trial here, and I will come and wake thee on the morrow.'

Afterlife

Did Newman really believe in demons, angels and purgatory? In a way, yes, he did; but he transformed our understanding of those ideas as only a poet could. In this Easter season, we may puzzle about our images of the afterlife. What will it feel like, to die? Are we really going to the heavenly Jerusalem? The answer is that Newman was a romantic, and described everything through the language of symbols. Yet those symbols convey a spiritual truth far deeper than any literal description ever possibly could. So we can rejoice that the indescribable God loves us and holds us in his loving arms, even when we die. And that's all we need to know. We can share in Newman's dream, and say the 'Amen' to the famous prayer based on words Newman wrote:

> O Lord, support us all the day long of this troublous life, until the shades lengthen, and the evening comes, the busy world is hushed, the fever of life is over, and our work is done. Then, Lord, in your mercy grant us safe lodging, a holy rest, and peace at the last, through Jesus Christ our Lord. Amen.

Suggested hymns

Firmly I believe and truly; Give me the wings of faith to rise; Lead, kindly light; Praise to the holiest in the height.

Fourth Sunday of Easter   21 April
Principal Service   Images of Salvation

Gen. 7.1–5, 11–18; 8.6–18; 9.8–13 Noah's flood (*if used, the reading from Acts must be used as the second reading*), or Acts 9.36–43 Peter raises Tabitha; Ps. 23 The Lord is my shepherd; Rev. 7.9–17 The Lamb their shepherd; John 10.22–30 My sheep hear my voice

> *'My sheep hear my voice. I know them, and they follow me. I give them eternal life, and they will never perish.' John 10.27–28*

Sumerian tablet

Recently the British Museum's expert on Ancient Mesopotamia was handed a clay tablet which had been bought in a bazaar in the

1940s. He was excited to find it was part of an ancient Sumerian account of a great flood, with God's instructions about building a boat in which human beings could escape from drowning. Other parts of this legend, from around 1700 BC, had been found, but this fragment said the boat should be a circular raft made of reeds. The Bible says Noah's ark was to be 300 cubits long by 50 cubits wide. In children's picture books it's always shown as an oceangoing boat, with a sharp end at the front; but it wasn't going anywhere, so a circular raft would make more sense.

Symbolizing resurrection

The story of Noah is set in our lectionary as the alternative first reading for this service. But as it's not printed out in some of the books of readings, and since the reading from Acts has to be used, many churches may not use it. It's obviously chosen for today, in the Easter season, because the story of Noah can be read as a symbol of the resurrection. The fact that a version of the story has been found, written in Mesopotamia some 1,000 years before the Hebrew Bible was written down, shows that it was already an ancient legend. Whether or not it had a historical basis we can't be sure, but the important thing is that the Bible writers retold the tale in such a way as to bring out several spiritual points. The first is that God saves. Even if the majority of the human race deserves to be punished for their wickedness, God can always find some who will co-operate in his plan of salvation. In fact, as we all know if we examine our consciences, nobody is completely innocent, and there's a mixture of good and bad in each of us. If God was to destroy the wicked, none of us would survive. Remember that, the next time you pray to God to remove all the wickedness in the world. Instead, God inspires us with his promise to save; then we start on the long struggle towards becoming the sort of people that God wants us to be. The story of our redemption begins when we pass through the waters of baptism, and the Christian Church has often been compared to the ark of salvation.

Tabitha

The Acts of the Apostles tells the story of how St Peter raised a dead woman, called Tabitha, to life again. Whether she was in a coma, or her heart had only just stopped and was restarted, I don't know. Either way, it was as much of a miracle as if she'd been dead for several hours. God has promised that the heartfelt prayers of a loving heart will always have a healing effect. Maybe in the first few years of the Church's existence, God enabled them to raise the dead like Jesus did, to encourage them and deepen their faith. Such events are pretty uncommon these days, because Jesus wants us to move on towards a deeper understanding of what resurrection means.

The Good Shepherd

In the Gospel, Jesus tells us that he is the Good Shepherd. 'My sheep hear my voice,' he said. 'I know them, and they follow me. I give them eternal life, and they will never perish.' Jesus took the familiar image of the twenty-third psalm, and retold it as a promise that all those who believe in him will rise to a new life, though not on earth like Tabitha, but in the spiritual world of eternity, which is much better. Pray to Jesus, and ask him to raise you to new life.

Ecology

One last word about Noah, then. The Lord took him into the ark with two of each kind of animal, so that he should 'keep their kind alive on the face of all the earth'. This turns out to be a very up-to-date ecological message. God has entrusted the human race with the care of all the other species, to prevent them from dying out as a result of human greed and selfishness. Mind you, I do wish Noah had swotted the mosquitoes!

All-age worship

Make a collage of pictures of endangered species, with stories from the papers about how we can protect them, for God's sake.

Suggested hymns

Above the moon earth rises; As water to the thirsty; Great is thy faithfulness; Lord, bring the day to pass.

Fourth Sunday of Easter 21 April
Second Service Heaven-Haven

Ps. 113 God raises the poor from the dust, 114 The Exodus;
Isa. 63.7–14 God led them through the depths; Luke 24.36–49
Words of the risen Christ

> '[The disciples] were startled and terrified, and thought that they
> were seeing a ghost. [Jesus] said to them, "Why are you fright-
> ened, and why do doubts arise in your hearts?"' Luke 24.37–38

Gerard Manley Hopkins

Gerard Manley Hopkins was a poet towards the end of the nineteenth century, and a Jesuit priest. His style reverted to that of
Anglo-Saxon poetry, with lots of alliteration, and instead of a regular rhythm, de-DAH de-DAH de-DAH de-DAH, he used what he
called 'sprung rhythm', with a pattern of so many stressed syllables
per line. In 1918 he wrote a poem called Heaven-Haven, or perhaps,
so that you can imagine what it looks like on the page, I should call
it 'Heaven-hyphen-Haven'. The subtitle is 'a nun takes the veil', and
he imagines the thoughts in the mind of a young woman when she
makes her vow to enter an enclosed convent. It's quite short, and
goes like this:

I have desired to go
Where springs not fail,
To fields where flies no sharp and sided hail
And a few lilies blow.

And I have asked to be
Where no storms come,
Where the green swell is in the havens dumb,
And out of the swing of the sea.

Peace

The postulant nun is fully aware that contemplative prayer is very
hard work; there are many domestic chores to be done daily; and
human nature doesn't immediately change when men or women
take vows of poverty, chastity and obedience. Yet despite all this,
she looks forward to her new life because of the peace it will bring
her. The first verse compares the contemplative life to a perpetual

springtime, free from the winter hailstorms, and she will have time to enjoy the flowers. The comparison in the second verse is to a ship returning to harbour, out of reach of the storms at sea, and no longer battling against the waves. Hopkins, in beautiful language, imagines the nun looking forward to the peace of the convent, out of the busy and stressful world.

Heaven

The contemplative life isn't for everyone, but we can all imagine the longing for peace. So look again at the alliterative title 'Heaven-Haven'. The nun looks forward to the peace of the enclosed life, imagining it as a haven, or harbour, away from the worries of the working world. (Apologies, alliteration's already awfully addictive!) And a haven, says the poet, is what heaven is like. Most of the time we enjoy our work, but who doesn't have moods when we long for a bit of peace and quiet? Gerard Manley Hopkins promises us that there *is* a time of rest for all of us at the end of the weary day: we call it heaven, and Jesus has promised it to all who trust him, when we die.

Doubt

Yet very few people these days behave as though they long for heaven. Fashionable atheism has taught many to disbelieve in an afterlife – it's only 'pie in the sky when you die', they cry in scorn. And Christians are put off by this, and no longer proclaim clearly our joyous expectation of a heavenly reward. Of course 'pearly gates' and 'streets of gold' are only metaphors to describe the indescribable. And nobody wants to become a ghost. But Jesus said, 'Why are you frightened, and why do doubts arise in your hearts?' His resurrection brings the promise of eternal life for all of us. Our ancestors had lives which were 'nasty, brutish and short'; most people died young. The bereaved were extravagant in their mourning, but soon consoled themselves that those they loved were at peace, and we shall all meet again in God's kingdom. Why can't we proclaim as boldly today that death is a blessed release? Instead, most people declare by their behaviour a belief that, if we can have the health care to which we are entitled, we shall live on earth for ever. Death has become an unmentionable tragedy, instead of a blessed hope.

Looking forward

Nobody should wish to go before God calls them. But perhaps we should regain the Christian longing for death, as the nun looked forward to peace, and proclaim boldly our belief in heaven-haven:

I have desired to go
Where springs not fail,
To fields where flies no sharp and sided hail
And a few lilies blow.

And I have asked to be
Where no storms come,
Where the green swell is in the havens dumb,
And out of the swing of the sea.

Suggested hymns

Alleluia, alleluia, give thanks to the risen Lord; Give us the wings of faith to rise; God sent his Son, they called him Jesus; This joyful Eastertide.

Fifth Sunday of Easter   28 April
Principal Service   **After We Die**

Bar. 3.9–15, 32—4.4 Wisdom, *or* Gen. 22.1–18 Abraham willing to sacrifice Isaac (*if used, the reading from Acts must be used as the second reading*), *or* Acts 11.1–18 Baptism of the Gentiles; Ps. 148 Nature praising God; Rev. 21.1–6 Death will be no more; John 13.31–35 The commandment to love

'See, the home of God is among mortals.
He will dwell with them;
they will be his peoples,
and God himself will be with them;
he will wipe every tear from their eyes.
Death will be no more;
mourning and crying and pain will be no more,
for the first things have passed away.' Revelation 21.3–4

Not yet

Some people are afraid to die. This is typical human fear of the unknown. Others are not afraid, but they don't wish to die just yet, because there are so many things still to be learned, to be experienced, and so much love yet to be given and received. This second attitude is a thoroughly praiseworthy one, but it's as mistaken as the first. If both sorts of people would read the words of Jesus, they would be reassured by his promise that there's a better life beyond death. As the Revelation to John poetically puts it, 'See, the home of God is among mortals ... Death will be no more; mourning and crying and pain will be no more, for the first things have passed away.'

The second death

Because Jesus, the Son of God, came to earth to live among us, says St John the Divine, there will be no more dying. Of course he doesn't mean that our bodies will cease to wear out, nor that a cure for every disease will immediately be discovered. But disease and bodily death are part of the 'former things', which will pass away when we enter the non-physical existence which the Bible calls 'eternal life'. Jesus came to dwell with us and be like us, so that we might go to dwell with him and be like him, in the timeless world of eternity. God's purpose in creating human beings was so that we might learn to love God and be loved by him, ready to inhabit the spiritual realm which we call heaven.

Heaven

Heaven is so much better than this life, that we have no words to describe it, and have to fall back on images and metaphors. When we describe life after death as 'eternal life', this sounds as though it's timeless, in which case nothing would ever change. But Jesus said, 'In my Father's house are many mansions' – or resting places – using the word for a wayside inn where a pilgrim might spend a night while on a long journey. He also promised that the Holy Spirit 'will lead you into all truth' – which implies a gradual process of learning, in this life and the next.

Fear not

Over and over Jesus calmed his disciples, saying 'Fear not – don't be afraid.' Our fear of death can be set aside, when we realize that the afterlife is a world where 'mourning and crying and pain will be no more'. We worry that death will rob us of the opportunity to go on learning and enjoying new experiences. Yet that's ridiculous – life's pilgrimage doesn't cease when we die. We continue the journey into God which we began here, in the company of friends, family, and great Christians past and present. In fact the biggest difference between our pilgrimage on earth and our journey through the here-after is that God is no longer invisible. The friendship with Jesus, which we have built up in our times of prayer, will be fulfilled, when we are fully aware of his presence with us, all the time.

Cheer up

So fear not – cheer up! The learning and the loving which we have so much enjoyed on earth will be transformed, when we die, into something even more wonderful. The work and the worship which give meaning to our life on earth are transformed into the angelic alleluias of heaven. As the Puritan, Richard Baxter, wrote:

> Lord, it belongs not to my care
> whether I die or live;
> to love and serve thee is my share,
> and this thy grace must give.
>
> If life be long, I will be glad
> that I may long obey;
> if short, yet why should I be sad
> to soar to endless day?
>
> Christ leads me through no darker rooms
> than he went through before;
> he that into God's kingdom comes
> must enter by this door ...
>
> My knowledge of that life is small;
> the eye of faith is dim;
> but 'tis enough that Christ knows all,
> and I shall be with him.

All-age worship

Cut out pairs of angels' wings, write on them the names of people you hope to meet in heaven, and hang them from a 'mobile'.

Suggested hymns

Alleluia, alleluia, hearts to heaven and voices raise; For ever with the Lord; Jesus lives – thy terrors now; Lord, it belongs not to my care.

Fifth Sunday of Easter   28 April
Second Service   Bede's Bird
Ps. 98 God has done marvellous things; Dan. 6.[1–5] 6–23 The lions' den; Mark 15.46—16.8 The resurrection

> '[The disciples] went out and fled from the tomb, for terror and amazement had seized them; and they said nothing to anyone, for they were afraid.' Mark 16.8

Mark

St Mark's Gospel ends abruptly with the words, 'For they were afraid.' It's no wonder that the disciples of Jesus were terrified when they found his tomb empty. No dead person had ever before come to life again, so they were confused, and told nobody what they had seen. At first. But Mark cleverly leaves us to work out for ourselves that the disciple didn't keep silent for long. Otherwise Mark himself would never have heard the good news that Jesus was alive; and neither would you nor I. Once they had overcome their initial fear, they couldn't wait to tell others that they had seen the risen Christ with their own eyes. And so the message came down to us. But that means that once we have come to believe that Christ is risen, keeping quiet about it isn't an option. We, too, must 'go, tell everyone' about the good news that we have discovered.

Bede

An awed silence is the natural human response to the mystery of life and death. So anyone who can explain it to us deserves a hearing. The Venerable Bede was a monk near Jarrow, in Northumbria. He compiled a *History of the English Church and People,* which he completed in AD 731. In it he wrote of the bewilderment of our non-Christian ancestors. Edwin, King of Northumbria, listened to the preaching of Bishop Paulinus, replying that he was willing to be baptized after he had consulted his advisors. One of the king's advisors added:

> The life of human beings, your Majesty, seems to me like the swift flight of a sparrow through the hall, where you sit at supper in winter with your officers and officials around a warm fire, while the storms of rain and snow rage outside. The sparrow flies in at one door and out through another. While he's indoors, he's safe from the winter's cold and wet. But after a short while in the warm, he vanishes into the freezing darkness whence he came. We humans, too, are on earth for a short while; but we know nothing of what happened before or what follows afterwards. So if this new religion can tell us something more certain about these things, we certainly ought to follow it.

Gratitude for the gospel

Hearing this, the King decided to become a Christian, and gave Bishop Paulinus permission to preach the gospel throughout the kingdom. The pagan priest personally destroyed the heathen temples, and burnt the idols. It's impossible to exaggerate our debt today to that anonymous counsellor with his tale of the sparrow in the hall. Those who are beset by doubts, and tempted to disbelieve in life after death, need to remember how gloomy and hopeless life was for our ancestors before the gospel of the resurrection was preached in this country. Like sparrows in the hall, we enjoyed for a brief while the light and warmth of life on earth, but had no idea where we came from or where we are going to. But now that we have heard that Jesus rose again, we know that there's a far better life waiting for us beyond the grave.

Where we came from

That sparrow that the Venerable Bede talked about – shall we call him 'Bede's Bird'? – he flew into the hall from the darkness outside. Where does the human soul come from? Christians have never been attracted by the idea of reincarnation – to rise to new life after we die is so much better than going round and round one life after another, until you have paid off the debt of your *karma*. Words-worth in his poem *Intimations of Immortality from Recollections of Early Childhood* suggests that 'trailing clouds of glory do we come from God, who is our home'. Yet it's also misleading to say that God gave us a soul at the moment of our conception – how can God allow so many miscarriages and spontaneous abortions to kill off his children before they are even born? Better say that God is building the spiritual side to our nature throughout our lives.

Where we go

But the Bible clearly tells us where we are going. The sparrow flies back into the cold, but the human soul flies up to the light and warmth of God's presence. God put us here to learn to love; then he teaches us to love our Creator. Thus we prepare ourselves on earth to enter the indescribable world of eternal love when we die. The lot of a human soul is so much *warmer* than that of Bede's Bird, thank God!

Suggested hymns

Do not be afraid, for I have redeemed you; God's Spirit is in my heart (Go, tell everyone); Love's redeeming work is done; O bitter the apostles' pain (Part 2 of Light's glittering morn).

Sixth Sunday of Easter (Rogation Sunday) 5 May
Principal Service   **Stress**
Ezek. 37.1–14 The valley of dry bones (*if used, the reading from Acts must be used as the second reading*), or Acts 16.9–15 The baptism of Lydia; Ps. 67 Let the peoples praise you; Rev. 21.10, 22—22.5 The heavenly Jerusalem; John 14.23–29 Going to the Father, *or* John 5.1–9 The paralysed man at the pool

> *'Do not let your hearts be troubled, and do not let them be afraid.'*
> *John 14.27*

Stress

The Risen Christ came to his disciples and said 'Do not let your hearts be troubled, and do not let them be afraid.' Are your hearts untroubled? Are you never afraid? If only! It's been estimated that 70 per cent of people in this country are stressed; 55 per cent of us have been clinically depressed at some time in our lives; 20 per cent have had therapy; 51 million antidepressant prescriptions are issued every year. If Jesus can tell us what to do about stress, we need to listen to him carefully.

Causes

Faith in God can relieve all types of stress. Stress can be caused by long working-hours, or by money troubles. It can come from worrying about your family, or fretting over your future. Stress may be due to loss or bereavement; or to success, and fearing you may be toppled off your perch. Your health can trouble you, and so can fear that you may die before you have achieved what you want to do, and put your affairs in order for those who survive you. Or you may be stressed because you feel alone. To all of these, Jesus has an answer.

Reactions

People react to stress in various different ways. Some are short-fused, angry at the least provocation. That's because we often put a paranoid interpretation on things which happen to us. We take offence when no offence was intended. Others are anxious and withdrawn, because they lack confidence. Some people are very controlled, and set themselves impossible targets. Some revel in stress, and find work situations and hobbies which cause the adrenalin to flow; but they may rely on smoking, alcohol or self-medication in order to carry on. Finally, some are very laid-back, and never allow their feathers to be ruffled; yet the result of this is that they may lack ambition, and others may find them unreliable, disorganized and unsympathetic. Except for the last type, each of these forms of stress may bring you bad health. Whereas the relaxation which comes from faith in Jesus may bring you unexpected relief from high blood pressure, sleeping problems, back pain, teeth-grinding and headaches, hand-wringing and skin complaints. The body which God has given us has amazing powers of healing itself; but these are often hindered by the degree of stress we endure.

Cure

So don't despise the doctor's advice. A course of cognitive behavioural therapy teaches you to be less self-centred, and to regard the world more positively. Occasional use of a few antidepressants may help, so long as you don't allow yourself to depend on them. Deep breathing and exercise helps. You can learn meditation from any guru, though I personally think a Christian retreat is the best way. Even something as simple as making a list of things you need to do, and tackling them one at a time, saves you from the feeling that the world is getting on top of you. But ultimately, the real cure for stress can only come from faith in Jesus.

Faith

The Bible tells you that God loves you. We have all heard those words, but have you taken them to heart? Jesus loves you enough to leave the glories of heaven and come to earth, then die on the cross to save *you, personally*. He wants to deliver you from many things, but included among them is, he wants you to be free from anxiety. If you really believe that Jesus loves you, you don't need to worry about lack of success. Jesus was a failure, in earthly terms, but spiritually he was the biggest success story of all time. Jesus will go on loving you, however many times you fail, however often you make mistakes, and however guilty you feel. The knowledge of his unconditional love will give you the confidence to step out and take risks. In the end, you know, everything's going to be all right, because Jesus will get us all into heaven, by hook or by crook, if we only let him. Why worry? Why all the stress? 'Let go, and let God' – let God carry the burden for you. Jesus said, 'Peace I leave with you; my peace I give to you. I do not give to you as the world gives. Do not let your hearts be troubled, and do not let them be afraid.'

All-age worship

Choose your favourite security blanket or cuddly toy. Write on it, or tie a label reading 'Don't worry – Jesus loves you!'

Suggested hymns

Dear Lord and Father of mankind; Let there be peace shown among you; Peace is flowing like a river; Peace, perfect peace, in this dark world of sin?

Sixth Sunday of Easter (Rogation Sunday)   5 May
Second Service   **The Third Man**
Ps. 126 The Lord has done great things for us, 127 Unless the
Lord builds the house; Zeph. 3.14–20 God is in your midst;
Matt. 28.1–10, 16–20 The ascension command

> *'Remember, I am with you always, to the end of the age.' Matthew
> 28.20*

Ascension

Jesus rose from the dead, and appeared to his disciples. Obviously
he couldn't appear visibly to everyone in the world for the rest of
time. An end-point to his visible appearances was necessary; it was
given by the ascension. Yet he reassured them that he is with us all
the time, but invisibly present. 'Remember,' he said, 'I am with you
always, to the end of the age.' Some people have visions of Jesus, or
hear his voice; many people have clear answers to prayer. But for
most of us, the invisible presence of Jesus is something which we
believe is possible, but we have no physical experience to fall back
on in times of doubt. We have to make an effort of will, determined
to behave as though Jesus is here, and speak to him, convinced that
he hears us.

9/11

Yet it's remarkable how many people, in moments of danger or
stress, have been absolutely certain that somebody was with them.
Ron DiFrancesco was working on the eighty-fourth floor of the
south tower of the World Trade Center in New York when the
second hijacked plane hit the Twin Towers on 11th September
2001, three floors below. Groping his way down a stairwell, he
found his way blocked by smoke, and sat down in despair. Then
he heard a man's voice calling, 'Ron, get up!' It wasn't the voice of
anyone in the stairwell, but he saw a point of light and followed
it, vividly aware of the physical presence of someone leading the
way. They came to the area which was burning, and the voice
encouraged him, against his better judgement, to run down three
storeys through the fire. What Ron, a deeply religious man, called
'his angel', left him when he reached a level which was safe, at least
temporarily. He had just got out of the building at ground level

when the tower collapsed. He woke up in hospital, convinced that God had sent someone to save him.

Shackleton

Many people in peril firmly believe that a mysterious 'other' is with them. Most famous was Sir Ernest Shackleton in the Antarctic in 1916. The crew of his ship were trapped by the ice, and he and a few others went in a small boat to fetch help. Through hurricane-force winds they got as far as South Georgia. But the whaling station he was aiming for was at the opposite end of the island; so Shackleton and two others walked there across the mountains and glaciers. Afterwards, he told a journalist that he'd had no doubt that God's Providence had guided them throughout. 'It seemed to me often,' he said, 'that we were four, not three.' One of his companions said, 'I had a curious feeling on the march that there was another person with us,' and the other agreed.

T. S. Eliot

T. S. Eliot, in his influential modernist poem *The Waste Land,* made a conscious and deliberate reference to Shackleton's experience, when he asked about a third person, always walking beside the traveller through the barren and challenging landscape which represented life after the 1914–18 war. He used poetic licence to change the number in Shackleton's party, but this type of experience is now always known as 'the Third Man Factor'. That's the title of a book by John Geiger, in which he quotes dozens of examples of people, some religious, others not, who were convinced of an unseen presence. He also quotes from physiologists who struggle desperately to find a scientific explanation. Their best effort so far is to say it is the two halves of the brain talking to each other. Of course there's no way of proving that this is true. It seems more logical to accept the simple explanation, that Jesus is keeping his promise: 'Remember, I am with you always, to the end of the age.'

Faith

So if you think you are alone, remember 'the Third Man Factor'. Believe that Jesus really is with us, wherever we go. If you need guidance, ask Jesus for advice, and act on whatever hints he gives you. If you are afraid, remember: your protector is always with you. If you are bereaved, understand that God may use the conviction that your loved ones are close to you, to persuade you of the divine presence. Don't pour scorn on those who believe they have a guardian angel – Jesus uses many ways to reassure us of his loving care. Let your prayer time be filled with faith that someone greater than you is listening to you. We must take seriously the promise Jesus made when he ascended into heaven, 'Remember, I am with you always, to the end of the age.'

Suggested hymns

Abide with me; Alleluia! Sing to Jesus; Be still, for the presence of the Lord; Great Shepherd of thy people, hear.

Ascension Day   9 May
Above the Clouds

Acts 1.1–11 The Ascension (*must be used as either the first or second reading*), *or* Dan. 7.9–14 The Son of Man; Ps. 47 God has gone up, *or* Ps. 93 The Lord is king; Eph. 1.15–23 Christ is seated beside God; Luke 24.44–53 The ascension

> 'As [the disciples] were watching, [Jesus] was lifted up, and a cloud took him out of their sight.' Acts 1.9

Clouds

Anyone who's taken off in an aeroplane knows that the great metal bird climbs up into a cloud, and outside the windows everything's white. Yet the cloud quite obviously isn't solid. Then your craft soars out of the top of the cloud into the bright sunshine, and a wonderful 'landscape' of clouds appears before you, away into the distance. Above the clouds is ... nothing! And lots of it. So we put out of our minds all those pictures in stained-glass windows of God sitting on a cloud, surrounded by angels. Heaven obviously isn't a place above the clouds. Heaven is a state of blessedness, when we shall be with God for all eternity – a spiritual existence, quite apart from the world of space, time and matter. If we have had a scientific education, we tell ourselves that heaven is another dimension.

The Disciples

But that's not how people spoke in Bible times. When Jesus rose again, he appeared to his disciples for forty days. Then, according to Matthew, he appeared to them on a mountain and gave them his final instructions. Mark's Gospel ends with the women running frightened from the tomb – two other writers later thought this was too abrupt, and added shorter and longer endings: the longer one says Jesus was taken up into heaven and sat down at the right hand of God. John ends with Christ's appearance at the lakeside. But Luke says that 'While [Jesus] was blessing [the disciples], he withdrew from them and was carried up into heaven.' The Acts of the Apostles, also by Luke, similarly says that 'as [the disciples] were watching, [Jesus] was lifted up, and a cloud took him out of their sight'. So only the longer ending of Mark, and Luke's Gospel, say that heaven is 'up'; and only Acts says it's above the clouds. Or at least, that appears to be the case. It shouldn't surprise us if the disciples of Jesus, never having seen an aeroplane, would think heaven was above the clouds; now we know better.

Symbolism

But wait. Even if you have never seen an aeroplane, you can look towards the horizon. On a clear day you can see a distant ridge of clouds. If there were any golden walls and pearly gates on the top of the clouds, *you would be able to see them*. The disciples weren't stupid. They knew as well as we do that there's nothing sitting on the surface of those fluffy things up there. They must have realized that talk of heaven being 'up' was symbolic language. The Old Testament says that 'the high official is watched by a higher, and there are yet higher ones over them'. Nobody thought that meant that the officials had their chairs on higher or lower platforms. 'Higher positions' is a metaphor for seniority in the hierarchy of power. So when Luke wrote that Jesus went 'up', he meant that our Saviour was promoted to a position of authority, equal to that of God his Father.

Clouds

The cloud is a symbol for God's presence. God spoke to Moses on Mount Sinai out of a cloud. God went before the Israelites through the wilderness as a pillar of fire by night, and a pillar of cloud by day. The disciples at the transfiguration heard God speaking out of the cloud. So I think all the disciples realized that their description of the ascension was symbolic language. Without the use of symbols you can't talk about the indescribable world of the Spirit.

Endings

The ascension was the ending for one phase of Jesus's life, and the beginning of another. His resurrection appearances were vital so that the disciples should realize he was alive; but they couldn't just peter out, there had to be what the psychotherapists call a 'moment of closure'. So Jesus caused his friends to see a vision of him being taken up into the presence of God. Maybe they knew it was a symbolic vision, which conveyed a true message, though not material facts. We have travelled in our imagination with Jesus from his birth at Christmas until today, when he was received back into the presence of his Father, and that's the end of a phase for us, too. But he promised to be invisibly with us, for evermore. We shouldn't go around with our heads in the clouds. But we should always set our minds on where Jesus is, in the spiritual world, where he's accessible to us at all times in our prayers.

Suggested hymns

Crown him with many crowns; Immortal, invisible, God only wise; Hail the day that sees him rise; See the conqueror mounts in triumph.

Seventh Sunday of Easter   12 May
(Sunday after Ascension Day)
Principal Service   **God's Love in Us**
Acts 16.16–34 Baptism of a jailer (*must be used as either the first or second reading*), or Ezek. 36.24–28 I will put my Spirit in you; Ps. 97 The Lord is king; Rev. 22.12–14, 16–17, 20–21 Come!; John 17.20–26 Church unity and love

> '[Jesus prayed to his Father for us, that] "I [may be] in them and you in me ... so that the world may know that you have sent me and have loved them even as you have loved me."' John 17.23

You're glorious

You're glorious! Yes, I'm talking about you. Even if you think of yourself as plain and ugly, you have a human body, which is a glorious thing, so complex, and yet it functions well most of the time in ways you hardly even notice. So look at you – you look glorious! If a sympathetic stranger asked you to tell them your life story, they would be fascinated to hear about the things you have done, your little successes and what you learnt from your failures. You have lived a glorious life. And what about your ideas and opinions? What do you think about? Yes, you have a glorious mind, too. But above all, you have a capacity to be loved, and to give love in return. That's the most glorious thing of all.

The prayer of Jesus

At the Last Supper, St John tells us that Jesus prayed to his Father in heaven. It was a long prayer, and it was all about glory. When Judas left the Upper Room to betray Jesus, Jesus knew he was going to die. Yet he said a surprising thing: 'Now the Son of Man has been glorified, and God has been glorified in him. If God has been glorified in him, God will also glorify him in himself and will glorify him at once.' So the cross was the glory of Jesus – not his power, but his weakness. Then in his prayer, Jesus said, 'Father, the hour has come; glorify your Son so that the Son may glorify you ... to give eternal life to all whom you have given him. And this is eternal life, that they may know you, the only true God, and Jesus Christ whom you have sent. I glorified you on earth by finishing the work that you gave me to do. So now, Father, glorify me in your own presence with the glory that I had in your presence before the world existed.' The glory of Jesus was his cross, his obedience, his love. He revealed his glory when people saw God's love shining in him.

Praying for us

Jesus prayed for the disciples gathered round the table with him. Next he said. 'I ask not only on behalf of these, but also on behalf of those who will believe in me through their word.' That's you and me he is praying for. 'The glory that you have given me I have given them,' he went on, 'so that they may be one, as we are one, I in them and you in me ... so that the world may know that you have sent me and have loved them even as you have loved me.' So that's what makes us glorious: that God loves us, and comes to live in our hearts. 'Father,' Jesus prayed, 'I desire that those also, whom you have given me, may be with me where I am, to see my glory, which you have given me because you loved me before the foundation of the world ... so that the love with which you have loved me may be in them, and I in them.'

God's glory is his love

So that's what glory is: it's the power of God's love. God loves you and me. When we realize this, he makes his home in our hearts. Then we are filled with his love; it pours from us onto other people. The more you love other people, the more glorious you become. That includes the poor and needy, the sick and the sad, the outcast and despised – Jesus loves them so very much, but he only has your hands to care for them with. We are part of God's plan to reveal his love to the world. Our glory will be when people see God's love in us.

Eternal life

We shall see God's glory clearly when we die. Glory is another word for love. The most glorious thing that can happen to you is when you know that you are loved, and you give love in return. Human love is wonderful, but to know that God loves you with a love beyond all telling is glorious, and returning it by loving God lasts through all eternity.

All-age worship

Make a lampshade. Write on it, 'God's love shines through my life'.

Suggested hymns

A new commandment I give unto you; Love is his word, love is his way; Rejoice, the Lord is king; The head that once was crowned with thorns.

Seventh Sunday of Easter   12 May
Second Service   **Bounty**

Ps. 68 Let God arise; Isa. 44.1–8 I will pour my Spirit; Eph. 4.7–16 Gifts of the ascended Christ; *Gospel at Holy Communion*: Luke 24.44–53 I am sending upon you

> 'Each of us was given grace according to the measure of Christ's gift. Therefore it is said, "When he ascended on high he made captivity itself a captive; he gave gifts to his people."' *Ephesians 4.7–8*

Bounty

'Bounty' is not a word you hear often these days. If you do, it's probably in the title of that marvellous old film, *Mutiny on the Bounty*. Historically, William Bligh was the brutal captain of a sailing ship named the *Bounty*, sent to fetch bread-fruit from Tahiti. On the return journey, in 1789, the crew mutinied under Fletcher Christian, and set Bligh adrift; the crew went on to populate Pitcairn Island, where their descendants still live. The ship was probably given that name in the hope that they'd bring back a bountiful harvest of fruit or other cargo. The word comes from the French for goodness, and means generosity in bestowing gifts.

God's bounty

God has been very bountiful in the gifts of nature. Yes, I know that in some places, poor peasants have to scrape away to produce a meagre harvest from the barren soil; but that's partly because we have destroyed the environment, and the human populations have grown to an unheard-of size. But looking at it in a worldwide perspective, the earth produces an amazing cornucopia of food for our species, and every other species as well. Hence, very many people marvel at the generous bounty of the Creator.

Ephesians

The Letter to the Ephesians in the Bible compares Jesus to a newly appointed emperor. When a new ruler succeeded to the throne, he would go up to his palace in a great procession, dragging his captive enemies in chains behind his chariot, and distributing free gifts of food and other necessities to the people who cheered him on his way. The support that he would receive during his reign was almost directly proportional to the bountifulness of his gifts. St Paul writes in his letter: 'Each of us was given grace according to the measure of Christ's gift.' Then he quotes from Psalm 68: 'When he ascended on high he made captivity itself a captive; he gave gifts to his people.' So Paul cleverly compares the ascension of Jesus into heaven, which we celebrated on Thursday, with a king going up to his throne, and giving bountiful gifts to his followers. The gifts which Jesus gives are the abundant gifts of the Holy Spirit, which we celebrate next Sunday.

Gifts of the Spirit

St Paul lists the gifts necessary for people to become apostles, prophets, evangelists, pastors and teachers. He always wrote to a specific group of people in a particular situation: Ephesus was a missionary church, sending members of its city congregation to plant churches in the neighbouring towns. The word 'apostle' means 'sent out' – in other words, men and women sent to be missionaries. They were followed by prophets – not necessarily those who foretold the future, but those who 'forth-told' God's words to the town where they were ministering. Then came evangelists: those who told the people the story of Jesus, and explained why it's good news for those who will listen. When these tasks had been done, the pioneers could leave and move to another town, while pastors were left to be shepherds of the new converts, and teachers explained to them how they should behave as Christians. Then they could hand over the missionary task to the new converts: the job of the experts was to equip God's people to do the work of ministry, building up the Church, the 'body of Christ', until *all* of us come to unity in faith and personal knowledge of Jesus, as fully mature Christians.

Lay ministry

'But how can ordinary lay Christians do this?' you ask, 'surely ministry is the work of trained professionals!' There *were* no professional ministers in Paul's day; and although training is important, it's possible for ordinary people to do God's work because of the bounteous gifts of the Spirit he gives to us all. It may take you a while to discern what particular gifts God has given you to make this congregation flourish and grow, but the Bible promises that God in his bountiful love gives some gift or other to everyone who believes. What Juliet said about her love for Romeo could be applied to God's love for us: 'My bounty is as boundless as the sea, my love as deep. The more I give to thee, the more I have, for both are infinite.' But we must be united. There must be no mutiny on this particular ship, or we shall all become castaways.

Suggested hymns

Jesus is Lord! Creation's voice proclaims it; Jesus, stand among us; Lord, enthroned in heavenly splendour; Spirit of holiness, wisdom and faithfulness.

Day of Pentecost (Whit Sunday) 19 May
Principal Service Words that Come Out and Words that Go In

Acts 2.1–21 The day of Pentecost (*must be used as either the first or second reading*), *or* Gen. 11.1–9 The tower of Babylon; Ps. 104.26–36, 37b The Spirit in creation; Rom. 8.14–17 Adoption, *or* Acts 2.1–21 The day of Pentecost; John 14.8–17 [25–27] The Spirit of truth

> *'I will ask the Father, and he will give you another Advocate, to be with you for ever.' John 14.16*

Misunderstanding

Have you ever said something to somebody else, choosing your words very carefully, and they have repeated them back to you later, but it's quite obvious that they have heard you say quite the opposite from what you intended to say? Perhaps it's because we all hear what we want to hear. We have made up our minds on various matters, and we either jump to the conclusion that everybody must agree with us, or we square up for a fight because we are certain that the person we are talking to isn't clever enough or wise enough to think things through as we have. Either way, the words that come out through the speaker's mouth can be quite different from the words that go into the hearer's ears.

The Holy Spirit

This may be a bad thing, or it could be a good thing. Most preachers have had this experience at some point in their lives. We give what we think is an absolutely brilliant sermon on, say, justification by faith, and someone in the congregation comes up to us afterwards saying, 'Your sermon on how we ask for God's guidance was just what I needed to hear.' Which makes me wonder whether the Holy Spirit isn't in charge of both, the words that come out of the preacher's mouth and those which go into the hearer's ears? Maybe the Spirit knew that that listener just needed a sermon on guidance on that particular day. So the Spirit made sure that the person in the pulpit said something sufficiently ambiguous, and also ensured that the person in the pew only picked out those words which would teach them something about guidance. To know that God's Spirit controls the words that come out and the words that go in is a great comfort.

Jesus's promise

Jesus promised us that he would give us another Advocate. An advocate is a lawyer whom you call to your side in a law court to speak for you. The counsel asks you questions which help you to give your evidence clearly, and then puts your side of the argument in words which appeal to the judge and jury. So an advocate is in charge of the words that come out and the words that go in. For some people, facing someone who is opposed to the Christian faith, and trying to defend their beliefs, is just as frightening as facing a court of law. But Jesus promised that the Holy Spirit will help you to explain your position clearly and attractively, without appearing to preach at them, and help your opponents to hear just as much as they can take in at that moment. Similarly, if you meet someone who is deeply troubled, you may feel lost for words to comfort them. Don't worry – just try to sound sympathetic, talk about your own experience of God's love, and listen to the other as they explain what's hurting them. Then leave it to the Holy Spirit, who controls the words that come out of your mouth, and the words which go into the needy person's ears.

God in us

That's what's so wonderful about the promise of the Holy Spirit. Jesus said, 'If you love me, you will keep my commandments.' It isn't a great struggle to obey God, because God's Spirit is inside you, giving you the strength to overcome temptation and guidance to show what you should do. The Spirit is 'with you for ever', he said. 'This is the Spirit of truth', which will lead you to understand the truth about the world and about God. 'You know him, because he abides with you, and he will be in you.' Christians don't have to struggle to find God – God is here already, in our hearts. The Spirit takes care of the words that come out and the words that go in. If God is in your heart, he will make sure you hear what you need to hear, and say what God wants you to say. Really, Pentecost, when we remember the gift of the Holy Spirit to everyone who believes, is the most joyful and wonderful time.

All-age worship

Play 'Chinese whispers', passing a difficult sentence from one to another. Then see how much better it goes if someone acts as the Holy Spirit, with a dove headdress, checking for accuracy at every stage.

Suggested hymns

Come down, O love divine; Spirit of God, unseen as the wind; Spirit of holiness, wisdom and faithfulness; Spirit of the living God, fall afresh on me.

Day of Pentecost (Whit Sunday)   19 May
Second Service   **Literal Interpretation**
Morning Ps. 36.5–10 In your light we see light, 150 Everything that breathes; Evening Ps. 33.1–12 The breath of his mouth; Ex. 33.7–20 My presence will go with you; 2 Cor. 3.4–18 Letter and Spirit; *Gospel at Holy Communion*: John 16.4b–15 The Spirit of truth

> 'God ... has made us competent to be ministers of a new coven-ant, not of letter but of spirit; for the letter kills, but the Spirit gives life.' *2 Corinthians 3.5–6*

Clear rules

When you are bringing up children, you give them clear rules of behaviour, for their own protection: 'Don't play in a busy street; don't talk to strangers; don't go near the water till you have learnt to swim.' Later, when they are teenagers, they will start to push the boundaries, trying to go just a little way into forbidden territory to see what happens. That's part of growing up. But you can't push the boundaries unless clear boundaries to your behaviour have been set when you are younger. Adults can base their behaviour on common sense, and the childish rules are subsumed in their mature thinking. Similarly, we are all God's children, and God treats us in the same way as we treat our own children. In the early stages of human history, he gave us laws for our own protection, such as the Ten Commandments. Human society will fall apart if you casually disobey God's laws. But Christians who insist on the letter of the law even for mature adults are an absolute menace. St Paul knew Christians like that in Corinth. 'God's covenant with Israel', they said – they were mostly Jewish – 'depends on every Christian – even those who aren't Jewish – obeying every word of the Hebrew Scriptures to the letter.' By their dogged insistence, they were splitting the church, Jews against Gentiles, Gentiles against Jews.

Paul

St Paul said this was an immature understanding of the Christian life, and he tried to heal the rift. 'God ... has made us competent to be ministers of a *new* covenant,' he wrote, 'not of letter but of spirit; for the letter kills, but the Spirit gives life.' There are still Christian busybodies today who go round telling everybody they meet, 'you mustn't do this, you mustn't do that, it's forbidden in the Bible'. To which Paul would reply, 'For Christ's sake, grow up! Govern your behaviour, not by the letter of the law, but by the Holy Spirit in your hearts, telling you what the loving thing to do is. The letter kills, but the Spirit gives life.' Then these literalists quote Paul's own words back to him: he wrote to Timothy, 'All Scriptures are inspired by God.' But it all depends what you mean by inspiration.

Inspiration

There's a lovely passage in the book of Exodus where Moses appoints inspired craftsmen to decorate the Tabernacle, the predecessor of

God's Temple. In particular, he says, God has filled Bezalel 'with divine spirit, with skill, intelligence, and knowledge in every kind of craft, to devise artistic designs, to work in gold, silver, and bronze, in cutting stones for setting, and in carving wood, in every kind of craft. And [God] has inspired him to teach [others] ... to do every kind of work done by an artisan or by a designer or by an embroiderer ...' So the inspiration of the Holy Spirit includes artistic skills. Many people have found this: they start doing something creative, and it turns out much better than they expected. They can only explain that they were somehow inspired. Yet that doesn't mean that God took away their free will to make choices, and even to make mistakes. Inspiration by the Holy Spirit goes much deeper than that.

Literal inspiration

Christians who insist on applying the dead letter of the law to our behaviour often justify it by claiming that God dictated every letter of the Bible, to remain true for all time. But the doctrine of literal inspiration presents many unnecessary problems. Is it necessary to believe that the sun goes round the earth, just because the Bible says so? Or that the hare chews the cud? If God dictated every word to the inspired writers, did he dictate every stitch to the inspired embroiderers in the Tabernacle, and every hammer blow to the inspired woodcarvers? Now I don't want to disturb the faith of simple Christians. But really this view of literal inspiration is a menace, because most people have had a scientific education these days. If you tell them they can't be a Christian unless they believe the sun goes round the earth, you have thrown away any chance of their ever being converted – they will just laugh at you. Whereas if you stick to the idea of the Holy Spirit inspiring writers and artists in the same way, that means that any of us can be inspired sometimes. The letter kills, but the Spirit gives life.

Suggested hymns

Angel-voices ever singing; Come down, O Love divine; Gracious Spirit, Holy Ghost; Spirit of holiness, wisdom and faithfulness.

Trinity Sunday 26 May
Principal Service **God as Metaphor**

Prov. 8.1–4, 22–31 Wisdom in creation; Ps. 8 Stewardship of nature; Rom. 5.1–5 God's love and Spirit; John 16.12–15 Spirit, Father and Jesus

> 'Does not wisdom call,
>   and does not understanding raise her voice? …
> "The Lord created me at the beginning of his work,
>   the first of his acts of long ago …
> When he established the heavens, I was there,
>   when he drew a circle on the face of the deep …
> then I was beside him, like a master worker;
> and I was daily his delight,
>   rejoicing before him always."'
>   *Proverbs 8.1, 22, 27, 30*

Wisdom

In the eighth chapter of the Old Testament book of Proverbs there's a passage, in which we are invited to imagine someone or something called wisdom, inviting us to understand that *she* was with God when the world was created. This is obviously poetry; wisdom is an abstract idea; you can't see wisdom, nor can wisdom speak in an audible voice. Of course you could take all the poetry out of that passage, and simply say that the natural world shows a remarkably clever arrangement of its parts to form an efficient universe. But who would listen to you if you did? We can't imagine abstract concepts until we put a face on them, and picture them as people. It's what's known as a metaphor. Do you know what a metaphor is? We all use them, and the dictionary defines a metaphor as a figure of speech, in which something is described as actually *being* what in fact it only *resembles*. If you say to an angry person, 'You are a real tiger, and when you roar and show your claws everyone runs a mile', you don't mean it literally. But you get much nearer to the truth about that person than by using bald statements of fact or psychobabble.

Ideas of God

If describing wisdom as a person is a metaphor, is God a metaphor, too? A young man who described himself as an atheist had a relative who was a convinced Christian. They both had a scientific education, and were very fond of each other, and loved to discuss religion; they called it 'sharpening their wits on each other' – another metaphor! The atheist remarked that sometimes people dismiss attempts to preserve a landscape because the concept of beauty isn't 'objective'. This implies that anything that can't be weighed and measured is merely subjective and therefore worthless. Whereas in fact many judgements are formed when different people agree to value something which lies beyond scientific study. So they support National Parks because they believe in the immeasurable importance of beauty. 'May not the idea of God be similar,' he asked his uncle, 'a metaphor which people used to agree on, but in our increasingly diverse society, they no longer do?' To his surprise, the Christian answered, 'Yes. Using the word "God" is a way of giving a human face to something we otherwise couldn't imagine.'

Unimaginable

They went on teasingly, the atheist suggesting that the Church had invented God to give it power over the people, and the Christian replying that regrettably the Church had never had any power, apart from a short period in the Middle Ages. But it makes you think, doesn't it? The *idea* of beauty is a metaphor, but beauty really exists: as the poet Keats said, 'Beauty is truth, truth beauty.' The force behind the universe, its beauty and remarkable cohesion, is something we could never get our minds around. So we give this force a name, 'God', and treat it as a person, though as C. S. Lewis said, God is 'beyond personality'. But God isn't *impersonal*; and he has revealed that, astonishingly, he wants us to have something resembling a personal relationship with him.

Depths

The author of the book of Proverbs had already realized that there are depths to the nature of God which you can't describe in terms of a person. So he separated off the idea of God's wisdom, and treated it as another person within the complex nature of God. Christians, trying to understand how the Jesus they'd seen was related to the Creator God and to the power they felt in their hearts, went further and described 'three Persons in One God', the doctrine of the Holy Trinity. But human beings will never understand God. All we can do is accept God's love, loving and worshipping him in return as our Father, Saviour and Inspiration.

All-age worship

Tie the ends of a piece of string together. Three people hold it as the corners of a triangle. A fourth person can only enter it if all three hold on; but once surrounded by the love of the three they will never be abandoned.

Suggested hymns

How shall I sing that majesty?; Immortal, invisible, God only wise; Love of the Father, love of God the Son; Majesty, worship his majesty.

Trinity Sunday   26 May
(For Corpus Christi, the Thursday after Trinity Sunday, see page 318.)
Second Service   I AM WHO I AM
Morning Ps. 29 The Lord enthroned; Evening Ps. 73.1–3, 16–28 Hard to understand; Ex. 3.1–15 I AM; John 3.1–17 God so loved

> '*Moses said to God, "If I come to the Israelites and say to them, 'The God of your ancestors has sent me to you', and they ask me, 'What is his name?' what shall I say to them?" God said to Moses, "I AM WHO I AM." He said further, "Thus you shall say to the Israelites, 'I AM has sent me to you.'"' Exodus 3.13–14*

Moses

Shepherding his sheep on the slopes of Mount Horeb, Moses saw a bush which was on fire but not burnt up – a symbol of God, ablaze with love, but quite imperishable. The God of his ancestors spoke from the burning bush, calling Moses to lead the Israelites out of slavery in Egypt to freedom in the Promised Land. Moses asked who was sending him on this daunting errand – how should he describe this God, what was his name? God replied, in capital letters, 'I AM WHO I AM.' The name the Israelites were to use for their particular God was 'I AM'. Believers have argued ever since about what these words mean. Perhaps God meant us to.

Yahweh

The original uses the first person singular of the Hebrew verb 'to be', pronounced eh-hyeh. The third person singular, 'he who causes to be', is 'Yahweh', the name of the God of Abraham, Isaac and Jacob. Mind you, you won't find that word used in most Bibles. It survives in the Psalms as 'Yah', and in people's names such as *Jeho*-saphat and Isa-*iah;* and a few centuries ago it was wrongly spelt as 'Jehovah'. But because of the commandment not to take God's name in vain, the Jews would never use his name at all. Instead they replaced it with 'Adonai', a word which means 'my Lord'. In English Bibles, we translate Adonai as 'the Lord' – printed in capital letters, as a sign of respect.

Existence

So God obviously enjoys a good pun. But why should he use the verb 'to be' to describe himself? A century before Christ, a Jewish philosopher called Philo paraphrased God's statement like this: 'There is no name whatever that can be properly assigned to me – I am the only being who really exists.' St Thomas Aquinas was familiar with the works of Philo, and he taught that God existed before the universe came into being, and he is not dependent on his creation in any way. This is called the 'ontological' argument for the existence of God – everything on earth that exists, exists because of something else. So there must be an otherworldly something or someone from whom everything else takes its existence. To put that more simply, arguing whether God exists is a waste of time – if anything exists at all, it must take its being from God. A much harder question is to ask whether I exist, and if so why?

Nature of God

In other words, the existence of God is a foregone conclusion; but what 'existence' means is hard for us to imagine. The nature of God, God's character, is a mystery which we shall never fully understand. 'I am what I am' is all God could tell Moses. Which would leave us up the creek without a paddle if it were not for one thing – God *wants* us to know him. So, bit by bit, God reveals his character to prophets and poets, to seekers and seers. It's taken centuries, each thinker basing their idea of God on what their predecessors had discovered, and adding another gem of understanding from what they have experienced of God in their lives. The turning point came when Jesus revealed that God's character is like that of a loving father.

Complex

But the character of God is at least as complex as that of the world of nature which he made. Yet beneath the diversity of the universe there is a basic unity, which we can't explain. Similarly, God reveals himself in many different ways, as the all-powerful Creator, as the loving Saviour, as the Spirit who inspires us – yet all these are one and the same God.

Trinity

So the doctrine of the Holy Trinity – Father, Son and Holy Spirit, three Persons in one God – isn't just a bit of complicated theology. It's a response to the diverse ways in which we experience God's love at different moments in our life. Yet although God loves each of us, responding to each one's varied needs and unique character, his love unites us into a single family, bound together in love on earth as the Trinity is bound together by love in heaven. You can say, like God, 'I am what I am, unique and special – now – but I'm gradually becoming united to God, and to the whole human race, by God's love, growing in my heart.'

Suggested hymns

Angel voices ever singing; Faith of our fathers, living still; The God of Abraham praise; Through all the changing scenes of life.

ORDINARY TIME

Pentecost and Trinity Sunday are the last of the major festivals in the rhythm of the Church year. They are followed by a season referred to as 'Ordinary Time', when we relax somewhat; but the Sundays after Trinity are important in keeping the rhythm of the Christian year. Other seasons prepare for or respond to Christmas and Easter; this is just a season of steady growth, which is why the church hangings and vestments are green, the colour of growing things. The Collect and Post-communion Prayer depend on the number of Sundays after Trinity Sunday, the date of which varies with the movement of Easter; but the Bible readings are 'Proper', or appropriate, to a particular range of dates. At the Principal Service, there are two alternative series of Old Testament readings and Psalms, and the minister may choose between them. The 'Continuous' series follow the chapters of an Old Testament book in sequence Sunday after Sunday. The 'Related' series are chosen to cast light on the set New Testament reading and Gospel. If a saint's day falls on the Sunday, the minister may choose to use the readings for the saint instead of those for the Sunday. In these cases, this book provides a sermon on the saint's day readings in place of the Second Service.

First Sunday after Trinity (Proper 4)   2 June
Principal Service   **My Daddy's the Pilot**
(*Continuous*): 1 Kings 18.20–21 [22–29] 30–39 Elijah and Baal; Ps. 96 Praise God all nations; *or* (*Related*): 1 Kings 8.22–23, 41–43 Solomon's Prayer; Ps. 96.1–9 God's greatness; Gal. 1.1–12 No other gospel; Luke 7.1–10 Healing a centurion's boy

'Only speak the word, and let my servant be healed.' Luke 7.7

Centurion

Jesus was living in the fishing village of Capernaum. If you visit Capernaum today you can see the white marble remains of a synagogue there, but it dates from a little later than the time of Jesus. Yet underneath it, you can see the foundations of its pre-

154

decessor, the so-called 'black synagogue' where Jesus worshipped, preached and healed. St Luke's Gospel tells us that the construction of the black synagogue at Capernaum was paid for by a Roman centurion. As you know, the Holy Land in the time of Jesus was part of the Roman Empire, and occupied willy-nilly by a powerful Roman army. Centurions were in charge of a hundred soldiers; they roughly correspond to the regimental sergeant-major in a modern army. A Roman historian wrote that centurions must be not so much 'seekers after danger, as men who can command; steady in action, and reliable; they ought not to be over-anxious to rush into the fight; but when hard-pressed they must be ready to hold their ground and die at their posts'. A centurion had to be trusted by those above him, and by those over whom he had command – and vice versa, he had to be able to trust them.

Non-racist

The Jews hated the Romans; several times groups took up arms against the occupying power, and some used to carry a dagger hidden in their clothes, ready to stab a Roman in the back in the crowd – they were the original terrorists. The Romans, in their turn, hated and feared the Jews, and eventually razed Jerusalem to the ground in punishment for the Jewish Revolt. They called the Jews a filthy race, and described their religion as a barbarous superstition. They passed on unfounded rumours that the Jews worshipped a donkey's head and made an annual sacrifice of a non-Jew to their God. Anti-Semitism is nothing new. So the fact that this officer had paid from his own money to build their synagogue proved that he was, unlike so many other Romans, totally non-racist.

Slaves

The Roman Empire was based on slavery. The centurion had a slave whom he was particularly fond of. According to St Matthew, the centurion called him his 'boy'; perhaps he was what British officers used to call a house-boy or batman. But the slave had fallen ill and was at death's door. Normally, when a slave couldn't work he was thrown out to die. But the centurion was so upset that he asked some of his friends in Capernaum to bring Jesus to heal the lad. Now, Jews didn't invite non-Jews into their homes, nor would they go into a foreigner's house. But Jesus was anti-racist, too, and he set out to visit the centurion's billet. When he heard this, the centurion sent a message telling him not to bother. 'I have soldiers under my command, and slaves in my household,' he wrote to Jesus. 'When I tell them to come, they come straightaway; or if I order them to go somewhere, they go without question. The same with you: you have the authority, and if you tell the illness to leave my boy, it'll do what you tell it.' Jesus exclaimed that this foreigner had a stronger faith in God than any Jew; and when the messengers reached the centurion's home they found the slave had just been suddenly and unexpectedly cured.

Faith

The centurion trusted that Jesus could perform a miracle, even from a distance. He wasn't interested in how Jesus would do it; he just had faith that Jesus was a man of his word. When we read of the miracles of Jesus, we have no idea how he did them. That doesn't matter. What counts is that the healings reveal what sort of person Jesus was, and we trust him to do what's best for us in all circumstances – even though that may not be exactly what we asked him for.

The pilot

To end, here's a little story about faith and trust. A small boy was on an aeroplane, and a stranger sitting nearby, thinking to comfort him, leant across and asked him, 'Is this your first flight? Are you feeling frightened?' 'Oh no,' answered the boy confidently – 'you see, my Daddy's the pilot!' If only we had the same trust that God is in charge of everything, as that boy did in his father, and as the Roman centurion had in Jesus, we should never be scared.

All-age worship

Draw the chain of command from school-children up to the Queen, then write, 'God's in charge of everything'.

Suggested hymns

At even, when the sun was set; At the name of Jesus; Majesty, kingdom, authority; When we walk with the Lord.

First Sunday after Trinity (Proper 4)   2 June
Second Service   **Ministers**

Ps. 39 Let me know my end; Gen. 4.1–16 Cain and Abel; Mark
3.7–19 The Twelve

> *'[Jesus] appointed twelve, whom he also named apostles, to be
> with him, and to be sent out to proclaim the message.' Mark 3.14*

Mark

St Mark's Gospel shows how it gradually dawned on his disciples
who Jesus was. They didn't understand at first – they needed to be
trained – 'disciple' means someone who is taught, and becoming a
disciple of Jesus is a steep learning curve. First they saw him as a
prophet, then as a healer, teacher, Son of Man, Messiah, and at last
they learnt that this man is the Son of God.

Apostles

Every Christian is called to be a disciple – and we all have to go
through the same rigorous education. When, at last, we have learnt
who Jesus is for us, we then have to tell the people around us, so
that they, too, can be 'discipled'. Then, out of the hundreds who
followed Jesus, he chose twelve to a special form of discipleship.
The number twelve was chosen because they were modelled on the
twelve sons of Jacob – that's why the Twelve were all men, though
there were many women disciples. Jacob's sons were the ancestors
of the twelve tribes of Israel; and these twelve were to be the beginning of the new Israel. They were disciples, like all the others, and
looking at poor Peter, you realize they still had a lot to learn. But
the task to which Jesus called them was that they were *'also'* to be
called apostles. 'Apostle' means 'someone who is sent', and they
were appointed 'to be with [Jesus], and to be sent out to proclaim
the message'. Every disciple, every Christian, is chosen by Jesus to
learn of him and to tell others, in the place where they live. An
apostle, however, is somebody who is sent somewhere else, to tell
the people there about the good news.

Ministers

There are millions of apostles working for Jesus today – people who
are sent to another place to make new disciples there. We usually

157

call them ministers, or clergy, or sometimes missionaries; they come in all shapes and sizes, but they all have the common call to go somewhere to make disciples. So when your minister helps you to learn who Jesus is, and what he means for you, she or he is doing the work of an apostle. None of us is perfect, any more than the first apostles were; we make many mistakes, and we still have a lot to learn. We are still disciples. But the fact that we have moved somewhere for the sake of the gospel, means that we are just as much apostles as St Peter and St Paul were. Then how should you, who are today's disciples, treat us? Not with hushed awe and reverence, please! We are all partners in Jesus and Co., working together as equals, but with specific tasks to carry out in order to make the firm successful.

Partnership

No minister can do everything. Some people expect us to be a brilliant preacher, teacher of the young, the chair of committees, maintainer of an ancient building, a fundraiser, home and hospital visitor, and God knows what else. Anyone can have a shot at all those things, but it's only human nature to say that nobody can be brilliant at every task. So we have to work together as partners, dividing the tasks according to each person's talents and abilities. The minister's task is to be a pastor or shepherd, helping the church members to learn and grow as disciples, until they are ready to make their friends into new disciples. The minister is to be the leader of the team – not bullying or browbeating the church members – but the congregation must be willing to be led, not insisting on always having everything their own way.

Covenant

In at least one church, when a new minister is appointed, they have a service establishing a 'covenant', or contract, between the minister and the people of God. The minister says, 'I covenant to serve and encourage this church and community', and the people respond, 'Today we bring ourselves and the gifts we have, and we covenant ... to respect and care for each other ... to encourage you as our minister as we make this journey together.' They outline what Christ calls them to be: 'a worshipping people ... working for justice, resisting violence and challenging the abuse of power ... an inclusive people, pulling down the walls of prejudice and welcoming the stranger ...'; then they pray: 'God of life ... we give ourselves today to each other and to you, trusting that as you call us, so you covenant to share this journey with us, to nurture and sustain our life together and to guide our paths.' To which I say a hearty 'Amen'.

Suggested hymns

Brother, sister, let me serve you; Captains of the saintly band; Make me a channel of your peace; O thou who camest from above.

Second Sunday after Trinity (Proper 5) 9 June
Principal Service Life after Death

(*Continuous*): 1 Kings 17.8–16 [17–24] The widow's jar; Ps. 146 God upholds the widows; *or* (*Related*): 1 Kings 17.17–24 Elijah heals the widow's child; Ps. 30 Resurrection from death; Gal. 1.11–24 Paul's conversion and authority; Luke 7.11–17 The widow's son at Nain

> *'The dead man sat up and began to speak, and Jesus gave him to his mother.' Luke 7.15*

Socrates

The philosopher Socrates was condemned to die, 400 years before Christ. He taught that there's no reason to fear death – 'for all we know, death may be the best thing that happens to us'. Either death is like a dreamless sleep, or else we go to a better world. If the dead go to a better world, just think how many wonderful people we shall meet after we die!

Nain

In a town called Nain, Jesus met a widow on the way to bury her only son. Jesus had compassion on her, and brought the dead man back to life again. With nobody to support her, this poor woman would probably have starved to death. But this story raises some difficult questions. How can you give fresh life on earth to someone in whom the processes of decay have already destroyed the linkages in the brain which are essential to life? And if Jesus could do that for this one man, why doesn't he bring everyone who dies back to life?

Miracle or coma?

The usual answer to the first question is that it was a miracle. God can do anything he wants to. You can't argue with that. But with modern advances in medicine, we may have a less mysterious answer. Sick people sometimes fall into a deep coma, which looks like death. A doctor can easily tell the difference, but it may not have been so easy then. In hot climates they always bury dead people within a few hours of death. Perhaps if the widow had waited a little longer, she would have seen that her son wasn't dead. In modern hospitals, if a patient's heart stops, they are officially pronounced dead. But sometimes, if resuscitation is applied very quickly, the patient's heart starts up again. Maybe the widow's son had only just died, and Jesus knew some way of making his heart start beating again. Neither of these is a very satisfactory explanation, and you may prefer to believe in a simple miracle.

Near-death experiences

In cases when a patient is clinically dead, and then returns to life, they often report what is called a near-death experience. Those with varied beliefs about an afterlife, or none at all, usually report rising above their body, then going down a dark tunnel towards a bright light. Sometimes they meet Jesus, or someone they know. Finally, when they realize they have to return to earth, nearly all say they were deeply disappointed. So in answer to Socrates, it really seems likely that we do go to a better world when we die. Atheists talk in terms of brain chemistry explaining why people have these experiences; but it's more scientific to accept the simplest explanation. It's hard to imagine why people from such different backgrounds all have similar experiences if they are making it up.

Why not all?

But if people who have been briefly dead agree that they would have preferred not to return to life on earth, that would explain why Jesus doesn't stop people we love from dying when we pray to him. He may have raised a few people to earthly life, like the young man in Nain, and his friend Lazarus; and indeed he himself returned from the dead for forty days. Sceptics often say, 'Well, no one's ever come back from the dead to tell us what it's like!' Actually, quite a lot of people, as it turns out, have done just that. But never-ending life on earth isn't our final destination, and these extraordinary cases may be given just as a way of convincing us that death is not the end. It's right to grieve; but those we grieve for, given a choice, would have no wish to come back to us; they would rather wait for us to go to them. Death is, as Socrates said, nothing to be afraid of.

A mother's dream

Finally, a true story. A boy of five had learnt in Sunday school about Our Invisible Friend called Jesus. He said, 'I believe that Jesus is alive in my heart. But I want to *see* Jesus.' That afternoon he was killed by a drunk driver. The same night his mother had a dream. She saw her dead child running towards her, holding somebody's hand. 'Mummy, Mummy,' he cried out. 'It's all right. Now I can see him.'

All-age worship

Act out the Old Testament story of Elijah and the widow's son. Then act the story of Jesus at Nain. What would you say to the widow?

Suggested hymns

Guide me, O thou great Redeemer; Lord, it belongs not to my care; Sometimes a light surprises; Thine be the glory.

Second Sunday after Trinity (Proper 5)   9 June
Second Service   **Global Warming**
Ps. 44 Come to our help; Gen. 8.15—9.17 God's covenant with Noah; Mark 4.1–20 Parable of the sower

> 'The LORD said in his heart, "I will never again curse the ground because of humankind, for the inclination of the human heart is evil from youth; nor will I ever again destroy every living creature as I have done.

As long as the earth endures,
  seedtime and harvest, cold and heat,
summer and winter, day and night,
  shall not cease."' Genesis 8.21–22

Noah

We often ask, 'Why does a loving God allow so much suffering?' Admittedly, a certain amount of pain is good for us – it helps us evolve physically, mentally and spiritually. And death, for those who believe in an afterlife, may be a blessing. Moreover, much of our suffering is caused by other people. There's a mixture of good and evil in everyone, and God can't stop us hurting each other without taking away our free will. If we ask God to destroy all the wicked people, the story of Noah tells us what would happen if he did. God himself says that 'the inclination of the human heart is evil from youth', so if God only allowed the perfectly virtuous to survive, how many would be left? Fortunately, God has promised that he will never go that far – 'seedtime and harvest shall not cease'. The bad news is that this leaves us free to destroy each other – and ourselves.

Nature

For although God swears that he won't bring the cycle of the seasons to an end, he doesn't promise that the human race will never become extinct. Maybe another species will replace us in God's planning; or maybe when God has enough candidates for heaven, he will have no further interest in earth. We may have no control over that; but we are certainly responsible for making life as pain-free as possible for coming generations. Which brings me onto the controversial subject of climate change.

Climate change

Recently, an iceberg the size of Luxembourg broke off from the Antarctic. It contained enough fresh water to sustain a third of the earth's population for a year. It broke off because it was hit by an even bigger iceberg, 60 miles long; together they are drifting northwards, and their effect on ocean life, ocean currents, and eventually on the high-altitude winds which control our climate is hard to predict. Although climate change can produce hot summers and cold winters, its effect on the growth of deserts and the shrinking of the Arctic are measurable, and increasing faster than they have done for centuries. Now, it's possible that this is a purely natural process, part of a long-term cycle. Maybe we are in for another ice-age sooner than we expected. *Homo sapiens* only just survived the last ice-age; we had better start planning for the next one now.

Human causes

Coming back to Noah, then, we should ask ourselves, is climate change God's punishment for our wickedness, or have we brought it on ourselves? Up until a couple of centuries ago, most of the land surface was covered by forest, and almost the only fuel was wood. Now, vast areas are desert and arid land where few people can survive, and we are burning huge quantities of coal and oil, polluting the atmosphere – until they run out – with smoke and carbon dioxide. Within the lifetime of some of us, the earth's human population has doubled. We travel long distances on business or holiday. A 200-mile flight in an aeroplane emits over 100lb of CO_2, more than three times as much as the same journey by train. In Britain, we cause emissions of almost ten tons of carbon per head per year; and we fly more than twice as much as people in any other country. Since 1980, the average global temperature has increased by about half a degree centigrade, and it's continuing to warm at an increasing rate. According to a new international study, warming in the twentieth century was so intense and widespread that there's a 95 per cent probability that climate change is largely due to greenhouse-gas emissions rather than natural variations.

Answers

We may never know the causes of global warming until it's too late. But God has put us in charge of the planet; it would be totally irresponsible not to do two things. The first is to cut our carbon emissions as much as we possibly can, just in case they are making things worse. And the second duty we owe to God is to take urgent steps to raise standards of living in poorer countries, before their people are driven to violence in searching for a fairer share of the earth's food-supply. God knows that human hearts are selfish, and he promised to Noah that he, God, would never bring an end to the cycle of harvests. But he said nothing about stopping us from destroying ourselves.

Above the moon earth rises; For the fruits of his creation; God, you have giv'n us power to sound; Lord, bring the day to pass.

See http://www2.ucar.edu/climate/faq

Third Sunday after Trinity (Proper 6)   16 June
Principal Service   **Complacent or Compliant?**
(*Continuous*): 1 Kings 21.1–10 [11–14] 15–21a Naboth's vineyard; Ps. 5.1–8 God's justice; *or* (*Related*): 2 Sam. 11.26—12.10, 13–15 David's repentance; Ps. 32 Forgiveness; Gal. 2.15–21 Law, faith and grace; Luke 7.36—8.3 A woman's repentance

> '*Her sins, which were many, have been forgiven; hence she has shown great love. But the one to whom little is forgiven, loves little.' Luke 7.47*

Complacent

Jesus was invited out to dinner. His host was a Pharisee, someone who was very strict in complying with the laws of the Old Testament. But he ignored the basic rules of hospitality, and didn't even wash his guest's feet when he came in from the dusty street. He despised Jesus, who rode lightly to the letter of the law, healed sick people on the Sabbath-day, and taught that love is more important than law. The Pharisee was a religious man, and smugly complacent in the knowledge of his own superiority.

Compliant

The courtyard where they ate was open to the street, and passers-by could wander in to listen to the conversation. A woman of the streets strolled in – a prostitute. The Old Testament condemns prostitution; one of the law books says, 'When the daughter of a priest profanes herself through prostitution, she profanes her father; she shall be burned to death.' In practice they were tolerated, but no respectable person would be seen speaking to a woman like that. The woman knew this, and felt guilty. Of course, we all know that it's men who turn women into prostitutes. Many widows and divorced women had no option but to become beggars or prostitutes, otherwise they would starve. Today, many do it to pay the price of an addiction from which they can't break free. But this woman knew she was considered a wicked sinner, and she felt worthless. Then she overheard Jesus saying that love is the fulfilment of the Law: strict adherence to the letter of the Law is impossible for some people; what counts is whether you comply with the law of love. From that moment she loved Jesus with all her heart: the friend of the friendless, he was the first man to treat this woman as a person. The guests were reclining on couches with their shoes off, so, standing behind Jesus, she poured a bottle of expensive perfume over his feet, washed them with her tears, and wiped them with her long, unkempt hair.

Parable

The complacent Pharisee was appalled that Jesus didn't chase her away – so Jesus told him a parable. It was about two debtors: one was let off an enormous debt, and was enormously grateful; the other only owed a little, and was quite casual when the money-lender cancelled the loan. It's gratitude that breeds love, said Jesus, not complying with the letter of the Law. The prostitute felt she was guilty, and when she heard of a God who forgives sinners, her heart filled with love. The religious man was complacent, believing that he'd done all the Law demanded, and had no need of forgiveness. But he failed absolutely to follow the law of love, which is the heart of morality. The upright man was complacent, but in fact, not compliant; the wicked woman complied with the only law that counts. Which is more important, asked Jesus – to be complacent or to be compliant?

Friend of the friendless

Jesus showed in his life what love means. He was the friend of the friendless, wherever they came from. Women had a raw deal in those days. They were despised, used, and then thrown out by men. Jesus was the only one who stood up for them. In the following verses, St Luke lists the women who travelled around with Jesus; probably the connection with the story of the prostitute was deliberate. Women weren't allowed to preach, but they had a vital function in preparing and serving the meals. So Jesus gave them work to do, to regain their self-respect. And what a mixed bunch they were! Joanna the wife of a high court official had access to plenty of cash; but Mary Magdalene, the former madwoman whom Jesus had healed – where did she get the money from to support him? The Bible doesn't tell us, but perhaps it was from the same source as the other woman's alabaster jar of expensive perfume. Yet Jesus was the friend of all; the posh and the poor, the wealthy and the wanton – and expected them to be friends with each other. The lesson for us all is obvious: don't judge or despise anyone, you don't know what has made them what they are. It's more important to be compliant to the law of love, than complacent, law-abiding, and totally without love in your heart.

All-age worship

Find out about charities which help drug addicts. Make red paper hearts and write on them: 'Jesus forgives me so I love him'.

Suggested hymns

And can it be?; Drop, drop slow tears; God forgave my sin in Jesus' name; Jesus, lover of my soul.

Third Sunday after Trinity (Proper 6)   16 June
Second Service   **Pascal's Gamble**
Ps. 52 A tree in God's house [53 Fools say]; Gen. 13 Abram and Lot; Mark 4.21–41 Parables and a storm

> *'Fools say in their hearts, "There is no God."' Psalm 53.1*

Pascal

Blaise Pascal, a French mathematician in the seventeenth century, invented the modern theory of probability, and his work has never been superseded. Pascal suggested we can decide whether a bet is worth taking, by multiplying the amount of the bet by the value of the prize. In other words if the probability of the horse losing is ten to one, it's hardly worth betting £1 on it, because if it wins you only gain a measly £10, and nine times out of ten you will lose your investment. Only the bookmakers make a profit in the long run. Yet if the odds are about even, and you know something the bookies don't know, bet as much as you can afford: the chances are more than 50–50 that you will finish with a fortune. But always stop when you are winning!

Global warming

The reasoning behind 'Pascal's gamble' applies to many areas of life. Take the controversial case of climate change [which I mentioned last week]. Some people believe that global warming is due to the normal cycle of rising and falling temperatures, and nothing to do with human activities. I hope to God they are right! But look at it in Pascal's way. If we reduce our carbon emissions by investing in solar energy and using our cars less, we shall suffer some inconvenience, and our already high standard of living will be reduced a bit. If global warming is cyclical, everything will return to normal eventually and we shall have lost very little. But supposing the rise in temperatures on land and sea is due to our carelessness. If we do nothing, our children will inherit an earth with large areas uninhabitable, and a worldwide shortage of food. So even if there's only a small probability of a human cause, our loss is small if we change our ways, but it's unimaginably dire if we do nothing. Multiply the value of the gain – a life for our children – by the value of the investment – limiting our carbon emissions – and you see that the gamble is overwhelmingly worth taking, whatever the odds.

Atheists

If you have followed the reasoning in that case, try applying the same logic to another. A group of atheists in the UK have paid to put a slogan on some buses, reading, 'There almost certainly isn't a God.' Yet, realistically, nobody can prove that there is a God, and nobody can prove that there isn't. But look at the probabilities:

- The universe exists, and is very beautiful. The Big Bang theory is a good suggestion for *how* it came to be there. But *why* does it exist at all? And why is it so mind-bogglingly wonderful? Is it more likely that it got that way by random chance, or because an intelligence was behind the process?
- If you accept the theory of evolution, then why is life progressing, instead of going backwards, or round in circles? Might it be because the creator intended from the very beginning for creatures to evolve who were capable of love?
- And why are humans able to love, and to think; why have there been so many fantastic human achievements? No computer has

167

yet created a computer cleverer than itself. The human mind can only be the result of an even greater Mind.

- Many people have revealed profound truths, and lived lives of triumphant goodness, saying that they were inspired by God. Is it possible that they were all the result of a colossal delusion?

Place your bets

There are many other features in our world which are easier to explain if there is some sort of God. But believing in God remains a bit of a gamble. If you want to know whether it's true, the only way to find out is to pray, give up your selfish habits, and join a community of believers. If changes for the better come in your life, the gamble has paid off. If you make the step of faith sincerely, and there isn't a God, you haven't lost much. But suppose there is a God, and you live as an atheist, and meet him when you die, you will be, to say the least, very sorry. There's a joke about the Scots atheist who came before the judgement seat, saying, 'Och, Lorrd, I didna ken!' 'Weel, Wullie,' replies the Almighty, in broad Scots, 'tha kens the noo!' As Pascal pointed out, believing in God is much the more worthwhile gamble. Multiplying the investment by the benefits, you stand to gain eternal life in endless bliss if you win. And if you are wrong, you have lost nothing by living as though virtue was its own reward.

Suggested hymns

Can we by searching find out God?; Do not be afraid; Forth in thy name, O Lord, I go; Lead, kindly light.

Fourth Sunday after Trinity (Proper 7)   23 June
(Eve of St John the Baptist)
Principal Service   **Label Free**
(*Continuous*): 1 Kings 19.1–4 [5–7] 8–15a The still small voice; Ps. 42 and 43 Faith and hope; or (*Related*): Isa. 65.1–9 God's judgement; Ps. 22.19–28 Salvation; Gal. 3.23–29 The Law our tutor till faith comes; Luke 8.26–39 Demons sent into pigs

> *'Jesus then asked him, "What is your name?" He said, "Legion"; for many demons had entered him.' Luke 8.30*

All except me

Some people used to hang humorous plaques on their walls. One read, 'All the world's mad save thee and me – and even thou'rt a little odd.' Of course, it's now incorrect to use these words, and we should be more considerate of those with psychological illnesses. But it makes you think, doesn't it? Perhaps it helps us to understand the people around us, to realize that they are all under psychological pressures of some kind. We should be more tolerant of the things in other people that annoy us, if we understood that absolutely anybody's thinking can go haywire when they are under stress. Bad behaviour is seldom caused by deliberate wickedness; more often it's due to immature thinking and uncontrolled emotions. Even if somebody does appear to be wicked, may not that, also, be due to a deprived upbringing, or defects in their brain? The last part of the human brain to develop is that which helps us to see things from other people's point of view; and that facility is what makes us different from the animals. Yet in some people that degree of empathy never develops at all, meaning they are less than fully human.

Tolerance and humility

So to believe that 'all the world's mad' may make us more tolerant of people under pressure. The sting, however, is in the tail: 'All mad save thee and me; and even thou'rt a little odd.' Anyone who can say that must be under the delusion that they are uniquely sane, and different from everyone else. It would be humbler to look for signs of psychological disturbance in our own behaviour, and try to put them right. Is it the fear of admitting that I myself may not be entirely rational that makes us so scared of meeting those who are disturbed?

Demons

In the old days people used to believe that psychological illness was caused by demon possession. Disturbed people were avoided from fear that the evil spirits in them would leap across to us, like germs, and drive us mad, too. Some were treated by having holes drilled in their skulls, to let the demons out. Sick people were, quite literally, demonized. Jesus met many people who were excluded from respectable society on the grounds that their odd behaviour meant they were possessed. But unlike his contemporaries, Jesus wasn't afraid of them; he went right up to them and healed them. Now it's a basic rule of medicine that the healer must use the same terminology as the patient. It wouldn't have helped anyone if Jesus had said to them: 'You are suffering from a bipolar disorder with behavioural symptoms' – they'd have put him in chains too! He was met by a man who said his name was 'Legion' – the language of Jewish people oppressed by legions of Roman soldiers. So Jesus replied in the same terms, and ordered the supposed demons, which the man thought were occupying his skull, into a herd of pigs, which were considered by the Jews to be unclean and unfit to eat. Immediately the man was healed – 'clothed, and in his right mind'. Psychological illness can often be cured, if treated early enough.

Psychological illness

If not treated, cognitive impairment becomes degenerative and the brain is permanently affected. Yet we put nothing like enough money into mental health to enable people who need it to receive courses of counselling, with the result that eventually we have to spend far more on hospitalizing them. The trouble is that psychological illness is invisible. Diabetes and cancer can be seen under the microscope; a disturbed psyche reveals itself in behaviour. New treatments are being examined which involve, not just sedation, but altering the action of dopamine and serotonin in the body.

Label free

Meanwhile we need to understand our sick neighbours, not shun them. One Mental Health Group publishes a magazine under the banner, 'Label Free'. Instead of labelling people as Psychotic, Bipolar, Mad, or Nut Cases, they say, let's treat them just as people. They are people like us, who just happen to have an extreme form of the problems which beset us all. This group even organize a fundraising event which they call, 'Sanity Fair'! This approach might even help us to look at our own thinking in a new way. Not so much 'All save thee and me'; rather 'All the world's disturbed, including thee and me – and we are all in need of help and understanding.' Jesus knew that; but we are rather slow to catch on.

All-age worship

Find out about charities such as www.mind.org.uk and www.sane. org.uk

Suggested hymns

As water to the thirsty; Dear Lord and Father of mankind; Thou whose almighty word; To God be the glory.

Fourth Sunday after Trinity (Proper 7) 23 June
Second Service **Despair and Hope**
Ps. [50 A sacrifice of thanksgiving] 57 In the shadow of your wings; Gen. 24.1–27 Isaac and Rebekah; Mark 5.21–43 Jairus' daughter

> *'Overhearing what they said, Jesus said to the leader of the synagogue, "Do not fear, only believe."' Mark 5.36*

Jairus

The story of Jesus is the tale of the triumph of hope over despair. In fact, that's the story of God's whole relationship with the human race he created: hope triumphing over despair. In the Gospels, we find one story enclosed within another, like meat in a sandwich. The bread is the story of Jairus, the ruler of the synagogue. When his 12-year-old daughter fell ill, he was in despair. So he fell at the feet of Jesus and begged him to heal her. Jesus immediately followed him home.

The sick woman

But before they got there, somebody else met Jesus – a woman with gynaecological problems. Her bleeding hadn't stopped for 12 years. She must have been worn out by the physical strain. She had spent all she had on doctors, but with all their best efforts, they couldn't stop the blood-loss. She too was in despair. Then she heard about Jesus, and hope returned to her heart. Surely this man, who seemed so close to God, could bring her God's healing? Women in her condition were forbidden by the Jewish Law from touching anyone, so she crept up behind Jesus in the crowd and touched the tassels on the edge of his robe. Immediately she was cured, and Jesus felt that power had gone out of him; he turned and asked who had touched him. Terrified, she owned up, but he reassured her that the cure was in response to her faith, and encouraged her to hope that her long-standing problem would never return. Hope triumphed over despair in that woman's heart.

Healing

Jesus, however, continued walking to Jairus's house. Some messengers met them to say that the little girl was already dead. Jairus's despair was now absolute; but overhearing what they said, Jesus encouraged him to hope still. When he got there, he found an uproar of wailing mourners, hanging over the girl's body, begging for a response from the silent lips. 'Why do you despair?' Jesus asked. 'She isn't dead, only asleep.' Did he literally mean that she was in a coma, or was this to teach them that every death is a falling asleep, ready to wake up in eternity? Bundling the mourners out of the way, Jesus went into the bedroom with the parents and a few of his disciples. St Peter must have been among them, for he told St Mark the actual words in the local dialect that Jesus had used: *Talitha cumi,* meaning, 'Little girl, get up!' Immediately, she sat up in bed! Once again, hope triumphed over despair.

Despair

Human beings have so little faith, that we spend most of our lives enslaved by what John Bunyan called 'Giant Despair'. We look at the world around us, and everything seems to be disaster and cruelty. We look at our own best efforts to deal with the world, and we feel weak and powerless. We are confronted by the death of those we love, and the inevitability of our own death, and we imagine that this is the end; the closing, not just of a chapter, but of the whole book. Then along comes Jesus the Giant-killer, and Giant Despair lies a corpse at his feet. Our hearts are freed from slavery to the ogre, whose place is taken by hope.

Hope

Jesus brings us hope, because he encourages us to have faith in God, like the sick woman who was cured by her faith. Hope, springing from faith, has two results. First, we believe that God will keep his promises, if we pray in faith. Of course, if you pray that today you might become the owner of a red Ferrari, you will be disappointed. God doesn't give us what we want if we don't actually need it. He only gives what he has promised in the Bible, and what he knows is best for us. If you despair, you won't even pray, because you will imagine it's a waste of time. If the sick person has already deteriorated to the point at which continuing to live would only be an agony, God won't prolong the misery. But if faith helps the sick person relax, healing may well follow. If not, then what? The Bible promises that death is followed by eternal life in a far better world, and who could begrudge a sick person a gift like that? So if we hope for heaven, we shall receive the strength to carry us through all life's trials and tribulations with head held high. Hope is always triumphant over despair.

Suggested hymns

All my hope on God is founded; As pants the hart for cooling streams; Be still my soul, the Lord is on thy side; Do not be afraid, for I have redeemed you.

Fifth Sunday after Trinity (Proper 8)   30 June
Principal Service   **Birds**
(*Continuous*): 2 Kings 2.1–2, 6–14 Elijah's spirit given to Elisha; Ps. 77.1–2, 11–20 Remembering God's saving acts; *or* (*Related*): 1 Kings 19.15–16, 19–21 Elijah calls Elisha; Ps. 16 The path of life; Gal. 5.1, 13–25 The fruit of the Spirit; Luke 9.51–62 Endurance in following Christ

'Foxes have holes, and birds of the air have nests; but the Son of Man has nowhere to lay his head.' Luke 9.58

Bird-lovers

Are you a bird-lover? Maybe you are a keen bird-watcher; or you just like seeing the creatures flutter around and listening to the birdsong, but you have no idea what species they are. These days, by watching the nature programmes on TV, or counting the birds in your garden and entering the numbers online in the RSPB Big Garden Birdwatch each spring, you can learn a great deal about our fine feathered friends, and discover how fascinating they are. The Darwinists can tell us how different coloured plumage and varied patterns of behaviour occur through random mutations of the genes, but that doesn't tell me why I find them so beautiful to look at. So I think God must be a bird-lover, too, and he made them to fill the airy section of his creation with colour and life – as it says in the book of Genesis – and then told human beings to care for them. When the robin-redbreast perches on my spade, and trills his song to me in the garden, I'm not sure whether he's thanking me for providing him with food, or whether he imagines that I'm another cock-robin and is warning me off his territory – but I prefer to think he knows somehow that God made him and cares for him, and that in his own way he's singing praises to his creator along with the rest of the dawn chorus.

Birds in the Bible

When you think of it, birds are often mentioned in the Bible, the word of God. In today's Gospel, Jesus said that 'Foxes have holes, and birds of the air have nests; but the Son of Man has nowhere to lay his head.' The birds work hard at building their nests and, barring accidents, they can live in them while they raise their brood. Jesus, on the other hand, was called to the life of a wandering preacher. Does that suggest that he has an especial sympathy with the many homeless folk in today's society; and those who have been thrown out of their homes because they couldn't keep up their mortgage payments? In the Old Testament, Elijah was fed by the ravens when he was hungry, as though they were obeying God's orders; and in that wonderful love-poem, the Song of Songs, the lovers recognize that spring has come when 'the voice of the turtle-dove is heard in the land'. In the Psalms, God welcomes the birds into his Temple:

Even the sparrow finds a home,
    and the swallow a nest for herself,
        where she may lay her young,
at your altars, O Lord of hosts,
    my King and my God.

In another psalm, the birds are a symbol of freedom: 'We have escaped like a bird from the snare of the fowlers; the snare is broken, and we have escaped.'

Learn from the birds

In the Sermon on the Mount, Jesus tells us to 'Look at the birds of the air; they neither sow nor reap nor gather into barns, and yet your heavenly Father feeds them.' He goes on to ask rhetorically, 'Are you not of more value than they?' We can learn from the birds: they simply gather what they need for food for their nestlings, and are satisfied, without needing to worry themselves sick about building up the enormous capital resources which are required of us in our materialistic society. Elsewhere Jesus says, 'Are not two sparrows sold for a penny? Yet not one of them will fall to the ground unperceived by your Father ... So do not be afraid; you are of more value than many sparrows.' He suggests that God cares for each individual bird among the billions who fly over the earth; so we should never doubt that God cares for us, too.

Caring for the birds

There's an email going round with photos of office workers helping a mother duck take her ducklings safely from their nest on a high ledge to the river several streets away. Surely the stories of birds in the Bible teach us to thank God for the wonderful diversity of his creation, and to care for our fellow creatures tenderly for God's sake.

All-age worship

Learn to recognize some common species of birds. Write a prayer thanking God for the world of nature.

Suggested hymns

All things bright and beautiful; Great is thy faithfulness; Morning has broken; O Lord my God, when I in awesome wonder.

Fifth Sunday after Trinity (Proper 8) 30 June
Second Service Legends
Ps. [59.1–6, 18–20 You are my fortress] 60 Human help is worthless; Gen. 27.1–40 Jacob cheats Esau; Mark 6.1–6 Jesus rejected at Nazareth

> *'Esau said to his father, "Have you only one blessing, father? Bless me, me also, father!" And Esau lifted up his voice and wept.'* Genesis 27.38

Legends and history

For centuries people believed that *The Iliad* and *The Odyssey* were fictional stories made up by a poet called Homer. Then Heinrich

Schliemann excavated the historical site of Troy. King Nestor was a character in the legend; in the Peloponnese you can see the remains of his palace, complete with his marble bathtub – evidence that he really existed. Odysseus was sent where the River Styx empties into a great lake; with nearby a cave where he offered sacrifices to the dead. In northern Greece there's an underground complex in just such a location, called the Nekromanteion, which was used for that purpose in very ancient times. So our view of Greek legends has changed. Doubtless they have been retold over the centuries and improved in the telling; but they seem to be based on genuine historical events. My question is, could we say the same thing about some of the stories in the Bible?

Jacob and Esau

Today we heard a story about Jacob and Esau, the two sons of Isaac. Jacob behaved abominably – cheating his twin brother out of his birthright *and* his blessing. Yet Jacob, whose other name was Israel, was considered to be the ancestor of the Israelite tribes, who lived in the northern part of what we now call the State of Israel. Esau was the ancestor of the Edomites, who lived on the other side of the River Jordan. The Edomites were great rivals of the Israelites, so what's this story doing in the Israelite Bible? I guess, comparing it with the Greek legends, that this story is based on historical events which happened to nomadic tribes fighting over land rights in ancient times; but it's been 'written up' to make a gripping tale, and to teach a number of moral lessons. It reminds those who live on a piece of land that they are there by the grace of God, not because they are morally superior to their rivals. They may have to admit that they treated their enemies appallingly in the past; and they should remember that they are genetically related to other tribes in the region, and need to treat them as brothers.

Racism

This was a message which the Israelites in biblical times needed to learn about their relations with the Edomites. It clearly applies to the politics of the Middle East at present. But its message has timeless significance. We *all* need to learn that our neighbours, our rivals, and even our enemies are, in fact, our brothers and sisters. From studying our DNA, we learn that every race of people in the world is descended from a small number of *Homo sapiens* who

176

evolved in Africa. This agrees with the Bible account that we are all descended from Noah, and before him from Adam and Eve. There's no such thing as a pure race – we are all mongrels! Moreover, however terrible the things which other countries do to us today, in most cases our ancestors have done equally bad things to their ancestors in the past. Hidden in the ancient legends of the Bible is a clear anti-racist message, and an appeal to tolerance and brotherly and sisterly love for all.

History and fiction

The Bible is full of stories like this one. Some people believe they are accurate history, because the Bible is the inspired word of God. All I can say is that, although most of my sermons are rubbish, just occasionally I write one which is much more moving when I preach it than I expected, and even brings *me* close to tears. That's nothing to do with how clever or stupid I am; it's because God inspired me to speak on his behalf. But I never feel he's taken away my freedom to choose the words I use. I believe the same is true of the biblical writers: God moved them to retell an ancient story in such a way as to teach us how we should behave; but he didn't dictate the words into their ears. What matters isn't where you place the stories on the scale between literal history like the Magna Carta and complete fiction like Harry Potter. That's irrelevant. What counts is whether you look hard at these legends, to see their inner meaning. And then put the moral lessons you have learned from them into practice. Thank God for where you live, by God's grace. But don't cheat and fight your neighbours of other races; the Bible says they are your brothers and sisters, and you must learn to love them as such.

Suggested hymns

God moves in a mysterious way; In Christ there is no east or west; O God of Bethel, by whose hand; The God of Abraham praise.

Sixth Sunday after Trinity (Proper 9) 7 July
Principal Service **Sent Out in the Spirit**
(*Continuous*): 2 Kings 5.1–14 Naaman healed from leprosy; Ps.
30 Healing; *or* (*Related*): Isa. 66.10–14 The motherhood of God;
Ps. 66.1–8 God's grace; Gal. 6.[1–6] 7–16 Righteousness; Luke
10.1–11, 16–20 Sending out the seventy disciples

> *'The harvest is plentiful, but the labourers are few; therefore ask
> the Lord of the harvest to send out labourers into his harvest.'*
> Luke 10.2

Community

In Europe and America we are too individualistic – '*I* think, therefore *I* am.' In other parts of the world people think more in terms
of communities: 'I am because *we are*.' In our approach to religion,
too, we think in terms of my personal relationship with God. There
must, indeed, be a moment when you decide for yourself to make
Jesus your personal friend. But Jesus saw this as a step towards
drawing the whole world into a community of love. At one point he
sent out seventy of his disciples on a mission – that must have been
quite a high proportion – virtually the whole community. The job
of mission wasn't restricted to the Twelve who were closest to him;
and as he sent them out as couples, they may have included women
and men together.

The gathering of the harvest

The job Jesus gave to these seventy disciples was to gather in a
harvest of souls – people who had accepted that God loved them,
and wanted to know more about Jesus's teaching. It would be tough
work, he said: 'I send you out like sheep among wolves.' But God
the Holy Spirit would be with them and in them to strengthen them.
This was by way of a trial run; Jesus started small, but with a global
vision. He assured them that millions would join the kingdom, from
all over the world: 'The harvest is plentiful, but the labourers are
few; therefore ask the Lord of the harvest to send out labourers into
his harvest.' As each new believer joined them, they were sent out at
once as missionaries, so that others might believe by their example.
They were to become a living, growing missionary community.

Synagogues

But in the period described in the Gospels, the believers weren't yet organized as a separate Christian Church. The first converts were almost all Jews. Jews were a well-organized community, meeting in each village and town in a gathering called a synagogue. The Jewish Christian converts remained members of the synagogues as long as they could, joining in the heated debates which characterized Jewish religious life, and trying to present the Christian point of view to other members. But the synagogues were exclusive clubs – only Jews who followed the Law of Moses were allowed to be members. Yet Jesus had taught by word and example that the fallen and the outcast, those on the margins of society, were welcome members of the kingdom of God. This must have caused uproar in the synagogues.

Gentiles

Nevertheless, in Judaea the followers of Jesus remained uneasily in the synagogues for several years after the resurrection, at least until the martyrdom of St Stephen. But the Acts of the Apostles tells us how non-Jews started joining the Christian movement – first of all the Samaritans, then the Roman centurion and the Ethiopian eunuch, then large numbers of Greeks in Antioch. What were these Gentile converts to do – join the synagogue? For that, they would have to be circumcised, stop eating pork, stay away from their work on Saturdays, and so on – no way could they do that! So they began setting up meeting places of their own, Christian churches, with all races welcome. St Paul was rejected in the synagogues, so he 'turned to the Gentiles', as he put it, and wrote letters to Greek Christian friends 'and the church which meets in your house'. Then these new converts began their mission to the world.

Acts

St Luke wrote his Gospel as a prelude to his other book: the Acts of the Apostles. The Christian mission which Jesus began when he sent out seventy followers, continued as the Church moved out into the Gentile world. Acts stops abruptly when Paul is a prisoner in Rome. This may be deliberate, to show that the mission of the Church can no longer be left to the first generation of Jewish converts, but continues to this day and includes every follower of Jesus, including you and me. Maybe you feel incapable of spreading the good news of Jesus on your own, and you are right. But you are not on your own; Jesus has given you his Holy Spirit to enable you, and the history of Christianity is the story of how the Holy Spirit spread to every corner of the globe.

All-age worship

On a map of the world, draw arrows showing how missionaries moved from one country to another, and still travel today.

Suggested hymns

God is working his purpose out; I the Lord of sea and sky; One shall tell another; The Kingdom of God is justice and joy.

Sixth Sunday after Trinity (Proper 9)   7 July
Second Service   **We Love Like God Loves**
Ps. 65 God in nature [70 Don't delay]; Gen. 29.1–20 Jacob loved Rachel; Mark 6.7–29 The death of John the Baptist

> *'Jacob loved Rachel ... so Jacob served seven years for Rachel, and they seemed to him but a few days because of the love he had for her.' Genesis 29.18, 20*

Falling in love

When two people fall in love, what a wonderful thing it is! They yearn for each other's presence, and feel incomplete unless they are together. They look for ways of pleasing each other, and enjoy being of service to one another. They are willing to climb mountains or swim oceans to prove how great their love is. The discovery that you are loved is astonishing, especially if you had never thought of yourself as particularly lovable. You ask yourself, 'What have I done to deserve this?' The answer, of course, is absolutely nothing. Love is never given because you have earned it; that's got nothing to do with it. It comes out of the blue, simply because your lover can't help loving you.

Jacob and Rachel

We see a wonderful example of human love in the Old Testament story of Jacob and Rachel. Jacob was talking with some shepherds, when Rachel came to the well to draw water for her father's flock to drink. It was love at first sight – Jacob rolled away the stone which was covering the well, and helped Rachel to water her sheep. Then he kissed her, and wept aloud. This was remarkable in the days when most marriages were arranged by the parents without the couple ever having met each other. So Rachel took Jacob home and told her dad. But he was a mercenary old so-and-so, and asked for the bride price; Jacob had no money, so they agreed that he could work for seven years to earn it. In one of the most beautiful phrases in the Bible, it says that 'Jacob loved Rachel ... so Jacob served seven years for Rachel, and they seemed to him but a few days because of the love he had for her.' Aaaah! The course of true love never does run smooth, though, and at the end of that time, her father tricked Jacob into marrying his older daughter first; so Jacob worked another seven years so that he could marry his first love. He certainly earned his bride, but she did nothing to earn her husband. They both learnt the hard way that love is given willingly; it can never be deserved. But our response to being loved is to try to become a little more deserving of it; even if it means working your fingers to the bone for 14 years.

Families

Perhaps that's why God made two sorts of people, male and female, and put us into families, to learn what love means. It's easy to fall in love; staying in love and growing in love is very demanding. Husband and wife find plenty of jobs that need doing around the house, even when they'd rather flop onto the sofa. Asking whether your partner deserves your love is a no-no; marvelling that you are loved and chosen is essential. Parents don't stop to ask whether the children deserve the sacrifices they make for them. Young children take it for granted that they are loved because they are lovable; later we begin to realize how much our parents did for us. Then the children start trying to be helpful to show how grateful they are. Love is never deserved. But our response to being loved is to try to become a little more deserving of it.

God's love

Human love is one of God's greatest inventions. In it, God has given us the deepest pleasure and a transcendent joy. Through being loved, we learn that however unworthy we are, we are all lovable. And that prepares us to understand what the Bible means when it says that God loves us. None of us can earn God's favour. When we realize that, nevertheless, God loves us because his heart is filled to overflowing with love for all his creatures, our whole world changes. Realizing that we are, after all, lovable, gives us self-esteem, the lack of which had been holding us back from loving other people. Discovering that God loves the undeserving fills us with a desire to do things for God, to show him how grateful we are for his love. Wonderful as the experience is of falling in love with another human being like Jacob and Rachel, I think God gave us this astonishing ability to love for a purpose. We love like God loves. Experiencing human love is the only way we can understand how God loves us. In that case, too, love is never deserved. But our response to being loved is to try to become a little more deserving of it.

Suggested hymns

Lord of all hopefulness; Love divine, all loves excelling; O Lord my God, when I in awesome wonder; The Lord's my shepherd.

Seventh Sunday after Trinity (Proper 10)   14 July
Principal Service   **When I Needed a Neighbour**
(*Continuous*): Amos 7.7–17 The plumbline: judgement on the city; Ps. 82 Justice; *or* (*Related*): Deut. 30.9–14 The word is near you; Ps. 25.1–10 Truth and guidance; Col. 1.1–14 Prayer, faith and works; Luke 10.25–37 The good Samaritan

> '*But a Samaritan while travelling came near him; and when he saw him, he was moved with pity.*' *Luke 10.33*

Jewish history

The hero of the story which Jesus told was a good Samaritan. Now that's astonishing! To understand why, you need to know a little history.

(Voice from the congregation) Oh, not again! History is so boring! (Reply from the pulpit) I find history fascinating, and I don't think you can understand Jesus and his teaching without putting them in historical context.
(Voice) Well, get on with it. But I'm timing you!

Two nations

The area we now call 'the Holy Land' was occupied for hundreds of years by a jumble of squabbling tribes, probably all closely related to each other. It's much more satisfying to hate your cousin than a total stranger! Two tribes, Judah and Benjamin, occupied the south of the country, and under King David they made Jerusalem their capital. Ten other tribes settled in the north and east. David persuaded the ten northern tribes to sign a covenant with him, and during his reign and that of his son Solomon, they were one nation based in Jerusalem, though with many other temples around the country. After Solomon's death, they split into two nations, the ten northern tribes calling themselves Israel and making their capital in the city of Samaria.

Post-exilic

Both the southern and northern kingdoms were at the mercy of the people of Mesopotamia – what we now call Iraq. The northern tribes, Israel, were defeated by the Iraqis in 722 BC; the leaders were deported to the Assyrian capital of Assur and absorbed into the Assyrian population; the rag, tag and bobtail of Israel stayed behind, and a mix of Syrians and Assyrians moved in with them, gradually intermarrying. Meanwhile, the Assyrian capital had moved to Babylon, and in 587 BC the southern kingdom of Judah was defeated by the Babylonians, and their leaders taken into exile there. Forty years later they returned to Jerusalem and started to rebuild. They dreamt that the mixed-race people in the north, whose capital was still in Samaria, could join them to recreate the United Kingdom of Israel and Judah with its capital in Jerusalem. They therefore gathered the Scriptures and legends of the northern tribes and merged them with their own, rewriting them to suggest that the Jerusalem Temple had always been the only valid centre of worship for all twelve tribes.

Samaritans

Most of the northerners weren't interested, and remained a separate group called the Samaritans. They recognized the five books of Moses as Scripture, and in many respects were quite similar to the Jews. But their independence made them an ideal hate-figure. We always need a scapegoat for our troubles, and now you can see why the Jews and Samaritans, though they were close neighbours, absolutely detested each other.

A 'good' Samaritan?

So when Jesus told a story about a Jew who fell among thieves, and was ignored by a Jewish priest and a Jewish Levite, but saved by one of the hated Samaritans, you can imagine how appalled his Jewish hearers were. To them, the words 'good Samaritan' were a contradiction in terms! And then to be told that the Samaritans were their neighbours, whom they should love as much as they loved themselves – it made them choke with fury. But it's true, isn't it? Anyone can love people who are 'just like us' – to love people who are just that little bit different, but your traditional rivals and sworn enemies – that's hard. Yet Jesus taught that the commandments to love God and your neighbour are the overriding rules – 'There is no other commandment greater than these.' So if you live an apparently moral and upright life, but can't bring yourself to love someone who's in need, just because they are different, the rest counts for nothing. 'When I needed a neighbour, were you there?' sings the hymn. 'For the name and the colour and the creed won't matter ...' So fill in the blanks for yourself. If a Frenchman needs your help, will you give it to him? Or a German, or a Black, or a Muslim, or someone who has been in prison, or the annoying family who live next door? Because that's the acid test; all other claims to be a good person pale into insignificance compared with this one, searching, question: 'When I needed a neighbour, were you there?'

All-age worship

On Post-it™ Notes describe groups of people you dislike. Stick the notes onto a 'Prayer Tree' labelled, 'Lord, help us to be good neighbours'.

Suggested hymns

A new commandment I give unto you; Hark, my soul, it is the Lord; Love is his word, love is his way; When I needed a neighbour, were you there?

Seventh Sunday after Trinity (Proper 10)   14 July
Second Service   **Jacob in Crisis**
Ps. 77 Remembering the past; Gen. 32.9–30 Wrestling Jacob;
Mark 7.1–23 Tradition

> *'Jacob called the place Peniel, saying, "For I have seen God face to face, and yet my life is preserved."' Genesis 32.30*

Crises

How should you behave in a crisis? Many types of crisis can happen in our lives. Some happen at work, when you have a row with your colleagues; or you are turned down for promotion, or – heaven forbid – you lose your job and spend a long time looking for another. Other crisis times happen in our personal relationships. Maybe you have a falling-out with your family or one of your close friends. Perhaps you have let them down, and feel they don't trust and respect you any more. Thirdly, you may have a health crisis. There are new pains where you have never felt them before; or an ongoing condition suddenly gets worse, and your GP sends you for tests and X-rays. When it comes to the crunch, we are often surprised by the depth of our fear, and can't decide what to do next. Where do we look for answers? Well, today's first reading from the book of Genesis, the very beginning of the Bible, might be 'a very good place to start'.

Jacob and Esau

Jacob's crisis was of his own making. He had cheated his brother Esau out of his birthright and his father's blessing. The rivals went their own ways, and both prospered. But Jacob was always afraid that Esau would come back for revenge; and now he was on his way, leading a force of 400 men. What should Jacob do? At first, he flew into a flurry of hyperactivity. He sent a deputation carrying presents to his brother, hoping Esau might forgive him. He divided his tribe in two, so that if one half was destroyed, the other might live to fight another day. He mouthed a quick prayer, no time for more. Yet Jacob's head of steam was rapidly approaching the 'Don't panic!' level. So he sent everyone away, hoping to calm down. This is his big moment; if he gets it wrong tomorrow, he's finished.

Wrestling Jacob

All night, Jacob wrestled with a mysterious figure. Who was his opponent – a man, or an angel? Modern psychologists might say he was wrestling with another side of his own personality. But Jacob felt that he had been wrestling with God. God told Moses that 'no one shall see me and live'. But Jacob called the place Peniel, which means, 'the face of God'. 'For I have seen God face to face,' he said, 'and yet I survived.' Our relationship with God is always a bit of a wrestling match. Is God really there in your moment of crisis? Does he really love you, because if so, why did he let this happen? But God doesn't deal in certainties – if you could be certain about the future, you would never learn to trust him. Faith only comes by wrestling with doubt. So Jacob needed the inner struggle in the dark hours, to give him strength to face the challenges of the day ahead. President Roosevelt said, when all seemed black in the Great Depression, 'the only thing we have to fear is fear itself'.

Bless me

At one point Jacob seemed to have his mysterious opponent in a headlock. What should he do, now that he'd got God where he wanted him? What would *you* do, if you thought you had killed off the idea that he's a God of love, or even the very possibility of God existing? Well, Jacob made a sensible choice. He said to God, 'I *will* not let you go, unless you *bless me*.' He traded his apparent victory for the opportunity to receive God's blessing.

Growth

Jacob wasn't disappointed. God blessed him in the most practical way possible: he helped Jacob to grow into a stronger personality. That was shown by the humble and generous way he treated his brother when they met. Every crisis holds within it the seeds of new birth. Stress forces us to look at ourselves honestly, to admit our faults and thank God for our virtues. We reassess our priorities. We make more realistic plans for the future. When the next crisis hits you, don't give in, and don't give up on God. Hold tightly to your faith, feeble though it may be, and trust God to see you through. Jesus almost lost his faith on the cross – 'My God, why have you forsaken me?' – but eventually he won through till he could say triumphantly, 'It is finished.' God will always bless you, if you ask him. Can you struggle with life's crises, when you have to, and come out the other side stronger and wiser? Wrestle with God – that's what to do in a crisis. And don't let him go till he blesses you!

Suggested hymns

Come, O thou Traveller unknown; Here, O my Lord, I see thee face to face; O God of Bethel, by whose hand; O Love, that wilt not let me go.

Eighth Sunday after Trinity (Proper 11)   21 July
(Eve of St Mary Magdalene)
Principal Service   At the Barbecue

(*Continuous*): Amos 8.1–12 Justice for the needy; Ps. 52 Justice for the needy; *or* (*Related*): Gen. 18.1–10a Abraham welcomes three guests; Ps. 15 Justice; Col. 1.15–28 Christ the head of the Church; Luke 10.38–42 Martha and Mary, works and prayer

> *'Martha ... had a sister named Mary, who sat at the Lord's feet and listened to what he was saying. But Martha was distracted by her many tasks.' Luke 10.39–40*

At the barbecue

Some well-meaning people were giving a barbecue, and invited their friend the vicar. One of them, however, waited until the clergyman had drunk a couple of glasses of wine, and then launched an attack on religion. 'Religion has caused most of the suffering in the world,' said the sceptic. 'It's religion, and specifically the monotheistic religions – Judaism, Islam and Christianity – which make people intolerant. Religious people put the stress on sin, and then call for vicious punishments for people who break their invented rules.' Fortunately, the vicar was still sober enough to make a courteous reply. Basically, he said, he agreed. But nobody, religious or irreligious, can ignore the need for morality, he continued, which is essentially about the way we treat each other. If we behave badly towards other people we can do a great deal of harm. So some guidance is needed to show people a better way of relating to others. Hinduism and Buddhism agree with the monotheists on that, and so do many humanists.

Laws

At first, moral guidance was given in the form of laws. Justice was administered by kings and tribal chiefs; but unless they were given some guidelines, their decisions could be very unjust. So early law-givers aimed to set a limit, which people who sought revenge must not exceed – no more than one eye can be demanded from someone who has taken your eye out, and a tooth for a tooth. But these decisions were made in the context of society at the time, and can't possibly be applied to the very different society today, without modification. For instance, both Muslims and Christians have to decide what to do with ancient Scriptures which recommend stoning to death as the punishment for adultery. Most Christians and, until recently, most Muslims have said that these were an attempt to deal with moral anarchy in a primitive society, and cannot be applied literally today. But both religions are at risk of being hijacked by extremists who call for a return to the 'old religion', thereby putting many sensible people off the idea of religion altogether.

Love

Jesus said that these laws had been superseded by the commandment to love your neighbour as yourself. Love is at the heart of all true religion; yet many people who call themselves religious are narrow and intolerant. This isn't a new problem. Jesus had far more trouble with the people who considered themselves to be religious, than with the actual sinners. The Pharisees interpreted the Scriptures literally; forbad practices which other people thought did no harm; and were intolerant of those who had a more liberal approach to religion than they did; St Paul, too, wrote many an angry letter, rebuking Jewish Christians, who wanted to impose obedience to *all* the laws of the Old Testament upon non-Jewish Christians, who lived in a totally different social context. 'Love does no wrong to a neighbour,' he wrote; 'therefore, love is the fulfilling of the law.' 'Sin will have no dominion over you, since you are not under law but under grace.' The trouble is, said the vicar at the barbecue, that many so-called Christians haven't begun to understand what grace means. If you know that Jesus loves you, God's love will flow through you into other people, and your heart will lead you into good behaviour, without any need for written rules. That, in summary, was how the vicar answered his critic.

Martha and Mary

There's a lovely story in the Gospels which points out clearly the difference between law and grace. Jesus went to dinner with two sisters, called Martha and Mary. Mary sat at Jesus's feet, soaking up his words and responding with all the love in her heart. Martha was so busy preparing the meal, that she had no time to listen. Jesus said to her, 'Martha, Martha, you are worried and distracted by many things; there is need of only one thing. Mary has chosen the better part, which will not be taken away from her.' Martha was so absorbed in doing the right thing, that she was intolerant of her sister. Mary let her heart lead her, and Jesus said this was the one thing necessary if we are to please God. We must all let grace, not law, rule our behaviour.

All-age worship

Draw on the back of one hand the stone tablets on which the Ten Commandments were written, and on the other a heart. Which will you follow when faced with what decisions?

Suggested hymns

Love is his word, love is his way; O love divine, how sweet thou art; Seek ye first the kingdom of God; When we walk with the Lord.

Eighth Sunday after Trinity (Proper 11)   21 July
Second Service   **You Got to Have a Dream**
Ps. 81 I rescued you; Gen. 41.1–16, 25–37 Interpreting dreams; 1 Cor. 4.8–13 Fools for Christ; *Gospel at Holy Communion*: John 4.31–35 Ripe for harvesting

> *'Joseph answered Pharaoh, "It is not I; God will give Pharaoh a favourable answer."' Genesis 41.16*

Dreams

A song from the musical *South Pacific* tunefully assures us that we must dream, otherwise how are we going to have a dream come true? You probably know the song I mean, but I'm not going to attempt to sing it to you. Richard Wagner, in his opera *The Mastersingers of Nüremberg*, says that poetry is nothing but the interpretations of dreams. So when we read in the Old Testament about God giving Joseph the power to interpret Pharaoh's dreams, we should look to see whether this is a unique and miraculous gift to Joseph alone, or whether something of the sort might be available to everyone.

Revealing the subconscious

Of course, we are using the word 'dream' to cover several types of experience. First, there's what happens to you when you fall asleep. The sleeping brain is often said to work through the choices and ideas that have been absorbing it during the waking hours. Sigmund Freud wrote that 'The interpretation of dreams is the royal road to a knowledge of the unconscious activities of the mind.' Skilled psychoanalysts can listen to what you tell them you have been dreaming about, and tell you a lot about your subconscious. Sometimes your dreams reveal your deepest fears, the things you don't dare to talk about while you are awake. Or they may be wish-fulfilment dreams, revealing what you hope will happen. Usually, dreams make use of symbolism, and a skilled interpreter will help you to work out what the symbols mean. Freud also said, 'Dreams are often most profound when they seem the most crazy.' Christians should look honestly at their subconscious motives, to make sure they are not deluding themselves, by pretending to do things in order to help other people, when really they are doing them for selfish reasons. Doing something which makes you feel what a virtuous person you are, may not in fact be any assistance to the people you are pretending to serve. Yet God may put dreams into your sleeping mind to guide you; St Patrick wrote an evening prayer including the lines:

Let your angels, God supreme,
Tell us truth dressed as a dream.

[St Patrick's prayer translated by Michael Counsell, from *2000 Years of Prayer* (Canterbury Press)]

Revealing the future

Less often, a sleeping dream may be caused by something outside the dreamer's mind. We shouldn't be surprised when bereaved people dream about the one who has died. If there is life after death, the deceased may actually want to communicate with us, to reassure us that everything is all right, and help us to look forward to meeting again in a very different world. God is the creator of time, so he may be said to sit outside time looking in, and all times are 'now' to the God of eternity. So God may occasionally wish us to know what will happen to us, so that we can prepare ourselves – and what better way to communicate this than in a dream? There are many accounts of people dreaming of possible accidents and calamities, and regarding it as a warning not to go to the place they dreamt about. Why, then, doesn't everybody hear these warnings? Perhaps because God *is* speaking to us all, but most of us aren't listening. So Pharaoh's dreams about the seven years of prosperity followed by seven years of hunger may have been sent by God, who also inspired Joseph to interpret them and warn Pharaoh what to do about it. Joseph said, 'It is not I; God will give Pharaoh a favourable answer.'

Daydreams

The third type of dream, and I think the most important, is the daydream. You may be accused of wasting time, but often the daydreamer is scanning the possibilities lying ahead. The lover dreams of the beloved, and the possibility of winning their love and getting married. The visionary reformer dreams of creating a more just society. They may be tempted to lose hope, thinking that it was just an idle dream. Only if they can be persuaded to take their dreams seriously will they build up the courage to try and bring them to pass. So God may be the giver of seemingly impossible daydreams, also. Arthur O'Shaughnessy wrote:

> We are the music makers,
> And we are the dreamers of dreams ...
> Yet we are the movers and shakers
> Of the world for ever, it seems.

Poetic symbolism is important, and we all need to dream, in the sense of having ideals to strive for. Otherwise, how can we know the joy of seeing our dreams come true?

Suggested hymns

As the deer pants for the water; God that madest earth and heaven; Nearer, my God, to thee; There is a land of pure delight.

Ninth Sunday after Trinity (Proper 12) 28 July
Principal Service **The Prairie Tortoise**
(*Continuous*): Hos. 1.2–10 Hosea's family; Ps. 85 Forgiveness; *or* (*Related*): Gen. 18.20–32 Abraham's prayer for Sodom; Ps. 138 Prayer for grace; Col. 2.6–15 [16–19] Resurrection with Christ; Luke 11.1–13 Our Father

> *'Father, hallowed be your name.*
> *Your kingdom come.*
> *Give us each day our daily bread.*
> *And forgive us our sins,*
> *for we ourselves forgive everyone indebted to us.*
> *And do not bring us to the time of trial.'* Luke 11.2–4

The Prairie Tortoise

One Sunday, a little girl asked her father, 'Daddy, what's a prairie tortoise?' 'I have no idea,' he replied. 'Why?' 'Because our teacher in Sunday school', answered the girl, 'said she was going to tell us about Jesus and the prairie tortoise.' The prayer which Jesus taught to us is usually known as the 'Our Father', or 'the Lord's Prayer'. That's what the Sunday school lesson was about!

Two versions

This prayer occurs in St Matthew's Gospel, in the Sermon on the Mount, and also in St Luke's Gospel, in a much shorter form – it's St Luke's version that we have heard today. Most people think the short version was the one that Jesus originally preached, and later, either Jesus expanded it to explain the pithy sayings of the original, or St Matthew realized it would need amplifying as the Christian religion moved out to new audiences who were unfamiliar with Jewish phraseology. The words which most of us know by heart are from one of the earliest translations of the Bible into English, long before the Authorized Version. They are the foundation of faith for many Christians, even young children, but we need the modern translations to understand what they mean. St Luke's version summarizes in 37 words the heart of what Jesus taught about prayer, and the relationship between human beings and our Creator. Yet the words are only there to guide us into wordless prayer. Mahatma Gandhi said, 'Prayer is not asking. It is a longing of the soul. It is better to have a heart without words than words without a heart.'

Father

First, Jesus teaches us that God loves us like a father; and that we should trust God as children trust their parents. We pray that God's 'name', a symbol for his reputation and nature, may be worshipped or hallowed, which means regarded as holy: 'Father, hallowed be your name.'

Kingdom

Next we pray, 'Your kingdom come'. The kingdom of God isn't a place – it's already there in every heart where Jesus is obeyed as our king. 'The kingdom of God is within you,' as Jesus said – or it could be translated as 'among you'. But the consequences of obeying God are that our selfishness is overcome, and injustice is banished from the world. That hasn't happened yet, but we are working towards it.

Bread

One of the major injustices in the world is that some people are starving while others eat too much. So when we pray, 'Give us each day our daily bread', we are asking that we ourselves may have the basic necessities of life, and also that the earth's resources may be more fairly distributed to those in greatest need.

Forgiveness

The reason our society is so unjust is because everybody is so selfish. This causes a breakdown in the relationships between human beings, between us and the natural world, and between us and God. To put this right, we have to learn to forgive, and to accept forgiveness. So we ask God to 'forgive us our sins, for we ourselves forgive everyone indebted to us'. That doesn't mean that we have to *feel* forgiveness emotionally, that would be too much to ask. But we can *practise* forgiveness without feeling it.

Testing times

It's easy to love God and our neighbour when things are going well for us; but in an imperfect world there are going to be some difficult times, when our faith is tested to the limit. So we ask God to give us the strength to endure them. That's what is meant by the words misleadingly translated, 'lead us not into temptation' – God would never deliberately tempt us, or 'bring us to the time of trial'. In a world full of sinners, testing times come to everybody, but if we pray, we may come through them with our trust in God made stronger by the experience. Jesus knew that we need to pray more often and more urgently; that's why these words are there in 'the prayer he taught us'.

All-age worship

Write a version of the Lord's Prayer on a large paper, and learn it by heart. Then write after each phrase, 'Especially ...', and add names or situations you should pray for.

Suggested hymns

'Forgive our sins as we forgive'; O God of Bethel, by whose hand; The kingdom of God is justice and joy; Thy kingdom come, O God.

Ninth Sunday after Trinity (Proper 12)   28 July
Second Service   **Jacob and Sons**
Ps. 88 Let my prayer come before you; Gen. 42.1–25 Joseph tests his brothers; 1 Cor. 10.1–24 Examples for us; *Gospel at Holy Communion*: Matt. 13.24–30 [31–43] Weeds

> *'Alas, we are paying the penalty for what we did to our brother; we saw his anguish when he pleaded with us, but we would not listen. That is why this anguish has come upon us.' Genesis 42.21*

Jacob and Sons

In Andrew Lloyd-Webber's musical, *Joseph and his Amazing Technicolor™ Dream Coat,* the twelve brothers are introduced as 'Jacob and Sons'. The idea is to compare them to a family firm, and to fix in the mind of the audience that they are all brothers. The young men themselves needed reminding of this too, because they were always falling out with each other. In particular, they had sold their brother Joseph as a slave. When they next meet him in Egypt he is a VIP, and they don't recognize him. He realizes that their bitter rivalry won't be overcome by reading them a lecture – they have to learn the lesson for themselves. So he tricks them by placing a valuable silver cup in Benjamin's sack, and threatens to make him a slave as a punishment for allegedly stealing it. Belatedly the brothers realize that deep down they love each other and need each other; they are reconciled, and live happily ever after. A charming story, obviously told so as to emphasize the importance of brotherly love.

Twelve tribes

But the story goes deeper than that. These brothers are the ancestors of the twelve tribes of Israel: Reuben, Simeon, Levi, Judah, Dan, Naphthali, Gad, Asher, Issachar, Zebulun, Joseph and Benjamin. Twelve brothers, twelve tribes. What a coincidence! So perhaps this story was repeated to remind the twelve tribes, in later years, of the danger of squabbling. We are all related, is the message: united we stand, divided we fall. An important political teaching. I'm leaving open the question whether or not the story is historically true – we can never be sure with these old legends. That doesn't really matter. What counts is the message which comes out of it, about brotherly love, within families, between tribes, between races and even between nations. We are all brothers and sisters, somewhere back in history: united we stand, divided we fall. Just like Jacob and Sons. The Old Testament writers may not have taken it that far – all they were interested in was unity between the northern and southern kingdoms after the return from exile. But the same principle applies in the United Nations today.

Twelve apostles

There's another link, which is often ignored in Christian preaching. Why did Jesus choose twelve apostles? Was it because he was thinking of the ancestors of the twelve tribes of Israel, namely, the twelve sons of Jacob? Just as they were the beginning and source of the twelve tribes, so the twelve men whom Jesus chose were the origin and foundation of the Christian Church, the New Israel. And it was equally important that they should stop squabbling, and be united. The churches they founded also needed to be united – perhaps Jesus was stressing the importance of brotherly and sisterly love between Christians. Different denominations, in different continents – we all spring from a common origin; we need each other and depend on each other – united we stand, divided we fall!

Women apostles

If you only take away from this sermon these three points, you will have learnt something: the importance of unity:

1 in family life,
2 in world affairs and
3 in the Church.

But I want to end with a controversial suggestion. Why did Jesus only choose men to be apostles, not women? Actually, apostle is a misleading word. It's Greek for a missionary. Many apostles are mentioned in the New Testament who weren't members of the Twelve, especially missionaries like Paul and Barnabas. They were not autocratic leaders, rather they were servants of the Church. The Twelve are usually referred to simply as 'the Twelve'; only in a few places are they described as 'the Twelve, who were also called apostles'. To emphasize that they were missionaries and servants, just like Paul. Of course the original twelve had to be men, because they were the origin of the New Israel, symbolizing the sons of Jacob. But there were many women among the early leadership in the Church: Mary Magdalene was the first to be sent as a missionary witness to the resurrection; and St Paul writes about one woman, Julia, who was 'prominent among the apostles'. The first time bishops are mentioned is when Paul writes to the church in Philippi, 'with their bishops and deacons'. In other words, the many 'overseers' in this tiny congregation were *all* called bishops – including Lydia, the merchant of purple cloth, in whose spacious house they met. If you want to stone me for propagating this heresy, please wait till after the service!

Suggested hymns

Blest are the pure in heart; Christ is the King! O friends rejoice; God of freedom, God of justice; In Christ there is no east or west.

Tenth Sunday after Trinity (Proper 13)   4 August
Principal Service   **Wisdom and Foolishness**
(*Continuous*): Hos. 11.1–11 Fatherhood of God; Ps. 107.1–9, 43 Guidance; *or* (*Related*): Eccles. 1.2, 12–14; 2.18–23 Vanity and wisdom; Ps. 49.1–12 Wisdom and death; Col. 3.1–11 Selfishness or unity; Luke 12.13–21 The rich fool

> *'[The rich man thought,] "I will say to my soul, 'Soul, you have ample goods laid up for many years; relax, eat, drink, be merry.'" But God said to him, "You fool! This very night your life is being demanded of you."' Luke 12.19–20*

Look around

Look around you. No, I don't mean here in church, I mean, look at the whole world situation. A few years ago, politicians and economists assured us that the world economy was all sorted out. Then we had the beginning of a recession. Queen Elizabeth was at an event at the London School of Economics, and gently asked a senior lecturer, 'Why didn't anyone notice?' Sometimes we think we are so wise, and imagine we have got the world under control. Then suddenly we realize that we are nothing like as clever as we thought we were. As Robin Goodfellow said in Shakespeare's *A Midsummer Night's Dream*, 'Lord, what fools these mortals be!'

Foolishness

The Bible has a lot to say about foolishness, and also wisdom, which is the opposite. Jesus told a story about a rich man who decided to tear down his barns, without calculating that he might be dead before he had time to build new ones, so leaving his children with nothing. God said to him, 'You fool!' It's sheer vanity which inflates us with the delusion that we know everything, and stops us taking sensible precautions based on the certainty that one day we shall have to die.

Vanity

'Vanity' is another word used in the Old Testament. But there it doesn't mean conceitedness. Literally it means 'a puff of wind', a triviality, mere nothingness. In the book we call Ecclesiastes, the Teacher says 'Vanity of vanities ... vanity of vanities! All is vanity. What do people gain from all the toil at which they toil under the sun? ... I saw all the deeds that are done under the sun; and see, all is vanity and a chasing after wind.'

Wisdom

In the Bible, the opposite of vanity is wisdom. Wisdom is insight into what really matters in life. In particular, it's wise to understand that becoming filthy rich never makes you happy. Wisdom is understanding the best way to live; it isn't the same as knowledge. A wise person recently said, 'Knowledge is knowing that tomatoes are fruit. Wisdom is knowing not to put them in a fruit salad!' The Bible tells us that 'the fear of the Lord is the beginning of wisdom'. Perhaps 'reverence' would be a better translation than 'fear'. If we remember always that God is wiser than we are, we shall put our trust in God, not in bankers, or governments.

Capitalism

No, there's nothing wrong with working hard so as to earn enough to feed, clothe and house your family, though it's not good for them to keep them in the lap of luxury. If you gain more than the bare necessities, you have a very heavy responsibility to use your money wisely. For a start, a tenth of your income should be given through the Church and other charities to do God's work. Seeking a modest amount of pleasure, and thanking God for it, is good. Then rich people should invest their money in such a way that it provides work and an income for as many other people as possible. That's how capitalism began: using your wealth so as to help others to improve their lot. But recently we seem to have lost sight of that, and instead capitalism has become a form of gambling. Bankers and investment agents put other people's money into one business after another, and then take it out again and invest it somewhere else, without any thought of how other people are hurt or benefited by their actions. Businesses aren't owned by people who care about the people who are employed in them, but by remote multinational corporations.

In God we trust

American coins carry the slogan, 'In God we trust'. We shouldn't trust only in governments or bankers or the growing value of our money. Like the rich fool, we may have to learn the hard way that these things don't last. But if we have the wisdom to put our trust in the only one who will never fail us, in God, in Christ, then we shall be truly blessed

All-age worship

Draw up a budget of how you think God would like you to spend your pocket money.

Suggested hymns

God of grace and God of glory; He that is down need fear no fall; Put thou thy trust in God; Take my life, and let it be.

Tenth Sunday after Trinity (Proper 13) 4 August
Second Service **Modern Prophets**
Ps. 107.1–32 Thanksgiving for deliverance; Gen. 50.4–26 Deaths of Jacob and Joseph; 1 Cor. 14.1–19 Tongues and prophecy; *Gospel at Holy Communion*: Mark 6.45–52 Walking on water

> *'Those who prophesy speak to other people for their building up and encouragement and consolation.'* 1 Corinthians 14.3

A broadcaster

A television producer was praised as 'a prophet for our time'. 'I'm a broadcaster,' he protested. 'That's all. A teller of tales. The primary thing is to get people interested in the things that matter.' But isn't that a definition of the prophet's task? Prophets in the Bible spoke out about corruption and injustice, trying to turn their hearer's attention away from trivialities. They were needed then, and they are essential today also, if we are to have a just and honest world. Obviously broadcasters and journalists have an important role in this, but it's something every Christian should be concerned about.

Old Testament prophets

Moses was described as a prophet, because he rebuked evil-doers and led his people in the way of the Lord. Women could be prophets, too: Moses' sister Miriam was a prophet because she sang a song by the Red Sea, a poetess; and so was Deborah, one of the rulers of the Israelites before the first kings were appointed by the prophet Samuel. Samuel anointed Saul, then rebuked him for putting his lust for riches ahead of obedience to God, and anointed David in his place. But David had Uriah the Hittite murdered so that he could marry Uriah's wife Bathsheba. So God sent Nathan the prophet, who told David a story about a poor man who possessed only one ewe-lamb, and a rich man who stole it from him. Like the parables of Jesus, this story ended with a question. David answered that the rich man deserved to die for the injustice, and Nathan replied, unforgettably, 'You are the man!'

Prophets in Israel

After David and Solomon, the kingdom split into two. In the northern kingdom of Israel, famous prophets continued to denounce wickedness and call the people back to the worship of the one true God. Elijah called down fire on Mount Carmel, triumphing over the prophets of Baal, and condemned the immorality of Ahab and Jezebel. Elisha, who lived in a commune called 'the sons of the prophets', denounced Ahab's descendants and anointed Jehu to found a new dynasty – like many prophets, he was deeply involved in politics. Amos criticized the rich people who did nothing to help the poor:

> they sell the righteous for silver,
>   and the needy for a pair of sandals –
> they ... trample the head of the poor into the dust of the earth,
>   and push the afflicted out of the way;
> ... they lay themselves down ... on garments taken in pledge;
> and in the house of their God they drink wine
>   bought with fines they imposed.

Prophets of Judah

You see how the same sins continue today, and how much we need prophets to rebuke them? Meanwhile, in the southern kingdom of Judah, prophets began to form their oracles into poetry: Isaiah,

Micah, Jeremiah and Ezekiel wrote books which are still relevant today. They also began to act out their parables: Jeremiah, for instance, smashed an earthenware pot to show that if any nation behaves unjustly, God can always, like a potter, start over again to create another people who will be more obedient. Tacked onto the end of the scroll of Isaiah are the writings of two other prophets whom we call 'Second Isaiah' and 'Third Isaiah'. They rebuked the Jewish exiles in Babylon, and those who returned. Their sin was not immorality but faithlessness – they thought God had no future purpose for them, and sank into depression.

New Testament prophets

Jesus was called 'the prophet from Nazareth'. Like many prophets, he spoke about the future, but prophecy isn't fortune-telling. Jesus told his contemporaries that if they continued with their narrow nationalism, the Romans were bound to destroy Jerusalem, which in fact happened 40 years later. So when St Paul describes prophecy as one of the gifts of the Spirit, he didn't mean *foretelling* future events – prophecy is better described as *'forth-telling'* – proclaiming God's view on the events of today. St Paul was writing about inspired, and relevant, preaching, unafraid to address contemporary issues.

Preaching today

How much we need that sort of discussion among Christians today! Aid agencies are often criticized for getting involved in politics, when they campaign against unjust trading patterns, and against global businesses which pay no taxes in the poor countries they exploit; against oppression of women, overpopulation, global warming, illiteracy, poor water supplies, and lack of medical treatment. Yet giving aid is only Elastoplast® unless it also addresses the causes of poverty. God condemns the unjust behaviour of power blocks, nations, organizations and individuals today. Are you willing to speak prophetically for him, whenever you have a chance?

Suggested hymns

Disposer supreme, and Judge of the earth; God has spoken to his people; Judge Eternal, throned in splendour; O God of earth and altar.

Eleventh Sunday after Trinity (Proper 14)

11 August

Principal Service   **Almsgiving**

(*Continuous*): Isa. 1.1, 10–20 Justice is better than sacrifice;
Ps. 50.1–8, 23–24 Covenant; *or* (*Related*): Gen. 15.1–6 Promise
to Abram and his faith; Ps. 33.12–22 Faith; Heb. 11.1–3, 8–16
Abraham's faith; Luke 12.32–40 Treasure in heaven

> '*Sell your possessions, and give alms.' Luke 12.33*

Treasure in heaven

In a *Punch* cartoon, a lady is giving tea to the vicar, and praising her domestic servant. 'She's an absolute *treasure*,' says the aristocrat. 'I do hope she will be able to work for me in the next life.' The vicar comments, 'When the gospel speaks of having your treasure in heaven, I don't think that's quite what it means!' He was right. Your 'treasure' is whatever is most important to you. If you have some precious possessions in your house, you will worry constantly about being burgled. In that case, owning expensive items is more important to you than anything else. Material possessions can easily become more important than God, in which case, goodbye to morality! There's no reason for being loving and honest, if being deceitful makes you richer. Whereas if your relationship with God is the most precious thing in your life, no thief can rob you of that. It's what Jesus called 'an unfailing treasure in heaven, where no thief comes near and no moth destroys. For where your treasure is, there your heart will be also.'

Monasticism

Jesus also said, 'Sell your possessions.' He exaggerated, because he knew that rich people wouldn't listen unless he spoke in striking phrases. Yet monks and nuns take this command literally. When the religious orders in the Middle Ages became worldly, St Francis, the son of a rich merchant in Assisi, recalled them to their ideals by literally giving away all he had inherited and living and dressing like a poor beggar. But this is not a recipe for every Christian. The economic order would collapse if the majority didn't remain, as Jesus said, 'in the world but not of the world'. To them, Jesus says, 'Give alms.'

Alms

This word, spelt A L M S, comes from a Greek word meaning compassion. It's related to the word we use in the chant, *Kyrie eleison,* meaning 'Lord, have mercy on us.' Almsgiving is giving some – not all – of your money, to people who are poorer than you are. But there's a problem with this. If you give to a solitary beggar on the street, it encourages them to become lazy, and tomorrow a dozen will be waiting for you. They will probably spin you a hard-luck story, then spend the money on drink or drugs. Some Christians have tried to draw a distinction between the deserving and undeserving poor. Unfortunately, you seldom meet the deserving poor, because they keep themselves to themselves. It's good to be generous to people whom you know to be genuinely needy, but they probably won't accept your help, because it's demeaning. There are subtle ways of helping people without insulting them, but it requires a great deal of thought. Get to know the *Big Issue* seller, encouraging him or her to move from the hostel into a bedsit, and helping them to find proper employment. You would do better helping the needy in non-financial ways, and giving your money to the Salvation Army. If beggars come to your doorstep, offer them a cup of tea, and invite them to earn a few pounds sweeping up leaves. And don't, whatever happens, ever expect to be thanked for your generosity: virtue is its own reward. Neither does God have a rewards-and-punishments balance sheet; 'treasure in heaven' means being certain that God loves you and the beggar equally, though neither of you deserves it.

Mental illness

But there's another problem. Most street-sleepers are there because of mental health problems. They may have an addictive personality, having wasted their money on drink and drugs. But breaking these habits takes a lot more counselling than is freely available in most towns. Someone writing to a newspaper expressed horror at seeing a down-and-out whipping his dog. A psychiatrist wrote in, explaining that this is typical – people with schizophrenia drive away those who love them, desperately trying to prove that your love is not dependent on their just deserts. The only way to help such people is to identify with them, and love them come what may – though probably not on your own. Then petition the government to provide more psychiatric help.

Humility

Being a Christian requires great humility. But we are all the same. Haven't you ever been difficult, just to test somebody's love for you? And isn't this why Jesus was crucified – because we can never quite believe that God loves us, until we have tested his tolerance to the limit? Identifying yourself with the dregs of society is what Jesus did; following his example, even a little, ensures your treasure in heaven.

All-age worship

Find out about local provision for the homeless, poor and addicted.

Suggested hymns

He that is down need fear no fall; O Lord of heaven and earth and sea; Will you come and follow me?; Will you let me be your servant?

Eleventh Sunday after Trinity (Proper 14)
11 August
Second Service **Now What's the Question?**
Ps. 108 Love as high as heaven [116 The cup of salvation];
Isa. 11.10—12.6 Return from exile; 2 Cor. 1.1–22 God's 'Yes';
Gospel at Holy Communion: Mark 7.24–30 The foreign mother

> *'The Son of God, Jesus Christ, whom we proclaimed among you ... was not "Yes and No"; but in him it is always "Yes". For in him every one of God's promises is a "Yes".' 2 Corinthians 1.19–20*

True love

'Darling, will you do something for me if I ask you?' 'The answer's yes, dear. Now what's the question?' That little dialogue is a sign of true love. If you really love someone, you will be anxious to please them, and your priority will be to seek what's best for them. What they ask you to do for them may possibly be inconvenient, or even unpleasant. But that's of secondary importance to the chance of making your loved one happy. So you say that you are eager to serve them, without waiting to find out what they want. When they tell you, you hurry off to do their will, without asking any questions. Well, there's one exception – you are allowed to ask, 'Are you absolutely sure that's what you want?' Not because you are trying to persuade them to change their minds, but helping to clarify their thinking, especially about what the effects will be of doing what they request, on them and on other people. The essence of true love is that no sacrifice is too great to make for the one you love.

Jesus is God's 'Yes'

St Paul was probably thinking about this when he wrote to his friends in Corinth that Jesus is God's 'Yes'. Paul had to postpone a promised visit to Corinth, and he's defending himself against any accusation that this proves him unreliable, vacillating between 'yes' and 'no' about doing what they ask him. But that leads him into a beautiful digression, in which he insists that God has no hesitation in giving us what we ask him for. Paul writes, 'The Son of God, Jesus Christ, whom we proclaimed among you ... was not "Yes and No"; but in him it is always "Yes". For in him every one of God's promises is a "Yes".' It's as though in our prayers we have been saying to God, 'Lord, will you do something for me if I ask you?' and God replies, 'The answer's yes. Now what's the question?'

The answer

When we pray, we ask God for guidance; for help in making decisions; for a pattern to copy in our living; to be loved; to be free from worry; for strength to undertake some difficult task. And Jesus is God's 'Yes' to all those questions. Jesus will guide us if we listen to him when we pray. He will help us to think through what the results of our decisions might be. He will show us that God is no remote despot, but that the love we see in Jesus is actually God's love for us. Knowing that we are loved will free us from worry about the future and guilt about the past. Knowing that Jesus is with us, and thinks us loveable, gives us the self-confidence to go ahead and succeed in things we thought were quite beyond our powers. To all these questions, Jesus is the answer, and the answer's 'Yes'. Nothing's too great a sacrifice for him to make on our behalf.

Here comes Mr Jordan

A marvellous film was made in 1941 called *Here comes Mr Jordan*. A prize fighter dies in a plane accident, but arrives in heaven many years earlier than he was expected, due to an administrative bungle. Mr Jordan, played by Claude Rains, is the heavenly supervisor who comes to sort this out, by finding another body for the dead man to inhabit. They choose a man whose wife and her lover are in the process of drowning him in his bath. When her husband reappears soon after, inhabited by the soul of the boxer, they are confounded. The reborn boxer starts training in his new body, so that he can defeat the rival champion. He sets off to do this, and Mr Jordan, who is beginning to seem more and more like Jesus Christ, asks him does he really want to go through that door, not knowing what might lie on the other side? Actually it's the wife and her lover who are waiting there to shoot him, which they do. The moral is that you should always be careful what you ask for, because you might not like it when you get it. Jesus answers 'Yes' to all our questions, but he hands us free will to ask for the wrong things, and gives them to us if we insist. All the more reason why we should ask for opportunities for self-sacrifice, as true lovers always do.

Suggested hymns

All ye who seek for sure relief; Father, hear the prayer we offer; O Lord, hear my prayer (Taizé); May the mind of Christ my Saviour.

Twelfth Sunday after Trinity (Proper 15)
18 August
Principal Service **Running the Race**
(*Continuous*): Isa. 5.1–7 The song of the vineyard; Ps. 80.1–2, 9–20 The vine; *or* (*Related*): Jer. 23.23–29 The word of God; Ps. 82 Justice; Heb. 11.29—12.2 Faith and perseverance; Luke 12.49–56 Interpreting the time

> *'Let us run with perseverance the race that is set before us.' Hebrews 12.1*

Sporting events

Sporting events are so exciting. Even if you know nothing about the sport you are watching, you can get quite carried away by the excitement of the crowd. Some will be supporting their own home-team; others will be trying to encourage competitors who aren't doing as well as they are capable of. Heartened by the cheering, the players or athletes will do their best, or possibly better than their best, even when they are out of breath and feel they can't go on. Runners can just see the judges standing by the tape at the finishing line, and nothing matters now except getting there before anyone else.

Arena

The writers of the New Testament were familiar with these sensations. The Olympic Games were just the most famous of the sporting events of the classical world; every city had some sort of competition, held in the local stadium. A 'stade' was a Greek furlong, 202 yards, and a stadium was an arena holding a circuit a furlong long. For important races, however, the finishing line might be in the middle of the city, so that the whole population could turn out to cheer the winner.

Hebrews

The writer of the Letter to the Hebrews used this as a metaphor for the Christian life. He wrote:

Since we are surrounded by so great a cloud of witnesses, let us also lay aside every weight and the sin that clings so closely, and let us run with perseverance the race that is set before us, looking to Jesus the pioneer and perfecter of our faith, who for the sake of the joy that was set before him endured the cross, disregarding its shame, and has taken his seat at the right hand of the throne of God.

He's already explained who the spectators are, since he's been speaking proudly of the heroes of the Old Testament, who bore witness to God despite opposition and suffering. These dead people are really alive, he says; we can't see them, but they can see us as we face the difficulties and discouragements of being a Christian.

Imagine yourself as a runner, he says, and these great heroes as the crowd willing you to win. In the twenty-first century, we'd add to our mental picture of the crowd the Christian saints down the ages, our childhood heroes, and even our loved ones who have died – they are all watching us and cheering us on. When you have a difficult decision to make, and feel utterly alone, remember that.

Sin

Athletes go into strict training and lose as much weight as they can, then strip off any unnecessary clothing which might get in the way. The Bible says that sin is what handicaps us – sinful habits, and feelings of guilt, stop us loving our neighbours as much as we would like to. So get rid of them, strip them away, by seeking God's forgiveness and the Holy Spirit's power. Then we must persevere in prayer and practical service, even when we feel like giving up, remembering that we are doing it for Jesus.

The tape

For Jesus is among those who are rooting for us. But he has a special place: he's one of the judges, standing by the finishing tape. His enthusiasm is justified, because he has run the race before us. He endured opposition and mockery, suffering and pain, and was often tempted to give up, yet he kept going. The winning athletes were taken to sit next to the Emperor or his local representative; Jesus triumphed, and is described as sitting on the right side of God. So we too must persevere, following the example of Jesus and hoping to share in his triumph in heaven.

Metaphor

It's a good metaphor. When you are tempted to do something you know to be wrong, you think nobody will notice. When religion is being made fun of, you shrink out of sight. When someone is having a hard time, you are reluctant to go to their defence. When someone needs your help, it's just too much trouble. So remember your heavenly fan club, and keep running the Christian race for as long as you have to. But there's one important difference. In the Christian life there are no winners or losers. Whoever reaches the finishing line without giving up gets the prize of eternal life. And that makes it all worthwhile.

All-age worship

Make a model stadium with Jesus standing at the finishing line.

Suggested hymns

Fight the good fight; Give thanks with a grateful heart; Give us the wings of faith to rise; The head that once was crowned with thorns.

Twelfth Sunday after Trinity (Proper 15)
18 August
Second Service **Salesian Meditation**
Ps. 119.17–32 Your decrees are my delight; Isa. 28.9–22 A foundation stone; 2 Cor. 8.1–9 Generosity; *Gospel at Holy Communion*: Matthew 20.1–16 Labourers in the vineyard

> *'Make me understand the way of your commandments, and so shall I meditate on your wondrous works.' Psalm 119.27 (Common Worship)*

St Francis de Sales

Geneva in Switzerland was the home of Protestantism, John Calvin dying there in 1564. But St Francis de Sales was the Roman Catholic Provost and then Bishop of Geneva from 1593 until 1622, and by his holiness and learning he won much of Switzerland back to the Catholic faith. His famous book *Introduction to the Devout Life* was assembled out of private instruction in prayer he gave to individuals whose spiritual director he was. In it he gives advice on meditation. He was born at the castle of Sales [Saarl] in Savoy in France, and since his name is spelt S A L E S, the adjective for describing his Method of Meditation is 'Sall-EE-zee-un'.

Meditation

Meditation is thinking about God in a structured way. Most people are not well trained in the art of logical thinking. When it comes to thinking about God, their mind goes blank, and they don't know where to begin. A retreat is a wonderful opportunity to learn how, but short periods of meditation can be included in the pattern of a busy week, such as on solitary walks, or before church worship begins. While much can be learnt from other religions about the techniques of relaxation, Christian meditation aims specifically for a personal encounter with a personal God. There's a long and little-known tradition of Christian teaching on meditation. A century earlier, St Ignatius of Loyola taught a rather better-known method, but the Salesian method is more concise than the Ignatian method, and easier for beginners to follow.

Preparation

It begins with a period of *preparation*: remembering the presence of God; and praying for inspiration. For example: 'Dear God, though I can't see you, I truly believe that you are here with me, loving me and listening to me. Give me your Holy Spirit, to help me to concentrate during this meditation, and to learn more about your love.'

Imagination

Second, you chose a passage from the Bible; read it; and using all your five senses, you try to *imagine* that you are there at the scene it describes. Supposing you chose the parable of the labourers in the vineyard, in Matthew chapter 20, you could begin by imagining you are beside the River Jordan where Jesus is telling the story. What can you hear? Imagine the sound of his voice; also the sounds of the river, the crowd, the birds and the insects. Imagine what you can see – smell – touch – taste. Then imagine you are in the vineyard in the story, with the labourers who'd been there all day arguing with those who'd only been there a short time. What are they saying?

Consideration

Now you use your *brain*, your intellect, to work out how the lessons of the passage can be applied to today. Do you feel resentful against those who have joined your church later than you did? Against Christians of other races? Do you feel you should get a bigger reward from God because you have worked harder for him than some other people have? Now you think about it, is that reasonable?

Resolution

Next, use your *will* to decide to make a practical response to what you have learnt. 'O God, I'm determined to resist the temptation to resent other people. I'll try to treat everyone equally. Please help me to keep these resolutions.'

Conclusion

In conclusion: 'Thank you, God, for this time with you. I offer myself in your service; use me in whatever way you choose. Please give me the grace to carry out my resolutions.' Then you can say the Lord's Prayer, and any other prayers you know by heart.

A 'spiritual nosegay'

You end by gathering what's colourfully called a 'spiritual nosegay'. A nosegay is a small bunch of flowers which you can put in your buttonhole, and sniff it at odd moments during the day. A spiritual nosegay involves selecting a phrase from the reading, memorizing it, and recollecting it occasionally during the day to enjoy again what the meditation has given you.

Summary

To summarize, there are five steps in your meditation:

* You say a prayer of *preparation*.
* Use your five senses in a time of *imagination*.
* Use your *brain* to learn the message of the reading for today.
* Use your *will* to decide what to do about it.
* The *conclusion* is to pray about it, and gather a nosegay of phrases you can keep coming back to all day long.

Finally, enjoy! Enjoy a period of peace and quiet among the bustle of life, and enjoy learning how to think constructively about God.

Suggested hymns

Be still, for the presence of the Lord; Dear Lord and Father of mankind; Let me have my way among you; O thou who camest from above.

Thirteenth Sunday after Trinity (Proper 16)

25 August

Principal Service **Praise, My Soul, the King of Heaven**

(*Continuous*): Jer. 1.4–10 Jeremiah's call; Ps. 71.1–6 Providence;
or (*Related*): Isa. 58.9b–14 The needy; Ps. 103.1–8 Forgiveness
and healing; Heb. 12.18–29 The mediator of a new covenant;
Luke 13.10–17 Healing on the Sabbath

> *'Bless the Lord, O my soul, and forget not all his benefits.'* Psalm
> *103.2 (Common Worship)*

Psalm 103

Everybody has a favourite Psalm – for most people it's the twenty-
third psalm. But for others, who know the Psalms well, the 'top
of the pops' has to be Psalm 103. It's such a joyful song, full of
gratitude for what God has done for us in his love:

> 'Bless the Lord, O my soul, and forget not all his benefits;
> who forgives all your sins, and heals all your infirmities;
> who redeems your life from the pit,
> and crowns you with faithful love and compassion ...'

The Psalmist admits that we are all sinners; yet God only reminds
us of this so that he can forgive us. Jesus ignored the Old Testament
regulations in order to heal a crippled woman on the Sabbath day.
Then he taught us that God is less concerned about people who
break the laws than with the breach in our loving relationship with
our heavenly Father, which is caused by our feelings of guilt. God
remembers our human frailty, and that we are only made from the
dust of the earth. Our lives are as short as those of the flowers, yet
God's love lasts for ever. The unspoken suggestion in this is that
God must have some loving purpose in mind for our souls when we
die, and join the angels in singing his praises in heaven.

Praise, my soul ...

This Psalm has been paraphrased into one of the most popular
hymns in our hymnbooks: *Praise, my soul, the King of heaven*. It
continues: 'Ransomed, healed, restored, forgiven, who like me his
praise should sing?' The message of God's eagerness to forgive us
is condensed into seven words: 'Slow to chide, and swift to bless'.

Father-like, he tends and spares us,
well our feeble frame he knows;
in his hands he gently bears us,
rescues us from all our foes.

Henry Francis Lyte

The hymn was written by Henry Francis Lyte, who was also the author of 'Abide with me'. He was born in Scotland in 1793, and studied at Trinity College, Dublin, where he repeatedly won the poetry prize. Ordained in 1815, he was appointed to the Devonshire parish of Lower Brixham, where he wrote hymns for the fishermen who docked their boats there. So successful was he that there were more than 800 students – adults and children – in his Sunday school. The level of literacy was low, so they couldn't read the psalms. He solved this by turning them into poetry which they could easily memorize. This hymn is popular at wedding services because couples have heard it at other weddings, or at school, and it gives a simple message of God's love and guidance in the days to come.

Tunes

Of course, a catchy tune makes a hymn popular, and the best known, called 'Praise my soul', was written by Sir John Goss, the organist of St Paul's Cathedral in London, especially to fit to these words. It's popular with musicians, too, because the first verse is in unison; the second verse is in harmony; the third is meant to be sung by women and children only; and the fourth has a descant. But in Nonconformist churches these words are often sung to the tune 'Regent's Square', which you may know as the tune to 'Light's abode, celestial Salem'.

Thankfulness and hope

Tune and words together make this one of the most positive and uplifting hymns in the book. The message is that God is like the best sort of parent, who will occasionally give their children a warning when their behaviour could have dangerous consequences, but quickly forgives them when they say 'sorry', and tenderly leads them in the right way. A few years ago a policeman was stabbed to death by a criminal whom he was trying to arrest. His widow asked to have this hymn sung at his memorial service. Her neighbours were puzzled how she could choose such a joyful hymn for such a sad occasion. She replied that it had been one of her husband's favourite hymns, and they'd sung it at their wedding. Of course she was devastated by what had happened; but the hymn helped her to remember that her husband was now in heaven, praising his Saviour along with the angels. 'It's the message of hope which this hymn gives us', she said, 'which has kept me going through the darkest days.'

All-age worship

Learn to sing the third verse of this hymn without any adult help.

Suggested hymns

Fill thou my life, O Lord my God; Praise, my soul, the King of heaven; Praise to the Lord, the Almighty, the King of creation; There's a wideness in God's mercy.

Thirteenth Sunday after Trinity (Proper 16)
25 August
Second Service   **Contemplation**
Ps. 119.49–72 I was humbled that I might learn; Isa. 30.8–21 This is the way; 2 Cor. 9 A collection; *Gospel at Holy Communion*: Matt. 21.28–32 The two sons

> *'In returning and rest you shall be saved;*
> *in quietness and in trust shall be your strength.' Isaiah 30.15*

Quiet

The world around us is so noisy. There's the noise of traffic which never stops, and of the radio and television which are never switched off. The ring tones of mobile phones, and people jabbering into them nineteen to the dozen. Words flood in through the newspapers and emails, or tweets sent on Twitter. The result of all this noise is that nobody has any time to think. Far less, to pray. Jesus told his disciples to go into their bedroom to pray, because that's the only place where you are unlikely to be interrupted. The prophet Isaiah reminds us that we become strong in our faith not by being busy, but by being quiet:

> Thus said the Lord God, the Holy One of Israel:
> In returning and rest you shall be saved;
>   in quietness and in trust shall be your strength.

Not thinking about God

The prayer of quiet is known as contemplation. Meditation is the art of thinking about God in a structured way. Contemplation, however, is the art of being quiet with God, and letting your mind go blank. The word means setting aside a space for a temple of quiet. Not talking or even thinking at all. It's the heart of Christian prayer, but sadly many Christians never even attempt it. It's not difficult; but it does demand a certain amount of self-discipline. When we stop talking and sit quietly, odd thoughts keep popping into our minds, and they need to be resisted. You can always make a note to think about them later, but for now, your object is to empty your mind completely.

The Jesus Prayer

Maybe you need some help to wind down. A prayer repeated as you thumb your way through some prayer beads may help, though the sequence of 'decades' of the rosary as traditionally taught, while they have their value in meditation, are more likely to be a distraction to somebody who wants to contemplate. Better is the 'Jesus Prayer' as taught in the Eastern Orthodox churches. Think it silently in it's long form to begin with, breathing in deeply on the first half and out on the second part:

> (IN:) O Lord Jesus Christ, Son of the Living God,
> (OUT:) Have mercy on me, a sinner, now and in the hour of my death.

Then gradually shorten it till you breathe Jesus in, then breathe out mercy. Soon the words, 'Jesus, mercy' become part of your breathing till you are no longer aware of them. If at this point you fall asleep, you obviously need it; pick up your contemplation when you wake up again. The object is to sit in total silence, becoming more and more aware of the presence of God with you. Don't even talk to him; but listen quietly. That doesn't mean listening for an audible voice, or struggling to understand what God's trying to say to you. He may just want you to be aware at the deepest possible level that he loves you. Occasionally, if God wants to say something special to you, then after a while, you will know what it is without any doubt. Always check what you think you have heard against the Bible, and the advice of other Christians. But you have had a successful contemplation if you simply enjoyed being quiet with God, and didn't receive any messages at all.

Ways to quietness

Of course, monks and nuns who live a contemplative life have developed techniques for quietening themselves down, but ordinary Christians can ignore these if they wish. The first step is the 'purgative way', in which you seek cleansing from sin. Next is when you put aside the pleasures of the five senses; it's sometimes called 'the dark night of the senses'. The 'dark night of the soul' is when we learn to do without even the feeling of God's presence. This leads into the 'vision of God', and the 'mystical union' of the soul with God. That's the aim, though it may take you many years before you reach this final phase.

Listening or awareness

To begin with, however, you just need to learn to be quiet. 'In returning and rest you shall be saved; in quietness and in trust shall be your strength.' Mainly, you just want to be aware of God's loving presence. In the back of your mind you are ready to hear what God wants you to do. But you know that already. After you have finished your contemplation, you will be inspired to love and serve your neighbour better than ever before, because you realize how deeply God loves you.

Suggested hymns

As the deer pants for the water; Be still and know that I am God; Be still my soul; Let me have my way among you.

Fourteenth Sunday after Trinity (Proper 17)

1 September

Principal Service   **Friend, Move Up Higher**

(*Continuous*): Jer. 2.4–13 Living water; Ps. 81.1, 10–16 God's justice; *or* (*Related*): Ecclus. 10.12–18 Pride and judgement, *or* Prov. 25.6–7 Pride and humility; Ps. 112 Righteousness; Heb. 13.1–8, 15–16 Righteousness; Luke 14.1, 7–14 Pride and humility

> *'When you are invited [to a dinner], go and sit down at the lowest place, so that when your host comes, he may say to you, "Friend, move up higher"; then you will be honoured in the presence of all who sit at the table with you.' Luke 14.10*

Humility

A famous man, when people burst into spontaneous applause as he walked onto the platform at a public meeting, used to step aside and allow the man behind him to go in front. Then he would join in the applause, unable to imagine that it was he himself whom the audience was clapping. That sort of natural humility is very noble, and very rare. More often, so-called celebrities not only claim to be important in their own field, but also consider that their views should be listened to with respect on subjects they know nothing whatever about. But it's plain common sense. Jesus pointed out that if someone with second-class talents arrives early for a dinner party, and annexes the top place at the table, in all probability someone more important than they are will arrive later, and the proud man will be forced to move down to make room for him. Then everyone will be sniggering behind their hands, because the arrogant man has been humiliated. Whereas if you humbly accept a place lower down, the host will come to you, begging you to move into a more important position, saying, 'Friend, move up higher.' Then the other guests will respect you, because you were humble, despite being more talented than they had realized.

Ambition

It's OK to be ambitious, and offer yourself for a more senior job when the opportunity comes, but you must leave the decision as to whether or not you are qualified for it to other people, and not be disappointed if they think you are not ready. Yet who would turn down a promotion if it's offered to them? Who wouldn't rejoice to hear those welcome words. 'Friend, move up higher' ... higher in the hierarchy at work, higher in the sense of taking on greater responsibilities. Granted, taking on a more important job may involve hard work and longer hours, researching your new responsibilities and mastering the art of management. There's a limit to the amount of time it's wise to spend away from your family. But even somebody who tries to be humble can graciously accept the rise when it's offered to them, because other people obviously think you are worth it.

God's work

Even more, you should accept responsibilities when God offers them to you. Working for God, whether as a volunteer or in the ministry, is no career choice for somebody who hopes to become rich. But if a voluntary post in the youth club becomes vacant, or the charge of a challenging church is offered to one, no false humility should cause anyone to hold back. If God trusts you to be able to do it, he will give you the necessary talents when the time comes.

God's kingdom

Yet we have very mistaken ideas about what promotion in God's kingdom actually means. James and John thought they could have thrones to the right and left of Jesus. They didn't realize that what wins you respect from God and your fellow Christians is willingness to suffer patiently and to sacrifice your time to the care of the needy. To be exalted in God's eyes may mean being lifted up on a cross.

Death

This changes our attitude to death, doesn't it? To the non-Christian, death seems like a disaster, the end of all our hopes and dreams. Yet the Salvation Army refer to death as 'promotion to glory' – moving up to a higher rank of being. You don't need to believe in the heaven of harps and haloes in medieval paintings, to realize that when God tells you the time has come for you to die, he is offering you a place of honour at his table, in a world far better than this one, in which relationships are renewed, and tasks left uncompleted

218

on earth can find their fulfilment in ways beyond our imagining. We call eternity a 'higher level of existence' than the world of time and space. It's a time for rejoicing, therefore, when God's angels say to us, 'Friend, go up higher.'

All-age worship

Pin a label on your chest reading 'I think I'm not important'. Then have a friend pin a label on your back, where you can't see it, reading 'God thinks I'm very important to him'.

Suggested hymns

Hushed was the evening hymn; Jesus, humble was your birth; Lord, it belongs not to my care; My God, and is thy table spread?

Fourteenth Sunday after Trinity (Proper 17)
1 September
Second Service   **Who was Jesus?**
Ps. 119.81–96 Like a wineskin in the smoke; Isa. 33.13–22 To see the king in his beauty; John 3.22–36 I must decrease

'Your eyes will see the king in his beauty.' Isaiah 33.17

Imagination

I want you to use your imagination. It's an everyday scene. Imagine you have just dropped into your nearest fast-food restaurant [or pub, or tea shop]. It's quite noisy, but at one table there seems to be a lot of laughter, and you peer across to see what the reason is. One of them beckons you across to join them. They are local men and women and you recognize some of them. They take it in turns to tell funny stories. One of them is particularly humorous, with a touch of satire to his jokes. You find yourself laughing at what fools people can be, and then you pull yourself up short, because you realize that you do daft things, too, and you are laughing at yourself. The storyteller looks quite ordinary, but gradually the others stop talking and everyone is listening to his stories. Sometimes they question him about embarrassing situations they have got themselves into.

Insight

The main feature of this man's tall tales is what I'd call insight. He seems to understand what makes people tick. He seems to understand your motives, as though he had known you for years. But he doesn't condemn people. In fact the only thing that makes him really mad is when folk are critical of others. We all say unkind things about the people down our street – after all, it would take the fun out of life if you stopped doing it. Then the storyteller asks you how you feel about people who say unkind things about you. *Touché!* We all slip into the habit of tit for tat, and he shows you how this sort of selfishness causes most of the misery in the world.

Travelling

You'd like to hear more from this unusual man, and ask if you can meet him again tomorrow. 'You will have to travel,' he replies. 'Tomorrow I'm going to [the next town] to share my stories with the folk who live there. Why not come with me?' So you find yourself following the storyteller all round the country, as far as your work allows, because you are fascinated. But his satire can be dangerous. Several people in government, and a few leading churchmen, complain about the critical things he has said about them. Crowds are now gathering round him, and some people on the edges seem to be making notes. Then he's arrested on a trumped-up charge. You have to make up your mind now whether you are going to admit to being his follower, and risk getting into trouble yourself. The funny stories have turned into dark tragedy. But it's still all about selfishness versus self-sacrifice.

Jesus

You have guessed by now that I have been telling you the story of Jesus, in modern dress. That's deliberate, because if I told it as ancient history, you would never get the idea of how approachable Jesus is, 'just like one of us'. Of course, he did live a long time ago, in a country far away, and speaking a language you have never learnt. But putting that aside for a moment, I want you to get to know him as easily as his contemporaries did, as your favourite friend. When you have done that, then you can begin to study the background. He lived in a country under occupation by a colonial power, where women were completely powerless. The language he spoke had several curious twists, like using 'son of' and 'daughter of' to mean 'of the same character as'. Once you have accepted Jesus as your friend, you can study all these things, so as to understand more accurately what he meant by what he said. Then, perhaps, you can look to see what he meant by 'my heavenly Father'. But don't rush it, otherwise your puzzlement about the words will get in the way of your learning that Jesus loves you. Just read the Gospels of Matthew, Mark, Luke and John in the Bible, ignoring the puzzles, and learning to talk to the most wonderful man that ever lived. Because it wasn't only his disciples who realized that you can go on talking to a man who has already died – billions of Christians have been doing that for 2,000 years: they call it 'prayer', and they have proved that it works. Now it's your turn to make the experiment. Assume that Jesus is listening to you, and ask him searching questions. Then think about what you would have expected him to reply. By the next day, you'll feel certain in your heart what his answer is. And you'll know that he is more than a friend: he's the king of all the earth, and he's incredible! You will have learnt, as the Bible puts it, to 'see the king in his beauty'.

Suggested hymns

A man there lived in Galilee; Fairest Lord Jesus; How sweet the name of Jesus sounds; Jesus, stand among us at the meeting of our lives.

Fifteenth Sunday after Trinity (Proper 18)
8 September
Principal Service   **The Purpose of Pain**
(*Continuous*): Jer. 18.1–11 The potter; Ps. 139.1–5, 12–18 God knows us; *or* (*Related*): Deut. 30.15–20 Choose life;
Ps. 1 Righteousness; Philemon 1–21 The runaway slave;
Luke 14.25–33 The call to take up the cross

> '*Whoever does not carry the cross and follow me cannot be my disciple.*' *Luke 14.27*

Evolution

Is suffering inevitable? I believe it is, because it's the only way that you and I could come into existence. Let me explain. Life emerged on this planet when the first cells began to divide and multiply. Then some cells developed variations. But there would have been no food for these more developed organisms, and no room for them to live, if the first cells hadn't begun to die. Development depends on death. Then the more complicated beings began to fight the others, to gain territory and the food which grows on it; often one creature eats another, and is itself preyed upon, setting up a food chain. Some creatures developed the ability to feel pain, which was very useful, because pain is how we learn to avoid danger. The faculty of memory developed, and lessons learnt by one generation were passed on to the next. The ability to choose between two alternative courses of action emerged among the higher animals.

Humans

Gradually, over many millennia, the complex creatures which we call human beings developed self-awareness and the ability to love. These features may not be unique to *Homo sapiens,* but we have them to a higher degree than anything else in the natural world. If there were no pain we wouldn't be able to learn from our mistakes; and if there were no death, there would be no room to live, and no new babies could be born. We have become what we are because of pain and death. Yet we were the first to ask why we should have to endure these things. So pain and death gave rise to suffering and grief.

Why?

According to the scientists, that's *how* it happened, and I have no dispute with their theories. But because we are human, we want to know *why* we have to suffer and grieve. And science can't answer the 'why' questions in life. Yes, scientists can say B happened because A happened. But there's a real difference in logic between that and saying that 'A happened in order that B should follow'. Moreover, there's no experiment which would test your theories of purpose. Yet it seems impossible that you and I should be what we are, unless there was some purpose for our existence, some great plan behind the whole process. Suffering and grief would be unbearable if they were accidental and meaningless. But if we can see some reason for our agony, we are enabled to bear it bravely.

Afterlife

I think the clue to the whole process lies in our belief in an afterlife. Human brains have developed the power to imagine a Supreme Being controlling the development of nature. As we have the ability to form loving relationships with each other, we can conceive of a loving relationship with the Supreme Intelligence, who designed the whole process. But because such a being is the Creator of space and time, he, she or it is not limited by time or space. So our relationship with him is timeless and eternal, as he is. Let's call him 'God', and say that he planned and controlled everything, from the Big Bang onwards, so that those who love him can live with him in eternity. There's room for everybody in heaven who wants to go there, because God is infinite. The purpose of creation was to populate heaven, and love is the meaning of evolution. Pain was necessary so that we should learn to love, and death was inevitable so that we can enter the next phase in God's loving plan for us.

Embracing your cross

Jesus said, 'Whoever does not carry the cross and follow me cannot be my disciple.' If you ask me, that means that suffering and death have an essential part to play on our path to heaven. Don't ask me why! If it was explained to us I doubt whether we could understand it. But in the light of Jesus's death on the cross, instead of railing against our mortality and pain, we can embrace them bravely as Jesus did, as an inevitable part of our progress towards a glorious eternity. A suicidal psychiatric patient once handed this poem to a visiting minister:

> The evening, after a day of suffering,
> I find myself, surprised,
> as though nourished.
> The soul breathes a clean air;
> the heart feels a sense of sweet plenitude.
> Then it looks impossible to me
> this pain should not, one day, give its fruits.

All-age worship

Draw (with matchstick men) a situation where the pain you felt helped you to avoid danger.

Suggested hymns

Lord of the years; Love is his word, love is his way; Take up thy cross, the Saviour said; We sing the praise of him who died.

Fifteenth Sunday after Trinity (Proper 18)
8 September
Second Service   **Fundamentalism**
Ps. [120 Deliver me] 121 I lift my eyes; Isa. 43.14—44.5 A new thing; John 5.30–47 Search the Scriptures

> *'You search the scriptures because you think that in them you have eternal life; and it is they that testify on my behalf.' John 5.39*

Pharisees

Jesus was having a row with the Pharisees. They insisted that theirs was a truly biblical religion; nothing was tolerable unless you could prove it from the pages of Scripture. Jesus seemed to them to be a dangerous liberal, introducing ideas which had no scriptural basis. Just look at the company he kept: his best friends were ignorant fishermen; he went to rowdy parties with the quisling tax-collectors, who overcharged their fellow Jews for customs duties, and gave the proceeds to their employers, the Roman state officials, to pay the occupying army. Jesus was said to mix freely with the people Pharisees called sinners – those who gave up trying to keep the elaborate food laws as impractical in the modern world – and was even said to have spoken respectfully to prostitutes! Jesus was known to be quite careless about observing the Sabbath-day regulations. God in his mercy had made a covenant with the Jewish people; their side of the bargain was to keep the laws of Moses to the letter, and Jesus was teaching people to ignore them!

Life

'You search the scriptures', replied Jesus, 'because you think that in them you have eternal life; and it is they that testify on my behalf.' Jesus respected the Scriptures; but the Pharisees were interpreting them wrongly. The Old Testament celebrates God's gift of new life; and all the Pharisees were interested in were narrow life-denying regulations. 'I came that they may have life,' said Jesus, 'and have it abundantly.' Fullness of life, to Jesus, meant celebrating the diversity of human nature, and exploring imaginative new ways of showing our love for our neighbours. Emphasis on conformity to regulations was in direct opposition to the purpose of the Bible.

Fundamentalism

Yet the Pharisees' narrow interpretation of Scripture is thriving today, in Christianity, Islam, Judaism and Hinduism. In 1910 some conservative evangelical Christians launched a series of pamphlets in America called *The Fundamentals.* The irreducible minimum of the Christian faith, they wrote, is to believe in the literal inspiration and inerrancy of the Bible; the creation of the universe in six days; the imminent return of Christ; and the belief that Jesus was punished on the cross in place of sinners to satisfy an angry God. These tracts brought a new word to the language – 'fundamentalism' – and led to a growth of narrow, fear-filled, judgemental conservatism in Christianity. In the Wahabi sect of Islam, among Orthodox Jews, and nationalist Hindus, similar exclusive movements grew up. Their common features are intolerance of those who are different from themselves, eagerness to use force against their enemies, and to impose fierce punishments on those who have broken what they regard as the moral laws of their religion. Christian fundamentalists have not yet ventured into terrorism, but their influence lies behind some of the warlike tendencies in the USA.

Tolerance

Now I hesitate to speak against the fundamentalists, and this is a dilemma facing many Christian preachers. If we preach in favour of diversity and tolerance, are we not being intolerant ourselves? The only answer to this is to say that 'I can tolerate everything except intolerance!' I respect the right of every Christian to interpret the Scriptures in their own way, and to practise the Christian religion in ways I don't like. But when they refuse to extend the same tolerance to those who disagree with them, it's time to stand up and say that theirs is a dangerous distortion of the teaching of Jesus. What's more, their skilful publicity leads many non-Christians to assume that fundamentalism is the only form of Christianity there is. They persecute lesbian and gay Christians and divorcees, and oppose contraception and abortion. It is not only among evangelicals:

many catholics oppose these things too, and reject the equality of men and women in the Church with equal vehemence. Thus many sincere Christians are being driven out of the Church, and anyone who is attracted to Christianity will draw back if they feel they have to turn their backs on openness and tolerance. It's being made harder for anyone with a scientific education to become a believer, if they are told they will have to reject the established discoveries of modern science.

Liberals

All I can say is that there *is* a much more liberal and comprehensive understanding of Christianity, open to science, reason and historical scholarship, stretching back to the time of the Gospels, and in tune with the tolerant teachings of Jesus. Don't let the fundamentalists put you off; look to see what Jesus actually said, and try to apply a Christlike love and sympathy for all sorts of people in your own life.

Suggested hymns

I danced in the morning; Lord, thy word abideth; There's a wideness in God's mercy; They shall come from the east, they shall come from the west.

Sixteenth Sunday after Trinity (Proper 19)
15 September
Principal Service   **They Did Not Find Themselves**
(*Continuous*): Jer. 4.11–12, 22–28 Judgement; Ps. 14 The fool has said; *or* (*Related*): Ex. 32.7–14 The golden calf and a prayer for forgiveness; Ps. 51.1–11 Prayer for forgiveness; 1 Tim. 1.12–17 Christ brings salvation; Luke 15.1–10 A lost sheep, a woman's lost coin

> *'What woman having ten silver coins, if she loses one of them, does not light a lamp, sweep the house, and search carefully until she finds it?' Luke 15.8*

Pharisees

They were good religious people – said their prayers, lived by the rules, and worshipped regularly. They knew that God had given special privileges to them and people like them. The trouble was, they thought they deserved it. They looked down their noses at folk who obviously didn't – those who had given up on the practice of their religion, and the lost souls who had even compromised with the filthy foreigners. They were the Pharisees, and it was these good religious people who gave Jesus the most trouble. It was no use arguing with them, they were so sure they were right. So Jesus told them stories.

Lost coin

St Luke recounts three of these parables – the lost sheep, the lost coin, and the lost son. Three things that were lost, and then were found again. Obviously symbols of the lost souls who collaborated with the Romans, even raising taxes to pay the occupying army. The only hope for these 'tax-collectors and other sinners', thought the Pharisees, would be if they gave up their wicked ways and rejoined the club of observant religious Jews. Yet, in none of the tales that Jesus told did the lost thing find itself. The shepherd had to search for the lost sheep; the prodigal son hoped for no more than a paid job, feeling that he'd never be readmitted as a family member. No lost coin has ever been known to get up and start looking for its owner.

God's a woman

In each case, it's the owner who hunts out his lost property, or who presses his son to become an honoured member of the family. None of them *deserves* to be found. Similarly, Jesus implies, none of the lost souls – tax-collectors and other sinners – *deserves* to be found by God, but our heavenly Father comes searching for us. So the shepherd in the story is a symbol for God. This idea's quite common in the Old Testament, where God is called 'the Shepherd of Israel'. The Hebrew Scriptures were also familiar with the idea that God is like a father to the nation, so the parable of the prodigal son won't have come as much of a shock. Except that Jesus makes God's loving care much more individual than previous generations had dared to do. What's really shocking, however, is the parable of the lost coin. It suggests that God's a woman! This must have been really offensive to the male-chauvinist Pharisees, who presided over a male-dominated society. Today we are quite accustomed to the idea that God, having no body, has no gender. But God shows many of the characteristics of women: tenderness to the weak; toughness and loyalty; patience and persistence in searching for the lost. In these ways God resembles the woman in the story. The ten silver coins were probably her dowry, given to her when she got married, and threaded on a string across her forehead. If anything happened to her husband, those coins were her life-support until she found somebody else to look after her; the loss of even one might make the difference between life and death for her. No wonder she turned the house upside down until she found it.

Precious, not deserving

The lost sheep, the lost coin and the lost son were all precious to their owners. Precious, but not deserving. They had no claim on the owner, and if the owner cared for them it was purely out of the kindness of his or her heart. What does this tell us about the Pharisees and the sinners? Jesus was telling the Pharisees not to be so stuck-up; they didn't deserve any special privileges. God loves everyone equally. Merit, good works, status, learning don't count – God just loves us anyway. Religious and irreligious alike. If you find a trace of Pharisaism in your nature, remember that the coin didn't go looking for the woman, the woman hunted for it because it was precious to her. The respectable and the disreputable are equally precious to God, yet neither of them deserves his love. Nobody can find themselves when they are lost; we are entirely dependent on God's grace. Remembering this may make us more tolerant of those we used to despise.

All-age worship

Play hide-and-seek. The seeker can be labelled 'God', and those who are hiding can be labelled 'sinner', 'rough-sleeper', 'alcoholic' etc.

Suggested hymns

Be thou my guardian and my guide; Just as I am, without one plea; Praise to the holiest in the height; Will you come and follow me?

Sixteenth Sunday after Trinity (Proper 19)

15 September

Second Service   **Feeling the Presence**

Ps. 124 If the Lord were not on our side, 125 Those who trust in the Lord; Isa. 60 Arise, shine; John 6.51–69 I am the living bread

> *'Arise, shine; for your light has come, and the glory of the Lord has risen upon you.' Isaiah 60.1*

Prayer

Sometimes people screw themselves up in agony about prayer. 'If I had any faith,' they say to themselves, 'I'd really be able to *feel* the presence of God with me. But I feel nothing! My heart's so dead, that no matter how hard I try, I can't really feel that anyone is listening when I pray. Obviously I haven't enough faith to be a Christian, and there's no hope for me.' The fallacy in this argument is that it confuses faith with emotion. If you have warm feelings when you pray, thank God for them. You have done nothing to deserve them; they are a gift of the Holy Spirit, and you can't create them for yourself. People who have a rosy glow when they pray are no better than those who feel cold and numb; they are just different. God has made each one of us unique, and some find it easier to express their emotions than others.

Faith

But faith is a matter of the will, not the emotions. You have looked at what the Bible says about God, and your brain, your reason, tells you that quite probably some of what it says is true – though you can't prove it. So you try an experiment, making up your mind to trust God to guide and direct you, and to try your best to follow his guidance. Having faith in someone is quite different from believing that something's true – it means trusting them absolutely not to mislead you. The same person may feel quite emotional during their prayer time one day, and the next day they are emotionally dead. There's no difference in their faith. What alters their emotional state is quite likely to be what they had for supper last night – did it lead to a feeling of well-being, or indigestion?

Isaiah

In the Old Testament, the Jewish people were driven out of their homes and taken away into exile in Babylon. They felt depressed, imagining that God had given up on them, and none of his promises would come true. They needed somebody to cheer them up, so God sent them a prophet. He reassured the people that God still had a plan for them, and one day they would return to their homeland of Israel. Now it wasn't safe to publish a message like that in Babylon, since it sounds like a call to rebellion. So the anonymous prophet secretly tacked his message of hope onto the end of the scroll of Isaiah. This new prophet's words begin at chapter 40: 'Comfort, comfort my people, says your God ...' We usually call him Second Isaiah. But when they returned home, they were still gloomy – there were so few of them, and they were weak in a world of powerful nations. So another prophet, whom we shall have to call Third Isaiah, added some more chapters later, we think, to cheer up the returned exiles. We heard some of this read today:

> Arise, shine; for your light has come,
>   and the glory of the Lord has risen upon you.
> For darkness shall cover the earth,
>   and thick darkness the peoples;
> but the Lord will arise upon you,
>   and his glory will appear over you.
> Nations shall come to your light,
>   and kings to the brightness of your dawn.

Other Scriptures

You will find similar messages of hope throughout the Bible, reassuring its readers that God really is present when we pray. In Psalm 125: 'Those who trust in the Lord are like Mount Zion, which cannot be moved, but stands fast for ever. As the hills stand about Jerusalem, so the Lord stands round about his people, from this time forth for evermore.' In St John's Gospel: 'Those who eat my flesh and drink my blood abide in me, and I in them.'

Arise, shine

So you are wasting precious time by worrying about whether you have the right feelings. God *is* with us, whether we can see him or not, whether we feel it or not. That's a statement of fact; we have his promises in the Bible. Forget your feelings, and get on with doing what God wants you to do. Trust and obey. Then people will see, shining from your faith, your calm certainty that the Lord our God is with us – which is far more likely to draw them toward the God who inspires you than any shallow emotionalism. 'Arise, shine; for your light has come, and the glory of the Lord has risen upon you.' That's fact, not feelings. Just act upon the facts, and your friends will want to discover where you find this new joy.

Suggested hymns

Awake, awake! Fling off the night; Break thou the bread of life; Darkness like a shroud; When we walk with the Lord.

Seventeenth Sunday after Trinity (Proper 20)
22 September
Principal Service   **'It's My Money'**
(*Continuous*): Jer. 8.18—9.1 Balm in Gilead, healing the nation; Ps. 79.1–9 Suffering, prayer for forgiveness; *or* (*Related*): Amos 8.4–7 The needy; Ps. 113 The needy; 1 Tim. 2.1–7 Those in authority; Luke 16.1–13 The shrewd manager

> *'Jesus said to the disciples, "There was a rich man who had a manager, and charges were brought to him that this man was squandering his property."' Luke 16.1*

Wealthy

Compared with the multi-millionaires we read about, you probably think you are quite poor. But compare yourself with people in the Third World, earning a dollar a day, and you realize that, in fact, you are rich beyond their dreams. But if I tell you what to do with your money, you will be very angry. 'It's my money,' you'll say, 'to do what I like with.' Most of us feel like that about our hard-earned cash. Yet Jesus told a parable about a shrewd manager. A millionaire owns several farms and workshops, he said. Each business is run for him by a manager. But one manager isn't entirely honest – this is fiction, of course! He creams off some of the profits for himself. 'It's my money,' he says, 'to do what I like with.' But it isn't his money, it belongs to the millionaire. Because he is a shrewd man, the manager goes round the people he has done business with, cooking the books to make it *appear* they owe his boss less than they do. That way, they are in debt to him, and when he's sacked, they help him out – you scratch my back and I'll scratch yours! When Jesus told the story, the people listening chuckled away. But the joke was on them.

The right use of wealth

We don't own our money, to do what we like with; it's been lent to us by God, who made everything. The world is God's creation, and we must do with it what God wants us to. We pray for daily bread, and God gives us enough to live on, and a roof over our heads. Over and above that, he lends us enough to live in comfort, and some to invest for the future. How does God want us to use it? The Bible suggests that the shrewd thing to do is to use it to make friends with those who are less well-off than us. If you use it to start a business which provides employment to others, and keeps them off benefits, they and their families will thank God for you every night. If you buy consumer goods, that at least provides work for people in factories around the globe. If you buy old master paintings and keep them locked in a burglar-proof cellar, this helps nobody. The dead artist can't benefit. You sell it at a profit in a few years' time, so the prices go up, and fewer art galleries can afford to buy good paintings for everyone to enjoy. If you spend your money on luxurious living, the makers of caviar and champagne will be happy, but food prices will go up all over the world, driving more people into starvation. It's hard, but before you spend money, always remind yourself that God has lent it to you. God wants you to enjoy his creation – don't be a Scrooge – but see if you can be helpful to others in the process.

Zambia

Many people invest their cash or their pension fund in things like the copper mines in Zambia. Recently the price of copper went up, so Christian Zambians campaigned for the mines to pay local taxes, keeping a greater share of the profits in Zambia. Then they lobbied their government to spend more tax money on health and education. Christian Aid in Britain advised them how to run an effective campaign, and publicized it among the shareholders in this country. Now Christian Aid is campaigning for all businesses that trade overseas to pay local taxes, to help with development. So your gifts to Christian Aid are a very effective way of using your limited wealth to help poor people in the long term.

The moral

The moral of the story is clear: spend what God has lent you responsibly. In old Bibles, the manager's called a steward. Christian Stewardship Campaigns call on church people to give 5 per cent of their after-tax income to their local church, and 5 per cent to other charities. But actually Jesus wasn't just talking about money. The people he was addressing had received the gospel, the good news of God's love, and they were keeping it to themselves. Jesus calls on us to pass the gospel on to others. Otherwise, we are as guilty as the crooked manager, who kept the boss's property for himself. If God has lent you time, talents, money or faith, share them with others, for your mutual benefit.

All-age worship

Learn about the fairer taxation campaign.

Suggested hymns

Be thou my vision; Forth in thy name, O Lord, I go; Lord, for the years; Take my life, and let it be.

Seventeenth Sunday after Trinity (Proper 20)
22 September
Second Service   **What if there were No Churches?**
Ps. [128 Domestic Bliss] 129 Cursing the persecutors; Ezra 1 Permission to rebuild; John 7.14–36 The one who sent me

> *'Thus says King Cyrus of Persia: The Lord, the God of heaven, has given me all the kingdoms of the earth, and he has charged me to build him a house at Jerusalem in Judah. Any of those among you who are of his people ... are now permitted to go up to Jerusalem in Judah, and rebuild the house of the Lord, the God of Israel ... and let all survivors, in whatever place they reside, be assisted by the people of their place with silver and gold ... besides freewill-offerings for the house of God in Jerusalem.' Ezra 1.2–4*

233

Cyrus

The Persian King wasn't a religious man, but he realized that his power depended on keeping all his people happy. Cyrus didn't worship the Jewish God, but he had a lot of Jewish subjects, and realized it was important to give them a temple to worship in. So he gave them enough money, encouraging their neighbours to help, too, and sent them off to build one.

Today

If our rulers today were as wise as Cyrus, they would realize that all religions in this country need places of worship, but usually the worshippers can't afford to maintain them on their own. Of course, governments mustn't favour one religion over another, but at present they only make grants to historic buildings, and then take away more than they have given by charging VAT on the repair bills. Taxpayers will grumble that they never go to church themselves, so why should their taxes go to buildings they never use? Yet we can answer that by asking another challenging question: what would the country be like if there were no churches?

What churches do

Imagine the landscape of this country if all the churches, through lack of funding, had fallen into dangerous ruins and were closed even to tourists. At present, the minority of people who are regular worshippers pay an enormous amount towards maintaining beautiful ancient buildings for others to enjoy. If there were no churches, there would still be believers, but they would have to worship in each other's homes. Businesses would lose the income from tourism. There would be nowhere for people to have a dignified wedding or have their children christened; all funerals would have to be secular. Church spires point the way to heaven: people would lose the inspiration that comes from knowing that there is a group of people there who will pray for the sick and help the needy. Among those who run our voluntary organizations, helping the aged and guiding young people, a far higher proportion are inspired to do so by what they learn in church than church-attendance figures would lead you to expect. Much of our history and tradition is centred on the churches, and many of the beautiful words and phrases in our language come from the Christian faith. Religion is no longer taught in schools, except as a cultural survival, so our children would no longer be taught about our heavenly Father, and about the importance of forgiveness, self-control and loving our neighbour. We can already see in the behaviour of some young people what effect the lack of moral teaching has – if that went on for a couple of generations I dread to think what our society would be like. Of course those who still believe would still bear witness, and teach those who were willing to listen. But with no centres of instruction, that witness would be obscured, and without the inspiration that comes from worshipping with others, those whose faith was weak would eventually lose heart and fall away.

Everyone's responsibility

In the past, when there was no other centre than the church building for community life and care, and no alternative way of passing an interesting Sunday, many people attended worship whose faith was purely nominal. Rich landowners built and repaired churches, and the contributions of the congregation were small. Today, although the numbers of committed Christians remains about the same, other things have changed in our society and people are reluctant to give time or money to an institution which seems increasingly irrelevant to their lives. Yet if even the Persian King Cyrus understood the importance of religious buildings in undergirding a stable society, perhaps secular people today can be persuaded to see the importance of spiritual values. The people of this land must be challenged, even those who say, 'I'm not religious, Vicar', to accept responsibility for the continuation of a spiritual life in our nation. The only way to do this is to ask them to imagine what it would be like if all the churches closed. Then perhaps they may realize that by avoiding any form of religious commitment, they are doing irreparable damage to the nation's future.

Suggested hymns

Angel voices, ever singing; Christ is our corner-stone; The Church's one foundation; We love the place, O God.

Eighteenth Sunday after Trinity (Proper 21)

29 September

(St Michael and All Angels)

Principal Service **A Rich Man and Lazarus**

(*Continuous*): Jer. 32.1–3a, 6–15 Buying a field; Ps. 91.1–6,
14–16 Providence; *or* (*Related*): Amos 6.1a, 4–7 Possessions;
Ps. 146 The needy; 1 Tim. 6.6–19 Possessions, the needy; Luke
16.19–31 A rich man and Lazarus

> *'The poor man died and was carried away by the angels to be with Abraham. The rich man also died and was buried.' Luke 16.22*

Jesus told a parable about a rich man, whom we call 'Die-veez', a poor man called Lazarus, and Abraham, their common ancestor. A parable is fiction; it doesn't tell us literally 'the furniture of heaven or the temperature of hell'. This dialogue, for two readers representing Dives and Abraham, is to make you think about what the story means to us today.

Dialogue

Dives   Father Abraham! Can you hear me? I can see you up there in the light. *(Louder)* Father Abraham! *(Shouting)* Abraham!

Abe   Hello, yes, that's me. Does somebody want to talk with me?

Dives   Yes, me! I've been calling 'Father Abraham', till I'm hoarse. Why didn't you answer?

Abe   Because I'm not your father. What's your name?

Dives   Mmm? My name? I'm sure I had one once. No, it's no good. Just can't remember. Everybody used to call me 'Die-veez', before I came down here. It means 'Rich'. My wealth mattered more than my personality to most people.

Abe   Which mattered most to you, your wealth or your personality?

Dives   Oh yes, tricky question. I was certainly proud of my money. It's the creators of wealth that make society what it is today!

Abe   Do you like society as it is today?

Dives   Oh, yes! Lots of food and drink for me to enjoy, nice clothes, people to wait on me.

Abe	But some people don't enjoy it much, because they are not wealthy.
Dives	Yes, it's disgraceful. You used to be able to walk down the street and admire the view, but these days there's beggars everywhere. I had a job to get in through my own front-gate last week. A beggar was lying across the gateway in a disgraceful state. Covered in sores! I even had to kick away the pi-dogs that licked off the pus, before I could get in. He wanted my leftovers to eat. I mean, people should work for their bread!
Abe	What was the name of this beggar?
Dives	Name? How should I know? I haven't got time to go round asking every beggar what his name is.
Abe	You've got all the time in the world now. I'll tell you. It's Lazarus. He's up here reclining at my table. In the place of honour, next to me. He died of starvation and disease, a couple of days before you ate yourself to death.
Dives	I ... It was apoplexy! ... Yes, I see the beggar-man now. What's he doing up there? Why should the poor be happy and a rich man like me have to suffer? I haven't had a drink for days. Where's the justice in that?
Abe	That's exactly what it is, simple justice. You had all the good things, and Lazarus had a bad time. Now the situation's reversed: fair's fair.
Dives	Well if everything here works by opposites, the idle beggar ought to be doing some work for a change. Tell him to get up off his ... couch, and bring me a drink.
Abe	Sorry, what's-your-name. Can't do that. Look, the scenery's like the Grand Canyon, between your bit of the after-life and ours. Never get across in an eternity of Sundays.
Dives	Why didn't someone tell me? Look here, one last favour. I've got five brothers back home. We were always scrapping and quarrelling. But I've got to warn them somehow. Send that idle Lazarus fellow to carry a message for me. Have him tell my brothers to change their ways – start giving pennies to the homeless. If they don't, all six of us might finish up here together for eternity. And that really would be hell!
Abe	No deal. It wouldn't work. Moses and the prophets left written warnings. Told them that God cares how we treat each other – that time's only a training course for eternity – that we make our own hell by cutting ourselves off

237

	from the people we could share heaven with. They paid no notice. Wrote off the writings as outdated moralizing.
Dives	But if Lazarus came back from the dead to warn them, surely that would do the trick?
Abe	We are planning to send God's own Son back from the dead, see if they believe in an afterlife then. I don't expect they will.
Dives	But I really wanted to ... Oh, if only ...
Abe	Your life was full of what you intended to do, if only you'd understood the urgency. On your way down, did you notice the paving stones?

All-age worship

Make toys to sell to help the homeless.

Suggested hymns

For the healing of the nations; From heaven you came, helpless Babe; O Jesus, I have promised; When I needed a neighbour, were you there?

St Michael and All Angels   29 September
Angels' Delight

Gen. 28.10–17 Jacob's ladder; Ps. 103.19–22 Bless the Lord, you angels; Rev. 12.7–12 Michael fought the dragon (*if the Revelation reading is used instead of the Old Testament reading, the New Testament reading is* Heb. 1.5–14 Higher than the angels); John 1.47–51 Angels descending on the Son of Man

> '[Jacob] dreamed that there was a ladder set up on the earth, the top of it reaching to heaven; and the angels of God were ascending and descending on it.' Genesis 28.12

Pudding

You know that there is a yummy sort of sweet-course called Angels' Delight? I don't know who first dreamt up the name, but it's a witty attempt to suggest that this pudding is the most delicious thing in all creation, and even the angels in heaven would be delighted to taste a portion. But joking apart, what do we mean by angels; and do we seriously believe in them?

Angels

The word angel comes from a Greek word meaning a messenger; the Hebrew word for an angel means the same thing. In Jacob's dream, he saw a ladder or stairway from earth to heaven, with angels coming down to bring God's messages of hope, joy and guidance to human beings, and returning to take our prayers up to God. The Bible says that angels are spiritual beings, created by God in the beginning, before the earth was founded, and they rejoiced when creation was completed. The Bible doesn't tell us what angels look like; in fact, sometimes they appear as ordinary human beings, and can't be recognized as angels, so that, as Hebrews tells us, 'some have entertained angels unawares'. Later, Jacob thought he was wrestling with an angel and only later did he realize that it was God himself, disguised as an angel. Abraham gave hospitality to three angels, who then became one, and Christians have seen this as an appearance of the Holy Trinity. But then, if there really are spiritual beings who carry God's messages, they don't have a physical body, and can appear in any form they choose.

Spirits

Hebrews asks, 'are not all angels *spirits* in the divine service, sent to serve for the sake of those who are to inherit salvation?' And spirits are not bound by the laws of time and space, as we are. So we can't expect to understand very much about them, and there is no scientific way of proving whether or not they exist. Jesus said that in the resurrection, we shall be like the angels in heaven, who neither marry nor are given away in marriage. All thoughts of property rights and inheritance are irrelevant when we are talking about beings without physical bodies. Some people seem to have a deep faith in God, but never give the angels a second thought. Others claim a close relationship with their own guardian angel. Jesus said there's joy in the presence of the angels when one sinner repents, and for some Christians that's enough to prove that they exist. But it may be better to think of them as a poetic way of saying that there are many things in the universe which we can never understand, but which have a great influence upon us. Poetic references to angels may be a way of leading us to contemplate the mystery of God and of the afterlife.

Poetry

Speaking of poetry, I'm going to read to you a little piece of light verse which I found in a book recently. But like most poetry, and much humour, it conceals a serious point. It's an attempt to talk about God's spiritual messengers in the language of modern science. And why not, if that helps modern, scientifically educated people to imagine the unimaginable – to conceive of beings which are not subject to the laws of science, but which act upon the physical world in ways beyond our understanding? But then the poem ends with a reference to the delight which angels experience in doing what God has created them for, and reminds us of the delicious pudding. It goes like this:

Angels' delight

We soar at a velocity
exceeding thought or sight,
with boundless curiosity
at twice the speed of light.
In new dimensions listening,
discovering God's will,
and then fly fast as glistening
his wishes to fulfil.

We travel without tarrying
through universal space,
obediently carrying
God's messages of grace;
and endlessly, with clarity,
through depth and width and height,
proclaiming heaven's charity,
the angels' one delight.

Suggested hymns

Angel voices ever singing; Hark! hark, my soul, angelic songs are swelling; How shall I sing that majesty?; Songs of praise the angels sang.

('Angels' delight' is © Michael Counsell and may be copied under the terms of the CCLI licence. It may be sung to the tune of 'O little town of Bethlehem'.)

Nineteenth Sunday after Trinity (Proper 22)
6 October
(Alternatively the Dedication Festival)

Principal Service   **Faith Amid Chaos**

(*Continuous*): Lam. 1.1–6 The nation, suffering; *Canticle*: Lam. 3.19–26 New every morning, *or* Ps. 137 Suffering in Babylon; *or* (*Related*): Hab. 1.1–4; 2.1–4 A watchman; Ps. 37.1–9 Faith and justice; 2 Tim. 1.1–14 Faith and justice; Luke 17.5–10 Faith and obedience

> *'For this gospel ... I suffer as I do. But I am not ashamed, for I know the one in whom I have put my trust, and I am sure that he is able to guard until that day what I have entrusted to him.'* 2 Timothy 1.11–12

Carousel

The song in the musical, *Carousel,* about walking through a storm and keeping your head held high, is so well known I needn't quote it in full. I think this is what the Bible means by faith. We tend to think about somebody arguing with an atheist, or sitting in a library weighing up evidence, when we talk of faith. It's true that before you can have faith in God you have to believe that there is a God to have faith in; and to believe this you have to weigh up the arguments for and against, and decide which is more probable. But you will never come to a conclusion if the process is entirely cerebral – there are no proofs of the existence of God. Eventually you have to take your head out of your books, and put faith to the test. This is called 'the leap of faith', when you step out in faith, and wait to see whether anyone catches you.

The leap of faith

A photographer was taking pictures of a hang-glider on a rainy day, and saw that he was leaping from the mountainside straight into a rainbow. What a perfect symbol of faith and hope! He had no proof that his wings would support him, but he trusted himself to the very strong possibility that they would, and made the leap of faith. Of course he'd tested all his equipment, and knew from his own experience and that of others that his forward momentum would create an upward pressure from the air on his sloping wing-surface. But he couldn't see the air, and he had to launch himself, trusting to the invisible forces to support him. Of course his faith was justified; he had an enjoyable afternoon and a superb view, and the photographer got the picture of his lifetime.

Christian life

The parallel between this story and living the Christian life is clear. We can't see God. But we know from our own experience and that of millions of others, that when you trust God he will always uphold you. That doesn't mean you will have a trouble-free life – there are many storms to walk through. But if you ask God for guidance and courage, and trust in him, he will give them to you, and you will emerge at the end 'bloodied but unbowed'. If you shrink back into your safe shelter and never step outside, you will live a dull life. But step out boldly, challenge the opposing forces, climb over the obstacles, and you will live heroically and receive your reward in eternity.

St Paul

The world around us often seems to be utterly chaotic. But the Bible begins with the image of God's Holy Spirit brooding over the chaos, which was 'without form and void', and bringing a beautiful creation out of the mayhem. Spirit-filled Christians can do the same. St Paul had a nice cosy number as a leading Pharisee, firm in his convictions and supported by his colleagues. Then Jesus spoke to him on the road to Damascus, and everything changed. He travelled by land and sea, keeping his head high amid shipwrecks, riots, imprisonment, opposition, exhaustion and extreme danger. He made the leap of faith; nobody could say his life was dull, but he counted the dangers his glory. In the Second Letter of Paul to Timothy, he wrote 'For this gospel ... I suffer as I do. But I am not ashamed, for I know the one in whom I have put my trust, and I am sure that he is able to guard until that day what I have entrusted to him.'

Example

Will you follow Paul's example, putting your trust in God amid the chaos and stepping out boldly to confront the challenges? Jesus said that even a tiny faith, no bigger than a mustard seed, is sufficient to bring you salvation; and, of course, the important thing about a mustard seed is that, given half a chance, it will grow. Faith in the midst of chaos will always result in triumph.

All-age worship

Learn the words of the song from Carousel – http://www.risa. co.uk/sla/song.php?songid=16078 – *Change them slightly so that they mention faith in Jesus. (NB it is illegal to publish the changes.)*

Suggested hymns

Be still, my soul; Father, hear the prayer we offer; New every morning is the love; Through all the changing scenes of life.

Nineteenth Sunday after Trinity (Proper 22)
6 October
Second Service   The Spirit Level

Ps. 142 My portion in the land of the living; Neh. 5.1–13 Social Justice; John 9 Spiritual blindness

> *'After thinking it over, I brought charges against the nobles and the officials; I said to them, "You are all taking interest from your own people." And I called a great assembly to deal with them.'* Nehemiah 5.7

What level?

At what level do you live your life? At the level of the Lowest Common Denominator? Some people live at an entirely *material level*, only concerned to become rich and enjoy earthly pleasures. Many of these people are miserable, for no matter how much you have got, you always want more. Or are you living your life on the level of people who are unselfish, who look for opportunities to help others, who create beauty and enjoy the simple things in life. These people think that spiritual values, like love, truth and beauty, are more important than material possessions. In Christian terms, they are inspired by the Holy Spirit. They live their lives at the *spiritual level*, and that's what we should all be aiming for. You could say they live at the *'Spirit level'*, except that people might think that you are talking about the carpenter's tool which we call by that name. And that's something entirely different. Or is it?

Spirit levels

Suppose you are building a set of shelves. You need to get them level or things will fall off. So you use a glass tube, mounted in a piece of wood, filled with alcohol except for a small bubble of air. Two lines are etched on the tube at the centre, and when it's precisely horizontal, the bubble sits between them. If it doesn't, you have got to raise one end of your surface until it does. You use the spirit level to ensure that both ends are at exactly the same height above floor-level.

Spiritual

Living at the spiritual level is also concerned with equality. Spiritual people believe that God made everyone, and loves them equally. Everyone is equally important to God. So we should try to affirm everybody's self-esteem, praising them until they regain their self-respect. We should care especially for the underprivileged and deprived, until they reach such a level that they can help themselves. Spiritually, we should regard everybody as at an equal level of importance in society, and equally precious.

Society

Does this mean everybody should be financially equal, with the same income? Probably not. When everything belonged to the tribe, the tribal chief ensured that it was shared out fairly. Under communism, some countries tried to reproduce this classless society; but communism failed because when you are all equally poor – no matter how hard you work – then nobody has any motive to work at all. The opposite extreme is when the richest own many times more than the poorest. A recent study has shown that societies where the gap is biggest have the most problems. The USA is one of the most unequal societies on earth. It imprisons 576 people per

100,000 of population, which is 14 times higher than the rate in Japan. The number of murders per million people in the population is 64 in the USA, 5.2 per million in Japan and 15 per million in the UK. Where the richest possess many times more than the poorest, we breed resentment and everyone lives in fear of theft and violence. Similarly, when rich countries overeat while poorer countries starve, we risk forcing the poor to take the law into their own hands.

Solutions

There are no easy answers to these problems. The first step is to recognize that there is a problem. We may never reach Marxist absolute equality, nor would we wish to. Levelling up is much better than levelling down. But when the Jewish leader Nehemiah was trying to rebuild Jerusalem after the return from exile, he called a national conference. The poor were in debt to money lenders, their sons were sold for slaves and their daughters as prostitutes. The rich realized that, for their own peace of mind, they needed to stop charging their poor neighbours an outrageous rate of interest, and they agreed to return their houses and their fields to them. Many of the prophets also preached justice for the poor. Charities involved in international development aim to restore to the poor their right to escape disease, to education, to share in community decisions and to self-respect. Christians fighting against the slave trade argued that injustice in society diminishes us all. The answer is not forced equality, but in recognizing that all are equally important in the eyes of God. Loving and caring for the poor isn't patronizing: it's trying to return to them the justice of which we have robbed them. With the help of the Holy Spirit, we want to return to a spiritual level, where all God's children are respected equally – a true 'Spirit level'!

Suggested hymns

God of freedom, God of justice; Judge eternal, throned in splendour; Restore, O Lord, the honour of your name; Thy kingdom come! On bended knee.

Twentieth Sunday after Trinity (Proper 23)

13 October

Principal Service **Contagion**

(*Continuous*): Jer. 29.1, 4–7 Support the city; Ps. 66.1–11 What God has done; *or* (*Related*): 2 Kings 5.1–3, 7–15c Naaman healed from leprosy; Ps. 111 The works of the Lord; 2 Tim. 2.8–15 Suffering and perseverance; Luke 17.11–19 The healing of a leper and his thanks

> *'As [Jesus] entered a village, ten lepers approached him. Keeping their distance, they called out, saying, "Jesus, Master, have mercy on us!" When he saw them, he said to them, "Go and show your-selves to the priests." And as they went, they were made clean.'*
> Luke 17.12–14

Contagion

Most people are terrified of contagious diseases. In wartime, the slogan was, 'Coughs and sneezes spread diseases – trap the germs in your handkerchief.' Now you have to put 'antibacterial rub' on your hands whenever you enter or leave a hospital. Until recently, leprosy was deeply feared. Anyone coming into close contact with a leper risked becoming infected. Painful sores were followed by lack of sensation, paralysis and death. So lepers were ordered to live outside the town, and to ring a bell as they moved around, crying 'Unclean, unclean!' Now that's all changed. By following simple rules of hygiene, the risk of contagion can be completely eliminated. With modern drugs, a sufferer from what's now called 'Hansen's Disease', if it's treated early enough, can be completely cured

Jesus

But when some lepers approached Jesus, St Luke tells us that they 'kept their distance'. St Mark and St Matthew tell us that there were occasions when, despite the risk of contagion, Jesus actually touched lepers, which must have shocked the onlookers. There was no known cure for leprosy in those days, and yet Jesus told the ten lepers to 'go and show yourselves to the priests', to prove that they were healed and no longer contagious. With remarkable faith, although they still had all the symptoms of leprosy, the ten set off towards the Temple, and 'as they went they were healed'. Was it a miracle? Well, yes and no. A miracle is something that makes us admire God, whether or not it breaks any so-called laws of nature. Scientific laws are simply our descriptions of how God normally works, but there's nothing to stop God occasionally working in a different way under special circumstances. There's plenty of scientific evidence for the 'placebo effect', when patients, who wouldn't otherwise have been expected to recover, are healed because they believe that an effective medicine has been given to them. So what! God has put many powers of self-healing into our bodies, which are inhibited if the patient is depressed or worried. Perhaps these lepers were prevented from recovering by the appalling effects of being outcasts from society. When Jesus showed them that he accepted them and loved them, this enabled them to heal themselves. If that doesn't make you admire God, what does?

Following his example

Many Christians have followed the example of Jesus. Blessed Father Joseph Damien gave his life in caring for the lepers in Hawaii. Many Christian medical missionaries have cared for lepers, to the astonishment of non-Christians who had been taught to shun them. Later they were formed into the Leprosy Mission. Some people have been converted to Christianity by the example of undiscriminating love which these Christian doctors showed to sick people of all faiths. In fact you could say that the example set by love is even more contagious than leprosy was. If you want to convert the world to Christianity, preaching comes second. First you must show the people around you an example of Christlike love to the sick, poor and needy, whatever their background. Then, when people ask you why you do it, you can reply that you are only following the example of Jesus.

St Francis

St Francis of Assisi was another who imitated Christ by kissing lepers. One time, as he turned away from the abhorrent, filthy and disfigured sufferer, Francis had a vision. He turned back and saw standing in the road, not the leper but Jesus himself. For ever after, he saw the image of Christ in all who suffer and are outcast. The love he showed to them was given, not just to them, but to Christ in them. 'All the world loves a lover', goes the proverb. If you are seen to be showing Christian love to those who don't deserve it, some of that love will 'rub off' onto those who see you, just as Jesus's love 'rubbed off' onto you. So the contagion of love will spread, until Christ's love infects more and more people, and this sick and sinful world is transformed.

All-age worship

Stand in a circle. One person hugs the person on their right, saying, 'I love you because Jesus loves you.' Then pass it on round the circle.

Suggested hymns

Give thanks with a grateful heart; Immortal love, forever full; One shall tell another; Thine arm, O Lord, in days of old.

Twentieth Sunday after Trinity (Proper 23)
13 October
Second Service　**Friendship**
Ps. 144 Prayer for peace; Neh. 6.1–16 Rebuilding the Temple; John 15.12–27 Friends of Jesus

> *'[Jesus said,] "You are my friends if you do what I command you."'*
> *John 15.14*

Friendship

A song about friendship by Cole Porter begins, 'If you're ever in a jam, here I am.' True friendship, then, involves making yourself available to help each other out, whenever you are needed. It's centred in self-giving, unselfishness and tolerance. Friendship is an enduring, intimate, trusting relationship between two people who may be very different. It's all the more remarkable, then, that Jesus called the disciples his friends. And that includes you and me. Jesus counts us as his close friends. He trusts you. He believes you are capable of the deepest of all human relationships with him. Listen:

> As the Father has loved me [he said], so I have loved you; abide in my love. If you keep my commandments, you will abide in my love, just as I have kept my Father's commandments and abide in his love ... This is my commandment, that you love one another

as I have loved you ... You are my friends if you do what I command you. I do not call you servants any longer, because the servant does not know what the master is doing; but I have called you friends, because I have made known to you everything that I have heard from my Father ... I am giving you these commands so that you may love one another.

Distant?

Have you been keeping your distance from Jesus? Don't! He wants a close, intimate relationship with you. Often, when someone offers you their friendship, you hold back, because you don't quite trust them. Friends can be so manipulative! But not Jesus. What he offers you is his deep, personal love, and all he wants in return is that you should love him in the same way. How you show that love is up to you. But I can tell you, once you realize how much Jesus loves you – enough to die for you – nothing is too much for you to do for your pal, to show how grateful you are. This isn't forced; it's your freely chosen personal response to the discovery that you are loved. Your friendship with Jesus will be as close as you will let it be – he will back off when you want to be alone, and come close to you when you feel lonely!

Ups and downs

The reason that Jesus came down to earth was so that he could make friends with you. There are ups and downs in every friendship, but when you have a row, you will take steps to heal the wounds as soon as possible. True friendship is the ability to have a heated argument and remain friends. There are times when you get very cross with our friend, Jesus – particularly when you had planned to go out and the rain comes sheeting down for hours on end! Well, tell him that you are *very* angry with him. Then you will pause, and begin to laugh at yourself when you realize how ridiculous you are being. You will say, 'Sorry, Jesus, I didn't really mean that!' Then you can imagine Jesus putting his arm round you, and saying, 'That's all right, my friend. I don't mind. I forgive you.' Forgiving, and accepting forgiveness, is an essential part of any friendship. Later, there may come more serious misunderstandings – you are in acute pain, or somebody you love dies. Then your friendship with Jesus is sorely tested. But if you hang in there, and trust him, come what may, eventually your friendship will be deeper than ever.

Other friendships

And you know what? The things that you have discovered about friendship, from your friendship with Jesus, will spill over into your other relationships. The friends you make at church; those you meet at the pub; your work colleagues; those you share sporting activities with. These are all friendships which you need, and which you can learn from. But they all have their ups and downs, and need preventive maintenance – sometimes serious emergency repairs. Then you can apply to them the habits of openness, honesty and forgiveness you learnt in your friendship with Jesus. And your family? Do you tell them, often, how much you love them? Do you ever say, 'You are a really good friend to me?' Do you have that true friendship with your loved ones which is the ability to have a heated argument and remain friends? It's the friendship of Jesus which teaches us how to manage all our other friendships. Thanks, Jesus – thank you, dear friend!

Suggested hymns

Come down, O love divine; Do not be afraid, for I have redeemed you; I come with joy a child of God; What a friend we have in Jesus!

Twenty-first Sunday after Trinity (Proper 24)
20 October
Principal Service **Persistence**
Jer. 31.27–34 The new covenant; Ps. 119.97–104 Love for God's Law; *or (Related)*: Gen. 32.22–31 Wrestling Jacob; Ps. 121 Providence; 2 Tim. 3.14—4.5 The word of God; Luke 18.1–8 Perseverance in prayer

> *'Jesus told them a parable about their need to pray always and not to lose heart.' Luke 18.1*

Corruption

Corruption in the legal system is not unknown today, in many countries of the world. We pride ourselves that justice in our own nation is entirely above board; elsewhere, however, the judges are not well paid, and expect an envelope stuffed with banknotes before they will give you a favourable judgement. Jesus told a story about a corrupt judge and a poor widow. Jewish judges sat in panels of three. Because the judge in the story was sitting alone, he must have been one of the magistrates appointed by King Herod or by the Roman Empire. These were notorious; unless the plaintiffs put down a hefty bribe, they stood no chance of winning. The poor widow couldn't afford this, so her only option was to dog the steps of the judge and make a real nuisance of herself.

Persistence

The judge complained that he got no sleep because of this. So, although it was against his selfish interests, he gave the widow what she wanted so as to get rid of her! Typical! The audience must have laughed knowingly when Jesus told the story. But what was the point? Did Jesus mean that God was like the unjust judge? Surely not! No, Jesus was saying that our heavenly Father is the exact opposite. God really wants to give us the very best in life. As the collect says, he is 'more ready to hear than we to pray'. But we have to ask for things, to remind ourselves that we are completely dependent on God's mercy. We are incapable of looking after ourselves. So like the importunate widow, we must be persistent in our prayers.

Ineffective

Everyone is disappointed sometimes about the apparent ineffectiveness of our prayers. We ask for something we desperately want, and nothing happens. It feels as though nobody is listening to our petitions. Why can this be, if God is as Jesus said he is? Well, the most loving parent has to refuse their children's requests sometimes. This is because the parent knows that what the child asks for may not be good for them. Too much sugary food may make the child obese and sickly. Dangerous toys might cause them to hurt themselves. There's nothing more unattractive than a seriously spoilt brat! Short-term indulgence may prevent long-term enjoyment, though children don't see it this way.

God knows

But compared with the all-seeing and eternal God, we are all like small children. We don't know what's going to happen in the next hour, let alone the next week, month or year. But God can foresee what will take place in our whole lifetime, and even into our eternal future. What God wants is for us to become so trusting of his love that we leave it to him to decide what's best for us. We can only hope to enjoy ourselves in the world to come if we have built up a deep relationship of love and faith, and a certain amount of adversity here below is essential if we are to learn what trusting God really means.

Spiritual gifts

That doesn't mean we should stop praying. The most important thing to ask for is the gift of perseverance – the strength and courage to keep on keeping on, however black the weather is. God has promised to give the spiritual fruit of love, joy, peace, patience, kindness, goodness, faithfulness, gentleness and self-control to all who ask for them. The best way to encourage them to grow is by using them – in that way gifts of character are like muscles: they need plenty of exercise. And the best way to realize just how much we need them is to keep on praying for them.

Don't lose heart

Of course, you should also persevere in asking for your daily bread; God knows that you need it, but we need to remind ourselves that we can't expect even basic nourishment except by the mercy of God. Ask for an occasional slice of cake, too. You may not always get it, but so long as you realize that, God doesn't mind you asking. The main thing is to build up that relationship of trusting dependence on God which follows from persistent prayer. Don't lose heart.

All-age worship

Write down things you want to ask God for: 2 things to eat; 2 things to play with; 2 changes in your character; 2 changes in your relationships. Against each mark either: Now, Later, or When you think I need it. Put them in God's Suggestion Box, then burn them.

Father, hear the prayer we offer; Great Shepherd of thy people, hear; Lord, teach us how to pray aright; Spirit of holiness, wisdom and faithfulness.

Twenty-First Sunday after Trinity (Proper 24)
20 October
Second Service   **Reasons for Staying Away**
Ps. [146 Freedom] 149 Justice; Neh. 8.9–18 Rejoice in the law; John 16.1–11 Stumbling

> *'I have said these things to you to keep you from stumbling.'* John 16.1

Stumbling

Jesus spoke about disciples who stumble. Whenever he uses this word, he means falling away from the faith; staying away from church. In every generation there are people who do this. Whether it's any worse now than at other times I'm not sure. In country districts people went to church because the squire would throw you off his land if you didn't. In smart suburbs they went because they wanted to look respectable. Church was often the only thing to do on Sundays. But the number of convinced believers is probably no less than it ever was. In Western Europe church attendance has slumped; but almost everywhere else the Church is growing rapidly. So why do people stay away? Jesus warned his disciples that they faced persecution and death for their belief. There's not much risk of that nowadays. But looking at the reasons why people stay away today may help us understand how to help them come back to church. It may also help us to analyse our own reasons for church attendance, so that we don't join the backsliders. Of course, listing the reasons why people stay away may encourage you to join them. In that case, we know that Jesus will be very, very sorry, because he loves you – and I shall be sorry for you too, because you will miss out on the deep joy and encouragement which comes from meeting up with these lovely people here.

Reasons

I have listed these reasons for staying away from church:

My friends make fun of me;
Church is boring, and I don't get anything out of worship;
I'd rather sleep in on Sundays;
Christianity has been disproved by science;
Christianity causes wars;
Christians tell me how to live my life.

Other reasons are often presented, but that will do for starters.

Mockery

The fear of mockery is a very mild disincentive, compared with the first disciples' fear of martyrdom. Many churchgoers are indeed made fun of for their faith; and many bravely bear it and try to show people that regular attendance makes them even nicer to know, because they become less judgemental and proud. Between cowardice and courage, I know which I admire most.

Boring

The charge that church is boring has some truth. Compared with television, which wants you to sit back and be entertained, church services require some effort by the worshippers. But in return for that you get a deeper satisfaction than any form of passive entertainment can give. What we get out of worship is the encouragement that comes from meeting up with other people who want to use love to make the world a better place; guidance on how to do it; and the affirmation that arises from knowing that God loves us.

Sleep

No doubt many would rather sleep in on Sundays, or catch up on the household chores; but looking back, couldn't you have used your time better?

Science and war

Science has certainly defeated those who believe the world was created 6,000 years ago; but many Christians and many scientists embrace both science and the Bible, sensibly interpreted. When Madame Marie-Jeanne Roland saw the bloodshed in the French Revolution, she exclaimed, 'O Liberty! What crimes are committed in your name!' But the fact that evil people used Liberty as an excuse for violence, doesn't mean that Liberty is a bad thing; and neither does the fact that some use religion to justify war discredit religion. If more people stood up for peace by coming to church, perhaps the movement away from violence might be even faster than it has been in the past 2,000 years.

Morals

Similarly, the fact that some Christians are moralistic and judgemental doesn't reflect on the teaching of Jesus, who told us not to judge others, but to forgive. It's a delusion to think that only respectable people are welcome at church; the outcasts and marginalized can be equally at home. However, Jesus did tell us that accepting the love of God means we have to love our neighbours. He expects us to work out for yourself what that means, and then try to put it into practice. This may be the real reason why people stay away: because they know churchgoing will involve changing to a more compassionate lifestyle, which they are not yet prepared for.

Affirmation

So hang on in there, sisters and brothers. Without church, your life would lack meaning, purpose, direction and encouragement. Then invite your friends to come with you one Sunday and give it a try. Tell them Jesus loves them, and wants them to know it. None of us is perfect; but coming to church helps us to improve. An atheist said, 'Churchgoers are all hypocrites', to which a Christian replied, 'Well, come and join us. There's always room for one more.'

Suggested hymns

Jesus! where'er thy people meet; One shall tell another; Spirit of holiness, wisdom and faithfulness; We have a gospel to proclaim.

Last Sunday after Trinity (Proper 25) 27 October
(Alternatively Bible Sunday or the Dedication Festival)
(Eve of SS Simon and Jude)
Principal Service **Defusing Crisis**

Joel 2.23–32 Harvest; Ps. 65 Harvest; *or (Related)*: Ecclus. (Ben
Sira) 35.12–17 Justice for the needy, *or* Jer. 14.7–10, 19–22
Repentance; Ps. 84.1–7 The Temple; 2 Tim. 4.6–8, 16–18
Fight the good fight; Luke 18.9–14 Pharisee's pride, taxman's
humility

> *'The Lord will rescue me from every evil attack and save me for his
> heavenly kingdom.' 2 Timothy 4.18*

St Paul

St Paul travelled all around the world spreading the good news of
God's love. In the process he upset some people, but Paul wasn't
afraid. He wrote to his friend Timothy, 'The Lord will rescue me
from every evil attack and save me for his heavenly kingdom.'
Defusing dangerous situations is an important Christian ministry.
It's very unlikely that any of you will be confronted with a serious
situation; but if you have thought over in advance how you would
react in a minor but worrying incident, you will cope competently
with anything which comes along. Remember, each one of you is
precious to God, and precious to each one of us here, and we don't
want you to come to even slight harm. That's why I want to talk
about such situations. I definitely don't want to make you alarmed,
as this would have the opposite effect to what I'm aiming for, which
is to enable you to stay calm in a crisis.

Anger management

Some problems can make the calmest individual become angry. If
this happens to you, count to ten, and make a deliberate attempt
to calm down. Then find an opportunity to talk it over calmly with
somebody else. If you become angry with somebody, take a deep
breath, lower your voice, and say something like, 'What you have
just said makes me feel angry, but I don't want a row. I shall control
my feelings now and, later, try to talk it over calmly with you.' If it
happens often, try to join a course of anger management. Jesus was
angry when he overturned the tables of the money-changers in the

Temple, but it was a very controlled anger. Uncontrolled anger is one of the seven deadly sins.

Angry strangers

If confronted by an angry stranger, follow a similar strategy. To be frank, there are a number of people with borderline psychiatric illness around, and we are called to deal with them sympathetically, but without risking anyone being hurt. If this happens in the church or churchyard, in the minister's house or on the doorstep, whether you are employed by the church or a volunteer, the same guidelines apply. There's an organization called National Churchwatch, who work with churches, dioceses, police forces and other groups to give them the confidence to deal with any crime issue they may have. They can be contacted at www.nationalchurchwatch.com and they issue a manual of advice. In brief, their advice is this – five don'ts and seven do's:

Never

Never give money to people, no matter how genuine their story is – be practical in your help.
Never get into an argument over any subject when on your own.
Never disturb the scene of a crime if you find one.
Never forget to report a crime to the police, no matter how trivial it may seem.
Never be afraid to run away.

Always

Always trust your instincts.
Always know your limitations.
Always report incidents to someone in authority, no matter how minor they may seem.
Always keep calm.
Always plan ahead – for example, try not be alone, and if approached by someone unknown be sure that a friend is close by and ideally can see you.
Always report any area of your work that puts you at risk.
Always remember that no item of property, even money, is worth coming to harm for.

Conclusion

In conclusion, if someone speaks to you angrily, don't interrupt. When they have finished, count to seven to see if they've got more to say. If not, try to repeat back to them what they just said, to show that you were listening respectfully, and ask them whether you have got it right. If they agree, say, 'Now, what you want me to do about it is this … Is that right?' If they say yes, promise to deal with it as soon as possible, and thank them for their help. If possible, escort them out of the building in the direction of their home. This has been a very down-to-earth sermon. But Jesus set us an example of practical love towards even the most disturbed people. It's not loving to allow them to do any harm to themselves or anybody else, so defusing a tense situation is a useful skill to learn. God bless you, and keep you safe.

All-age worship

Remind children how to contact Childline 0800 1111, and of the rules on speaking to strangers, e.g. http://www.safechild.org/strangers.htm.

Suggested hymns

A safe stronghold our God is still; Be still my soul; Guide me, O thou great Redeemer; When I needed a neighbour.

Last Sunday after Trinity (Proper 25)   27 October
Second Service   Old and Young Together
Ps. 119.1–16 How can young people be pure?; Eccles. 11, 12 Remember your Creator in your youth; 2 Tim. 2.1–7 Crowning an athlete; *Gospel at Holy Communion*: Matt. 22.34–46 Love God and love your neighbour

> *'Remember your creator in the days of your youth, before the days of trouble come.' Ecclesiastes 12.1*

Ecclesiastes

There's a book in the Old Testament called 'Ecclesiastes', meaning 'the Teacher'. It's one of the books known as the 'Wisdom literature' – the author had gathered a collection of proverbs and wise sayings to use in instructing the next generation. Traditionally he was called Solomon, but it's more likely that a scribe was writing in the name of Solomon at a very much later date. He keeps repeating that everything under the sun is vanity, which sounds cynical, but he's probably trying to draw the reader away from concentration on material things, and turning them to the things of God.

Young

In chapter 11, the author encourages young people to enjoy their youth, but remembering that it won't last for ever:

> Rejoice, young man, while you are young, and let your heart cheer you in the days of your youth. Follow the inclination of your heart and the desire of your eyes, but know that for all these things God will bring you into judgement. Banish anxiety from your mind, and put away pain from your body; for youth and the dawn of life are vanity.

Balancing enjoyment of youthful frivolity with adult seriousness isn't easy, but then, youth has never been an easy phase of life for anybody. There are high ideals, much to learn, hormones rushing madly round the bloodstream, and great puzzlement about to how to reconcile the conflicting desires which characterize young people.

Old

Yet immediately following this there's one of the world's most beautiful and touching descriptions of old age:

> Remember your creator in the days of your youth, before the days of trouble come, and the years draw near when you will say, 'I have no pleasure in them'; before the sun and the light and the moon and the stars are darkened and the clouds return with the rain; on the day when the guards of the house tremble, and the strong men are bent, and the women who grind cease working because they are few, and those who look through the windows see dimly; when the doors on the street are shut, and the sound of the grinding is low, and one rises up at the sound of a bird, and all the daughters of song are brought low; when one is afraid of heights, and terrors are in the road; the almond

tree blossoms, the grasshopper drags itself along and desire fails; because all must go to their eternal home, and the mourners will go about the streets; before the silver cord is snapped, and the golden bowl is broken, and the pitcher is broken at the fountain, and the wheel broken at the cistern, and the dust returns to the earth as it was, and the breath returns to God who gave it. Vanity of vanities, says the Teacher; all is vanity.

Old and young together

The writer sounds old, and knows the disadvantages of growing old, but also understands that the old have, in a long life, learnt wisdom which could be very useful to the young. Yet he thinks back nostalgically to the time of his youth, and wishes he still had the enthusiasm and energy which he had then. Linking the two passages together, perhaps he's saying that neither youth nor age are of any value on their own; but if young and old will come together and learn from each other, they can rise above their limitations, and achieve things together which neither could do on their own. The young shouldn't dismiss their elders as old fogies, past it, with nothing but outdated ideas. Nor should the elderly write off the young folk as dangerous innovators, wanting to change everything for no good reason. Young folk should question their elders about their life, and what they have learnt from their experience which might be of value to the young. Old people should try to learn from the novel ideas of the young, and harness their enthusiasm for the benefit of all. Thus old and young, pulling together, can make the world a better place for future generations. Dreams of individual wealth are nothing more than a puff of wind, and there's no new thing under the sun. Yet to everything there is a season ... cast your bread upon the waters ... eat your bread with cheerfulness, and drink wine with a merry heart ... The end of the matter is this ... fear God, and keep his commandments, for that is the whole duty of everyone.

Suggested hymns

According to thy gracious word; Faithful vigil ended; O God, our help in ages past; Give rest, O Christ, to thy servant.

All Saints' Sunday 3 November
Principal Service **Putting God on Hold**

(*These readings are used on the Sunday, or if this is not kept as All Saints' Sunday, on 1 November itself; see p. 353.*)
Dan. 7.1–3, 15–18 The people of God will receive power; Ps. 149 The victory of God's people; Eph. 1.11–23 Christ rules with the saints; Luke 6.20–31 The sermon on the plain

> '*Blessed are you when people hate you, and when they exclude you, revile you, and defame you on account of the Son of Man. Rejoice on that day and leap for joy, for surely your reward is great in heaven.*' *Luke 6.22–23*

The Sermon on the Plain

Many sayings of Jesus about how we should live our lives are found in three chapters in St Matthew's Gospel which we call the Sermon on the Mount. St Luke has a similar but shorter collection, when Jesus had come down a mountain to stand on a level place. I would call it 'the Sermon on the Plain', except that somebody might think it was preached when Jesus was on an aeroplane! Both collections are intended to make you sit up and think – the people who are described as 'blessed' are the very opposite of what the world would consider to be lucky. St Luke writes: 'Blessed are you who are poor ... Blessed are you who are hungry ... Blessed are you who weep ... Blessed are you when people hate you, and when they exclude you, revile you, and defame you on account of the Son of Man.' Not a job description which would attract many applicants today!

The easy life

But Jesus is trying to suggest that the easy life is not good for us. If we live in the lap of luxury, there are no stimuli to our imagination, and we are seldom creative. Spoilt children are horrid. Our best work is done when we are up against it, and challenged to meet a deadline. We may be tempted to ask God to give us our heart's every desire, but it's a jolly good thing that God ignores that sort of prayer, because to get everything we ask for would be the ruin of us. Whereas when bad times come, that's often a time of growth, as we learn to endure hardship bravely. Adversity builds character. At this time of year we think of the great saints of the past. None

261

of them lived an easy life, yet each of them showed greatness in the way they coped with adversity.

Putting God on hold

The most serious aspect of this, however, is the effect it has on our relationship with God. Have you ever used a telephone helpline, when, after listening to a lot of computerized messages, and pressing a long sequence of buttons, you eventually get through to a real human being at last? You carefully explain your problem to them, and they blithely say, 'I shall have to put you on hold for a moment while I consult with my superior.' Then you have to listen to the same snatch of awful music played over and over, interrupted by another computer saying to you, 'Our customers are important to us. Please do not hang up; you are in a queue, and we will deal with your query as soon as one of our operatives is available.' It's at this point that you realize that your call, instead of being free, is being charged to your account at a high cost per minute. Aargh! The fact that you have been 'put on hold' makes you feel totally worthless – nobody is interested in you. Well, when things are going well in our life, we often put God on hold! We tell him we'll deal with him when we have got time, but sorry, we are much too busy to give him our time and attention at present.

Good out of evil

By contrast, when thing go badly, we turn back to God, and realize our need of his help. God brings good out of evil, because he turns our misfortune into a reminder of our total dependence on his love. When we are in trouble, God brings good out of it, because we turn back to him.

Example

So learn a lesson from the example of the saints. We may wish that God would let us live in a garden of roses, but every rose bush is full of sharp thorns. If we accept the prickles when they come to us, and learn our lesson from them, God may be trying to tell us something. In fact, God is always trying to tell us something – usually because he wants to ask us to do something for him, such as looking after someone less fortunate than we are. Listen out for God's call, and do what he wants you to at once. Don't tell God you will call him back when you are less busy. Never put God on hold!

All-age worship

Practise speaking politely to grown-ups on an imaginary telephone. What would you say if God called you?

Suggested hymns

Christ for the world we sing; God has spoken by his prophets; God has spoken to his people; God moves in a mysterious way.

Fourth Sunday before Advent   3 November
Principal Service   **Forgiveness**
(*For use if the Feast of All Saints is celebrated on 1 November, see p. 353.*)
Isa. 1.10–18 Forgiveness; Ps. 32.1–8 Forgiveness; 2 Thess. 1.1–12 Justice; Luke 19.1–10 Salvation for Zacchaeus

> '*All who saw it began to grumble and said, "He has gone to be the guest of one who is a sinner."*' *Luke 19.7*

Zacchaeus

Tax-collecting in the time of Christ was very different from the honourable practices of the Inland Revenue today. For a start, Zacchaeus, who was a tax-collector in Jericho, worked not for his own government, but for the hated Roman occupying army. Admission to the profession was not by competitive examination – the job went to whoever could bid most for it at an auction. Zacchaeus had paid over a lot of cash for the right to fleece his fellow Israelites who passed through Jericho. So he had to recoup his investment by charging the highest rates he thought he could twist out of them, to anyone who passed through his town. Jericho, at 1,300 feet below sea level in the rift valley of the River Jordan, is the lowest city on earth – and Zacchaeus was the lowest crook in Jericho. The crowd was being quite mild when they said, 'Zacchaeus is a sinner.' They were appalled at the idea that a respectable man like Jesus should dine at his house. Jesus was under no delusions about his host's morals. But Jesus wanted to promote Zacchaeus from the status of 'notorious sinner' to that of 'forgiven sinner'. The first step along that path, Jesus knew, was to treat the sinner with respect and understanding. So he invited himself to dinner at Zacchaeus's villa.

Sin

You see, we get it all wrong about sin and sinners. If you or I do something wrong, we kid ourselves it doesn't matter – we ignore it, and go on hurting ourselves and other people by our misdeeds. Whereas the first step is to acknowledge that sin is serious, and confess it. God is on tenterhooks to restore our loving relationship with him, and as soon as we confess, he immediately forgives us, and the sin is forgotten as far as God is concerned. The next mistake we make is to doubt his forgiveness, refusing to forgive ourselves. Which is merely egocentric: you know the verse:

Once in darkest anguish I cried in bitter grief,
'O Lord, my soul is black with guile, of sinners I am chief!'
But then my guardian angel whispered from behind,
'Vanity, my little man, you're nothing of the kind!'

Avoidance

If we know we are forgiven sinners, we never forget it, and we take steps not to repeat the same sins over and over, by avoiding the situations in which we are tempted. I have been talking about when *we ourselves* have sinned. When *other people* sin, however, we condemn them outright, demanding that they should be punished. Which only alienates them further. Instead, what Jesus did was to have dinner with the sinner, and forgive him before he had even got round to confessing. Forgiveness can't change the past, but it makes all the difference in the world to the future. Forgiving somebody is nothing to do with the bitterness and anger you feel in your heart: it's a matter of the practical care and respect you show to the wrongdoer as a human being. Once Zacchaeus realized he was loved, the repentance followed, and he confessed he was a sinner. What's more, he imposed his own punishment, at considerable financial cost to himself. When he knew he had been forgiven, he resolved to avoid sin in future, and was saved. That's why Jesus told us to forgive others, just as we have been forgiven by God – who doesn't wait for our repentance before showing us his love.

As we forgive them

God can't get through to us, so long as we have a spirit of bitterness in our hearts towards somebody else – not because God doesn't want to, but because we shut our hard hearts against him. We all need forgiving: you can't say that one sin is worse than another. We have all fallen short of the standard and example of perfect love set us by Jesus. If two men try to jump a river, the one who falls short by a little bit will get just as wet as the one who falls a long way short! Many people are cut off from God by their failure to forgive others; and don't receive the love he longs to give them because they won't forgive themselves. Jesus died so that *everyone* can be forgiven. So the highest dignity and status that's given to any human being is that of the forgiven sinner who is loved by God.

All-age worship

Make a list of naughty deeds. Write against each the punishment you think you should receive if you did them. How would you feel after that?

Suggested hymns

All ye who seek for sure relief; 'Forgive our sins as we forgive'; I heard the voice of Jesus say; O for a closer walk with God.

Third Sunday before Advent   10 November
The Changing Face of Marriage
(*For a service which is not a Service of Remembrance.*)
Job 19.23–27a My redeemer lives; Ps. 17.1–9 Prayer for salvation; 2 Thess. 2.1–5, 13–17 Perseverance; Luke 20.27–38 The wife of seven brothers

> *'Teacher, Moses wrote for us that if a man's brother dies, leaving a wife but no children, the man shall marry the widow and raise up children for his brother.' Luke 20.28*

Old Testament

Some Sadducees came to Jesus with a story about a woman who had seven husbands, one after another. 'In the resurrection, whose wife will she be?' they asked. Jesus answered that when we rise from the dead we shall be like angels, loving everybody; and questions of legal marriage and inheritance won't matter any longer. This story depended on an obscure law in the Old Testament. If a woman is left a widow, but has no children, who is going to look after her when she's old? So her late husband's brother was ordered to marry her, and give her children who would care for her later. *Even if he was already married to somebody else.* In other words, the law of Moses *ordered* people to practise polygamy, in some circumstances. Was Jesus going to disagree with Moses? He cleverly avoided the challenge by counter-attacking on the Sadducees' attitude to resurrection. This law arose out of a situation in which there was no social security, and widows frequently starved. Abraham had two wives, and David and Solomon had many. Polygamy was necessary, in a society where many men died in battle, leaving women unprotected unless they were taken in as somebody's second wife. The situation had changed by Jesus's time, when most marriages were monogamous. According to the Latin proverb, 'Times change, and we change with them.' We talk about the unchanging Christian attitude to marriage, but in fact our attitude has changed many times.

Slave marriage

In Roman times, the rich were notoriously casual about sex, and the poor were mostly slaves, doing what their masters told them to. In the Middle Ages, everywhere there were feudal societies. The serfs, as they called them, were in fact slaves, owned body and soul by their liege-lord, who was often of a different race: Celts owned by Anglo-Saxons, Saxons owned by Normans and so on. When we talk about the suffering of black slaves in Africa and the Caribbean, it's easy to forget that white people, too, have ancestors who were slaves, and many of them were born 'on the wrong side of the blanket'.

Property rights

Legal marriage only really matters when people own property. When a landowner dies, if there's a dispute as to which of his children are legitimate, the estate is fragmented into units too small to be viable. Romantic love emerged during the Renaissance, influenced by what Jesus said about self-sacrificing, caring love for our neighbours. Yet even when parish registers were first kept in the sixteenth century, far more couples had their babies baptized than appeared in the church marriage registers.

Today

In our own day the situation has changed again. Many people divorce and remarry; so, many couples don't bother to marry because, supposedly, 'living together' makes it easier if you ever want to split up. Homosexual relationships, which were always there beneath the surface, have become more open. What should the Christian reaction be to this more relaxed view of sex?

Relationships

Jesus condemned easy divorce, but that was to protect women, who could be abandoned to starve on the flimsiest of excuses in his days. He wasn't so much concerned with strict rules, as with healthy relationships which could make people happy. Children feel more secure if their parents stay together, at least until the children are grown; men and women need the emotional security of knowing that their partners are loyal, and not sharing their affections with somebody else. So the Christian attitude to marriage shouldn't consist of condemning irregular life patterns, but should concentrate on relationships more than rules. Love, for the Christian, is a matter of behaving caringly to someone, whatever your feelings may be. Falling in love is an effect of the emotions – anyone can do it. Growing in love as the years go by is only possible if you both make an effort of will to be loyal, whatever your feelings may be.

Unselfish love

So despite the changing face of marriage down the ages, the attitude of Jesus remains unchanging. Love, Jesus taught, must always be unselfish, even self-sacrificing. Though we are all fallible, God leaves us free because he trusts us. If we are to make each other happy, we must be able to trust each other; so we must be trustworthy. Marriage is always changing – love never changes.

All-age worship

Play at weddings. Write your own marriage vows.

Suggested hymns

Dear Lord and Father of mankind; I danced in the morning; Lead us, heavenly Father, lead us; Love divine, all loves excelling.

Remembrance Sunday   10 November
The Old Soldier

(The readings of the day, or those for 'In Time of Trouble' can be used. These readings are for 'The Peace of the World'.)
Micah 4.1–5 Swords into ploughshares; Ps. 85.8–13 God will speak peace; James 3.13–18 The harvest of peace; John 15.9–17 No greater love

> *'A harvest of righteousness is sown in peace for those who make peace.' James 3.18*

The old soldier

This is the story of one soldier who fought in the First World War. It draws on his sketchy diary, the official records, and the few things he told his family. He was one of many; but to concentrate on the individual helps us imagine what it was really like. He was not quite 18 years old in 1914, on the day when war was declared between Britain and Germany. He cycled 20 miles to the recruiting office, where he lied about his age, and volunteered to be a soldier. Then he stayed in England for three frustrating years, training to fire guns for the Royal Artillery.

Battle

In France, he found the battlefield a terrifying place. Shells flew directly over the observation post where he was hiding. Several times everyone had to put on gasmasks, because the enemy fired shells containing chlorine gas – if you breathe it in, chlorine burns up the lining of your throat so that you can't breathe, and you die a slow and agonizing death. The officers had to decide what to do with soldiers who were so frightened that they tried to run away. Their noble ideas of fighting bravely for their country didn't last long in those conditions; all they wanted was to live long enough to get home again. They lived in trenches and bunkers dug into the fields. In the heavy rain, the earth turned to mud, and it was freezing cold in the winter. Many dead soldiers were left lying there in the mud because it was too dangerous to bury them. The food was appalling and there was never enough. The smell of raw sewage made them want to vomit.

Wounded

One day in 1917 they came under heavy fire from the enemy, and were ordered to pull back a couple of miles. They couldn't dig the guns out of the mud, and they didn't want the Germans to capture them and use them against them. So this soldier and another soldier were ordered to stay behind, and when the Germans were nearly on them, to blow up their own gun by pushing a shell backwards down the muzzle, putting another in the breech, then pulling a long cord tied to the trigger. They survived this and got away, but on their way back to join the others they were hit by flying shrapnel – heavy bits of red-hot iron, part of an exploded shell. It tore through the soldier's right arm, damaging it beyond repair. In appalling pain he was carried on a stretcher to the field hospital, where the only thing they could do was cut the arm off just below the shoulder. Then he was taken in a rattling railway train to the boat which carried casualties back to England.

Casualty

This probably saved his life. Many of those who were still there for the final year's fighting were killed, and often nobody knows where they were buried. The two-minute silence is to give us a chance to think about those who sacrificed their lives that we might be free. The soldier I have referred to was taken to a hospital near his childhood home, where the hospital cook was an old school friend with whom he'd quarrelled. She must have forgiven him, because a couple of years later they were married. But it took a long time for the British and the Germans to forget *their* quarrel and live together as friends. And still people go on fighting, despite knowing how it tears to shreds the bodies and the families of the millions who are wounded and killed.

Laying down your life

Jesus said, 'Abide in my love … love one another as I have loved you. No one has greater love than this, to lay down one's life for one's friends.' People used to say that the soldier I have been talking about lost an arm in Belgium – he replied, 'Don't say "lost", it sounds careless! Can't you say, I "gave" it?' Many people sacrificed more than an arm in that war and others since. Their sacrifice, to give us freedom, deserves to be remembered on Remembrance Sunday – alongside the sacrifice of his life that Jesus made on the cross, to give us a place in heaven. What would please them most would be if we, their children and grandchildren, could stop fighting, and learn to love each other instead.

All-age worship

Find photographs of servicemen who have fought in battle. Find out all you can about them.

Suggested hymns

For the healing of the nations; Judge eternal, throned in splendour; Make me a channel of your peace; Peace is flowing like a river.

Second Sunday before Advent   17 November
Principal Service   **The End**
Mal. 4.1–2a Judgement; Ps. 98 A new song; 2 Thess. 3.6–13 No idleness; Luke 21.5–19 The end

> *'Beware that you are not led astray; for many will come in my name and say, "I am he!" and, "The time is near!" Do not go after them.' Luke 21.8*

Dashed hopes

Between now and Christmas, our Bible readings seem to refer to the end of the world. Every few years some group of Christians climb a mountain to wait for the Second Coming of Jesus. And he doesn't come, at least not in the way they were expecting. Often their disappointment completely destroys their faith in Christ. Yet when his disciples asked Jesus when the events he had predicted would happen, he replied: 'Beware that you are not led astray; for many will come in my name and say, "I am he!" and, "The time is near!" Do not go after them.'

Confusion

The confusion arises because Jesus spoke about four different things, and they have been placed side by side in the Gospels as though they were all about one event. Jesus predicted:

1 The Day of the Lord, which separates the present age from the age to come;
2 The destruction of Jerusalem by the Roman army in AD 70;
3 The coming of the Son of Man;
4 God's judgement.

Day of the Lord

First, the Jews thought that time was divided into two: the present age, when good people suffer at the hands of cruel tyrants; and the age to come, when God would reign as king and his people will live in peace. These would be separated by the dark and terrible Day of the Lord, a final battle in which there will be great suffering. Jesus spoke often about the kingdom of God, but you will notice he redefines it. The kingdom of God, for Jesus, exists here and now in the hearts of everyone who obeys God as their king. Jesus said: 'The kingdom of God is not coming with things that can be observed; nor will they say, "Look, here it is!" or "There it is!" For, in fact, the kingdom of God *is* among you.'

Destruction of Jerusalem

Second, Jesus foretells the destruction of Jerusalem. This, in fact, happened 40 years later, in AD 70, when the Roman army, exasperated by the Jews' rebelliousness, besieged the city, then set it on fire, until it appeared to observers that there was not one stone standing on top of another. No miraculous foresight was needed for Jesus to see which way things were going, and he warned his listeners to flee Jerusalem before the worst happened. Over a million people died in the debacle, and 97,000 were carried away into captivity.

Son of Man

The third subject which is mixed with these two in the minds of many Christians is 'the coming of the Son of Man'. When Jesus used these words he was quoting from the prophecy of Daniel, in which the great empires of the ancient worlds are symbolized by horrible beasts. Then a human figure, 'one like a son of man', comes on the clouds *to* God, representing the People of God. They are rewarded for their faithfulness when 'To him was given dominion and glory and kingship ... His dominion is an everlasting dominion that shall not pass away, and his kingship is one that shall never be destroyed.' For Jesus, this was fulfilled in his own birth, crucifixion, resurrection and ascension – *that* was the coming of the Son of Man; we don't have to wait for a 'Second Coming'. You may be surprised to learn that this phrase is never used in the Bible.

God's judgement

Fourth, there's the idea of God's judgement. This is poetically imagined as happening at the end of human history and the destruction of the universe. St Paul was among those who, in his early letters to the Thessalonians, thought it would happen in his lifetime. By the time he wrote to the Corinthians, however, he'd decided it happens in a spiritual realm: 'flesh and blood cannot inherit the kingdom of God'. Jesus himself said that unbelievers have already judged themselves: 'And this is the judgment, that the light has come into the world, and people loved darkness rather than light because their deeds were evil.'

Eschatology

Theories about the last things are called 'eschatology'. I was brought up short recently by a reference to the traditional Advent hymns with their 'now dated eschatology'. The old language allowed people to procrastinate, imagining the end as something in the distant future. It's much better to challenge people to realize that God is judging us right now, taking the old words poetically, and not literally.

All-age worship

Set a simple exam about right and wrong. Which is better: discuss the questions now, or leave it till the end of the lesson?

Suggested hymns

In a world where people walk in darkness; The Kingdom of God is justice and joy; The Kingdom is upon you!; The people that in darkness sat.

Second Sunday before Advent   17 November
Second Service   **Parables of the Kingdom**
Ps. [93 The Lord is king] 97 The Lord is king; Dan. 6 The lions' den; Matt. 13.1–9, 18–23 The parable of the sower

> '[Jesus] told them many things in parables, saying: "Listen! A sower went out to sow."' *Matthew 13.3*

The kingdom

What do you think Jesus spoke about more than anything else? It was the idea of the kingdom. He used the word 123 times in the Gospels. The kingdom of God isn't a territory; it's wherever God is obeyed as King. The kingdom of God can therefore be found in the homes of the poor.

Obedience

But God requires total obedience from his subjects. If we are members of God's kingdom, we have to use every effort to find out what God requires of us, and then sacrifice our interests to do it. There was an old-fashioned verse entitled 'God First'. Sometimes parents would hang it over a child's bed, and it could make a deep impression on someone growing up with those words before them every evening and morning. Putting God before everything else is what being in the kingdom of God means.

Among you

Jesus told his followers to proclaim that 'the kingdom of God is among you'. This means that it's here and now. Not something you have to wait for, coming a long time hence. Wherever a group of Christians are prepared to ignore their differences, swallow their pride, and meet together round the Lord's Table, then they are doing what Jesus commanded us to do, and the kingdom of God is already there in the relationships between them.

The kingdom of heaven

The Ten Commandments tell us not to take the name of God in vain. Some Jews in Jesus's day took that literally, and wouldn't even speak the word 'God'; they would use words such as 'heaven' or 'the power' to represent the deity. So Matthew's Gospel represents Jesus as calling the kingdom of God, 'the kingdom of heaven'. This has misled many people into thinking that he was talking about something we wait for until after we die. No, it starts here and now, and it challenges us to obey God as our King on earth, so that we can remain in his kingdom after death.

Parables

Many of his parables start, 'The kingdom of God is like ...'; here are six examples are from Matthew chapter 13:

the kingdom of God is like a man who sowed seed;
the kingdom of God is like a grain of mustard seed;
the kingdom of God is like leaven which a woman hid in some dough – it was hard to obtain pure yeast so, in bread-making, people used to save some of the fermenting dough from the last baking, with live yeast in it, which they called leaven, and use it to start the next batch;
the kingdom of God is like a treasure hidden in a field;
the kingdom of God is like a merchant searching for pearls;
the kingdom of God is like a net which is thrown into the sea.

Context

Before we can apply these stories to ourselves, we must see what they meant to the first hearers. In fact that's true of all the teaching of Jesus; only by seeing it in context can we work out its real meaning. Jesus would have used stories about twenty-first-century life if he had been speaking to us today; but as he wasn't, we have to translate the stories he did use, into our own culture.

Artists

All the great artists paint Jesus in clothes of their own day. It is right to think of Jesus as completely human, one of us, and our friend. But we distort his message if we assume there were no differences between his attitudes and those which are now fashionable. Jesus, and the people he was talking to, knew much of the Old Testament by heart. So he could allude to a verse in the Scriptures without quoting it in full, and everyone would know what he was talking about. Moreover, theirs was a much more poetic way of speaking than our fact-based, science-influenced language; so it's a misunderstanding to treat his statements about personal relationships as though they were scientific fact. We must beware of interpreting Jesus as if he was just like us.

Accuracy

The Gospels were written not as disinterested records of historical fact – in fact there's probably no such thing, because all history is interpretation by selection. But because of their insistence that Jesus was truly human, they were not free to distort history. They are a better record, closer to the events, than we have for most of the personalities in history. There's no question but that the people they describe were historical, and that they said roughly what the documents tell us they said. There's no doubt that Jesus told us to obey God as our King, and the parables are illustrations of what that means.

Suggested hymns

Happy are they, they that love God; Tell me the old, old story; Tell me the stories of Jesus; To thee, O Lord, our hearts we raise.

Christic the King   24 November
Principal Service   **St Dismas**

Jer. 23.1–6 Bad and good shepherds; Ps. 46 God is our refuge
and strength; Col. 1.11–20 Forgiveness in the Son through the
cross; Luke 23.33–43 The thief on the cross

> '[Jesus] replied, "Truly I tell you, today you will be with me in Para-
> dise."' Luke 23.43

Penitent thief

It's very hard to say what we mean by 'a saint'. One definition is
that a saint is someone whom we know to be in heaven. On these
terms, the person we are most certain about is a most improbable
candidate for sainthood. Probably he had a deprived childhood,
got into bad company, started by pinching things from the market
stalls, and graduated to breaking and entering. It got really serious
when he and his pals became highwaymen, armed bandits who
attacked travellers on the road and robbed them of their belong-
ings. When they beat up some high officials, the government had
to take action. Two of them were hunted down, arrested, and condemned to death. Execution in those days was done by the painful
method of crucifixion, and in between the two of them, they hanged
another, who was accused of starting a revolution and claiming to
be a king – probably he was placed between the thieves in order to
humiliate him and rank him among the robbers. Jesus and one of
the thieves struck up a friendship in these unlikely circumstances.
Most people would be incapable of thinking of anything beyond
their agony; but they held a conversation on the meaning of kingship. The thief frankly admitted that he deserved to die; but he
recognized something kingly in the crucified man beside him, and
called out, 'Jesus, remember me when you begin your reign as king.'
Jesus replied, 'Today you will be in paradise.' Both knew there was
no hope of an earthly kingdom now; but Jesus transformed the
language of the kingdom to refer to a heavenly paradise. So the
penitent thief became the only person whom we know with absolute certainty to be in heaven now with Jesus. The wickedest of
sinners became the first among the saints.

Dismas

The Bible doesn't tell us what his name was. A hundred years or so later, he was named as Dismas in the apocryphal *Gospel of Nicodemus*, and ever since, the penitent thief has been called *Saint Dismas* – the sinner who was promised a place in paradise because he recognized the man hanging next to him as some sort of king. Jesus promised that it only takes a tiny expression of trust, faith as small as a grain of mustard seed, to flip us over the dividing line, enabling us to enjoy eternal life. But there's also a lovely legend about St Dismas, showing that even the wickedest of people may have one redeeming feature. It was said that Dismas was a sort of Jewish Robin Hood, stealing from the rich to give to the poor. When Mary, Joseph and baby Jesus were escaping from Herod's persecution on their flight into Egypt, they were attacked, the legend says, by a band of robbers. Dismas was the captain of the band, and was so touched by the loveliness of the Holy Child, that he told his followers not to lay hands on him. 'Blessed child,' said Dismas to the infant, 'if ever there comes a time for you to have mercy on me, then remember me and what I have done for you today.' If that incident ever happened, I don't think it was the cause of Christ's forgiveness, which he would have offered anyway – but it may have been the reason why St Dismas had the courage to ask for it.

Christ the King

The penitent thief asked for a place in God's kingdom, and it was granted to him forthwith. 'This day,' said Jesus, 'you will be with me in paradise.' 'Paradise' is a Persian word. meaning the garden where the king walks with his friends in the cool of the evening. Dismas and Jesus were both shortly going to die, and King Jesus promised his new friend, not just a seat in an earthly throne-room; not everlasting boredom in a misty dream-world; but the most wonderful thing imaginable: eternity in the company of friends, basking in the love of our heavenly King. That offer is open to you, too – and your neighbour, and your enemy. However wicked you may have been, just one word of trust, a simple prayer for mercy, and like the Penitent Thief, you will find yourselves, together with all whom you love, in a world where you are so happy that time seems to stand still. The human race is pictured by the Bible as beginning in paradise – and that's where God wants us all to end.

All-age worship

List people you'd like to meet in heaven when we are all dead.

Suggested hymns

Awake, my soul, and with the sun; Meekness and majesty; The kingdom of God is justice and joy; Were you there when they crucified my Lord?

Christ the King   24 November
Second Service   Jesting Pilate

Morning Ps. 29 Enthroned, 110 The king at your right hand; Evening Ps. 72 An ideal king; 1 Sam. 8.4–20 The demand for a king; John 18.33–37 My kingdom is not of this world

> *'Pilate ... asked [Jesus], "Are you the King of the Jews?" Jesus answered, ... "My kingdom is not from this world ..." ... Pilate asked him, "So you are a king?" Jesus answered, "You say that I am a king. For this I was born, and for this I came into the world, to testify to the truth. Everyone who belongs to the truth listens to my voice." Pilate asked him, "What is truth?"' John 18.33–38*

Pontius Pilate

Jesus was brought before Pontius Pilate, the Governor, charged with starting a revolution. The Roman wasn't interested in Jewish arguments about blasphemy, but he was very concerned about any threat to the authority of the Roman Emperor. 'Is it true?' he asked. 'Do you claim to be the King of the Jews?' 'King is your word,' answered Jesus the Anointed One, the 'Christ'. Pilate had quite the wrong idea of kingship. Jesus was not a this-worldly king, so he was no threat to the Romans. To Jesus, kingship meant witnessing to the truth about the love of God, and his plans to draw us all by love into his heavenly kingdom. 'Everyone who belongs to the truth listens to my voice ...' Jesus began, but Pilate interrupted him – 'You say you are a witness to the truth? Ha! What is truth?' For Pilate the politician, truth was whatever he wanted it to be, and he could twist words until they meant the opposite of what the speaker had intended. Kingship, to Pilate, meant domination of others by force and cruelty. 'And that's the truth!' he thought, as he walked away.

Francis Bacon

This incident was mentioned by Francis Bacon, who was a philosopher in the sixteenth and seventeenth centuries. He was a pioneer of scientific thinking, insisting that repeated experiment is essential in trying to understand the workings of nature. Proper regard, he said, must also be paid to any possible evidence which runs counter to the theories you hold about the world around us. 'What is truth? asked jesting Pilate,' wrote Bacon in the first of his great volume of essays ... 'What is truth? asked jesting Pilate ... and would not stay for an answer!' Bacon's words are devastating satire – Pontius Pilate claimed the right to discuss truth, but he was only frivolous, and wasn't interested in any views which contradicted his own. Bacon's Essay 'Of Truth' continues:

> It is not the lie that *passeth through* the mind, but the lie that *sinketh in*, and *settleth* in it, that does the hurt ... [Whereas] the *inquiry* of truth, which is the *love-making*, or *wooing* of it – the *knowledge* of truth, which is the *presence* of it – and the *belief* of truth, which is the *enjoying* of it – is the sovereign good of human nature ... Certainly, it is heaven upon earth, to have a man's mind ... turn upon the poles of truth.

Jesus is the truth

Jesus Christ said, 'I am the Way, and the Truth, and the Life.' Jesus is truth at its profoundest, because he is the truth about the universe, and about human life – about why we are here, how we should live, and what the future holds. Now you may say that this is subject to Bacon's objection that nothing is true unless you can test it by experiment. Yet you *can* test the truth of what Jesus said – but the only way to do so is to put his teachings into practice and base your way of life upon what Jesus taught. If this brings you happiness, a sense of purpose, the fellowship of other believers and awareness of the love of God, then you have proved that what Jesus said was the truth. But you can't test this by half-hearted dabbling in Christianity – you have to commit your life to it. Much of what humans claim to be truth is merely a form of words, and you can waste precious hours arguing over words. Whereas the important truths are often too deep to put into words, and can only be expressed in a life of self-sacrifice and service to others. That is the truth which Pontius Pilate met face to face when Jesus was brought before him, for Christ is the true King of the Universe. But this evidence ran contrary to Pilate's existing prejudices – so he ignored it. Are you open to new ideas which can radically shake your long-held views? If so, read the Gospels, and find out what Jesus really said. Follow his example, not that of Pontius Pilate, regarding whom Francis Bacon wrote: 'What is truth? asked jesting Pilate ... and would not stay for an answer!'

Suggested hymns

Come, my way, my truth, my life; Morning glory, starlit sky; The head that once was crowned with thorns; Thou art the Way, by thee alone.

Sermons for Saints' Days and Special Occasions

SAINTS' DAYS

The friends of St Polycarp, in about AD 156, declared their intention of 'celebrating the birthday of his martyrdom' every year in the future. When churches were built to enshrine the relics of the martyrs, they were often dedicated on the anniversary of the saint's death, and a dedication festival was held on that date every year. Other churches soon celebrated the day of the saint whose name they bore as their 'patronal festival'. The Bible describes the heroes of the Old Testament as a 'cloud of witnesses' around us, and says that all believers are united as 'fellow citizens of the saints'. Christians believe that those who have died heroically are praying for those who are alive, the Church Triumphant interceding for the Church Militant. It seems natural to ask the departed for their prayers, and to talk to our dead friends just as we did when they were alive. But superstition grew up in the Middle Ages around devotion to the saints, and it was rejected by many Protestants. Yet many congregations still wished to honour the saints, especially on their own patronal festival. The Book of Common Prayer was at first printed in two colours, and the more important saints' days were listed in the Calendar as 'Red Letter Days'.

St Stephen, Deacon, First Martyr

26 December 2012

Boxing Day

2 Chron. 24.20–22 The stoning of Zechariah, *or* Acts 7.51–60 The death of Stephen; Ps. 119.161–168 Persecuted without a cause (*if the Acts reading is used instead of the Old Testament reading, the New Testament reading is* Gal. 2.16b–20 Crucified with Christ); Matt. 10.17–22 Persecution

> *'Princes have persecuted me without a cause,*
> *but my heart stands in awe of your word.'*
> Psalm 119.161 (Common Worship)

1066 and All That

1066 and All That was a parody of British history as it was taught in schools, published in 1930 by W. C. Sellar and R. J. Yeatman. It famously divided the nation's rulers into 'Bad Kings' and the rest, who were usually categorized as 'a Good Thing' – capital G, capital T! Such a division is simplistic, because many rulers have mixed motives; some act with good motives but the results are disastrous; and there are some who make grand promises, then become so corrupted by power that they finish up as definitely not a Good Thing. We shouldn't be hasty in judging those in authority, yet it's good to be reminded that with power goes responsibility. Those who are leaders should recognize that they are entrusted with the well-being of those under them.

St Stephen

The High Priests and the Council in Jerusalem who condemned St Stephen to death were certainly not a Good Thing. Society had changed, and there was no longer a royal family in Israel, but Stephen could well have applied to those who sat in judgement on him the words of the psalm: 'Princes have persecuted me without a cause, but my heart stands in awe of your word.' In spite of what those in authority did to him, Stephen had more respect for Jesus, the Word of God, than for them. Like his Saviour, Stephen identified with the poor and powerless, and preferred death at the hands of the rich and powerful to compromising over the truth.

Riches

You see, there's no surer route to power than possessing wealth. If you have money, you automatically have power over those who possess less. All the poor can do is to remind you that power brings responsibility. Society continues to change. The powerful in St Stephen's day had mostly inherited their wealth, or were appointed by those who had. Today, in a democracy things are different. Our leaders are elected by the people; but it costs money to stand for Parliament, so the wealthy leaders of industry still wield great power. And even the poorest in this country are something like 30 times richer than most people in the Third World. What responsibilities does that lay on us? The best we can do is to elect only those MPs who make a real effort to straighten out the world's trading patterns.

Victorians

International problems didn't trouble our nineteenth-century ancestors. They were in fact exploiting poorer nations by removing their raw materials without raising the standard of living of the people, but they didn't have television to show them how the other half lives, as we do. Yet they could see all round them people on lower incomes, and it became a tradition to pay tips and gratuities to those who serve you on St Stephen's Day. That's how it got its alternative name of 'Boxing Day'. 'Christmas Boxes' were first mentioned in the 1620s, when they were earthenware receptacles with a slot for coins, rather like a piggy-bank, which had to be broken to get the money out. In these so-called 'boxes', servants and apprentices used to collect their annual tips. Later, any annual payment or present was called a Christmas box. They were not gifts, but gratuities paid by masters or customers to those who served them. Anyone who served, looked after, or delivered goods to the public expected a tip. Parson Woodforde in 1782 ungrudgingly gave two shillings and sixpence to each of the bellringers, and a shilling each to the butcher's boy, the blacksmith's boy and the maltster's man. By the 1830s the 26th December was widely known as Boxing Day. But in towns the burden on the middle classes became unsupportable, with the postman, the newspaper boy, the beadle, the milkman and the baker's man all ringing the bell on Boxing Day and demanding to be paid.

Nowadays

In consequence, after the Second World War the practice of giving Christmas boxes died out. But there are still people who serve us who are not well paid. A tip left on the table for the waiter, or the people who clear the tables in the snack bar, or telling the minicab-driver to keep the change, all these are generous gestures, especially if we are not very well off ourselves. They show that we realize that money gives power, and with power goes responsibility to care for those who serve us. Then we should certainly be considered a Good Thing! Happy Boxing Day!

Suggested carols

Good King Wenceslas; Long ago prophets knew; Love came down at Christmas; See him lying on a bed of straw.

St John, Apostle and Evangelist   27 December
Patmos

Ex. 33.7–11a The tent of meeting; Ps. 117 Praise God, all nations; 1 John 1 The word of life; John 21.19b–25 The Beloved Disciple

> *'This is the disciple who is testifying to these things and has written them, and we know that his testimony is true.' John 21.24*

Patmos

The island of Patmos is one of the Dodecanese islands belonging to Greece; yet it's only 30 miles from the coast of modern-day Turkey. In biblical times Turkey was called Asia Minor and was part of Greece. Not far from Patmos is the site of ancient Ephesus. Letters to seven churches, situated a day's travel apart around Ephesus, are included in the biblical book of the Revelation: Ephesus, Smyrna, Pergamon, Thyatira, Sardis, Philadelphia, and Laodicea. In chapter 1 of the Revelation, the author writes, 'I John ... was on the island of Patmos ... because I had been witnessing to Jesus.'

Two Johns

Today is the feast day of St John, who is called 'the Evangelist' because he wrote the Gospel of John – *evangelion* is Greek for 'good news', and 'gospel' is Anglo-Saxon for 'good news'. Until recently, Christians believed that the Gospel of John and the three Letters of John in the New Testament were written by one of the twelve apostles, John the brother of James and son of Zebedee – though the author is nowhere named in the text – and that this was the same John who wrote the book of Revelation. The Greek church still believe this, claiming that John the Evangelist preached in Ephesus and the nearby churches, and was then sent as a prisoner to work in the quarries on Patmos. In the nineteenth century, with a more scholarly approach, came the realization that Revelation was written by a Jew who spoke a rough, ungrammatical Greek, in the form of a vision. The Gospel and Letters, however, are written in fluent literary Greek, like that spoken by the Greek philosophers. John was a common Jewish name, so most scholars now think that they were written by two different people, neither of them the Galilean fisherman. But nothing is certain. Yet there's only one saint's day for both of them, and I thought we'd pay some attention this year to the author of the Revelation.

John the Divine

The island of Patmos is only eight miles long. At the highest point, today, there stands a massive fortress, the Monastery of St John the Theologian. A theologian is someone who thinks logically about God, a good description of the author of the Revelation. In Shakespeare's time, theologians were called divines, so in old Bibles the book was headed 'The Revelation of St John the Divine'. The word is used in quite a different sense from that in the joke about the actors' church being dedicated to 'St John the too, too, divine'!

Apocalypse

On the road up to the fortress on Patmos is the entrance to the Cave of the Apocalypse. In Greek, *calypto* means to cover, so an apocalypse is an uncovering or revealing – my, what a lot of Greek we are learning today! This is where St John had his vision, in which God's view of history was revealed to him, or uncovered – that's why some people call the book of the Revelation 'The Apocalypse'. It's written in a style that was quite common in Jewish writings of the time, both in and outside the Bible, called 'apocalyptic literature'. These books describe a vision of the future. Probably they have no more to do with a magical insight into the future than modern science fiction does. Rather, they give God's 'take' on what was happening when they were written.

Roman Empire

So St John was writing to the seven churches, to give his friends a God's-eye view of events at the end of the first century AD – John was exiled to the concentration camp on Patmos because he was one of a small minority of Jewish and Greek Christians who were just beginning to feel the weight of persecution. Before long, the authorities thought, the Christians might become dangerous terrorists. John wanted his friends to remain law-abiding, but faithful to God's commandments. After all, the kingdom of God would last for ever, whereas the Roman Empire would one day collapse.

Babylon

Of course, anyone who said so openly would be executed for treason. So John disguised Rome under the name of Babylon, an ancient empire which no longer existed. Like Rome, it's described as seated on seven hills; John's readers would have known exactly what he meant. There's no time today to interpret what the Revelation means to you and me; you will have to do that for yourselves. But be sure, it's much more to do with being loyal to God in adversity today, and our reward when we die, than with the distant future. You may be quite surprised. But all honour to St John, whoever he was, who gave us such a thought-provoking book.

Suggested hymns

At the name of Jesus; Jerusalem the golden; My soul, there is a country; Soon and very soon.

Holy Innocents   28 December
Children in Wartime

Jer. 31.15–17 Rachel weeping for her children; Ps. 124 When our enemies attacked us; 1 Cor. 1.26–29 God chose what is weak; Matt. 2.13–18 The massacre

> *'A voice is heard in Ramah,*
>   *lamentation and bitter weeping.*
> *Rachel is weeping for her children;*
>   *she refuses to be comforted for her children,*
>   *because they are no more.' Jeremiah 31.15*

Bethlehem

The children of Bethlehem in the time of Jesus died because King Herod wanted to wage war against what he feared was a resistance movement which would tumble him from power. A rival for the post of King of the Jews? The only way he could see to deal with that was by violence. Yet it was not his real or imaginary enemy that suffered. It was a group of innocent children who, as we would say today, became collateral damage. Meanwhile two-year-old Jesus became a refugee, homeless in a foreign land among people who didn't speak the same language as his parents. Can you see a pattern here? Eglantyne Jebb, the founder of the Save the Children charity, used to say: 'All wars, just or unjust, disastrous or victorious, are waged against the child.' A brief look at history forces us to agree with her. Those who suffer most in wartime are always the innocent children. It's been so since the days when Jeremiah wrote, 'A voice is heard in Ramah, lamentation and bitter weeping. Rachel is weeping for her children; she refuses to be comforted for her children, because they are no more.' Ironically, the children of Bethlehem today are still suffering as a result of the strife between Palestinians and Israelis.

The First World War

Eglantyne Jebb was arrested for distributing leaflets in Trafalgar Square, protesting against child suffering. After the First World War, the British government kept up a blockade that left children in cities like Berlin and Vienna starving. Tuberculosis and rickets were rife. 'The children's bones were like rubber,' wrote one doctor.

'Clothing was utterly lacking. In the hospitals there was nothing but paper bandages.' With her sister, Dorothy Buxton, Eglantyne Jebb called a meeting in the Royal Albert Hall, and founded a charity, the 'Save the Children Fund'. Ever since, SCF has been relieving child suffering, and drawing the world's attention to innocent child victims in wartime.

Armenia

In 1921, an Armenian refugee child reported seeing 'thousands of people ... tired, sick and hungry. I had to carry my youngest brother,' he said. 'One day I saw that he was not moving or crying for bread any more. I showed him to my mother and she saw that he was dead. We were glad that he was dead because we had nothing to feed him on.' Eglantyne Jebb drafted a 'Declaration of the Rights of the Child', which inspired the present United Nations Convention on the Rights of the Child.

The Second World War

SCF worked with refugees from the Spanish Civil War, and were part of the committee that organized the Kindertransport of Jewish refugees. During the Second World War, however, they were forced to withdraw from projects in occupied Europe. After the war, they had 105 staff working with children, displaced people, refugees, and concentration camp survivors in devastated areas of France, Yugoslavia, Poland and Greece.

Korea

The Korean War left over 100,000 homeless children in South Korea, and over a million people with active TB. In Austria in 1956, Hungarian refugees were fleeing after the failed revolution. SCF worked there, and in Somaliland, Syria and Lebanon.

Refugees

SCF did valiant work in dangerous situations during the Vietnam War. They helped children on both sides of the civil war in Nigeria. Unaccompanied children were among the boat-people from Vietnam, and suffering children were refugees from the Chinese invasion of Tibet. Fernando, a boy of 14 from Mozambique, said, 'The bandits killed my father. They killed my mother. And my brother. They took me to their base camp. Yes, I was with the bandits. I had a gun.' During the 1990s and the beginning of the new millennium SCF continued to work with children affected by war in Iraq, Sudan, Somalia, Mozambique, Nicaragua, Colombia, Sri Lanka, Sierra Leone, Angola and the Balkans. They work in over 50 countries worldwide. Of children born in some parts of Sierra Leone, one in four won't make it to their fifth birthday.

Today

There are wars going on today; you can find out about them by reading your newspaper. Think about the innocent children who suffer most, wherever there's conflict, like the children in Bethlehem did in Jesus's lifetime. Pray for them, and agitate to bring an end to their plight. Check out the Save the Children website to see where they are working today, and support them in any way you can, for the sake of Jesus the refugee.

Suggested carols

I cannot tell why he, whom angels worship; It came upon the midnight clear; Lully, lulla; Unto us a boy is born!
See www.savethechildren.org.uk

Naming and Circumcision of Christ   1 January 2013
Identity
Num. 6.22–27 Aaron's blessing; Ps. 8 From the mouths of babes; Gal. 4.4–7 Born under the Law; Luke 2.15–21 Naming and circumcision

> *'After eight days had passed, it was time to circumcise the child; and he was called Jesus, the name given by the angel before he was conceived in the womb.' Luke 2.21*

Circumcision

A week after Jesus was born – the Jews count inclusively, so this was the eighth day – Jesus was circumcised. This little operation, removing a few centimetres of the foreskin, had become symbolic.

It was part of God's covenant with Abraham; any boy who had received this sign was considered a member of God's chosen people. So were his descendants – it was only after the Jewish wars with the Romans, when so many rapes had left Jewish children uncertain who their father was, that the definition of a Jew changed to 'anyone with a Jewish mother'. At circumcision, the boy was given his name – more recently, a naming ceremony has also been introduced for girls. The Christian equivalent is infant baptism. Some sort of naming ceremony is essential, because until then the child has no identity. If nobody knows what to call you, you don't know who you are. An unnamed child is a nonentity. We all know the dangers of identity theft; those who commit this crime can not only steal your money; they can take away your sense of being a unique person. Here are some profound questions to which we all need an answer:

Who am I?
Why am I here?
How am I connected to those who came before me?
To what community do I belong?
How do I fit into the customs and traditions of that community?

Community

Religion is especially good at answering these questions. Religions tell stories, and celebrate rituals, which confirm your identity and build up community loyalties. They tell stories of the saints, to give us role models to imitate, showing how we should behave as a member of that community. But other things, as well as religion, give you a sense of identity. Which nation do you belong to? What work do you do? What is your ethnic origin? Some people even find their identity in terms of which football team they support – Bill Shankly said, 'Some people believe football is a matter of life and death ... I can assure you it is much, much more important than that!'

Conflict

Trouble begins, however, when people define who they are *over against* someone else. Their identity becomes a matter of who they are not. If your identity comes from your nationality, you will mock all other nations, and easily go to war against them. If you define yourself by your ethnicity, this leads to racism. Supporters of a particular cause quickly oppress those who don't agree with them, as happened in communist Russia. Even football can lead to terrible violence. It was for this reason that Socrates said, 'I am not an Athenian or a Greek, but a citizen of the world.'

Roots

In any circumstances where you have no community to belong to, you soon feel rootless and alone. That's why a religion, especially one which welcomes members of all nations and races, is a good place to put down roots. With a firm faith, you know that you are loved, by God and your fellow members, and you know how you are expected to behave. There's a security in being members of a faith community, which non-believers may not understand. Religion has become important in the twenty-first century because all the other sources of identity have been shown to be divisive.

Religious wars

Of course, religion can also be divisive, and religious wars show the dangers of defining yourself by what you can't possibly accept. Yet there are signs that these divisions may be fading as religious people come to realize their need of each other, to support each other against the attacks of a godless world.

Diversity

A visitor to Strasbourg recently was invited to an international festival of folk dance and folk music. He was deeply moved by the pride that each of those present showed in their own culture, coupled with their willingness to learn about and enjoy the cultures of other people. Pride in your distinct identity needn't lead to conflict. Tolerance enables us to celebrate our own identity, while respecting what makes others distinct. Religion ought to be the best place to foster that sort of tolerance, if only we understand that this is what God calls us to be. The name given to Jesus at his circumcision means 'God saves'; yet he didn't see himself as the Saviour of the Jews only, but the Saviour of the world. When we become Christians, this shouldn't narrow our horizons, but lead us to share the love that we have received from God through Jesus with everyone, no matter how different from us they may be.

All hail the power of Jesus' name; At the name of Jesus; How sweet the name of Jesus sounds; O God, whom neither time nor space.

Epiphany   6 January
(See page 37.)

Week of Prayer for Christian Unity   18–25 January
Backwards and Forwards
Zeph. 3.16–20 Bring you home; 1 John 4.9–15 We ought to love one another; Ps. 133 Brothers at unity; John 17.11b–23 That they may be one

> *'At that time I will bring you home, at the time when I gather you; for I will make you renowned and praised among all the peoples of the earth … says the* LORD.*' Zephaniah 3.20*

Stories

I'm going to tell you some true stories about unity and disunity in the Church. The first story is about an Eastern Orthodox church in the UK, worshipping in a Central European ancient language which nobody else understands. In the Week of Prayer for Christian Unity, they celebrate the Liturgy, praying for the Unity of Christ's Church throughout the world. Visitors come from many denominations, to admire the ceremonial, and the icons, wall-paintings and chanting. At the end the priest gives a little speech in English, saying: 'We pray for Church unity. Unity is very simple. All that is necessary is for all of you to become like us, and then we shall be united!' The visitors gasp. His ceremonial dates from the Byzantine Empire. Other churches also have centuries of cultural tradition behind them; must they forget it all and become Slavs, to fulfil the prayer of Jesus 'that they may all be one'?

Traditions

The second story's about a Greek Orthodox priest who was showing some English friends around a shrine on one of the islands. He was stopped by another priest who lectured him in Greek for half an hour. When he'd gone, they asked their friend what it was all about. 'He's an Old Calendarist,' replied the Greek priest. 'He was telling me that I'm not a Christian, because I celebrate Easter on a different date than he does!' On such trivial issues, thought his friends, are Christians willing to tear apart the Body of Christ.

Anglicans

My third story concerns a small black-led church which was suddenly denied the use of the building where they had been worshipping. An Anglican congregation offered to let them use their church on Sunday afternoons, saying that they hoped the two congregations could co-operate in mission. When the black pastor met the Anglicans, however, someone in the congregation asked him why he remained separate, why didn't he join the Anglican Church? People were being prevented from becoming Christians, said the questioner, by the scandal of our disunity. The black pastor felt he was under attack, and needed to justify himself. We already are one Church, he replied, but just as St Peter and St Paul were called to evangelize different groups of people, so different ministers may be called to different ministries in the same town. And so the arguments about unity go backwards and forwards.

Backwards and forwards

So that's what I'd like to do now: go backwards then forwards. The black pastor took us back to the New Testament; I'd like to start there and come forwards again to the present day. He was right; the unity of the Church was important to Jesus and St Paul, because the Church is called to unite the world in love. Yet different Christians have different understandings of what unity means. Writing to the Corinthians, Paul rebuked them for their divisions. The things they disagreed about were important: inspiration and reason, methods of spiritual healing, the way the congregation was led, and so forth. But none of them was important enough to split the Church over. The divisions in the early centuries, usually called heresies, died out eventually. Then in 1054, at the Great Schism, the Greek Orthodox Church and the Roman Catholic Church split; mainly, some say, because one spoke Latin and the other Greek. The Protestant Reformation, I suggest, was about the newly independent nation states, which didn't want a centrally controlled Church. But maybe the Protestants wouldn't have formed a new church if they hadn't been excommunicated. The Church of England started with the aim of being one Church for the whole people; but refused to tolerate the Independents, who then fled to America. There, having a row of different denominations on Main Street is considered a commendable witness to religious freedom. The World Council of Churches raised hopes of unity, but initiatives such as the Anglican–Methodist conversations were rejected.

Hope

And so the arguments go backwards and forwards. The road to unity is a long one, needing perseverance. Who knows what the future shape of Christ's Church will be? Meanwhile, it's vital that we treat each other with courtesy, and never appear to compete. Others judge us, not so much by our beliefs as by our tolerance and love. Zephaniah promised that God will bring us home, when he gathers us into one; and then the Christian Church will be 'renowned and praised among all the peoples of the earth'.

Suggested hymns

A new commandment I give unto you; Jesus stand among us at the meeting of our lives; Lord of our life, and God of our salvation; Thy hand, O God, has guided.

Conversion of St Paul   25 January
Lost in Translation

Jer. 1.4–10 The call of a prophet; Ps. 67 Let all the peoples praise you; Acts 9.1–22 Saul's conversion (*if the Acts reading is used instead of the Old Testament reading, the New Testament reading is* Gal. 1.11–16a Called me through his grace); Matt. 19.27–30 The reward of eternal life

> 'The Lord said ... "[Paul] is an instrument whom I have chosen to bring my name before Gentiles."' Acts 9.15

Lost in Translation

Lost in Translation and *Still Lost in Translation* are two books by Charlie Croker. They tell of some of the comical results when those who don't speak English very well try to write public notices in English. For example, in a Chinese tailor's shop: 'Order your summers suit. Because is big rush, we will execute our customers in strict rotation.' In a hotel in Paris: 'Please leave your values at the desk.' In a Korean airliner: 'Upon arrival at the airport, please wear your clothes.' In an advertisement for a Scandinavian airline: 'We take your bags and send them in all directions.' And on an elevator: 'Please do not use the lift when it is not working.' Mind you, English-speakers are so bad at learning foreign languages, I'm sure we make even worse blunders when we try. As anyone who's tried translating from one language into another knows, it's not easy. Even if you use the exact dictionary equivalent of the words in English, you will get them in the wrong order. And there are subtle differences in the way the same word is understood in each language which causes the true meaning to be ... 'lost in translation'. They sell computer programs which claim to translate into any language – but just try asking it to translate an English sentence into, say, German and then back again, and you will see it bears hardly any relationship to the original. 'Lost in translation' was a common phrase in English long before the film with that title was made – misunderstandings between people who speak different languages has been a problem since the Tower of Babel fell down!

Apostle to the Gentiles

St Paul knew all about the problems of translation. He was brought up in a good Jewish family, and learnt passages of the Hebrew Scriptures by heart for his bar mitzvah. But Jews in his day spoke Aramaic; Tarsus was a Greek-speaking university town; and the administrators in the Roman Empire spoke Latin. So Paul was probably at least bilingual; he may have had to learn four languages even. But God called him to be the apostle to the Gentiles – he was sent to proclaim the good news about Jesus to people of every race and language except Hebrew. Jesus, however, was also a Jew, and to understand what he was doing, you need to understand the Hebrew Old Testament. Yet many Hebrew sentences, translated literally into Greek, which is the tongue that Paul wrote his letters in, are either incomprehensible, or mean something totally different from the original. To answer God's call, Paul had to translate not only the words but the ideas of the Christian faith into idioms that non-Jews would understand. It's untrue to say that Paul invented a new religion; but he had to be very creative in expressing Christian ideas in a way that would be understood by people all over the world. Otherwise they would be lost in translation.

Today

The challenge continues today. Many Christians grew up learning about Jesus from what they heard in church. In some cases that means the 1611 Authorized Version of the Bible and the 1662 Book of Common Prayer. Even for those who used modern translations, the teaching was often explained in words like redemption, atoning sacrifice, covenant, coveting, purity, eternal life, justification, and so on, which are hardly ever heard in modern language, or if they are, they mean something quite different from what they mean in Christian teaching. This is the language of medieval and Reformation theology, and it means nothing to the man or woman in the street. Yet Jesus died for everyone, not just the theologians and scholars. Unless we put his message into words and ideas which can be understood by ordinary people, we are, in effect, blocking the love of Jesus from getting through to them. Small wonder so many people think churchgoing is out-of-date nonsense, and totally irrelevant to day-to-day life.

God's call

God's call to you is the same as it was to Saul of Tarsus: experience the love of Jesus in your life, and try to put what it means to you into your own words, avoiding technical terms, using picture-language with images from the common experience of ordinary people today. God never changes – the message of the gospel never varies – but the words we express it in must be chosen anew from generation to generation. Otherwise what God is trying to say through us to the people around us will be lost in translation.

Suggested hymns

Disposer supreme and judge of the earth; God is working his purpose out; Let all the world in every corner sing; Tell me the old, old story.

Presentation of Christ in the Temple (Candlemas)

2 February *(or may be observed on 3 February)*
Time Flies
Mal. 3.1–5 The Lord shall come to his Temple; Ps. 24.[1–6] 7–10
Open the gates for the Lord; Heb. 2.14–18 Jesus became like
the descendants of Abraham; Luke 2.22–40 The presentation of
Christ in the Temple

> 'There was also a prophet, Anna the daughter of Phanuel, of
> the tribe of Asher. She was of a great age, having lived with her
> husband for seven years after her marriage, then as a widow to
> the age of eighty-four. She never left the temple but worshipped
> there with fasting and prayer night and day. At that moment she
> came, and began to praise God and to speak about the child to all
> who were looking for the redemption of Jerusalem.' Luke 2.36–38

Old and young

Time was very precisely measured out for little Jewish boys. On
the eighth day of their life, that is, when they were a week old, they
were circumcised, made a member of the Covenant community, and
given their name. Then, 33 days after that, the child was brought
to the Temple in Jerusalem for the ritual sacrifice. This showed that
it was safe for the mother to leave her house without risking infec-
tion. But if the boy was the firstborn son, he was God's property
– this had been agreed at the time when the Egyptian firstborn had
died during the ten plagues. So on the fortieth day after his birth,
a firstborn son was brought to the Temple to be presented to God,
and then the parents were allowed to buy him back from God at
the price of another sacrifice! If Jesus was born on December 25th,
the fortieth day was February 2nd which we call the feast of the
Purification of the Virgin Mary and the Presentation of Christ in the
Temple. I expect 40 days feels an age to a newborn baby. But there
were some very old people in the Temple on that day. Simeon was
an elderly priest who recognized that baby Jesus was the Messiah
he'd waited all his life to see. He sang a song, thanking God for the
wonderful things he'd seen in his time, culminating in holding the
infant in his arms. He hailed the baby as 'a light to the Gentiles' –
which is why we call it Candlemas – and made his farewell to life,
which I bet he thought had absolutely whizzed past. Then there was
an old lady called Anna – we are told exactly how old she was, and

how many years she'd been married before she became a widow.
But her childhood probably seemed like yesterday to her. Time flies
when you get older.

Time flies

When you are young, the next birthday, the next Christmas, the
holidays, all seem an age away. When children are travelling, they
are impatient – 'Are we there yet?' You can't wait to be grown
up. Yet as you grow older, you complain that there's so much to
do, and not enough time to do it in. A wise old teacher said to his
pupils, 'Never plead that you didn't have enough time to finish your
project. You have all the time there is.' A famous comedian used to
joke, 'They tell me, time flies. But you can't – they go too quickly.'
Given time, you can work that one out for yourselves.

Using time

But God gives us all the time in the world. Sixty minutes in each hour,
24 hours a day, 365 days in the year, every year of our life. What
we have to do, is to work out the best way of using the time we
have. Wasting time is an extravagant misuse of a commodity which
seems to be in increasingly short supply. At the end, we have to ask
ourselves what we have achieved in the time we had. Have we been
selfish with our time, or have we made time for others, to help them
and listen to them? How much time have we set aside for God?

Henry Twells

In Chester Cathedral there's an old clock, with an appropriate verse
displayed on it, written by a Victorian clergyman called Henry
Twells. He's best remembered as the author of the hymn, 'At even,
ere the sun was set'. The poem is all about time, and I heard it once
read on the radio by an old clockmaker in his workshop, with the
sound of a couple of dozen clocks ticking away behind him. Listen:

> When as a child I laughed and wept, time crept.
> When as a youth I dreamed and talked, time walked.
> When I became a full grown man, time ran.
> And later as I older grew, time flew.
> Soon I shall find while travelling on, time gone.
> Will Christ have saved my soul by then? Amen.

At even, ere the sun was set; Come, thou long-expected Jesus; Faithful vigil ended; Hail to the Lord who comes.

St David, Bishop of Menevia, Patron of Wales
c. 601   1 March
Abstinence

Ecclus. (Ben Sira) 15.1–6 Whoever holds to the Law will obtain wisdom; Ps. 16.1–7 I have a goodly heritage; 1 Thess. 2.2–12 Entrusted with the gospel; Matt. 16.24–27 Take up your cross

> *'Jesus told his disciples, "If any want to become my followers, let them deny themselves and take up their cross and follow me."'*
> *Matthew 16.24*

Egyptian connection

St David, or Dewi, founded the monastery at Menevia, now called the city of St David's, and at least a dozen other monasteries, in the sixth century AD. He compiled a Rule to govern the life of the monks, but the original was lost because of 'age, carelessness and attacks by pirates'. It's said that it emphasized abstinence, and was based on that of the Egyptian desert monks. Which is remarkable, when you remember that Egypt is a long way from Wales! It shows that Wales was not an isolated backwater, even then.

Asceticism

The Egyptian hermits fled to the desert because they could pray better when they were not distracted by the temptation to rich living. They obeyed the warning given by Jesus in the gospel: 'If any want to become my followers, let them deny themselves and take up their cross and follow me.' Self-denial includes giving up things you enjoy, so it's appropriate that this passage should be read on St David's Day, during Lent. But it means more than that; Jesus told us to deny our very selves: to say no to the desire to have our own way, and learn instead to live our lives in God's way. Going without things we like during Lent isn't an end in itself; it's a way of learning to put God's wishes before our own. There's nothing wrong with sensual pleasures: God wants us to enjoy his creation, and thank him for the wonderful sights and tastes and feelings he's given us. But sometimes the task of spreading the gospel, and loving our neighbours for God's sake, has to come first; then we may have to forego the pleasant things of life, for a while at least, so as to concentrate on the task in hand.

Monasteries

So St David chose groups of shock troops to fight the battle against evil, calling them monks. He gathered them together into communities, to make a combined effort to convert the Welsh people. Today, believers who have to earn their living in the world of business may set aside a day or two to go on retreat, so that they can learn to pray better when they are free from distractions.

Hard work

Can we learn other lessons for today from the Rule of St David? We are told that he emphasized hard work, abstinence from alcohol, and not talking. He was talking about physical work. Some people get plenty of that in their employment; they should work hard to the glory of God. They may not have much time left over to pray, but they can silently offer up their labours to the glory of God in odd moments, until their work itself becomes their prayer. Others who are desk-bound during the day may need to set aside time every week to go for a long walk, say, so that they can have time to become aware again of God's presence with them. Without this they are not going to be much use to God as witnesses to the unbelievers.

Alcohol

For God has given each of us a body to use in his service. We must look after ourselves, regarding our body as something God has lent us. Regular exercise is essential to keep us fit, so that we can show other people that Christians can enjoy a full life. As for abstaining from alcohol, St David taught this, because of the danger of drunkenness, which gradually destroys the body. There's nothing wrong with a quiet drink with your friends; but if you suspect you can't manage without alcohol, Lent might be a good time to try giving it up. If you find that hard, maybe you should go to Alcoholics Anonymous to find a solution. Because St David never drank alcohol, he was nick-named 'the Waterman'; for the same reason he taught his followers to eat only very simple meals.

Silence

His third emphasis, on silence, is quite impractical for those who live in the world, except on retreat. Yet perhaps we chatter away too much, and need to learn that our words are more effective when there are fewer of them. We should treasure the moments of quiet, in church and in the countryside; and learn to listen to God in silence. Then let's thank God for all that St David has taught us about how to live in the twenty-first century.

Suggested hymns

Be still, for the Spirit/presence of the Lord; Disposer supreme, and judge of the earth; Guide me, O thou great Redeemer/Jehovah; Teach me, my God and King.

St Patrick, Bishop, Missionary, Patron of Ireland
c. 460   18 March (transferred)
Potato Famine

Deut. 32.1–9 Let my teaching drop like rain, *or* Tob. 13.1b–7 In the land of my exile; Ps. 145.12–13 Make known to all peoples; 2 Cor. 4.1–12 This ministry; Matt. 10.16–23 Warnings for missionaries, *or* John 4.31–38 Ripe for harvest

'Always carrying in the body the death of Jesus, so that the life of Jesus may also be made visible in our bodies.' 2 Corinthians 4.10

Potato famine

St Patrick was born in England, and taken as a slave-boy to Ireland, where he suffered great hardship. Yet he learnt from his suffering to trust entirely in God, and returned when he was a man to share that faith with the Irish people. He had learnt not to bear a grudge against the people who treated him so cruelly. In this he resembled St Paul, who wrote that he was 'Always carrying in the body the death of Jesus, so that the life of Jesus may also be made visible in our bodies.' Fourteen hundred years later, the Irish people themselves endured a period of great suffering, one of the worst the world has ever known. From 1845 to 1852 Ireland was in the grip of the Great Potato Famine. Up until the eighteenth century, the Irish people had grazed cattle and grown grain on their land, to feed themselves and their families. Then the landlords, most of whom were of English descent, seized the best land to raise quality beef to sell in England, making the indigenous population almost entirely dependent on the potatoes which could be grown in poorer soil. When potato blight destroyed the crop, around a million people died, and another million were exiled by sea in appalling conditions to America. The population dropped by almost 25 per cent in seven years. This created resentment among the Irish against the English, which is still felt to this day by some. The potato famine was even described as an act of genocide. However, others, pointing to St Patrick, say we shouldn't go on hating those who have oppressed us, but try to share with them what we have learnt from our sufferings. There's right and wrong on both sides.

Literature

The events of a century and a half ago may seem very distant, but you have only to read some of the books about the potato famine to see how it seared the soul of the Irish. A few years ago, Joseph O'Connor wrote a novel with the title *Star of the Sea*. It became an international bestseller. The book describes the suffering passengers of a famine ship, carrying, from Ireland to New York, people who had lost everything. *Star of the Sea* was the name of the ship, a translation of *Stella Maris*, one of the titles of the Virgin Mary. Like any good novel, it doesn't oversimplify the characters of the protagonists. Instead it shows through a truly tragic story that there's good and bad in everyone. The same message comes over in the classic novels of Anthony Trollope. Employed by the Post Office, he was sent to work in Ireland during the years of the famine, and wrote his early books *The Macdermots of Ballycloran* and *The Landleaguers* there. His novel *Castle Richmond* took the famine as its theme. It's an eyewitness account of the people's agony at that time, and like O'Connor, he recognizes that although many absentee landlords exploited the Irish wickedly, there were others who did what they could to help, suffering deeply with their tenants.

Learning through suffering

The potato famine is a strange subject to preach about on St Patrick's Day. But it's essential to understand how it shaped Irish attitudes, and is still in the background of many people's thinking today. We have to face up to how deeply the Irish people have suffered, and to the guilt of their oppressors. And still today in the Third World, people starve because the produce of their land is exported to feed prosperous people in other nations. So what can people learn from their suffering? Whatever race we are descended from, just like St Patrick, we can learn how to bring good out of evil. To repent, forgive and love. As a result of the potato famine, Irish people spread all around the globe. Like the Jews of the Dispersion, including the first Christians, they have a unique opportunity to spread what they have learnt of the love of God to people among whom they live.

Jesus's suffering

This is the message of the cross. Jesus suffered agonies on the day he died, yet we call it Good Friday. Human beings have a remarkable ability to turn defeat into victory, to use suffering in a way that causes love to grow. Jesus was the supreme example of this. St Patrick, the patron saint of Ireland, based his life on the pattern of forgiving love set us by Jesus. So can you.

Suggested hymns

Captains of the saintly band; Christ triumphant, ever reigning; God, whose city's sure foundation; My song is love unknown.

St Joseph of Nazareth   19 March
Children of the Law

2 Sam. 7.4–16 Descendants of David; Ps. 89.26–36 David's line; Rom. 4.13–18 Abraham's descendants; Matt. 1.18–25 Joseph's dream

> *'[Our salvation] depends on faith, in order that the promise may rest on grace and be guaranteed to all [Abraham's] descendants, not only to the adherents of the law but also to those who share the faith of Abraham.' Romans 4.16*

Raising kids

Joseph was a model father. He was an example whom his children could copy, and from whom all of us can learn a lot about raising kids. He brought up Jesus, and his brothers and sisters, to be proud of their Jewish heritage, and to obey the Law of Moses. The Gospels tell us they were descendants of King David, and, before him, of the Israelites who followed Moses out of Egypt, and received the Ten Commandments at Mount Sinai. When Jesus was 12, Joseph and Mary took him up to Jerusalem for the ceremony when Jewish boys became 'Children of the Commandment' – that's what 'bar mitzvah' means. Later, Jesus said, 'Do not think that I have come to abolish the law or the prophets; I have come not to abolish but to fulfil. For truly I tell you, until heaven and earth pass away, not one letter, not one stroke of a letter, will pass from the law until all is fulfilled.' I think he learnt this respect for the Law from his earthly father.

Conflict

When we speak of God's Law, most people think of the Ten Commandments, which are at the heart of the Old Testament. For Jews, however, these ten laws are only part of God's revelation of how he wants us to behave. They call the whole of the Hebrew Scriptures 'the Torah', the Law which God gave to his people, to show us how we should treat each other. This includes the moral law, the ritual law, and suggestions for a state legal system. Jesus was brought up by Joseph and Mary to respect the Law, but he joined the Rabbis in fierce debate about how the Law should be applied. In some circumstances, two laws contradict each other, and you can't apply one without breaking another. Jesus cut through the undergrowth, and said that the law of love is supreme. Unloving behaviour, suggested by any other law, must give way to the command to love our neighbours. For instance, if a law tells you not to heal the sick on the Sabbath, but the law of love says you should, then the Sabbath law must take the back seat. The Pharisees thought this was shocking; but some Jews today agree with Jesus.

Culture

Jesus remembered that Joseph took pity on Mary, the unmarried mother; even though the Law said he should divorce her. So when they brought a woman caught in the act of adultery to Jesus, he found a loophole in the Law saying that the first stone must be thrown by someone sinless. Culture is constantly changing, and state laws must adapt to new circumstances. Jesus pooh-poohed the idea of applying such an antiquated law in a more settled society. When non-Jews started becoming Christians, the Church, under the chairmanship of Jesus's brother James, decided that Jewish ritual law doesn't apply to other nations.

Commandments

The moral law itself was subject to interpretation. Jesus had learnt how to be loving from his parents. Morality always begins in the family, not in laws imposed by others. Society today is crumbling, because the only laws which people learn are the laws of politics and greed. We don't teach children about human relationships, our motives for goodness, or the grace we need to behave unselfishly. In the Sermon on the Mount, Jesus went to the heart of the Ten Commandments: 'People of old were told not to kill,' he said, 'but I tell you not to hate. They were told not to commit adultery in their bedroom, but I tell you not to plan adultery in your heart.' And so on. I think St Joseph, who brought up his children to be children of the Law, would have been proud of the way his son interpreted the commandments, not literally, but as suggesting ways in which we can love our neighbours. We can honour Joseph by teaching our own children the law of love, and setting them an example by our own behaviour.

Suggested hymns

Children of Jerusalem; I want to walk with Jesus Christ; Lord, hear the praises of thy faithful people; There's a song for all the children.

Annunciation of our Lord to the Blessed Virgin Mary   8 April (transferred)
A Normal Family?

Isa. 7.10–14 The sign of Immanuel; Ps. 40.5–11 I love to do your will; Heb. 10.4–10 I have come to do your will; Luke 1.26–38 The angel's message

> '*I delight to do your will, O my God; your law is within my heart.*'
> Psalm 40.8

A normal family?

Was the Holy Family a normal family? It consisted of the boy Jesus, his parents, and possibly some brothers and sisters. They were unusual in that the firstborn was born out of wedlock, though his parents knew the secret reason for that. Yet for his humanity to flourish, it was essential that Jesus should share the ups and downs of normal family life – 'smiles and tears like us he knew'. In the Middle Ages, however, Mary was held up as a symbol of mystical purity, a superhuman heroine of the celibate life, way above the concerns of mortal folk. Perhaps that doesn't do her justice. What impresses many about Mary is that she was a perfectly ordinary young woman, called by God to do a quite extraordinary job. And when she was challenged, she replied, 'Let it be according to God's will.' In other words, whatever God wants me to do, I'm willing to give it a try. Perhaps she was familiar with those words from today's Psalm, 'I delight to do your will, O my God; your law is within my heart.' The fact that she made the difficult choice is what we admire her for; the possibility that it was a struggle for her as well as for us gives us hope that we, too, may come through the hard decisions as triumphantly as Mary did.

Feminism

Modern feminists feel a bit ambivalent about Mary. The medieval picture of her as an icon of purity can make some women feel that God is setting an impossibly high standard for other women to imitate. It may be that this image grew up in an age when women were regarded as chattels – when they were expected to have nothing to do with worldly affairs. Possessive husbands had a double standard, claiming freedom to behave as they wished, themselves, but to keep their wives and daughters locked in a metaphorical chastity belt. So they held up the ideal of Mary Ever-Virgin for their women-folk to imitate. This was exacerbated by the celibacy of the clergy – though this was a slow development, and didn't happen all at once. So the celibate priest, struggling to be faithful to his vows, fell down in adoration before the statue of the Virgin, and was comforted to think that his vocation was to be as pure as she was. Yet Jewish society was never like that, and Jewish women had a great deal of power. So some feminists feel that the cult of the Blessed Virgin is putting them back into a straitjacket of male oppression.

Laughter

Unfair, you may say. Yet wherever you are coming from, you must agree that there's much to be gained by looking on the human achievements of Mary. She was a good mother, and the sound of children laughing is one of the most charming aspects of family life. Surely the home at Nazareth must often have rung with the sound of Mary laughing with her children. Our exaltation of Jesus's mother shouldn't lead us to think that earthly concerns are beneath our consideration. Jesus showed a sharp wit in some of his parables; where did he learn it from if not at his mother's knee?

Emulate

So the Mary of the annunciation is not an impossible model for us to emulate. She was a busy housewife, caught by surprise – in her kitchen, they say in Nazareth today. The angel told her she was to have a child, but not just any child – God's own Son. She was to feed him and clean up after him as any parent does for their children. She was to comfort him, teach him, set him an example, cry with him when he was sad, and yes, laugh with him when he was happy.

The only way to survive

Laughter is often the only way to survive. Brian Keenan, the Belfast man who was taken hostage in Beirut by an Islamic jihad organization from 1986 to 1990, speaks in a typically exaggerated way. He has said that the only way to come through a grim experience like that is to believe that God is a comedian – if you don't have a sense of humour, you are dead. So if God has a sense of humour, surely God's mother can be allowed one also? Without denying the hardships of her life, and the courage of her obedience, let's fill out the picture by imagining her having a good chuckle from time to time with her perfectly normal family.

Suggested hymns

For Mary, Mother of our Lord; Jesus, good above all other; Sing we of the blessed Mother; The angel Gabriel from heaven came.

St George, Martyr, Patron of England *c.* 304

23 April

Marching Songs for Soldier Saints

1 Macc. 2.59–64 Be courageous, *or* Rev. 12.7–12 Michael fights the dragon; Ps. 126 Restore our fortunes; 2 Tim. 2.3–13 A soldier of Christ; John 15.18–21 They will persecute you

'Share in suffering like a good soldier of Christ Jesus.' 2 Timothy 2.3

Soldier saints

An army marching into battle is encouraged and strengthened by the marching songs they sing. Christians too, in our battle against sin, the world and the devil, gain spiritual strength from the hymns we sing together. Today is St George's Day, and George was a soldier-saint. Surely the hymns we choose for today should be marching songs, shouldn't they? Yet there's a problem here. Hymns using military metaphors can sound dangerously like glorifying war. Christianity doesn't encourage us to kill our enemies. Choosing hymns is great fun; but it can also be a serious matter, because of the risk of misunderstanding. There's an added danger with St George, for he's England's patron saint. Hymns chosen for St George's Day take on almost the importance of national anthems.

God save the Queen

'God save the Queen (or King)' has been the UK's national anthem since the eighteenth century. National anthems are not noted for brilliant music, but this one must surely have the dullest melody of any! The verse we always sing is a prayer, reminding us to pray for our head of state in the difficult task she has to fulfil. But other verses are more bloodthirsty: few today would be happy singing 'Scatter her enemies, And make them fall: Confound their politics; Frustrate their knavish tricks ...' and so on.

Land of hope and glory

Many people prefer to sing 'Land of hope and glory', or 'Rule Britannia'. In the first we sing: 'Wider still, and wider, shall thy bounds be set; God, who made thee mighty, make thee mightier yet!' Does this mean that God approves of one nation having dominion over another? A similar problem occurs with 'Rule Britannia', which, although it mentions Guardian Angels, doesn't mention God at all.

And did those feet

'Jerusalem' begins by asking a question about Jesus, the Lamb of God. But it's a question expecting the answer 'no' – Jesus didn't visit England when he was a boy – and neither has the New Jerusalem been 'builded' here – yet! William Blake suggests it's up to us; until we let loose our desire to bring justice to the poor, England will never become a 'green and pleasant land'.

Hymns about fighting

Several well-known hymns make use of military metaphors, and would be suitable for St George's Day: 'Fight the good fight'; 'Stand up, stand up for Jesus'; 'Soldiers who are Christ's below'. Yet the word 'fight' is seldom used in the New Testament; does singing it in our hymns encourage violence?

Remembrance Sunday

Some of the hymns used on Remembrance Sunday are quite critical of using warfare to solve our problems. Rudyard Kipling, often accused of imperialistic jingoism, wrote his Recessional, 'God of our fathers, known of old', warning empire-builders never to forget that God alone rules the world, and any power we have is lent to us temporarily.

Jesus, Lord of our salvation

'Jesus, Lord of our salvation' is a hymn by Frederick William Newman which thanks God for St George, but would be suspect today, not only for the self-righteousness of praying that 'we may all our foes subdue', but also because it forgets the female half of the human race, as in: 'Teach her manhood to confess thee as the Master, Lord and King.'

When a knight won his spurs

Political incorrectness is narrowly avoided by the superb hymn, 'When a knight won his spurs in the stories of old'. It concerns our spiritual battle against 'the dragons of anger, the ogres of greed'; and both girls and boys can regard the romantic legends of the medieval knights as an example to copy.

Loving your country

'I vow to thee, my country' is a popular patriotic hymn, but loyalty to our country should always be a critical love; the line about 'the love that asks no questions' is very dubious. Better are 'Judge eternal, throned in splendour' with the words 'purge this realm of bitter things'; and 'O God of earth and altar', with 'our earthly rulers falter' and 'the walls of gold entomb us'. It's not our brave service men and women who are to blame when our country makes mistakes; in a democracy it's not even the politicians; it's our fault, for electing leaders without constantly examining their policies.

Lessons

Jesus praised the Roman centurion who asked for prayers, and St Peter gladly baptized the centurion Cornelius. St Paul told Timothy, 'Share in suffering like a good soldier of Christ Jesus. No one serving in the army gets entangled in everyday affairs; the soldier's aim is to please the enlisting officer.' We can learn from St George, and other soldier-saints, to stand up bravely for what's right, at all costs.

Suggested hymns

Any of the above.

St Mark the Evangelist 25 April
Gospel Truth

Prov. 15.28–33 Good news, *or* Acts 15.35–41 Paul rejects Mark; Ps. 119.9–16 How can young people keep their way pure?; Eph. 4.7–16 The gift of an evangelist; Mark 13.5–13 Staying-power

'We must no longer be children, tossed to and fro and blown about by every wind of doctrine, by people's trickery, by their

craftiness in deceitful scheming. But speaking the truth in love, we must grow up in every way into him who is the head, into Christ.'
Ephesians 4.14–15

True?

St Mark was the first person ever to write a Gospel. Not just a Life, not a Biography, but the story of Jesus told as good news for those who read it. But is it true? Did Mark write 'the gospel truth'? Or did he change and improve it, inventing new stories and distorting the history so as to impose a theological theory which wasn't there to begin with? To hear some people talk, you'd think there's very little truth in the Gospels, and that those who wrote them made it all up!

Craftiness

Well, if they did, they must have been very cunning indeed. St Paul, in the passage in Ephesians in which he talks of some having the gift of an evangelist, warned his readers against craftiness. 'We must no longer be children,' he wrote, 'tossed to and fro and blown about by every wind of doctrine, by people's trickery, by their craftiness in deceitful scheming. But speaking the truth in love, we must grow up in every way into him who is the head, into Christ.' St Mark was a pupil of St Paul, and if he'd twisted the narrative to make a point of doctrine, he'd have been disobeying his teacher. Furthermore, it would have been counterproductive. Once a writer is caught out in one lie, nobody believes anything else they have written.

Holocaust

In Jerusalem, and several other cities, there's a 'Holocaust Museum'. This *is* telling history to make a theological point! They want everyone to know how the Jews suffered during the Second World War, so that other people should sympathize with them. But for that very reason they have to make certain that everything they say is absolutely spot-on true, incapable of being demonstrated as a lie, or even a distortion of what happened. Similarly, the very fact that the Gospels were written to show that Jesus is our dependable Saviour, is the reason that they must never be caught out in a fabrication.

Lee Strobel

An American journalist called Lee Strobel wrote a book, listing the evidence for the truthfulness of the Gospels. He was experienced in reporting on court cases for his newspaper, and told how his prejudice against an accused man changed when he saw the full evidence. A similar process had changed him from a convinced atheist into a believing Christian. The book is called *The Case for Christ*. He lists the reasons for believing that the four Gospels in the Bible are based on eyewitness accounts, unlike the more fanciful Apocryphal Gospels. He shows that the apostles would never have sacrificed their lives for teaching that Jesus was risen if they hadn't persuaded themselves that it's absolutely true. Later Jewish writings attack Christianity, but they don't deny the facts of Jesus's life and miracles. Archaeology has confirmed the accuracy of the Gospels' descriptions of places. Early accurate copies of the Gospels have been found dating to within 30 to 40 years after they were first written. Strobel lists 39 different non-Christian writings from the early centuries which confirm more than 100 facts about the life of Jesus. And he demolishes one by one the arguments of those who allege that the Gospels are inaccurate.

Thank you, Mark

So I think we owe a vote of thanks to St Mark, for having the brilliant idea of writing down an account of the life of Jesus, and calling it 'the Good News'. We should thank him for the care and trouble he took to make it accurate. And for inspiring the other Gospel writers to prepare their own versions, expanding and confirming the truthfulness of what Mark had written. Based on Mark's writings, we should try to find out what Jesus said, and why he died and rose again, and why that's good news to me as an individual. Mark wrote that Jesus sacrificed his life for your sake. Because the Gospels are so true to history, we can't read them and remain unmoved by his love. Jesus knows you as an individual; he knows what makes you tick. He died to show you how much he loves you. Also, writes St Mark, Jesus reveals in himself the character of his heavenly Father. So, however unworthy of it you may feel, the Gospels reveal God's personal love for you. Thank you, Jesus, for loving me so. Thank you, Mark, for writing such a precise account. Thank you, God, that you gave your Son, that whoever believes in him may have eternal life.

Suggested hymns

Lord, thy word abideth; O the deep, deep love of Jesus; Thank you Jesus; We have a gospel to proclaim.

SS Philip and James, Apostles   1 May
Inchworm

Isa. 30.15–21 This is the way; Ps. 119.1–8 The way of the Lord; Eph. 1.3–10 The mystery of forgiveness; John 14.1–14 Show us the Father (I am the way)

> *'[Jesus said to Thomas,] "I am the way, and the truth, and the life. No one comes to the Father except through me. If you know me, you will know my Father also. From now on you do know him and have seen him."' John 14.6–7*

The inchworm

The 'inchworm' is another name for the looper caterpillar, which moves its rear set of legs forward by bending the centre of its body up in a loop, then moves its front legs forward, for all the world like a tailor measuring out his cloth with a tape measure. Danny Kaye, in the biographical film *Hans Christian Anderson,* sang a song by Frank Loesser, called 'Inchworm'. It begins with children learning their tables: 'Two and two are four', and so on. Then it compares one of them to the inchworm, which is measuring the marigold. But although the child's love of arithmetic will certainly lead to worldly advancement, so much of what makes life enjoyable and worthwhile is being lost because the child won't stop to see how beautiful the flowers are!

Truth

There are many types of truth. Mathematical, measurable, material truth is important. In recent centuries, we have learnt a lot about the material world, and how it works. But other types of truth are just as important. It's true that the marigolds are beautiful; and it's true that human love is more profound than that of even the higher animals. Yet neither of those things can be measured or explained in scientific terms. But if scientists say they enjoy flowers and love their kids, they don't have to produce a scientific explanation for what they say to prove that it's true! Nor can science prove it's untrue. The truths of love and beauty are different types of truth from scientific truth; but they are just as true. The theory that nothing happens unless there's a scientific explanation for it is called 'materialism'. Materialists have caused much suffering in recent years. Yet scientists who fall in love, and admire the sunset together, disprove the theory of materialism every day!

Jesus is the truth

Jesus was discussing truth with two of his apostles, Philip and Thomas, at the Last Supper, and speaking about going to heaven after we die. 'You know the way to reach the place where I am going,' he said. Thomas was out of his depth. 'We don't even know where it is you are going to,' he wailed – 'so how *can* we know the way to get there?' Jesus's answer rocked them back on their heels: '*I* am the way,' he said. While they were still struggling with that, he continued, 'And I am the truth – and I am the life.' Jesus wanted them to understand that after his crucifixion, he would lead us to eternal life with our heavenly Father. The way to get to heaven is by following Jesus, believing and trusting him, and imitating his life of self-sacrificing love. This was too much for Philip. He was having an 'inchworm moment' – he couldn't believe anything was true unless he could see it and measure it – and he couldn't see God. 'Just *show us* the Father,' Philip howled, 'that's all I ask!' Patiently, Jesus replied, 'If you have seen me, you have seen the Father.' The truth about heaven, and God, is embedded in Jesus, because the man Jesus is so like God that we call him the Son of God – whatever is true about Jesus, is also true about his heavenly Father, and vice versa. Heaven is being united with God in love. That's what *we* long for – but that's what *Jesus* already is! We hope to gain that life one day by following Jesus the Way, and believing in him who is the Truth; but Jesus already *is* that Life!

Spiritual truths

The truth about eternal life is a spiritual truth. So are the truths about beauty and love. John Keats wrote in his 'Ode on a Grecian Urn': '"Beauty is truth, truth beauty," – that is all ye know on earth, and all ye need to know.' God's love for us is a spiritual truth; you can neither prove nor disprove it by scientific argument. There are many types of truth, beside those you can measure. Scientific truth is important, as the songwriter told the studious child: 'You and your arithmetic, you'll probably go far.' Yet the other sorts of truth are equally valuable: the truths of love and beauty, and the spiritual truth about God. Inchworm, inchworm, don't ever become so absorbed in measurable truths, that you miss the equally important ones that can never be measured in a month of Sundays! The truth about love is summed up in Jesus; so are the truths about the creation, and about the Creator. How beautiful they are!

Suggested hymns

Dear Lord, we long to see your face; Fairest Lord Jesus; The spacious firmament on high; Thou art the Way: by thee alone.

St Matthias the Apostle   14 May
Judas Killed Himself
Isa. 22.15–25 Eliakim replaces Shebna; Ps. 15 Who shall dwell in your house?; Acts 1.15–26 Matthias replaces Judas (*if the Acts reading is used instead of the Old Testament reading, the New Testament reading is* 1 Cor. 4.1–7 Stewards of God's mysteries); John 15.9–17 I have appointed you

> *'Judas acquired a field with the reward of his wickedness; and falling headlong he burst open in the middle and all his bowels gushed out.' Acts 1.18*

Suicide

When we read in the Acts of the Apostles about Judas Iscariot 'falling headlong', it sounds like an accident. But we know it wasn't, because St Matthew writes: 'Throwing down the pieces of silver in the temple, he departed; and he went and hanged himself.' Suicide is frighteningly common. We don't like to talk about it, because we feel powerless to do anything. Then, when someone we know seems suicidal, we don't want to believe it, not knowing what to say to them. So although you will probably find it distressing, may I talk about what to say to someone who's suicidal, so that you will be ready if ever you come across somebody like that?

Take it seriously

The first piece of advice is: take it seriously. People often say, 'Those who talk about suicide don't do it.' That's a complete myth. Anyone who even hints that they are thinking around the idea of suicide needs immediate attention, and you may be the only person they will talk to.

Mental illness

The second myth is that anyone who tries to kill themselves must be psychologically disturbed, and so you are not qualified to deal with it. About 10 per cent of all suicidal people are psychotic or delusional, and their main problem is facing up to their illness, which you can help them with, persuading them to seek treatment. The rest mostly suffer from depression, which is a recognized mental illness, and very common. Yet many depressed people don't commit suicide. The friendship of someone like you, who is concerned about them and wants to help, may carry them through the suicidal phase until the depression can be dealt with.

A cry for help

Don't tell yourself that this person's problems aren't serious enough to commit suicide over. They may not seem serious to you, but to them they may seem overwhelming. It's not how bad the problem is that counts, but how badly it's hurting the person who has it. Remember: suicidal behaviour is a cry for help.

Half and half

Another myth is that 'If someone is going to kill themselves, nothing can stop them.' A suicidal person is ambivalent – one half of them wants to live, and the other half wants, not so much death, as an end to their pain. If someone who is feeling suicidal turns to you, they probably believe that you are more caring than anyone else they know, or more informed about coping with misfortune, and that you can be trusted to protect their confidentiality. However negatively they speak, no matter how angry they seem, they are doing a positive thing and have a positive view of you. It's your responsibility to respond positively.

Immediately

So agree to listen at once. Preventing suicide can't be left to the last minute. Unfortunately, suicidal people are afraid that trying to get help may bring them more pain. Give them the chance to talk, and avoid arguing or giving advice. Show by your voice and manner that you are concerned; be patient, sympathetic and tolerant. Ask how they feel – you needn't worry that you are putting the idea of suicide into someone's mind, it's there already. Avoid leaving them alone, and remove all pills and poisons from their home. Urge them to seek professional help.

No secrets

Respect their privacy, but reserve your right to ask advice. Don't try to go it alone. Learn by heart the number of The Samaritans: 08457 90 90 90 – and don't leave the house until they have rung them. If only one of the other apostles had understood all this, poor Judas might not have committed suicide, and Matthias wouldn't have needed to step into his shoes. But don't let the suicidal person make *you* feel guilty for what *they* do; you can only do your best.

Come to Jesus

Poor Judas thought that Jesus was the problem, but in fact, Jesus is the solution. We rebel against him until we are in deep trouble, and then, 'out of the depths' we cry to him, and we find he's not the remote, disapproving tyrant we had feared, but a loving, sympathetic friend. Jesus is willing to absorb our anger, sympathize with our pain, accept us as we are, and forgive us all our sin. If only people who are depressed could understand that, Jesus would throw them a lifeline, and they would have no wish to turn their backs on such a loving heart. And without preaching at them, you may be the only person who can share with them from your own experience the knowledge of Jesus's love.

Suggested hymns

Art thou languid, art thou weary?; I heard the voice of Jesus say; There's a wideness in God's mercy; When morning gilds the skies.

Day of Thanksgiving for the Institution of Holy Communion (Corpus Christi) 30 May
Panis Angelicus

Gen. 14.18–20 Melchizedek brought bread and wine; Ps. 116.10–17 The cup of salvation; 1 Cor. 11.23–26 The Last Supper; John 6.51–58 Living bread

'I am the living bread that came down from heaven. Whoever eats of this bread will live for ever; and the bread that I will give for the life of the world is my flesh.' John 6.51

Manna

Jesus fed five thousand people from five loaves and two fish. This was not only a miracle, but a symbol. They were reminded of the time when the Israelites were hungry as they crossed the wilderness, fleeing from Egypt towards the Promised Land. Moses prayed, and God sent small round pieces of bread, falling from the sky, which they called manna. Referring to this, Psalm 78 reads, 'Mortals ate the bread of angels.' Perhaps this was the heavenly equivalent of the 'Bread of the Presence', kept in the Temple where God lived on earth. Questioned by the crowd, Jesus said, 'I am the living bread that came down from heaven. Whoever eats of this bread will live for ever; and the bread that I will give for the life of the world is my flesh.' He was not only looking back to the manna, but also forward to the Holy Communion in which we eat bread together in memory of him.

Ambrosia

Thus, already in the Psalms, the gift of bread to save the people from starving has become associated with the legend that we are allowed to share in the food which immortal spirits feed upon. In the Garden of Eden, there was supposed to stand the Tree of Life, whose fruit would give immortality to those who ate it. The Greek gods were supposed to eat 'ambrosia', and drink 'nectar'. If a mortal managed to taste these, they would confer eternal youth and beauty. So when Jesus said that he was the bread of life, and whoever eats this bread will live for ever, he was linking what happens when we receive Holy Communion with the legendary bread of angels, and the gift of eternal life. It isn't magic – it doesn't work if you have absolutely no faith – but you can be sure that if you have faith as small as a grain of mustard seed, your place in heaven is confirmed every time you eat the sacramental bread.

Corpus Christi

In 1208, a nun called Sister Juliana, in Liège, was devoted to the mystery of the Blessed Sacrament, but complained that there was no day in the year on which we could thank God for this special gift. Maundy Thursday is when we celebrate the Last Supper, but on that day we are also thinking of Christ's new commandment of love; of the foot-washing; of the priesthood; and of the events in Gethsemane. So, responding to her request, her bishop founded the feast of Corpus Christi, which is Latin for 'the Body of Christ'. Quickly it became popular throughout the Western Church. It falls on a Thursday, because the Last Supper was on a Thursday; but to avoid all the competing attractions of Eastertide, it was placed on the Thursday after Trinity Sunday. In the Church of England, it's called the Day of Thanksgiving for the Institution of Holy Communion.

Aquinas

When the new festival had become established, special prayers were needed, and St Thomas Aquinas wrote a complete liturgy for Corpus Christi. He was the greatest Christian philosopher of his day – some would say, the greatest ever. But the prayers and hymns he wrote, although they contain some philosophical terms, are sublime poetry, and many of them have become famous in other contexts. The Collect of the Day begins, 'O Lord, in a wonderful sacrament you have given us a memorial ...' The hymn, 'Now, my tongue, the mystery telling', contains the verse 'Therefore we, before him bending ...' Another hymn, 'The heavenly word, proceeding forth', includes a verse, 'O saving victim, opening wide ...' These all have Latin titles, but the best known of all is the verse, 'Panis angelicus' meaning 'Bread of the angels'. In 1872, César Franck, a famous choirmaster and composer in Paris, added these words to one of his Mass settings. He set it for tenor solo, chorus, organ, cello, harp and double bass, and it's become one of the best-loved solos in the tenor repertoire. Here's a rough translation; would you make it your prayer today?

319

Bread of the hosts above,
now down from heaven streams,
for humans, God's pure love,
fulfilling all our dreams.
Wonderful spectacle!
Poor humble folk, it seems,
touch God, our daily miracle.
Dwelling in heaven's height,
grant what we beg you for:
visit us here below.
You whom we kneel before,
lead us, who seek your sight,
that we may evermore
live in your everlasting light.
Amen.

Suggested hymns

Now, my tongue, the mystery telling; O saving victim, opening wide; The heavenly word, proceeding forth; Therefore we, before him bending.

The translation is © Michael Counsell 2010.

Visit of the Blessed Virgin Mary to Elizabeth
31 May
My Magnificat
Zeph. 3.14–18 Sing, daughter Zion; Ps. 113 Making her a joyous mother; Rom. 12.9–16 Hospitality; Luke 1.39–49 [50–56] Magnificat

> *'Mary said,*
> *"My soul magnifies the Lord,*
> *and my spirit rejoices in God my Saviour."' Luke 1.46–47*

Gratitude

When somebody asks you to do something for them, how do you answer? Your boss at work, or one of your family, makes a polite request for help. Do you say, 'I'm too busy just now.' Or, 'I don't feel like doing that today.' Or, 'I'm exhausted, I'll think about it tomorrow.' Or even, 'Not on your life! Who do you think I am? If you want it done you can jolly well do it yourself!' Occasionally one of those may be the best answer in the circumstances. But not every time, or you will get a reputation for being a selfish curmudgeon. So do you sometimes say, 'Certainly, I'd love to do that, right now. Thank you for giving me the opportunity to help you. It's a pleasure.' If you answer like that, people will say, 'What a kind and helpful, unselfish person!' But suppose it's a really big ask, something which will change the course of your whole life? Most of us would need time to think about that one. At last we might grudgingly say, 'Oh well, if I must ...' But the Virgin Mary wasn't like that at all. When God asked her to spend the next 30 years looking after God's Son for him, she answered, 'Here I am, the servant of the Lord; let it be with me according to your word.' Then she sang a song of gratitude to God for asking her – we call it the Magnificat.

Magnificat

Mary sang her song when she went to visit her cousin Elizabeth, a meeting which we commemorate on this day, the 31st May. It's a wonderful hymn of praise, a heartfelt thank you to God for the honour he had paid her. When Mary says she is magnifying God, she means that by praising him, she's making God's reputation greater throughout the earth. First she thanks God for looking favourably on his humble handmaid. Every generation from then till the end of the world will say that Mary is the luckiest girl on earth, because the Mighty and Holy One has done a wonderful thing for her. God is kind and forgiving to everyone who respects him. By choosing an ordinary working-class girl for such an honour, God has turned the social order upside down. The powerful people are removed from their positions, and the underdogs are given honour and authority in their place. The outcast are accepted, the starving are fed, but the rich are sent away with nothing. The Jewish people, if they are faithful to God, receive, when Jesus is born, the Messiah whom God promised them centuries ago. The Magnificat is a very revolutionary manifesto, but young Mary realizes we get nowhere by trying to seize power by ourselves; it's God in his mercy who gives honour to the poor and humble like Mary, while denying it to those who follow the path of violence.

My Magnificat

So Mary's response to the task that God had laid upon her was to give God thanks and praise. Oughtn't we to look to see how many things in our own lives we have to thank God for? Then, instead of grumbling at what a hard furrow God has given us to plough, we should thank him for the compliment of choosing us to serve him. Thank God for trusting you to bear an extra burden of hard slog and suffering without complaint, and make up your own thanksgiving prayer. It won't be the same as Mary's, because God has chosen you to fulfil some quite different tasks than she was called to do. But there are always things to thank God for. Call your hymn 'My Magnificat'. Write it down if you want to; or you can make it up in your head every day afresh when you come to your prayer time. Think of all the things you have received from God, and thank him for them. For your family and home when so many are alone or homeless; for your health and strength, which, though it may not be perfect, is always better than that of so many poor people in this troubled world. The gifts and talents God has given you, and the things you enjoy doing. The Venerable Bede said of the Magnificat, 'These words of praise, therefore, may be fittingly uttered by all of God's creatures.' Will you join Mary in her hymn of thanksgiving today, along with all the other people whom God has blessed, with the song of the birds and the roar of the lion, all singing together, 'My soul magnifies the Lord, and my spirit rejoices in God my Saviour.'

Suggested hymns

For Mary, Mother of our Lord; Her Virgin eyes saw God incarnate born; Tell out, my soul, the wonders of the Lord; Ye watchers and ye holy ones.

St Barnabas the Apostle   11 June
Who Is and Who Isn't a Christian?

Job 29.11–16 Like one who comforts; Ps. 112 Generous; Acts 11.19–30 Barnabas encourages Saul (*if the Acts reading is used instead of the Old Testament reading, the New Testament reading is* Gal. 2.1–10 Barnabas and me); John 15.12–17 Love one another

'It was in Antioch that the disciples were first called "Christians".'
Acts 11.26

Gentiles

We owe everything to St Barnabas. A Jew brought up on the Greek island of Cyprus, he was one of the first followers of Jesus, the Jewish Messiah. But he spoke Greek, and when the church in Jerusalem heard that Greek-speakers were joining the church in Antioch in large numbers, they sent Barnabas to help in caring for them. The Acts of the Apostles calls these new converts Hellenists. They certainly spoke Greek, but they may have been ethnically Jewish yet knowing little of the Jewish religion and speaking little Hebrew; or they may have been from the many races in the Roman Empire who spoke Greek as their second language. It quickly became apparent to Barnabas that you can't restrict the message of Jesus to pious Hebrew-speaking Jews; and once you open the church doors to outsiders, anybody can come in. Even you and me, thank God.

Sects

Thanks to the work of Barnabas, and his friend Saul of Tarsus, they had a new situation in Antioch. There were Jews all over the Empire, and changes had been made in Roman law to exempt them from, for instance, making sacrifices to the Emperor as though he was a god. Everybody knew who the Jews were: they had Jewish parents, and worshipped in the synagogue. Within the Jewish community there were many sects: Pharisees, Sadducees, Essenes, followers of John the Baptist, and so on; but they were all Jews. But what were they to call this new group, who followed a Jewish prophet called Jesus Christ, yet were not of the Jewish race? Their friends made fun of them – 'followers of King Herod are called Herodians,' they said, teasingly, 'so we shall have to call followers of this man Christ "Christ-ians", or Christians!' So a new word came into the language. Few people knew what 'Christ' meant – something to do with anointing, they said – but here was a convenient label for his followers. Then, when the Hebrew followers of Jesus were expelled from the synagogues, they too became known as Christians. Applied in mockery, it became a badge of pride, and a third of the world's population now call themselves Christians. Thanks to St Barnabas.

Exclusive

But who is a Christian? And, equally important, who isn't a Christian? Originally the term was applied indiscriminately to everyone who wanted to learn more about Jesus, and meet with others who were also interested in what he taught. Then, when they were ready to trust him, they were baptized. After that they could be called 'the baptized', or 'the saints', meaning those who belong to the holy family of Jesus, or simply 'the Church'. But they still had a lot to learn, and they argued among themselves incessantly about what Jesus had said. That was all right so long as they remained inclusive – as long as they allowed those who disagreed with them to share the label of Christian. But before long, some were baptized, and then revealed that what they believed was nothing like the beliefs they'd learnt from Jesus – even plain contrary to what Jesus had taught. They tended to split off, when they were called schismatic, or form quite separate communities, known as heretics.

Divisive

Sadly, the process continued down the centuries, and the name of Christian, which was intended to show how inclusive the family of God is, welcoming all and sundry, soon became divisive. You will hear Christians today telling other people, 'you aren't really a Christian!' They talk about, 'the day I became a Christian', which was probably a wonderful emotional experience, when they committed their life to Christ and accepted certain doctrines as true. But then anyone who hasn't had the identical experience is told that they are not Christian. Somebody who was on the point of becoming a follower of Jesus may be driven to despair because they don't express their emotions in that way, and then they may be lost for ever, because of the narrow-mindedness of those who want to make the title of 'Christian' exclusive to 'people like us'. This must make St Barnabas, 'the encourager', very sad. Jesus too, who told his apostles to 'go and make all people my disciples', must weep when what was meant to be the open, tolerant and diverse family of God is turned into an exclusive coterie. Who is a Christian? Who isn't a Christian? God only knows! All we need to know is this: that all men and women are our sisters and brothers, and the love of Christ embraces us all.

In Christ there is no east or west; O happy band of pilgrims; O happy day; Thy hand, O God, has guided.

The Birth of St John the Baptist 24 June
The Forerunner

Isa. 40.1–11 A voice in the wilderness; Ps. 85.7–13 Salvation is at hand; Acts 13.14b–26 A baptism of repentance, *or* Gal. 3.23–29 The law our schoolmaster; Luke 1.57–66, 80 Birth of the Baptist

> *'You, child, will be called the prophet of the Most High; for you will go before the Lord to prepare his ways.'* Luke 1.76

Benedictus

Zechariah sang a song when his son, John the Baptist, was born – we call it the Benedictus. At one point the old man sang to his son, baby John: 'You, child, will be called the prophet of the Most High; for you will go before the Lord to prepare his ways.' This is a quotation from the prophet Malachi, according to whom God said, 'See, I am sending my messenger to prepare the way before me.'

The forerunner

When a king, in Bible times, was making a royal progress through his realm, he needed someone called a forerunner to sprint down the road ahead and warn the king's subjects to make preparations to receive him. Buildings needed to be vacated, tents erected, supplies of food brought in and water drawn from the well, at least a day before His Majesty arrived at their town; the forerunner ran ahead to give them fair warning of what was expected when the king arrived. The forerunner announced the imminent arrival of the king; and John the Baptist, while still a tiny baby, was told by his dad that he was to be the forerunner for God's Messiah.

A prophet

But even before Malachi wrote, Moses had promised, 'The LORD your God will raise up for you a prophet like me, from among your own people; you shall heed such a prophet.' Moses, the great law-giver, revealing God's wishes for how his people should behave, was also described as a prophet. And he predicts that another prophet will one day come, like him revealing God's will, and he was to be obeyed in all things. Malachi, also, predicted the coming of a prophet; according to him God said, 'Lo, I will send you the prophet Elijah before the great and terrible day of the LORD comes.' But Elijah had prophesied about 350 years before Malachi; so the prophecy is that Elijah would *return* to earth to prepare for the Day of the Lord. So when John the Baptist appeared in the wilderness, calling on his fellow countrymen and women to repent and be baptized, they readily recognized that John the Baptist was fulfilling these promises – a prophet preparing the way for the coming of God's king, the Messiah.

John's testimony

John was a very common name in those days, and we mustn't confuse the author of 'The Gospel according to John' with John the Baptist. According to the Gospel, the 'baby Baptist', when he grew up, was asked whether he was Elijah, come back to earth. Or the prophet that Moses predicted, or the Messiah? To all these questions John answered 'No! ... I am the voice of one crying out in the wilderness, "Make straight the way of the Lord."' Here he was quoting from Isaiah, who predicted the return of the Jewish exiles from their captivity in Babylon to their homeland. A great army like that, crossing the wilderness, would need a broad highway, so the forerunner warns the people to start road-building: 'A voice cries out: "In the wilderness prepare the way of the Lord, make straight in the desert a highway for our God" ... Then the glory of the Lord shall be revealed, and all people shall see it together.' In Jesus, God revealed his glory; so John is to be the forerunner for his cousin Jesus, the glory of God in human form.

Are you ready?

If a herald ran into your street, and told you that Jesus would be there soon, what would you do? Panic, I expect! But once you'd calmed down, you would try to tidy the place up a bit. Then you'd realize that it wasn't the mess in the street that Jesus was concerned with, but the mess in your heart, and in your life. So you'd set about tidying that up as quick as you could. That was what John the Forerunner did, warning people to repent, and be washed, as a symbol of making a clean start, ready for the new age beginning when God's Messiah arrived. Don't put it off, he warned. Similarly we mustn't delay our preparations for the coming of Jesus just because we can't see him yet; he's invisibly here all the time. Don't be frightened and guilt-ridden; the warning is given along with the promise that as soon as you repent, God will forgive you. But start clearing out the clutter in your life right now; that's what John the Forerunner was sent to tell you to do.

Suggested hymns

Hark, a thrilling voice is sounding; On Jordan's bank the Baptist's cry; Sing we the praises of the great forerunner; The great forerunner of the morn.

SS Peter and Paul, Apostles 29 June
Did Jesus Intend to Found a Church?

Zech. 4.1–6a, 10b–14 Two anointed ones; Ps. 125 Stand fast for ever; Acts 12.1–11 Peter released from prison (*if the Acts reading is used instead of the Old Testament reading, the New Testament reading is* 2 Tim. 4.6–8, 17–18 Poured out); Matt. 16.13–19 Peter recognizes the Messiah
or for Peter alone: Ezek. 3.22–27 Preaching to his own; Ps. 125; Acts 12.1–11 (*if the Acts reading is used instead of the Old Testament reading, the New Testament reading is* 1 Peter 2.19–25 Suffering for God); Matt. 16.13–19

> *'You are Peter, and on this rock I will build my church.'* Matthew 16.18

Jesus

Peter was the first to recognize Jesus as the Messiah, the Son of God. Jesus gave him a new name: 'You are Peter, and on this rock

I will build my church.' The word 'church' only occurs in Matthew's Gospel here, and once again two chapters later where the church is to mediate between two Christians who are having an argument. The word is *ekklesia,* from which we get our word 'ecclesiastical', and means those who are called out. Coined in Athens, where democracy was invented, it describes the gathering of all the free men of the city, called out to vote on civic policy. It seems an unusual word for Jesus the Jew to use; but in the Greek translation of the Old Testament, *ekklesia* was used to translate the Hebrew word for the Assembly of the People of God. Maybe Jesus was thinking of any assembly of believers, who, to begin with, were all Jewish.

Paul

It was St Paul who extended the Christian gospel to include non-Jews also. Until then, the Christian believers were a group worshipping among other Jews; years later, those Jews who wouldn't accept that Jesus was the Messiah threw the Christians out of the synagogues. But following Paul's ministry, large groups of non-Jewish Christians all over the Roman Empire had no intention of converting to Judaism. They met in people's homes, and Paul writes to them as the Church or assembly of believers in each town. Paul uses the word 62 times in his letters, mostly referring to local churches; but he sometimes speaks of persecuting 'the church of God'. In his Letter to the Ephesians, he writes about the worldwide church as a mystery, one body, holding one faith and worshipping one Lord. But at this stage, there was no organization, bureaucracy, priesthood, or hierarchy – just local self-governing fellowships with a sense of responsibility to each other and a common mission to the world.

Organized religion

A cartoon in the *Church Times* showed a vicar sitting at a desk piled high with papers, answering the telephone. 'Well, Mr Smith,' he replies, 'you don't believe in organized religion, you say? You should come here; this is the most *dis*organized religion I have ever come across!' Indeed, the Church today has become a huge organization. So the question arises, when Jesus spoke to St Peter, did he intend to found that sort of organized religion? The answer is, almost certainly, no. But inevitably changes came about. First, the missionary who had founded their church appointed overseers in each large town, to make sure none of the groups flew off at a tangent; and the word for overseers is 'bishops'. Then the bishops from different towns met together in a synod, to plan a common strategy for evangelism. Deacons, meaning 'servants', were appointed to take the burden of administration off the shoulders of the missionaries. The leading deacon was called an archdeacon, and next ... well, you can see the way it was heading. The larger the group, the more it needs an organized structure. But the more organized it becomes, the more opportunities there are for squabbling, strife, power-seeking and even corruption. Jesus wouldn't have wanted that ... we need constantly to simplify and reform our church structures. But forming a breakaway church is no answer, because they, too, eventually become top-heavy.

No other plan

When Jesus ascended to heaven, the angels are supposed to have asked him who would continue his ministry on earth. 'I have chosen twelve fishermen,' Jesus answered. 'Twelve fishermen,' gasped the angels. 'It will never work!' To which Jesus replied, 'I have no other plan!' Some sort of Church is necessary, to teach the world that God loves them. Yet because it's made up of sinful individuals, it will always be far from perfect. Nevertheless, with all its faults, we need the Church if we are to do the work to which God has called us. Peter and Paul were right. So, did Jesus intend to found a Church? Yes – and no! But if we are to be effective in evangelism and ministry, we *must* stay within its walls, trying to reform the Church of God from within. Jesus has no other plan.

Suggested hymns

Lord of the Church, we pray for our renewing; The Church of God a kingdom is; Thy hand, O God, has guided; We love the place, O God.

St Thomas the Apostle   3 July
Questions Science Cannot Answer
Hab. 2.1–4 The righteous live by faith; Ps. 31.1–6 I trust in
the Lord; Eph. 2.19–22 The foundation of the apostles; John
20.24–29 Doubting Thomas is convinced

> *'Jesus said to [Thomas], "Have you believed because you have
> seen me? Blessed are those who have not seen and yet have come
> to believe."' John 20.29*

Curiosity

Human beings have always wanted to make sense of the world in
which we live, and our place in it. Why is the world so beautiful?
Why are we here? What's the aim and purpose of my life? Why do
we love? Is there any purpose to suffering and death? Might God
be part of the answer? These are fundamental questions, and as far
as we can discover, we have been asking them since writing was
invented and probably long before. We ignore them for a while;
we 'eat, drink, and are merry, for tomorrow we die'; but they keep
niggling in the background. As Socrates said, 'The unexamined life
is not worth living.' Searching for answers to these questions helps
us decide how to live today and tomorrow.

Science

Around the seventeenth century, in the period known as the Renaissance, people came up with a new tool, which they hoped would
answer some of these questions. They would gather observations
over a period of time about how things behaved, and try to see a
pattern in them. Then they would guess at an explanation for this
pattern – a 'hypothesis' they called it. Then they tried to predict, on
the basis of this hypothesis, how other things would behave in different circumstances. Next, they tested these predictions by repeat-
able experiments in controlled conditions. If the measurements
were what they predicted, they called the hypotheses a theory,
which would stay in place as an explanation of how things came to
be as they are, until some measurements were made which didn't fit
the prediction. If this happened, they either scrapped their theory,
or, more likely, modified it to fit the new facts. They called this the
scientific method, and earned the right to call themselves 'scientists', from a Latin word meaning 'to know'. St Thomas, whom we

commemorate today, has been called the patron saint of scientists, because he wouldn't believe that Jesus was alive until he'd seen him.

Limitations

Scientific method was responsible for some very useful and life-saving discoveries. But notice two limitations. First, science, to begin with, dealt only with things you could observe, measure and repeat. Second, it deals only with questions of *how* things came to be as they are, rather than with *why* it happened like that. Most of the fundamental questions are 'why' questions, and science, by its very nature, can't answer those questions. A little later, various disciplines arose calling themselves sciences, but which couldn't test their hypothesis by controlled experiment. Such are the behavioural sciences, like psychoanalysis and sociology. They can give statistical estimates of the probability of certain outcomes, but they can't be sure what will happen in individual cases. The new science of genetics is a sort of in-between case: observations of large numbers of births, like fruit flies or fossil seashells, appear to confirm evolution by natural selection. The presence or absence of a particular gene in the DNA makes certain medical conditions more or less likely. But a lot of different genes are involved in the development of each individual, and we are a long way off saying that our physical characteristics, let alone our behaviour, are inescapably determined by our genetic inheritance.

Questions science cannot answer

Scientists, like St Thomas, look for material proof of their theories. In the process they have made millions of useful discoveries, developing our understanding of the universe and our ability to heal diseases. But none of their theories address the fundamental questions I mentioned earlier. That's because science can only answer the 'how' questions – *how* do things come to be as they are? Whereas the things we really care about need 'why' answers. The material world is important for us. But questions about love, beauty, meaning, and truth itself are questions science can't answer. Some atheists think that science proves there is no God; many other distinguished scientists consider that belief in science and belief in God go hand in hand. We need science *and* faith if we are to understand the world about us.

My Lord and my God

St Thomas saw the wounds in Christ's body, and was the first to hail Jesus as 'my Lord and my God!' His observations led him to faith. Many scientists have wondered at the marvels they see revealed, and draw the same conclusion. Jesus said to Thomas, 'Have you believed because you have seen me? Blessed are those who have not seen and yet have come to believe.'

Suggested hymns

Fairest Lord Jesus; Light's glittering morn (Part 3); Lord of beauty, thine the splendour; The mighty firmament on high.

St Mary Magdalene   22 July
The Penitent Sinner

S. of Sol. 3.1–4 Seeking and finding; Ps. 42.1–10 As deer long for water; 2 Cor. 5.14–17 A new creation; John 20.1–2, 11–18 Go and tell

> *'Upon my bed at night*
> *I sought him whom my soul loves;*
> *I sought him, but found him not;*
> *I called him, but he gave no answer.' Song of Solomon 3.1*

Penitent sinner

Titian's picture of Mary Magdalene, painted in the 1560s, depicts her as a penitent sinner. Most of the art and literature of the Western Church imagine her as a reformed prostitute. While this tradition may not be strictly true, it performed a useful function in days gone by. By showing that Magdalene, who was honoured to be the first to see Jesus after his resurrection, had left a guilty life behind, it proclaimed the message that nobody is beyond redemption. No matter what deplorable things we may have done in the past – says the Church – provided we are genuinely penitent, we can be forgiven. We can make a fresh start, with a clean sheet, and begin our lives again, certain that God loves us as much as he loves those who seem beyond reproach. Mary Magdalene's story reminded respectable Christians not to shun even the most debauched sections of society, who are, after all, human beings still. Instead we must offer them the opportunity of reform. Within living memory, the Church provided a home for so-called 'fallen women' in most big cities.

Feminists

Then came the feminists, who pointed out how patronizing and sexist all this is. Why did it have to be a woman who represented the most deplorable aspects of human behaviour? Why not a man? After all, prostitutes only live that way because men wish to patronize them. Often they have been driven to it after betrayal or desertion by the men in their lives; or because the inequalities of man-made society made it impossible for them to avoid starvation by any other means.

The Gospels

As the feminists pointed out, the four Gospels say nothing about Mary Magdalene being a prostitute. All they tell us is that Jesus had driven seven devils out of her – which we would call today healing her from mental illness; that she was sufficiently wealthy to join with other women in paying for the expenses of Jesus's travels; and travelled with the apostles, looking after them; and that, in the garden where Jesus had been buried, the Risen Christ sent her out to bear witness to his resurrection. This last fact is such a privilege for Mary Magdalene that some would say it shows that Jesus treated the women in his team as equally important with the men, well qualified to take important roles in the mission of the Church.

Other women

What happened was that Mary Magdalene was confused with three other women mentioned in the Gospels:

- One is Mary of Bethany, near Jerusalem, the sister of Martha and Lazarus, who, according to St Luke, sat at Jesus's feet while Martha was busy preparing the meal. St John tells us that, when Jesus saw this Mary crying over the death of her brother Lazarus, he was moved to tears himself. And when he came to supper with them just before the crucifixion, Mary took some expensive perfume, poured it over Jesus's feet, and wiped them with her hair.
- This led to her being confused with another, unnamed woman, who, according to Matthew and Mark, poured ointment over Jesus's head, also at Bethany, but in the house of Simon the leper.

- Also, according to St Luke, 'a woman of the city, who was a sinner', poured ointment over Jesus's feet in the house of Simon the Pharisee, but this was in Galilee, not in Bethany.

There's no reason to assume these three women had anything to do with each other, still less with Mary Magdalene.

Reputation

So it's an unjustified slur to imply that poor Mary Magdalene had been a prostitute. In a short passage added later to St John's Gospel, about a woman taken in adultery, who was due to be stoned to death, Jesus shows his sympathy with women who are unfairly blamed by men, and says, 'Neither do I condemn you – go and sin no more.' Magdalene had quite enough to put up with, as she had to live down the reputation of being psychologically unstable. Yet although the confusion is regrettable, we can still learn from it that the mercy and forgiveness of Jesus reaches out to everyone, man or woman, who repents of the mistakes they have made. Neither should we condemn those whose sins are open and notorious – in the eyes of God our little secret sins are just as serious, yet we are all equally loveable, whatever we have done.

Suggested hymns

All hail the power of Jesus' Name; Father of heaven, whose love profound; Mary, weep not, weep no longer; Walking in a garden.

St James the Apostle   25 July
Answering a Question with a Question
Jer. 45.1–5 Seeking greatness; Ps. 126 Sow in tears, harvest in joy; Acts 11.27—12.2 Herod kills James (*if the Acts reading is used instead of the Old Testament reading, the New Testament reading is* 2 Cor. 4.7–15 Treasure in clay pots); Matt. 20.20–28 Seeking greatness

> 'The mother of the sons of Zebedee ... asked a favour of [Jesus] ... She said to him, "Declare that these two sons of mine will sit, one at your right hand and one at your left, in your kingdom." But Jesus answered, "... Are you able to drink the cup that I am about to drink?"' Matthew 20.20–22

Jewish joke

Jewish people tell this joke: A non-Jew asked his Jewish friend, 'Why do Jews always answer a question by asking another question?' To which his friend replied, 'Why shouldn't we answer a question with another question?'

James and John

If this is so, the apostles James and John showed that Jesus was characteristically Jewish. They asked him a very urgent question. According to St Mark, 'James and John, the sons of Zebedee, came forward ... and said to him ... "Grant us to sit, one at your right hand and one at your left, in your glory." But Jesus said to them, "... Are you able to drink the cup that I drink, or be baptized with the baptism that I am baptized with?"' You see? Jesus answers their question by asking them another question. According to St Matthew, their mother asked the question on behalf of her sons; but she got the same answer. Yet Jesus wasn't playing tricks. He was helping them to see that they were asking the wrong question. Before he could give an answer, they had to understand what leadership in the kingdom of God involves.

Leadership

In any walk of life, the leader's role is very demanding. The foreman of a gang, the CEO of a company, the teacher of a class or the head of the school, all have to put a great deal of effort into what they do. Often they will work longer hours than the people they lead; they have to wrestle with difficult decisions; they frequently take their work home with them. If you accept a post of responsibility, hoping that you will live a life of leisure, surrounded by luxury, and supported by the praises and devotion of your colleagues, you have a nasty shock coming! Junior employees sometimes work their fingers to the bone for nine hours a day, enduring the insults of some of those around them, so that they can gain ... what? Promotion to a senior position, where they work their fingers to the bone for 14 hours a day, *hated* by everyone! Of course, in the top jobs you know that your talents and abilities are being used to the full, and have the satisfaction of making a real contribution to the world. But a rose garden it ain't.

335

Kingdom

James and John, however, were asking for a very different type of responsibility. They wanted leadership in the kingdom of God. They probably thought that Jesus would shortly head up an army, driving out and defeating the hated Roman legions which were occupying their land. Then, they expected, he'd form Israel into a Jewish state, with himself as king, and a court full of honoured subordinates around him. Many Jews thought that this was what messiahship involved. If so, their request to be given the seats of honour, on either side of the king's throne, was quite reasonable.

Suffering

So Jesus asked them whether they were able to drink from the same cup as he did, and be baptized with his baptism. These were probably conventional phrases, understood by everybody, for a life of suffering. As we might say, to drink the cup of sorrow to the very dregs, and to be plunged into agony up to your neck. That pulled them up short. That wasn't at all what they were thinking of. For Jesus himself, being Messiah led to a painful death; only after that did it lead to eternal life. James and John needed to grow up, and realize that the only way to gain spiritual rewards is to live a demanding life, and the only way to heaven is through the gate of death.

Don't ask

You can ask Jesus any question you like. If you are puzzled, pray about it. He always answers, but his answer may not be what you expected. Jesus always leads you beyond your naive enquiry to a more mature understanding of what the world demands. Like James and John, we should be cautious about what we ask God for, because sometimes he gives it us, but we don't like it. God always puts us on the road to glory; but the journey there isn't an easy one.

Suggested hymns

Brother, sister, let me serve you; From heaven you came, helpless babe; Take up your cross, the Saviour said; 'The Kingdom is upon you!'

The Transfiguration of our Lord 6 August
A Transformation Scene

Dan. 7.9–10, 13–14 The Son of Man; Ps. 97 Clouds are around
him; 2 Peter 1.16–19 We saw; Luke 9.28–36 The transfiguration

*'About eight days after these sayings Jesus took with him Peter
and John and James, and went up on the mountain to pray. And
while he was praying, the appearance of his face changed, and his
clothes became dazzling white.' Luke 9.28–29*

Pantomime

All the best Christmas pantomimes have a transformation scene.
Pantomimes are a peculiarly English tradition, with the Principal
Boy played by a woman, and the Dame – a comical old woman –
acted by a man. Once an Englishman was asked to sing the part of
the witch, in Humperdink's opera of *Hansel and Gretel*, in drag,
of course. The American producer asked him how he interpreted
the role, and he replied, 'Rather like a pantomime dame.' 'Like a
what?!!' she exclaimed. I'm sure you know that pantomimes are
based on traditional fairy tales. At some point there is a scene in
which, by clever stagecraft, things are metamorphosed into something else. The frog is changed in the transformation scene into a
prince, which is what he always truly was. Or Cinderella is changed
into a princess, which she was always going to become, and her
mice into horses and the pumpkin into a coach. At midnight they
are changed back again, which humorists misquote as the basis for
a cliché: 'If I stay any later I'll turn into a pumpkin.'

Transfiguration

I wonder whether it would help us to think of the transfiguration of
Jesus as a transformation scene? He took his disciples to the top of
a high mountain, where, the Gospels tell us, 'the appearance of his
face changed, and his clothes became dazzling white'. The aston-
ished disciples also saw Moses and Elijah, representing the Law and
the Prophets, standing beside him, discussing 'the Exodus which
he was about to accomplish in Jerusalem'. This is code language:
as the Israelites, crossing the Red Sea, were led to freedom in the
Promised Land, so the crucifixion of Jesus leads us out of slavery to
sin and death, into what Hamlet called 'the undiscovered country'
of heaven. In other words, the disciples were seeing everything for

the first time as it really was. Jesus was a human being, a good friend and a great teacher and healer. But he was also much more than that. Daniel describes God as an 'Ancient One [who] took his throne, his clothing was white as snow.' So the description of Jesus at the transfiguration shows us that the human Jesus was, in actuality, very like God – later the disciples would say that he was really one with God.

Everything's changed

In the pantomime, it's not only Cinderella who's changed; everything around her and the circumstances of her life are altered too. Jesus was on his way to the most acute suffering in Jerusalem. Yet his willingness to lay down his life for others was the most glorious manifestation of love that the world has ever seen. His suffering was, in reality, his glory. St John, in his Gospel, wrote, 'the Word became flesh ... and we have seen his glory, the glory as of a father's only son ... Jesus did this, the first of his signs ... and revealed his glory.' Jesus asked Martha, 'Did I not tell you that if you believed, you would see the glory of God?' Then Jesus prayed at the Last Supper, 'now, Father, glorify me in your own presence with the glory that I had in your presence before the world existed ... Father, I desire that those also, whom you have given me, may be with me where I am, to see my glory.' In other words, the pain of the Suffering Servant is his greatest glory, and suffering and death are the way into the glory of heaven.

A glimpse of reality

At the transfiguration, the disciples had a vision of reality: the reality of who Jesus actually was, and what he was about to become. The same is true of us. In Jesus, we see who we really are, and what we are destined to become. We *are* ordinary human beings, not very beautiful or clever; and yet we are also a wonder of evolutionary development, capable of loving, and being loved. Because God loves you, you are the most wonderful creature on earth. St John also wrote, 'Beloved, we are God's children now; what we will be has not yet been revealed. What we do know is this: when he is revealed, we will be like him, for we will see him as he is.' The transfiguration gave the disciples a vision of who Jesus really was and what he would become. It also enables us to see the reality of ourselves – not grubby Cinderellas, but shining with glory, now and in the world to come.

Suggested hymns

Immortal, invisible, God only wise; Jesus, these eyes have never seen; Lord, the light of your love is shining; 'Tis good, Lord, to be here.

The Blessed Virgin Mary   15 August
Icons

Isa. 61.10–11 As a bride, *or* Rev. 11.19—12.6, 10 A woman in heaven; Ps. 45.10–17 You shall have sons; Gal. 4.4–7 Born of a woman; Luke 1.46–55 Magnificat

> *'A great portent appeared in heaven: a woman clothed with the sun, with the moon under her feet, and on her head a crown of twelve stars. She was pregnant and was crying out in birthpangs, in the agony of giving birth.' Revelation 12.1–2*

Iconoclasts

The Greek word for a picture is 'icon'. Long before the word was applied to a symbol on your computer, icons of Jesus, Mary and the saints were treated with great reverence in the Eastern Church. Orthodox Christians feel that the icons convey the presence of the saints, almost to the same extent as the bread and wine convey the presence of Christ in the liturgy. The walls of their churches, and the screen called the *iconostasis,* are covered with icons which they call 'windows to heaven', reminding them of the continual presence around us of the communion of saints. The icon of Mary always has a place of honour. Yet from the eighth to the tenth centuries, a wave of Puritanism swept the Eastern Church, arguing that honouring the saints who were represented in the icons meant that the pictures, far from being innocent visual aids, had become idols. So the 'iconoclasts', or icon-smashers, destroyed or defaced all the icons they could. Those icons which survived this terrible time were of course doubly precious, and the end of iconoclasm is still celebrated as the birth of the Orthodox Church as we know it today.

Pictures of Mary

Very few examples of Christian art survive from the first three centuries, understandably, because of persecution and the iconoclasts. In the catacombs in Rome, Christian tombs were marked by Christian symbols, and there are a few paintings of Jesus as the Good Shepherd. Only a handful of images of the Blessed Virgin Mary have survived. But the wonderful Sister Wendy Beckett, who was so popular and successful with her television programmes about art, has made a special study of the early icons of the Virgin. She travelled to see eight, in Rome, the Ukraine and the Sinai desert in Egypt. She calls it 'reading' an icon, and writes that these visits are conduits for prayer; her book is called *Encounters with God.*

Portraits by Luke

St Luke is the source of most of our information about Mary, maybe because he met her soon after Christ's resurrection. There's a very widespread tradition that Luke painted her portrait. There are five places which claim to have an original portrait of St Mary by St Luke. They are:

- In Jerusalem, the Jacobite Church belonging to an Eastern denomination which still uses the Aramaic language that Jesus spoke.
- In Egypt, a Coptic monastery belonging to the ancient church of Egypt, founded, they claim, by St Mark.
- In Rome, the ancient basilica of Santa Maria Maggiore [soft 'gg'].
- In Cyprus, a very old church.
- In Russia, the *Theótokos* in the Russian Orthodox Church of Vladimir.

Mary's title of *Theótokos,* or 'the bearer of God', was given to her at the Council of Ephesus, to emphasize that Jesus was already the Son of God when he was in her womb, as opposed to those who taught that he became divine at a later date.

Styles

Icon painting is a solemn ritual, and every step is accompanied by the correct observations of prayer and fasting. The artists are only allowed to innovate within recognized limits, and mainly see themselves as making faithful copies of their predecessors' work. Nevertheless, a number of different presentations of the Blessed Virgin have emerged. Mary is always known in Greece as the *Panagía*, [hard 'g'] which means the all-holy-woman. Each of these styles of painting has a beautiful name, showing the different aspects of her motherhood. They are:

- The *Panagía Kyriotíssa* ['y' = 'ee'], which shows her enthroned.
- *Hodegétria* [hard 'g'], meaning 'showing the way', which depicts Mary looking at the observer.
- *Ele-óusa* ['ou' pronounced 'oo], showing Mary touching her Son tenderly (this is the type found at Vladimir).
- *Orans*, which means praying.
- And most beautifully named of all, *Glyko-philóusa* – meaning 'sweetly kissing'!

Other images

Most of the depictions of Mary during the Romantic Movement, such as those drawing on the image in Revelation of a woman in heaven crowned with 12 stars, strike most observers as being in poor taste. More recently, however, artists have produced simple and graceful images which seem fully worthy to honour the mother of our Lord. The feminist movement has led to a re-evaluation of Mary's importance to modern women. Now we are beginning to see that Mary is herself an icon: a symbol for all time of the importance of motherhood.

Suggested hymns

Her Virgin eyes saw God incarnate born; Lord of the home, your only Son; The Angel Gabriel from heaven came; The God whom earth and sea and sky.

St Bartholomew the Apostle   24 August
Butchered

Isa. 43.8–13 My witnesses; Ps. 145.1–7 Speak of your wondrous acts; Acts 5.12–16 The apostles heal (*if the Acts reading is used instead of the Old Testament reading, the New Testament reading is* 1 Cor. 4.9–15 The shame of the apostles); Luke 22.24–30 Judging the twelve tribes

> '*A great number of people would also gather from the towns around Jerusalem, bringing the sick and those tormented by unclean spirits, and they were all cured.*' Acts 5.16

Skinning

Have you ever watched a butcher removing the hide from a carcass? It's called 'flaying' the carcass, and it's a bloody business; but fortunately the animal is dead, so it feels nothing. Or maybe you have actually had to skin a dead rabbit or some other sort of game yourself, and you marvel at what hard work it is. But just imagine if the animal was still alive. You couldn't do it, could you, while watching the poor creature screaming with pain? Now I suggest you skip quickly over the next scene, because it's too unbearable to imagine the process of flaying a live human being. But that's how St Bartholomew the apostle died, according to the tradition; and what's more, he didn't complain. The saints regarded martyrdom as the highest honour, because it leads to eternal glory. Such courage is almost impossible to imagine. He is said to have converted the local king Polemius and his family. This infuriated the king's brother, Astrages, who captured him and ordered Bartholomew to be flayed alive and then beheaded – in a word, he was butchered. A statue of Bartholomew in San Gennaro in Italy shows him with a large butcher's knife in his scalp; and Michelangelo's *Last Judgement* in the Sistine Chapel in Rome shows the saint, now alive again after the general resurrection, holding his own flayed skin high, as a badge of triumph! Wow!

Healing in Rome

His remains were brought to Rome, and buried on an island in the River Tiber. Tiber Island, as it was called, was already famous as a place of healing. It was probably used as an isolation hospital for people who were dying of infectious diseases. In 293 BC, the plague was so bad that a temple to the healing-God Aesculapius was built there, and the island was joined to the city on either bank of the river by two bridges. Medicine was primitive in those days. Lindsey Davis, in her detective novel *Saturnalia,* lists the different schools of ancient Roman medicine, including the dream therapists, the Hippocratic pneumatists, the empiricists, the dogmatists, and the charity workers from the shrine of Aesculapius. Among all this hocus-pocus, the dogmatists turned to invasive surgery, though of course without anaesthetics.

Christian healing

When the butchered remains of St Bartholomew were brought to Tiber Island it must have caused a sensation, for here was a new sect, called Christians, invading the headquarters of Roman medicine with a completely new technique. Jesus had been known as a healer, laying his hands on the sick and praying with them. The apostles followed his example. After Peter and John had healed the lame man at the Beautiful Gate, in the Jerusalem Temple, the Acts of the Apostles says: 'A great number of people would also gather from the towns around Jerusalem, bringing the sick and those tormented by unclean spirits, and they were all cured.' Christians showed, by the courage with which they faced martyrdom, that they weren't afraid to die, because they believed that death leads to eternal life.

St Bartholomew's Island

In AD 998, the Roman Emperor built a church over the ruins of the Aesculapius temple on Tiber Island, and dedicated it to St Bartholomew. So the island is now known as St Bartholomew's Island. It became one of the first Christian hospitals. Spreading out from there, many of the medieval monasteries were the only places where sick pilgrims could receive hospitality and healing, which is where the word 'hospital' comes from. So it was natural that when a large church and priory were founded in London, it should be dedicated to St Bartholomew, giving rise to St Bart's hospital. But that's another story.

Christian healing

Christian healing isn't superstitious – Christians teach that the work of the physicians and surgeons is at its best when it's accompanied by prayer. Mind, body and soul each affect the other parts of our personality. To surround a sick person with love and prayer speeds up the natural processes of healing that God has put in the body. When a sick person ponders on the universal love of God, they become more relaxed, and the medicines that the doctors have prescribed are more effective. Moreover, the willingness of saints like Bartholomew to suffer butchery for the sake of Christ helps us to see our own suffering as a willing sacrifice to God our Father, and a sign of our love.

Suggested hymns

At even, when the sun was set; As water to the thirsty; Make way, make way, for Christ the king; Peter and John went to pray.

Holy Cross Day   14 September
The Sign of the Cross

Num. 21.4–9 The bronze serpent; Ps. 22.23–28 All the earth shall turn to the Lord; Phil. 2.6–11 Obedient to death on the cross; John 3.13–17 God so loved the world

> *'Being found in human form,*
>   *he humbled himself*
>   *and became obedient to the point of death –*
>   *even death on a cross.*
> *Therefore God also highly exalted him*
>   *and gave him the name*
>   *that is above every name.'*
>   *Philippians 2.7–9*

Orthodox

A rather ill-educated Greek Orthodox Christian was asked what he thought about the Roman Catholics. 'We have a list of ten points', he replied, 'at which they have departed from the orthodox faith, as held by us, who are the original church founded by the apostles. One of these is that they make the sign of the cross all wrong. No wonder God doesn't answer their prayers, when they sign themselves from left to right, when everybody knows the correct way to do it is as we do, from right to left, finishing over the heart!' That may be the opinion at the grass-roots level – officially the two churches have excellent relations, having officially cancelled the mutual excommunications issued in the eleventh century. But for *hoi polloi* – Greek for 'the ordinary people' – these details matter. Making the sign of the cross is a very powerful symbol.

History

That's because it has a very long history. Tertullian in about AD 200 wrote that 'We Christians *wear out our foreheads* with the sign of the cross!' Bishops and priests used the sign in giving blessings, and especially at baptisms. Christian people sign themselves during the Mass and at private prayers. The practice remained in common use after the split between East and West. Reasons given for the left–right versus right–left split are ingenious, even including the parable where the good sheep were on the shepherd's right and the naughty goats on the left, but probably it was just one of those historical accidents. In the West the gesture is made with the whole hand, or the 'small blessing' is done with the thumb on the forehead, lips and breast. In the East the blessing is always made with three fingers, symbolizing the Holy Trinity. Priests and bishops give the blessing the opposite way from the people, so that when they are facing their flocks it looks the same, and dip their fingers in water for baptism blessings, holy oil at confirmations, and ashes on Ash Wednesday, saying, 'In the name of the Father, and of the Son, and of the Holy Spirit. Amen.' The people sign themselves in the Mass at the greeting and the blessing, and use the small blessing at the Gospel – but there are many other circumstances in which people like to cross themselves. Martin Luther approved of the practice, and Lutheran Christians still do it regularly; the Book of Common Prayer instructed Anglicans to use the sign of the cross at baptisms. But many Protestants regard it as superstition.

Reasons

Undoubtedly some people regard crossing oneself as an almost magical act. Somehow they think it will automatically protect them from danger, and the more often they do it the safer they will be – a frightened woman crossing herself over and over when she hears

345

a blasphemy is a favourite figure of fun. But for sincere Christians there are many good reasons for crossing ourselves. We do it to remind ourselves of the covenant we made with God at our baptism; to ask for God's blessing and protection on ourselves and on the things we use, and to pray for success in the projects we undertake. We claim for ourselves the blessings, following from the crucifixion of God's Son, which Jesus promised in the Gospels, and which the priest is pronouncing at the altar. We remind ourselves that we are nothing on our own, and completely dependent on God's grace.

Holy Cross Day

We try to worship God not only with our lips, but with our hearts and our whole bodies. So we use all five senses in worship: sight, hearing, taste, smell and touch. Making the sign of the cross is a form of physical, but wordless, prayer. On today, Holy Cross Day, we remember that, according to Paul, Jesus 'became obedient to the point of death – even death on a cross. Therefore God also highly exalted him.' Paul also wrote, 'May I never boast of anything except the cross of our Lord Jesus Christ, by which the world has been crucified to me, and I to the world.' And in another place he wrote, 'I am not ashamed of the gospel; it is the power of God for salvation to everyone who has faith.' When we make the sign of the cross, we are not ashamed to proclaim publicly that God has forgiven and saved us, not due to any merit of our own, but because of the death of Jesus Christ on the cross.

Suggested hymns

From heaven you came; Faithful cross, above all other; In the cross of Christ I glory; On a hill far away.

St Matthew, Apostle and Evangelist   21 September
Matthew's Audience

Prov. 3.13–18 Wisdom more precious than jewels; Ps. 119.65–72 Better than gold; 2 Cor. 4.1–6 The open statement of the truth; Matt. 9.9–13 The call of Matthew

> *'As [Jesus] sat at dinner in the house, many tax-collectors and sinners came and were sitting with him and his disciples.' Matthew 9.10*

Jesus's audience

Jesus spoke to a very strange audience. If someone comes to talk about God, you might expect him to gather a group of religious people to speak to. But those who listened to Jesus were very different. St Matthew in his Gospel tells us that Jesus sat down to dinner with tax-collectors, sinners and his disciples. 'Disciples' means learners, and they came from all walks of society. But there were very few from the leaders of the nation among them. The twelve 'apostles, who were also called disciples' were mostly Galilean fishermen – businessmen in a small way, with little education though not illiterate, and able to deal with merchants who came from other countries to buy their salt-fish. The 'sinners' may have included a few who had been very wicked and now repented of their wrongdoing. Mostly, however, those whom the Pharisees called sinners were the little people, those who had no time or opportunity in their busy lives to complete all the washings and strict food laws which were involved in obedience to the laws of the Old Testament. So they gave up, remaining nominally Jewish but not observant of the ritual. Typical of these were the tax-collectors. The Gospel of Matthew tells us that Matthew himself was a tax-collector. Some of them were crooked, making false tax demands for their personal enrichment. But what put them beyond the pale in Jewish eyes was that they collected cash from their own countrymen, to give to the Roman Emperor to pay the occupying army which was oppressing the Jews. To be religious, the Pharisees thought, you had to cut yourself off from the corrupting influence of the non-Jewish world – and Jesus was friendly with tax-collectors actually employed by the Romans! A mixed bunch, then – much like us.

Greek

Probably the reason why St Matthew mentions in his Gospel the assortment of people who listened to Jesus, is because he wrote for a readership who were equally diverse. Matthew quotes from the Old Testament more than any other Gospel, though he usually subverts the traditional understanding of its message: 'Go and learn what this means: I desire mercy, not sacrifice.' This ploy would only have worked if there were many Jews, or Jewish-Christians, in the congregation of the church where Matthew worshipped. But the Old Testament was written in Hebrew – Matthew wrote in Greek, the language spoken by most people in the Roman Empire – Latin was only spoken in Italy and in legal matters. So Matthew's audi-

347

ence must have included foreigners who spoke no Hebrew, and Jews who had lived so long abroad that they were equally fluent in both languages. 'Abroad' includes Galilee, which had such a mixed population that it was referred to as 'Galilee of the Gentiles', or 'Galilee of the nations'. They were not what you'd call very observant Jews.

Fulfilment

Yet St Matthew's Gospel emphasizes that Jesus was the answer to the promises of the Old Testament: 'All this took place to fulfil what had been spoken by the Lord through the prophet: "Look, the virgin shall conceive and bear a son, and they shall name him Emmanuel," which means, "God is with us."' And Jesus said, 'Do not think that I have come to abolish the law or the prophets; I have come not to abolish but to fulfil.' Many non-Jews were hugely attracted by the contrast between the high ethical standards of the Jews and the lax morals of the Romans, and by the simple challenge of worshipping one good God, as against the many competing deities of classical religion. These factors also made multicultural Jews reluctant to desert their ancestral faith. Yet neither group wanted to be bound by the strict laws imposed by the Old Testament. What was needed was a new slant, faithful to history, but willing to look at it in a new way. Maybe most of us, in a changing, multicultural society, where religion is under constant attack, find ourselves equally torn. So Matthew has the answer for us today, too. Jesus re-emphasizes the scriptural demand for kind, loving behaviour, and for loyalty to the One God. But he challenges us to find a new interpretation of these things, suitable for modern people, which brings out the inner meaning of the Bible without enslaving us to its literal interpretation. So thank you, Matthew, and the audience for whom Matthew wrote, for the challenge you set us – to keep on reinterpreting God's will for today, fulfilling the old as we strike out towards the new.

Suggested hymns

He sat to watch o'er customs paid; Oh Lord, all the world belongs to you; One more step along the road I go; Will you come and follow me?

St Michael and All Angels   29 September
(See Eighteenth Sunday after Trinity p. 238)

St Luke the Evangelist   18 October
Luke the Healer
Isa. 35.3–6 Healing in the new age, *or* Acts 16.6–12a The
Macedonian call; Ps. 147.1–7 God heals the broken-hearted; 2
Tim. 4.5–17 Only Luke is with me; Luke 10.1–9 Sending out the
seventy

> *'Luke, the beloved physician, and Demas greet you.' Colossians
> 4.14*

The beloved physician

In his Letter to the Colossians, St Paul refers to Luke as 'the beloved
physician'. In other words Luke was a doctor. Medical knowledge
was quite primitive, but it was useful to have somebody nearby
with medical experience when you fell ill. St Paul, as we can tell
from his letters, was often unwell, and Luke undertook exhausting
and dangerous journeys with him so that his personal doctor was
always at hand. Luke is regarded as patron saint of doctors and
surgeons. Jesus told his disciples, 'Whenever you enter a town and
its people welcome you, eat what is set before you; cure the sick
who are there, and say to them, "The kingdom of God has come
near to you."' Healing the sick and proclaiming the kingdom of
God are closely related activities.

Need for healing

Our estrangement from God causes inner tensions which may stop
us recovering from illness. Yet many sick people don't realize that
their physical sickness may have a spiritual cause. Others who are
physically well don't recognize their need of spiritual healing. The
things from which we need healing are many. For some, it may be
unhappy memories of the past; for some it may be sorrow for cruel
actions or words regretted; for some it may be a broken heart; for
some it may be anger because someone they loved has died; for
others, it may be an abuse in early years; for some it may be an
anger that an injustice has happened, and there's no sense of rec-

349

ompense. Yet unless we know we are ill, we don't go to the doctor. In the same way, until we realize that the sadness and tension in our life is a disease which needs spiritual healing, we are not likely to realize our need of Christ's healing. How can we know the joy of forgiveness, how can we rejoice in reconciliation, how can we be happy and healthy, if we don't realize first that there's something wrong?

How Christ heals

Christ heals us by showing us that we are loved and valued; forgiving us for our sins; and helping us to trust that he will make everything right in the end. Through the cross, we are reconciled to God – we're saved by Christ; we are healed and made whole in body, mind and soul. So healing is the central act of God's redeeming love in Jesus. Jesus reconciles us with God, showing us that the maker of the universe is our loving heavenly Father and our friend. In that way, he takes away all the tension and loneliness which prevent our healing, both physical and mental. God has put wonderful powers of recovery in our bodies, but they can't work when we are all twisted up with fear and guilt.

The Church's call

The Church today is called, just as the first disciples were, to continue Christ's work of healing. We can co-operate with the medical profession by visiting people who are sick, at home or in hospital, showing them that they are not forgotten, cheering them up, and helping them to relax. If it seems appropriate, we may be able to share with them the good news that God loves them. Before you leave, you can ask them whether they'd like you to say a simple prayer with them. There are also special services of prayer for healing in many churches; and centres for quiet prayer and withdrawal if they want it. The good news, the gospel of Jesus Christ, which we are called to share with our neighbours, is that we are reconciled to God through him. That message of reconciliation, and the power to reconcile people with their heavenly Father, has been granted to his Church – Jesus said, 'If you forgive the sins of any, they are forgiven them.' If you go to a Christian minister and ask for advice about the problems in your life, the minister will often end with the words, 'Through the authority vested in me at my ordination, I declare that your sins are forgiven. Go in peace, and pray for me, a sinner also.'

In the same boat

Healing is the heart of the gospel – the medicine of the gospel – and we all need it, every one of us. Whether it is physical, spiritual or emotional healing, we are all in the same boat. We all need to be healed, reconciled, saved, and 2,000 years ago, St Luke recognized that salvation was in Christ Jesus, and that the gospel had to be preached in every land.

Suggested hymns

At even, when the sun was set; Be still and know that I am God; Healing God, almighty Father; Thine arm, O Lord, in days of old.

SS Simon and Jude, Apostles   28 October
Maturity

Isa. 28.14–16 A foundation stone; Ps. 119.89–96 I am yours, save me; Eph. 2.19–22 The foundation of the apostles; John 15.17–27 You have been with me

> *'If they persecuted me, they will persecute you; if they kept my word, they will keep yours also. But they will do all these things to you on account of my name, because they do not know him who sent me.' John 15.20–21*

Martyrs

I warn you, I'm going to make a terrible pun. Whenever I look at the fruit called a tomato, I think of a Roman emperor looking at a line of Christians, and soliloquizing, 'To martyr, or not to martyr, that is the question.' Sorry! That's a frivolous start to a serious subject. Many of the early Christians were faced with that dilemma: should they speak up boldly for their faith, and risk being killed, or should they stay quiet, so that they should live to serve the Lord another day, and for many more days to come? To be a martyr, or not to be? It's not an easy question to answer. Jesus warned his disciples that the people of the world would do to them as they had done to him. Bad people resent anyone who is good, and find them an embarrassment. The good people show up how bad the bad people are, by contrast; so they must be got rid of. The only way to get rid of Jesus was to kill him; the commonest way that bad people

351

have for getting rid of Christians today is by pretending that you have to be stupid to be a believer, and pointing the finger of scorn at us. Yet if you endure mockery for the sake of Jesus, you can be proud that you are walking in his footsteps.

Simon and Jude

Saints Simon and Jude, whom we commemorate today, were both martyred. Both of them were members of the Twelve, the disciples who were closest to Jesus. Traditionally, St Jude was supposed to have written the Epistle which goes by his name in the New Testament, and to have been clubbed to death. Simon was supposed to have been sawn in two. They were cousins, and there's a book called *The Passion of Simon and Jude* which describes them travelling round Persia together, preaching the gospel, and meeting their deaths together there. That's why they are commemorated on the same day, the 28th October. But the book could possibly have been written many years later, which is why it's called 'apocryphal'. There's very little evidence that this was how they died, and many other stories are told about their deaths; Simon is variously said to have been stabbed to death, or to have died in battle when he was Bishop of Jerusalem, while others claim that he trekked across North Africa until he reached the age of 120, and only then was he martyred. The Eastern Orthodox Church commemorates them on the 10th May and the 19th June respectively. But everyone venerates them as martyrs.

A good thing?

But that brings us back to our first question: is martyrdom a good thing? Certainly the witness the martyrs give to their faithfulness is a wonderful example, and many have been converted by it, so that the early Christians used to say, 'The blood of the martyrs is the seed of the Church.' It's as though, wherever you kill one Christian, a hundred new Christians spring up in their place. People today in many lands who kill others for being Christians should beware. But some people in the early days began to go out of their way to *seek* martyrdom, because of the honour it would bring them, and the certainty of a place in heaven. This makes you think of Muslim terrorists today, who cause great embarrassment to peace-loving Muslims. Similarly, the early Church found that they were becoming unpopular with the authorities, because the martyrs provoked them. By seeking martyrdom, they might unwittingly cause the death of other Christians. So the Church issued warnings that Christians should not 'court martyrdom', as they put it. If you are challenged, admit to your faith and risk the consequences. But don't go out of your way to become a martyr if it isn't strictly necessary.

Motives

A person's motives for doing something are so hard to analyse. A psychologist called Wilhelm Stekel is quoted as saying that 'the mark of the *immature* man is that he wants to die nobly for a cause, while the mark of the *mature* man is that he wants to *live humbly* for one'. Pray that all Christians should become mature Christians, and prefer living humbly to dying unnecessarily, or even suffering unnecessarily. To martyr or not to martyr, that is the question. And the Church, with the example of Simon and Jude before us, has given the answer, 'Never court martyrdom, and accept death only if it's impossible to avoid it without denying your faith.'

Suggested hymns

For all thy saints, O Lord; How bright these glorious spirits shine; Lo, round the throne of God, a glorious band; Lord, it belongs not to my care.

All Saints' Day   1 November
Bless You

(If 3 November is not kept as All Saints' Sunday, the readings on p. 261 are used on 1 November. If those are used on the Sunday, the following are the readings on 1 November)
Isa. 56.3–8 My house for all people, *or* 2 Esd. 2.42–48 Crowned by the Son of God; Ps. 33.1–5 Rejoice, you righteous; Heb. 12.18–24 Come to Zion; Matt. 5.1–12 The Beatitudes

> *'When Jesus saw the crowds, he went up the mountain; and after he sat down, his disciples came to him. Then he began to speak, and taught them, saying: "Blessed are the poor in spirit, for theirs is the kingdom of heaven."' Matthew 5.1–3*

Bless you

When somebody sneezes, we say 'Bless you'. It's simply a phrase that sounds like 'atishoo', and we never stop to think about what it means. What would we be like if God blessed us to the full? The answer is given in the Sermon on the Mount, where Jesus made eight statements, each beginning 'Blessed are ...'. We call these eight sayings 'the Beatitudes', from the Latin word *beati* meaning blessed. Jesus teaches that God will bless those who show these characteristics in their life. Some Bibles translate this as 'happy'. These are not laws; they describe the character that God wants us to have, our 'attitude' to life. If you asked most people to say what things would make them truly happy, they'd reply in terms of wealth, success, health, popularity and celebrity. But these are transient pleasures. Jesus startles us into looking at things differently: he says that what produces deep inner happiness is to be poor, grieving, humble, hungry, forgiving, pure, peacemakers, and, most astonishing of all, persecuted! Quite the opposite of what we should expect.

'Blessed are the poor in spirit, for theirs is the kingdom of heaven.'
'Poor in spirit' doesn't mean 'spiritually deficient'! It means having the same attitude that poor people have. The poor are grateful for what they are given, humble, and aware of their dependence on God. We should be like that, even if we are comparatively wealthy, says Jesus. Then we shall receive the kingdom of heaven. When other Gospels speak of the kingdom of God, Matthew often uses 'heaven', to avoid taking the name of God in vain. But probably, here, Jesus was actually speaking about the afterlife.

'Blessed are those who mourn, for they will be comforted.'
If Jesus was talking about the afterlife, those who 'mourn' for departed loved ones can be comforted by the certainty that they are with Jesus, out of pain, and we shall see them again when we die. But Jesus was probably also referring to those who grieve over the terrible state of the world – they are more blessed than those who ignore it, and through their concern, things will slowly get better.

'Blessed are the meek, for they will inherit the earth.'
'Meek' means humble, not pushy, not always demanding to have our own way. 'They shall inherit the earth' is a quotation from Psalm 37. Many Jews interpret this as 'the land', meaning that they will possess the Holy Land. But God's not interested in land-grabs;

he promises those who are humble that the whole world will be theirs to enjoy.

'Blessed are those who hunger and thirst for righteousness, for they will be filled.'
'Righteousness' is good behaviour in ourselves, justice for others, and victory for God's kingdom of love – we should long for these things as a starving man desires food.

'Blessed are the merciful, for they will receive mercy.'
If we are forgiving and kind to others, God will forgive us; Jesus explained this in the parable of the unforgiving servant, and in the Lord's Prayer.

'Blessed are the pure in heart, for they will see God.'
Our heart is the very centre of our being; the seat of our will and our personality. (Not, in the Bible, by the way, of the emotions, which reside in the liver!) Pure in heart means avoiding impure thoughts, but it also means single-mindedness.

'Blessed are the peacemakers, for they will be called children of God.'
Peacemakers resemble God our Father, who is always trying to bring reconciliation between his children.

'Blessed are those who are persecuted for righteousness' sake, for theirs is the kingdom of heaven.'
We should be happy when people persecute us, mock us, oppose us and make life difficult. That's how they treated the prophets; that's how they treated Jesus; we are in good company. Like Jesus, if we accept persecution without complaining, we may win our persecutors to be ashamed, and even to ask God for forgiveness. Many of the saints whom we commemorate today were persecuted. I pray that none of you may suffer as they did, but in every other respect, may you be like the saints in imitating the eight beatitudes.

Suggested hymns

Blest are the pure in heart; Breathe on me, breath of God; Happy are they, they that love God; Seek ye first the kingdom of God.

Commemoration of the Faithful Departed
(All Souls' Day) 2 November
Death, Be Not Proud

Lam. 3.17–26, 31–33 New every morning, *or* Wis. 3.1–9 Souls of the righteous; Ps. 23 The Lord my shepherd, *or* 27.1–6, 16–17 He shall hide me; Rom. 5.5–11 Christ died for us, *or* 1 Peter 1.3–9 Salvation ready to be revealed; John 5.19–25 The dead will hear his voice, *or* John 6.37–40 I will raise them up

> *'Indeed, just as the Father raises the dead and gives them life, so also the Son gives life to whomsoever he wishes.' John 5.21, or*

> *'This is indeed the will of my Father, that all who see the Son and believe in him may have eternal life; and I will raise them up on the last day.' John 6.40*

John Donne

John Donne [pronounced Dun] was one of England's greatest romantic poets. Soldier and lover, he was converted, and in 1614 he was ordained, and became Dean of St Paul's Cathedral in London. He wrote a wonderful poem beginning, 'Death, be not proud', which actually makes fun of death! Death is imagined as a person, but the poet warns death not to be too cocky, not to get above itself!

Interpretation

Some people speak of mighty, dreadful death, but really, there's no need to be afraid, writes Donne. Addressing death, he writes that when death thinks it has won a victory over those whom it kills, it is mistaken – they are not really dead, only on their way to heaven. Nor can you kill me, he adds. Resting and sleeping, which give us great pleasure, are images we use to describe dying. So death, too, if we think of it as the gateway to eternal life, is a great gift. Even the best human beings are not reluctant to go to rest, and have their souls set free from imprisonment in the body. Death depends on others to do its dirty work for it: fate, luck, kings and rebels. All death can do, he writes, is to send us to sleep. But so can opiates, or hypnotism; and they do it rather more efficiently. So what's death got to be proud about? We go to sleep, and wake up again, after a short while, in heaven, where death is no more. In a final stabbing thrust of four short syllables, John Donne ends his poem with the mocking words: 'Death, thou shalt die.'

The poem

Let me read the whole poem to you. Its quite short, only 12 lines:

Death be not proud, though some have called thee
Mighty and dreadful, for, thou art not so;
For those, whom thou think'st thou dost overthrow,
Die not, poor death, nor yet canst thou kill me.
From rest and sleep, which but thy pictures be,
Much pleasure – then from thee much more – must flow,
And soonest our best men with thee do go,
Rest of their bones, and soul's delivery.
Thou art slave to Fate, Chance, kings, and desperate men,
And dost with poison, war, and sickness dwell,
And poppy or charms can make us sleep as well,
And better than thy stroke; why swell'st thou then?
One short sleep past, we wake eternally,
And death shall be no more; death, thou shalt die.

All Souls

Today is the day of the Commemoration of the Faithful Departed, commonly known as All Souls' Day. We think about all those who have died; not just the famous saints, but every Christian believer, and even those who didn't have a strong Christian faith, or any faith at all. Of course, if we loved them, we grieve that we can no longer see them and hug them here on earth. It's not for us to judge, but if God is the loving Father that Jesus spoke of, we can be sure that he wants to find a way of getting all those who wish it into heaven with him. So death is nothing to be afraid of; we fall asleep, and either we shall never wake up, and there's nothing more to bother us, or we shall wake up to a better life than we had ever dared to imagine. Death, thou shalt die.

An old man

An old man had seen many of his colleagues die a terrible death in the First World War. In his eighties, he was being driven to hospital by his son for an operation. Like many Englishmen, he was not good at expressing his inner feelings. But his son remarked that even if we die, as Christians we have nothing to fear, because we shall wake up in heaven. The old man said clearly, 'Yes, that's definitely true.' The son knew that was the nearest to a confession of faith he would ever get out of his father; a few days later the old man died peacefully in his sleep, having won the final victory, over the last enemy – death itself.

Suggested hymns

Alleluia, alleluia, give thanks to the risen Lord; Christ the Lord is risen again; Love's redeeming work is done; The strife is o'er, the battle done.

Saints and Martyrs of (our own nation)
8 November
The Reformation

Isa. 61.4–9 Build up the ancient ruins, *or* Ecclus. (Ben Sira) 44.1–15 Let us now praise famous men; Ps. 15 Who may dwell in your tabernacle?; Rev. 19.5–10 A great multitude invited; John 17.18–23 To be with me to see my glory

> *'Then I heard what seemed to be the voice of a great multitude ... And the angel said to me, "Write this: Blessed are those who are invited to the marriage supper of the Lamb."' Revelation 19.6, 9*

Crowds in heaven

St John, in the book of Revelation, describes people from every nation welcomed into heaven. We can be sure that includes our own nation, and that there are many of our own 'tribe, and race, and tongue' among the heavenly host. We honour some of our famous compatriots by calling them saints, and on this day we celebrate the saints and martyrs of our own nation. The Roman Catholic Church continues to canonize saints up until our own day; the Church of England and the Protestant churches honour heroes of the faith, but have stopped drawing a distinction between those to whom we give the title of 'saint' and those to whom we don't.

Reformation

At the time of the Reformation in the sixteenth century, many Christians stood up boldly for what they believed in, and some of them died for it. We can't deny the title of 'Saint' to those who were burnt at the stake for refusing to deny what they believed to be true, even those with whom we disagree. The ironic thing is that many of them disagreed with each other, and some of those we honour as saints and heroes were the direct cause of the death of some of the others. How can we call them saints when they caused other saints to die a martyr's death? Before we can answer that question, we need to go a little deeper into the lives of these men and women.

Wolf Hall

The winner of the 2009 Man Booker Prize for fiction was a novel called *Wolf Hall,* by Hilary Mantel. It tells the story of the English Reformation from the point of view of Thomas Cromwell, who rose from a poor and violent childhood, son of a Putney blacksmith, to become the Agent of Cardinal Wolsey, then King Henry the Eighth's Chancellor of the Exchequer. He was not related, apparently, to the more famous Oliver Cromwell, though both, a century apart, rose to the top and were then disgraced. Thomas Cromwell is represented in most history books as being an unscrupulous fixer with no principles, but the novel makes him a much more complicated person. If fact, what made the book a bestseller, as well as the vigorous language and the detailed description of life at court, is the way it reverses the common judgement on the people involved, and shows them all as complex characters torn apart by difficult decisions.

King Henry

The Reformation in Europe was a religious movement, which had political consequences; the English Reformation was a political movement with religious consequences. King Henry was undoubtedly a womanizer, but didn't need to marry the women he fancied. Why he needed a divorce was because his first wife, Catherine of Aragon, didn't bear him any children, and if he died without a male heir, amid the complex rivalries of the time, everybody believed England would become subject to a foreign king. The Pope had bent the law to allow Henry to marry his deceased brother's widow; now

His Holiness was enmeshed in alliances with the European royal families, and refused to admit he had been mistaken. The King, fed up with having English law controlled by a foreign prince, got Thomas Cranmer to persuade the European universities to vote that Henry had never been legally married. It was all part of the rise of the independent nation-state. Yet Henry remained the Defender of the Roman Catholic faith until he died. St Thomas More, praised in the film *A Man for All Seasons*, was a fervent supporter of the Pope, and was directly responsible for the martyrdom of several Protestants. Thomas Cromwell assisted Henry in his projects, including the condemnation of More, though he tried to save him from martyrdom. Yet because he arranged the King's marriage with Ann of Cleves, 'the Flanders Mare', Cromwell was himself beheaded.

Saints

What does all this show? That everybody's motives are complex, and nobody's perfect. These complexities continued through the next three reigns, with martyrdoms on both sides. I think we should avoid favouring those who supported 'our side' exclusively, but instead, honour all who believed in their faith enough to die for it, and sympathize with those who struggled to find an honest way through the maze. All deserve to be called saints, whether we agree with them or not.

Suggested hymns

For all thy saints, O Lord; Give us the wings of faith to rise; God, whose city's sure foundation; Rejoice in God's saints, today and all days.

St Andrew the Apostle   30 November
The First-Called

Isa. 52.7–10 The messenger who announces peace; Ps. 19.1–6 The heavens declare God's glory; Rom. 10.12–18 God's messengers reconcile Jew and Greek; Matt. 4.18–22 The call of the fishermen

> *'[Jesus] saw two brothers, Simon, who is called Peter, and Andrew his brother, casting a net into the sea – for they were fishermen.*

And he said to them, "Follow me, and I will make you fish for people." Immediately they left their nets and followed him.'
Matthew 4.18–20

Two brothers

The Gospel for St Andrew's Day tells how Jesus saw two brothers, Andrew and Simon Peter, catching fish. He called them both to follow him, saying they were to start fishing for people. Thus the task of an apostle was defined, which is to be a travelling missionary. This is the version from St Matthew's Gospel, and Mark and Luke are very similar. But St John's Gospel is rather different. Here, John the Baptist is talking to two of his followers when Jesus walks by; and John says 'Behold the Lamb of God'. The two who heard this left John the Baptist, and went after Jesus. They had been disciples of John – now they became disciples of Jesus. One of the two is never named; but the other is identified as Andrew. Jesus invited them to come and see where he was staying, and they spent the day with him. Then they left Jesus for a while, and the first thing that Andrew did was to fetch his brother Peter. So the two brothers weren't called at the same time, as Matthew had said – Andrew was called first, according to John, and a few hours later he went and fetched Peter, introducing him to the wonderful new rabbi that he had discovered. St John writes:

> One of the two who heard John speak and followed him was Andrew, Simon Peter's brother. He first found his brother Simon and said to him, 'We have found the Messiah' (which is translated Anointed). He brought Simon to Jesus, who looked at him and said, 'You are Simon son of John. You are to be called Cephas' (which is translated Peter).

The first-called

I don't think you should read too much into these discrepancies. Jesus must have met his disciples several times before they decided to follow him, and two separate stages in the call of Andrew and Peter may be represented in these different traditions. All four Gospels say that Jesus gave Simon the nickname of 'Peter' or 'Rocky'. It may have been a private joke; he was a big craggy sort of fellow physically, but morally, when it came to admitting to being a disciple of Jesus, Peter became all crumbly, and denied even knowing who Jesus was. Nothing very rock-like there. Perhaps Andrew really was the first one to be called, but Peter was the first to say to Jesus, 'You are the Messiah, the Son of the living God', and it was on the rock of Peter's faith that Jesus was going to build his church. But the Greek Orthodox Church always refer to Andrew as the 'Protoclete' which means 'the first-called'.

First on the scene

You have a great responsibility if you are first on the scene. You have to tell others, who come later, how it was in the very early days. Often you have to call them back to the purity of the first principles of the movement. Yet we are deluded if we think everything was simple at the beginning. Andrew came from a Jewish family, but he had a Greek name, Andreas, which means 'manly'. He and his brother came from the town of Bethsaida, which stood on the northern shore of Lake Galilee, where the river Jordan flowed in; right on the border between Hebrew-speaking Capernaum and the Greek-speaking Decapolis. All Jewish boys had to learn to read Hebrew for their bar mitzvah at the age of 12, but the fisherman had to be able to do business in Greek, too. So Andrew was an interpreter, a go-between, helping people from different cultures to learn from each other. He began by evangelizing his own brother, and he finished his life as a travelling missionary once more. So St Andrew's-tide is kept by some churches as a time of prayer for overseas missions. Though the word missionary is out of fashion, small churches in many countries still desperately need the help of Christians from old-established churches to help them in their task of making new converts.

Fishing for folk

So Andrew the first-called became the first to call others. All his life he served the Lord by fishing for folk. Sooner or later, whenever you hear in your head the voice of Jesus calling you to do something for him, or simply work out that there's something he needs you for, you have to obey at once. Andrew did; and we must follow his example.

Suggested hymns

Captains of the saintly band; Disposer supreme, and judge of the earth; God is working his purpose out; I will make you fishers of men.

Sermon for Harvest Festival
Principal Service **Hawker of Morwenstow**
Deut. 26.1–11 First fruits; Ps. 100 Enter his gates with thanks; Phil. 4.4–9 Rejoice!, *or* Rev. 14.14–18 The harvest of souls; John 6.25–35 Work for the food that lasts

> *'Jesus said to them, "Very truly, I tell you, it was not Moses who gave you the bread from heaven, but it is my Father who gives you the true bread from heaven."' John 6.32*

Harvest

It's amazing how popular Harvest Festival is, even in urban parishes where many in the congregation have never visited a working farmyard. Lustily we sing, 'We plough the fields and scatter', when most of us wouldn't have a clue how to operate a plough. Yet it feels right to affirm our unity with nature, and to remember that even in the days of tinned and frozen foods, we are entirely dependent on the harvest of the land. We celebrate in church because we know that ultimately we depend on God's mercy to keep us alive.

Hawker

Harvest Festival feels like a survival of an ancient pagan celebration, so it comes as quite a surprise to learn that it was a Victorian invention. It was Robert Stephen Hawker, parson-and-poet, vicar of Morwenstow in Cornwall from 1834 to 1875, who dreamt up the idea. On the 13th September 1843 he put up a notice informing his flock that, from then on, a special Sunday would be set apart for thanksgiving, and that the old custom of making eucharistic bread from the first ears of the wheat-harvest would be revived. It read, 'Let us gather together in the chancel of our church, and there receive, in the bread of the new corn, that Blessed Sacrament which was ordained to strengthen and refresh our souls.'

Life

It has been said that the ministry of the Church of England is the last refuge of the great British eccentric. Hawker of Morwenstow was certainly odd. He was born in 1803, the son of a Cornish curate. His family was so hard-up that it was only by marrying his rich godmother, when he was 19 and she was 41, that he was able to pay his way through Oxford University. There he won the Newdigate Prize for poetry, and soon after he was ordained, and after a short curacy, he became vicar of Morwenstow, where he spent the rest of his life. It was hardly a plum living; when he arrived he was the first vicar for over a century. But he loved the old church, with its Saxon font and decorated Norman arches, where he could stand in the sanctuary and hear the waves breaking against the rocks hundreds of feet below. He was also a faithful and compassionate pastor to his flock – quixotic and mischievous, with the mixture of shrewdness and naivety which is often the mark of a saint.

Wreckers

Most of the people were smugglers and wreckers. If a ship got into trouble, they would wait for it to break in pieces and the crew to drown before rowing out to gather the cargo for themselves. Meanwhile their parson was shouting above the gale, rebuking them for being so cruel, and demanding that they should pick up the bodies of the drowned so that he could give them Christian burial.

Poet

He built himself from driftwood a small hut in the cliff-side, where he could write his poetry. Hawker's 'The Song of the Western Men' included the famous lines, 'And shall Trelawny die? There's 20,000 Cornish men shall know the reason why!' 'Hawker's Hut' is now the smallest property in the care of the National Trust. His first wife died in 1863, and the next year, aged 60, he married a young woman of 20. The marriage brought him some happiness, three daughters and great anxiety about money. He talked to the birds, invited his nine cats into church and then excommunicated one of them for catching a mouse on Sunday, and kept a huge pig as a pet.

Spiritual

But Hawker of Morwenstow is justly remembered chiefly for inventing the Harvest Festival. After spending many hours in silent meditation, he felt very close to God, and wanted to thank our loving heavenly Father for the ample way he bestows on us his children the necessities of life. As we bring forward our harvest goods, use them to help the poor and needy, and sing the marvellous harvest hymns, let's also give thanks to God for the simple saint who invented the festival, as a way of expressing our gratitude for the food in our store-cupboard. Everything we have, everything we eat, the raw materials of our daily existence, all come from God; and once a year we have a chance to remind ourselves of that fact. Jesus told his disciples that our daily bread comes from no human agency, but from God our loving heavenly Father.

All-age worship

Plait grasses into harvest crowns.

Suggested hymns

All things bright and beautiful; Come, you thankful people, come; God, whose farm is all creation; We plough the fields and scatter.

Sermon for a Wedding
The Pilot
John 15.9–17

> *'[Jesus said,] "This is my commandment, that you love one another as I have loved you."' John 15.12*

The Flight into Egypt

A Sunday school teacher once told her class how Joseph and Mary were so frightened of the persecution by wicked King Herod that they fled with Baby Jesus into Egypt. Then the teacher asked the children to draw 'the Flight into Egypt'. Inevitably, one child drew an aeroplane with four people in it. Startled by this imaginative approach, the teacher asked, 'Who are those people?' 'That's Mary, Joseph, and Baby Jesus,' was the reply. 'And who's the fourth one.'

'It would be stupid to start on a journey without someone to drive the aeroplane,' replied the child. 'So that's *Pontius, the pilot.*'

The journey of marriage

The bride and the groom today are beginning a journey: the journey of marriage. Actually, it started when they fell in love. Today they promised to love each other 'as long as they both shall live'. Now anyone can fall in love, that's easy. Falling in love is as easy as falling off a log, and a good deal less painful! But to go on loving someone for the rest of their life, that's difficult. Staying in love, and growing in love, takes a lot of hard work and imagination, give and take, willingness to say sorry and to forgive, to make sacrifices, to show your feelings. And a lot else, besides.

We all need help

And because it's so hard to love each other for ever, every married couple needs help. That's why some couples like to get married in church. They like to invite their friends to share in their joy and their happiness, and to have a good party, because that deepens friendship. Then they hope that because they have been kind to their friends, their friends will be kind to them. If they strike a sticky patch in their marriage, they hope their friends will give them practical help; a listening ear; and good advice *if,* and only if, they ask for it. We are their support team, to be their friends always, and to help them if required. We can begin, today, by praying for them, and asking God to help them to have a long and happy life together.

Jesus our friend

Now you remember what the Sunday school child said? 'It would be stupid to start on a journey without someone to drive the aeroplane.' Well, can't we draw a moral from that about the journey of marriage? The bride and groom are starting out today on the journey of marriage, a journey of exploration, a journey of trust. It would be stupid to begin without someone to point them in the right direction. The best person to do that is Jesus. Jesus said, 'I have called you friends, because I have made known to you everything that I have heard from my Father. You did not choose me but I chose you.' That's amazing! However naughty we have been, however much we have ignored Jesus and turned our backs on him,

Jesus has chosen you and me to be his friends. Particularly today, we think that Jesus is the friend of this happy couple, the sort of wise friend they need to show them the way. Jesus is their direction finder, their pilot.

How to love

Couples learn how to love from each other. They also learn from the example of their friends. Jesus said, 'This is my commandment, that you love one another as I have loved you.' Our love for each other needs to be like his love for us, that's his suggestion. We would be well advised to follow his example. Jesus cares for his friends, and listens to them. He even sacrificed his life for us, so that we can have eternal life with him in heaven. Very, very few people are called upon to sacrifice their lives for other people. But we can all learn from Jesus's example to live a life of self-sacrifice – taking trouble for those we love, and not demanding to have our own way all the time.

Stupid not to

Taking the childish words of the story I began with, it would be stupid to start on a journey by air without someone to drive the aeroplane. So, if I dare say so, it would be stupid to start out on the journey of marriage without having someone to guide you, fill you with the fuel of his love, and show you by his example what love really means. Let Jesus be the pilot in your married life together. May you have a long and blessèd life together – enjoying your love for each other, and enjoying the love of Jesus, your guide, your example and your friend.

Suggested hymns

Guide me, O thou great Redeemer; I danced in the morning; Lead us, heavenly Father, lead us; The Lord's my shepherd.

Sermon for the Baptism of Infants
Why Baptize Babies?

'The word of God came to John son of Zechariah in the wilderness. He went into all the region around the Jordan, proclaiming a baptism of repentance for the forgiveness of sins.' Luke 3.2–3

Origins

Today we are sprinkling some water over a baby's/some babies' head(s). A peculiar thing to do; what does it mean? Some people never bother their heads over this question – it's what we have always done, and what everybody else does, why make it complicated? Others, with more claim to be thinking, reasonable people, answer that it's what Jesus did; it's there in the Bible, isn't it? Well, I'm sorry, Jesus may have baptized babies, but the Bible doesn't actually say so. So let's go back to the origins and ask where baptism came from.

Chosen People

The Bible says that the Jews are God's Chosen People – chosen to get to know God, and tell the world about him. Everyone who was born of Jewish parents was automatically one of the Chosen People: little boys were admitted to the People of God when they were eight days old, though in those days there was no similar ceremony for girls. But someone who wasn't born a Jew could also become one of God's people if they wanted to. For this, they had to make a public statement that they believed in God and would obey the Ten Commandments. Then they were washed. It was a symbol – it meant that they were washing away all the wrong things they had believed about God when they were heathens, and were washed clean of all the wrong things they had done in the past. They called this, the washing or *'baptism'* of converts.

John the Baptist

John the Baptist took this over and said that everyone should be baptized, even Jews, to show that they had made a personal decision to obey God and worship him; that they were sorry for their sins, and wanted God to forgive them – the Bible calls it 'a baptism of repentance for the forgiveness of sins'. This means it was basically meant for grown-ups, those who were old enough to make this personal decision. What the Bible does say, however, is that on different occasions, a man called Stephanas in Corinth; Crispus, a jailer in Philippi; and a widow called Lydia, were 'baptized along with their whole household'. That probably included the children, but we can't be absolutely certain.

Why baptize babies?

The Reverend Michael Green, in a book called *Baptism: Its Purpose, Practice and Power,* listed seven reasons for baptizing the babies of parents who are believing Christians. They are:

- Children were admitted into the Jewish people when they were babies.
- The whole family was baptized when heathen converts became Jews.
- Complete households were baptized in New Testament times.
- Jesus blessed the children, saying, 'Let the children come to me, don't try and stop them.'
- Throughout its history the Christian Church has baptized babies.
- Infant baptism stresses that God actually does something for us when he welcomes us into his family, and it makes a change in us, even if we don't understand.
- God takes the initiative: he reaches out to us long before we are able to reach out to him.

Preparation

Many people are convinced that these are good reasons for baptizing babies; others are not so sure, and say that people should only be baptized after they have made an adult decision to follow Jesus. The Baptist Church, of course, are well known for this. But you notice that if you do accept these seven reasons, every one of them assumes that the parents are Christian believers. The words of the Christening service ask the parents and godparents to make some very solemn promises about bringing up the child as a Christian. It would be unfair to them to expect them to stand up and make these promises in public, without knowing in advance what they had to sign up to. So most ministers, before baptizing a baby, meet the parents, and if possible the godparents, beforehand to explain the service to them. Some churches even offer a series of meetings to discuss what christening is all about. It's usual to invite the parents to bring their baby to one or more of the normal Sunday services, so that they know what family their kid is joining – and so that the congregation can show they are willing to help the parents teach their offspring about Jesus. Without such preparation, sprinkling water on a baby's head would be a bit of a nonsense. With it, baptism becomes a glorious way of showing God's love for the child, and for each one of us, whether we understand it or not.

Suggested hymns

A little child the Saviour came; Child of blessing, child of promise; Loving Shepherd of thy sheep; There's a song for all the children.

Sermon for the baptism of those who can answer for themselves
Why Wash?
Luke 3.2–6 The baptism of John

> *'The word of God came to John son of Zechariah in the wilderness. He went into all the region around the Jordan, proclaiming a baptism of repentance for the forgiveness of sins.' Luke 3.2–3*

Why wash?

'Wash your hands before you come to the table.' We have all had it said to us sometime, and being rebellious, we replied, 'Why?' Then some grown-up explained that if we don't wash we might swallow germs which would make us ill. Or we might pass on our infections to others, who, in any case, don't like looking at somebody's dirty hands while they are eating. Finally – and here's the real clincher which sent us off obediently to use the wash basin – we smell! Once the reasons have been explained to us, we shall never again raise the question, 'Why wash?'

John the Baptist

I bet some clever-clogs asked the same question of John the Baptist – 'You are telling us to go down to the River Jordan and wash ourselves,' they must have said. 'Why? What's the point? Why wash?' To which John gave a forceful answer. You see, the Jews are God's

Chosen People, chosen to learn about God, and tell the rest of the world about God. But they became exclusive. Yes, it was possible for anyone to become one of God's people if they really wanted – even the smelly foreigners, like you and me. But first we would have to wash – washing away all our wrong deeds and mistaken beliefs, to make a clean start. But John said to his fellow Jews, 'Don't be so proud and complacent! Just because you have Jewish parents doesn't automatically make you one of God's Chosen People. Just like the foreigners, you too have done selfish and unkind things. You have had wrong ideas about God. In fact, as far as God's concerned, you stink!' That made them sit up! So John told everyone, even respectable Jews, to wash their hands before they came to God's table. Only it wasn't just their hands, they had to wash all over, to show they were really sorry for all their wrong deeds. Then, God would be only too happy to forgive and forget what they had done. The heart of John's message was 'a baptism of repentance for the forgiveness of sins'.

John's cousin

Then John's cousin took charge. Jesus took over as leader of the People of God. He himself was baptized, even though he hadn't done anything wrong that needed to be washed away. This was to show that baptism was the way to become a member of God's family, for Jews and for the rest of us. Jesus's best friend Peter was baptized in the river Jordan, with all his family, though they were very careful not to drown the children. (We know Peter was married because Jesus healed his sick mother-in-law, and you can't have a mother-in-law unless you have a wife.) And then when Peter's wife presented him with another bouncing baby, they couldn't tell the baby to wait until he (or she) was old enough to understand what it meant before they let him become a member of God's family. They probably baptized children at eight days old, the age at which little Jewish boys became members of the Jewish nation.

A game of two halves

So they turned joining God's family into a game of two halves. Part one is baptism, which can happen at any age, just as soon as you are ready. This shows that it's not you who decides to be a Christian, but God who calls you and invites you to join his family, before you even fully understand what it means. Jesus said, 'You have not chosen me, but I have chosen you.' Then some godparents or sponsors are appointed to help you grow as a Christian. They and the parents promise to show, by their example and their teaching, the Christian life of love and obedience, prayer and regular worship, and to share the knowledge of God's love for us found in the Holy Bible. You take the promises for yourself if you are grown-up enough. The congregation here also promises to care for you as you grow into a mature, thoughtful Christian. The second half is when you confirm the promises that were made at your baptism, and the bishop confirms your membership in God's family the Church. We call that Confirmation.

Why wash?

So if you ever wonder what we are doing today, pouring water over people's heads – if you ask, 'Why wash?' – that's the answer. It's part one of the process of joining God's family, with your naughty deeds washed away by God's forgiveness. It's the first step in living the Christian life, which eventually becomes the highway to heaven. God bless you all.

Suggested hymns

As the deer pants for the water; As water to the thirsty; O happy day; O Jesus, I have promised.

Sermon for a Funeral or Memorial Service
Being Helpful
Matthew 25.34–40

> *'Now may our Lord Jesus Christ himself and God our Father, who loved us and through grace gave us eternal comfort and good hope, comfort your hearts and strengthen them in every good work and word.' 2 Thessalonians 2.16–17*

Sick visiting

Visiting somebody we know or love, when they are on their sick-bed or in hospital, is a way of showing them that they are loved. Yet it's not easy to know what to say to a sick person, that will be helpful to them. No doctor can be absolutely sure what will happen to one of their patients. A lot depends on whether the patient is relaxed, and is determined to try hard to recover. So we should always try to calm them down by our words, and encourage them to work on the process of healing.

Death

But should we mention the possibility of dying? Probably not, it would be too discouraging. But there comes a time when it's evident that the sick person hasn't got long to live. Then, if you try to speak to them about death, you will soon know whether they want to talk about it or not – if not, they will quietly change the subject.

Religion

One of the proud traditions of this country is freedom of religion. I believe that freedom is a Christian virtue, and comes from the belief that God has left us free to believe in him or not, or to have a partial belief which may be a different aspect of the truth from what I believe in, though they are all parts of a truth which goes beyond words. So when I'm sick-visiting, I offer people an opportunity to talk about God, but if they prefer not to, I give them my best wishes and change the subject.

Being helpful

But I want to be as helpful to the sick person as I can. Anyone who calls themselves even vaguely a Christian has heard the good news that God loves us. Jesus told us to share this good news with anyone who is willing to listen. So, with due respect for the beliefs of others, as I have said, all Christians are duty bound to mention God's love to sick people if they are allowed to. This doesn't mean preaching at them, or ramming religion down their throats, or telling them off. But it often takes the form of saying, 'I have been very much helped myself, during the difficult times in my life, by praying, hearing or reading one of the sayings of Jesus about God's love for us. Do you think it might help you? Would you like me to pray for you?' Then I may thank God for happy memories, for those who care for us, friends, family and medical staff. Finally I say something like, 'May God give you freedom from pain, peace of mind, and deep trust in his promises of love, now and into eternity.'

Funerals

Not infrequently, the relatives of people who have died have told me their loved one spoke about the last conversation he or she had with me, and said how much it had helped them. Sometimes they ask for me to conduct their funeral. And then I'm faced with the same opportunities and problems when deciding what to say at the service. Because there are sure to be people present of all beliefs and none, and courteous respect for this diversity is essential. But it would be dishonest of me not to mention my belief that God, or whatever we mean by that word, loves each one of us, and wants us to love God in return, and love other people for God's sake. I leave it there, in the certainty that everyone will interpret those words in the way that's most helpful to them.

Jesus

Jesus told people that God loves us, and forgives our sins as soon as we say sorry. He promised eternal life to everyone who is willing to accept it, without tying us down to any particular form of words to describe what eternal life means. He taught us to love God with all our hearts, and to love our neighbours as much as we love ourselves. Jesus loves us for what makes each one of us unique, and different from anyone else, and pays us the supreme courtesy of leaving us free to interpret his words in our own way. Then he faced death himself, in the unimaginable pain of the cross, with courage, and with consideration for others. After that, many of his friends became sure that he is alive still, and can hear our prayers, and will give us courage to bear our grief patiently if we ask him to. Jesus wants to help you, and my fumbling attempt to be helpful to you is intended to spread his great love to all who listen.

Suggested hymns

A new commandment; Immortal love, forever full; Let there be love shared among us; Now the green blade riseth.

Could you be their Chaplain?

Since the formation of the Royal Air Force Chaplains' Branch in 1918, chaplains have been an integral part of the RAF 'story' and have taken the Church to where it's needed most. As an RAF Chaplain you'll be involved in the lives of our personnel, regardless of their rank or religious background. Your personal sacrifice may be considerable as you'll serve with our people wherever they go, providing vital spiritual, pastoral and ethical support in places of conflict, including on the front-line. Your home-based duties will be equally important in support of personnel and their families on RAF stations. While exploring innovative ways of engaging with your community, you can also expect to fulfil the more traditional roles of leading worship and officiating at weddings, baptisms and funerals.

A whole new congregation awaits you. **Be part of the story. Contact us now.**

www.raf.mod.uk/chaplains

The Royal Air Force values every individual's unique contribution, irrespective of race, ethnic origin, religion, gender, sexual orientation or social background.

⊙ **ROYAL AIR FORCE**

Produced by Air Media Centre, HQ Air Command. 0357_11RD © UK MOD Crown Copyright, 2011

Fresh!

AN INTRODUCTION TO FRESH EXPRESSIONS OF CHURCH
AND PIONEER MINISTRY

**DAVID GOODHEW, ANDREW ROBERTS and
MICHAEL VOLLAND**

Fresh! offers a strong rationale for fresh expressions and pioneer
ministries rooted in scripture and the breadth of the Christian
tradition. It combines a serious theological engagement with
earthy practicality to offer guidance in starting and sustaining
fresh expressions of church in the long term.

"This is a gift of a book – well constructed, aimed and timed for all those serious about the need
of the hour and seeking to see the re-evangelisation of western society."

Pete Atkins, a director of Ground Level network of churches

David Goodhew is Director of Ministerial Practice, Cranmer Hall, Durham.

Andrew Roberts is Director of Training, Fresh Expressions. A Methodist Minister who has
planted a number of fresh expressions.

Michael Volland is Director of Mission and Tutor in Pioneering, Cranmer Hall.

  978-0-334-04387-4   paperback   200pp   RRP £19.99

ALSO...

Church for Every Context

AN INTRODUCTION TO THEOLOGY AND PRACTICE
MICHAEL MOYNAGH

**The first comprehensive textbook on the theology and praxis
of Fresh Expressions and new forms of Church.** Combines
sustained theological reflection with practical guidance and case
studies while addresses the theology and methodology of Fresh
Expressions/church planting. Fresh Expressions is a key initiative
of several major mainstream denominations, including the
Church of England.

  978 0334 04369 0   £25   paperback   512 pp

**SPECIAL PRICE FOR BOTH TITLES £35. Please quote FRCC1
Orders through Norwich Books & Music tel: 01603 785 925 or
email orders@norwichbooksandmusic.co.uk**

P&P rates: Orders under £25 a p&p charge of £2.50 will apply. Orders for £25.01, p&p charge is £5

Scripture Index to Sermon Texts

An **inclusive society** for male and female priests within the **Anglican tradition** seeking to promote priestly spirituality and **catholic evangelism**

the
Society of Catholic Priests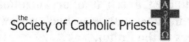

Further information about the Society as well as the Dearmer Society for ordinands in training and the Company of Servers for male and female servers of all ages from the Membership Secretary:

The Revd John Joyce scp,
The Rectory, 21 Cuckfield Road,
Hurstpierpoint, BN6 9RP
rector@hurstrectory.co.uk

Helping people on their Christian journey

Short talks for adults and children
Devotional resources
All free and no registration required

www.holyfaith.org.uk

English Clergy Association

www.clergyassoc.co.uk

Patron: The Rt. Rev'd and Rt. Hon. The Lord Bishop of London;
President:
Professor Sir Anthony Milnes Coates, Bt., B.Sc., M.D., F.R.C.P.

The Association seeks to be a Church of England mutual resource for clergy, patrons and churchwardens requiring information or insight. We publish for Members usually twice yearly Parson & Parish – an independent, reflective eye on what is happening in the Church as an organization, with editorial and comment, general articles, book reviews and letters to the Editor.

Men and women clergy and laity are equally welcome. Our stance is to support the historic integrity of the Church.

Clerical and Lay Membership at £10 p.a. includes the magazine and the A.G.M. in London at St. Giles-in-the-Fields, on the second or third Monday in May, with speakers after a Service and Buffet lunch, who have recently included: the Bishops of London and Rochester, the Marquess of Salisbury, the Rt. Hon. Dominic Grieve, Q.C., M.P., (Attorney-General), Chancellor Dr. James Behrens, Dr. Brian Hanson, Professor Norman Doe, Mrs. Margaret Laird, and Patrick, Lord Cormack.

Our charitable activity is to make Holiday Grants to Clergy, employing Donations to the Benefit Fund, Gifts, Legacies, Church Collections — all the more appreciated when interest rates are so low.

Registered Charity No. 258559

Benoporto-eca@yahoo.co.uk for Membership enquiries.

The Old School House, Norton Hawkfield
Bristol BS39 4HB

Chairman: The Rev'd John Masding, M.A., LL.M.

Subject Index

Entries in *italics* are sermon titles

378

379

The Sign

The Sign, published by Hymns Ancient & Modern, is the leading nationwide magazine supplement for church and parish.

For less than **10p** a copy when bought in bulk, and with lively, topical articles, this inset will help you improve the look and content of your own parish magazine.

For a **FREE** sample copy or to find out more details about our subscription rates:

Please call 01603 785910 or email louiseh@hymnsam.co.uk Please quote 'SG1203'

NEED HELP WITH YOUR CHURCH'S FINANCES?

Grow Your Church's Income

BY MAGGIE DURRAN

Is your church facing new financial challenges because of the recession? This utterly practical handbook will help you manage your church's resources in difficult times, whatever the size of your budget.

Maggie Durran outlines well-tried and effective approaches to safeguarding, managing and maximising your income, as well as some innovative ways to strengthen financial stability. Avoiding quick-fix solutions, she focuses firmly on long-term strategies that will free you up to concentrate on mission and ministry.

978 1 84825 039 0 · 216x138mm · 80pp · £12.99

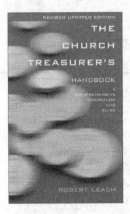

The Church Treasurer's Handbook

BY ROBERT LEACH

This clear, user-friendly guide to the duties and responsibilities of the church or charity treasurer is essential reading for anyone in this important position.

This new edition includes all the latest updates on the many issues affecting churches and charities, including accounting, banking, expenses, tax, insurance, charity law, employment and fundraising. It assumes no specialist knowledge and will help treasurers meet the requirements of current legislation.

978 1 84825 019 2 · 234x172mm · 288pp · £16.99

To order: tel: +44 (0)1603 785925, fax: +44 (0)1603 785915, write to: Norwich Books and Music, 13a Hellesdon Park Road, Norwich, Norfolk NR6 5DR, email: orders@norwichbooksandmusic.co.uk, or visit: www.canterburypress.co.uk

UK orders: to cover p&p, £2.50 on orders below £25; £5 for orders between £25-£75: P&P is free for orders over £75. For details of overseas carriage, please contact our Norwich office or email: admin@norwichbooksandmusic.co.uk **Please quote code CBDDTR13**

 **CANTERBURY** PRESS Norwich

Canterbury Press is an imprint of Hymns Ancient & Modern Ltd. Regd. Charity No. 270060. Regd. in England No. 1220696. Regd. Office: 13a Hellesdon Park Road, Norwich, Norfolk NR6 5DR. VAT Reg. No. GB 283 2968 24.

Author Index

383

Notes

Notes

Notes

Notes

Advance order for the 2014 editions *(available May 2013)*

Order the 2014 editions now, to avoid disappointment! *(All to be published in May 2013)*   quantity
Prices are subject to confirmation and may be changed without notice

CANTERBURY CHURCH BOOK & DESK DIARY 2014 *Hardback*	£17.99 + p&p*	....
CANTERBURY CHURCH BOOK & DESK DIARY 2014 *Personal Organiser (loose-leaf)*	£17.99 + p&p*	....
CANTERBURY CHURCH BOOK & DESK DIARY 2014 *Personal Organiser (A5)*	£17.99 + p&p*	....
CANTERBURY PREACHER'S COMPANION 2014 *Paperback*	£17.99 + p&p*	....

For details of special discounted prices for purchasing the above in any combinations
or in bulk, please contact the publisher's Norwich office as shown below.

Order additional copies of the 2013 editions

Subject to stock availability

Hardback Diary **£17.99***.............   Organiser **£17.99***............

Preacher's Companion **£17.99***............   A5 Personal Organiser **£17.99***............

Ask for details of discounted prices for bulk orders of 6+ copies of any individual title when ordered direct from the Publisher.

Sub-total £................

*Plus **£2.50** per order to cover post and packing (UK only): £................

All orders over £50 are sent POST FREE to any UK address.
Contact the Publishers office for details of overseas carriage.

TOTAL AMOUNT TO PAY: £................

I wish to pay by ...

... **CHEQUE** for £ .... made payable to **Hymns Ancient and Modern Ltd**

... **CREDIT CARD**   All leading credit and debit cards accepted *(not American Express or Diners Club)*
Your credit card will not be debited until the books are despatched.

Card number: ....   Expiry: ____ /____

Issue No: ____ Valid from: ____ /____
Switch or Maestro only

Signature of
cardholder: ....   Security code:_____
Last three digits on signature panel

Please PRINT all details below.

Title: ....   Name: ....

Delivery address: ....

....

....

.... Post Code: ....

Telephone or e-mail: .... Date: ....

Please ensure you have ordered the edition you require for the correct year. No liability will be accepted for incorrect orders

Return this order form or a photocopy – with details of payment – to

Norwich Books and Music, 13A Hellesdon Park Road, Norwich NR6 5DR
Telephone: 01603 785900   Fax: 01603 785915   Website: www.canterburypress.co.uk